Renewing America's Food Traditions

Renewing America's Food Traditions

Saving and Savoring the Continent's Most Endangered Foods

EDITED AND INTRODUCED BY

Gary Paul Nabhan

CONTRIBUTORS

Ashley Rood, Anne Minard, Makalé Faber Cullen, Don Bixby

FOREWORD BY

Deborah Madison

Chelsea Green Publishing Company • White River Junction, Vermont

"Evil Tendencies Cancel" and excerpt from "Blueberries" from THE POETRY OF ROBERT FROST edited by Edward Connery Lathem. Copyright 1930,1939, 1969 by Henry Holt and Company, copyright 1936, 1958 by Robert Frost, copyright 1964, 1967 by Lesley Frost Ballantine. Reprinted by permission of Henry Holt and Company, LLC.

Managing Editor: Emily Foote
Project Editor: Benjamin Watson
Copy Editor: Margaret Pinette
Proofreader: Nancy W. Ringer
Indexer: Christy Stroud
Designer: Peter Holm, Sterling Hill Productions
Design Assistant: Abrah Griggs, Sterling Hill Productions

Printed in the United States of America
First printing, April 2008
11 10 09 08   1 2 3 4 5

Our Commitment to Green Publishing

Chelsea Green sees publishing as a tool for cultural change and ecological stewardship. We strive to align our book manufacturing practices with our editorial mission and to reduce the impact of our business enterprise in the environment. We print our books and catalogs on chlorine-free recycled paper, using soy-based inks whenever possible. This book may cost slightly more because we use recycled paper, and we hope you'll agree that it's worth it. Chelsea Green is a member of the Green Press Initiative (www.greenpressinitiative.org), a nonprofit coalition of publishers, manufacturers, and authors working to protect the world's endangered forests and conserve natural resources. *Renewing America's Food Traditions* was printed on 68# Renew Matte, a 20-percent postconsumer-waste recycled paper supplied by RR Donnelley.

Library of Congress Cataloging-in-Publication Data

Renewing America's food traditions : saving and savoring the continent's most endangered foods / edited and introduced by Gary Paul Nabhan ; contributors, Gary Paul Nabhan ... [et al.]; foreword by Deborah Madison.
     p. cm.
  Includes bibliographical references and index.
  ISBN 978-1-933392-89-9
  1. Cookery, American. 2. Endangered plants--United States. 3. Endangered species--United States. I. Nabhan, Gary Paul. II. Madison, Deborah. III. Title.

TX715.R42157 2008
641.5973--dc22

2008000276

Chelsea Green Publishing Company
Post Office Box 428
White River Junction, VT 05001
(800) 639-4099
www.chelseagreen.com

For Marty and Mary Teitel, the David Smith family, Amy Goldman, and Mary Ann Mott,
who have given their blessings to this project in innumerable ways

CONTENTS

5: Clambake Nation, 105

Quahogs of Great South Bay • Berry Berry American Cranberry • Bronx Seedless Grape • Gaspé Flint Corn • Harrison Cider Apple • Meech's Prolific Quince • Milking Devon Cattle • Narragansett Turkey • Rubel Northern Highbush Blueberry • Waldoboro Green Neck "Turnip" • Boston Marrow Squash • Gloria Mundi Apple

6: Cornbread Nation, 133

Yellow Hickory King Dent Corn • Tennessee Fainting (Myotonic) Goat • Early Golden Persimmon • Magnum Bonum Apple • Chickasaw Plum • Nickajack Apple • Mulefoot Hog • Southern Queen Yam • Tennessee Sweet Potato Cushaw Squash • Honey Drip Cane Sorghum

7: Crabcake Nation, 157

Blue Crab of Chesapeake Bay • Fish Pepper • Choppee Okra • White Maypop Passionfruit • Zimmerman's Pawpaw • Ossabaw Island Hog

8: Gumbo Nation, 175

Sassafras Leaves for Handmade Gumbo Filé • Centennial Pecan • Clay Field Peas • Cotton Patch Goose • Datil Chile Pepper • Goliath Grouper • Pre–Civil War Peanut • Gulf Coast Native Sheep • Seminole Pumpkin • Pineywoods Cattle

9: Maple Syrup Nation, 199

Sugar Maple of the Allegheny Plateau • Java Chicken • Cayuga Duck • Oldmixon Free (Clearstone) Peach • Seneca Hominy Flint Corn • Buckeye Chicken

10: Moose Nation, 211

Moose of Northwestern Minnesota • Northern Giant (McFayden) Cabbage • Short and Thick Parsnip

11: Pinyon Nut Nation, 219

Nevada Single-Leaf Pinyon Nut • Cui-ui Sucker • Colorado Pikeminnow • Death Valley Devil's Claw • Paiute (Speckled) Tepary Bean

FOREWORD

It seems that most of us humans are not content with eating only what grows on or walks the earth around us, but that we long to put new foods in our pantries. Many things determine what we eat: where we live and the climate, soil, and geography of place; human factors like social status; whether we live in times of war or times of peace; and whether we ourselves or our communities live in isolation or in proximity to others. These are only a few of the factors that have a bearing on what we eat. But perhaps the qualities that have most influenced what's in our collective pantries are simple human curiosity combined with the quest for reliable nourishment. Was there ever an explorer who sailed across the ocean or a pilgrim who trekked home through the desert without bringing back a stash of plants or seeds? What about the ancient Spice Route, or the newfound appetite for coffee, sugar, and chocolate that blossomed in Europe once those foods had arrived from afar? Without a doubt, there's long been curiosity about food, especially when it comes from somewhere else.

When I came of cooking age in the 1970s I remember the excitement generated by the arrival of the first jars of sun-dried tomatoes from San Remo, the first goat cheeses, sherry vinegar, walnut oil, and a host of other food firsts that have by now become securely embedded in our culture. Today far more than spices moves around the globe, and I mean not just common commodities like chicken and snow peas, but delicacies meant to excite the palate. The waves of commerce never cease to deposit their dazzling culinary treasures on our shores. With unfailing enthusiasm, we lap them up and have ever done so.

The Renewing America's Food Traditions (RAFT) collaborative, however, suggests a different scenario, one in which foods that are old might well be new again; these unfamiliar products from our own country's regional food traditions can be every bit as compelling as the exotic foods we import from afar. The collaborative effort of seven partners, RAFT has focused on foods that were thriving on our native shores, and in our fields, long before any of us or our ancestors can remember. In this book you'll discover foods that have deep roots to place and people, especially native peoples, and foods that are good to eat—in some cases, really quite good indeed. (A smoked and braised Mulefoot hog shoulder enjoyed by some of the RAFT partners at one memorable dinner in Iowa was almost unbearably delicious.)

Some of the RAFT foods exist only in this country, such as the true hand-harvested wild rice *(manoomin)* of our northern lakes, while others, like the Navajo-Churro sheep, originally came from elsewhere but have been in America for so long that they are pretty much regarded as native. Having about 500 years to adapt to the arid Southwest climate makes the Churro sheep a part of our native food culture by almost anyone's standards.

Many of these foods bear colorful names. I especially like the Waldoboro Green Neck turnip, the Death Valley devil's claw, and the Pike's Peak squash. And all of them come with stories—stories of origin as well as tales of near disappearance and, sometimes, almost miraculous reappearance. These stories make you want to connect, to bring these foods literally into your own life, and in many cases we can do that. But not all of these RAFT foods are still with us today. Some, like the passenger pigeon, are fully extinct, while others teeter on the brink: white abalone, leatherback sea turtle, goliath grouper, Cotton Patch goose, and masked bobwhite quail, to name a few. They are emblematic of the misfortune that falls on a food when ignorant consumption rules over intelligent use of a plant or animal resource. (We do not recommend eating them again until their populations are fully recovered and their habitats are restored.)

At the other extreme, though, are RAFT foods that, with little more than a trip to the Web and maybe a phone call, we can find ourselves feasting on: hand-parched wild rice, Santa Maria pinquito beans, Narragansett turkeys, Pixie tangerines, Sierra Beauty apples, and Black Sphinx dates. In fact, I can't imagine my cupboard without those beautiful gray grains of *manoomin,* pebbly tepary beans, and Sonoran desert oregano, or my freezer without its share of Navajo-Churro sheep and American bison. The meats I can buy at my farmers' markets, and that's also true for the wonderful Santa Domingo casaba melon. The RAFT foods I know well provide such deep nourishment and stunning flavor that I eat them often or whenever they're in season, and over time they have secured their own honored place, front and center in my culinary repertoire.

Yet there are also those RAFT edibles that remain elusive, and for the moment anyway, they must live mostly in the imagination, amid hopes that more farmers will soon begin to plant or raise them. For instance, I long to taste Jack's Copperclad Jerusalem artichoke, but this plant is such a rarity that some other cultivar will have to stand in for what promises to be a fine tuber. And I'd dearly love to make George Washington Carver's peanut cake with blackstrap molasses using pre–Civil War peanuts. Alas, there are only a few seed sources for this old legume, but then, the promise of such plants leads one to know the importance of seed savers—whether they are individual gardeners or RAFT partners like the Seed Savers Exchange and Native Seeds/SEARCH—for reintroducing old varieties back into the culture. We shouldn't forget, of course, that the farmers who grow out these traditional varieties then have to get people to give them a try and establish a market for them. And that can be hard work, for while we may like new foods, we are also nervous about trying them if someone, like a chef, hasn't led the way and popularized them. But really, in the case of these classic foods, the trail was blazed long before now; it's just that most of us don't know that—not yet.

While we often talk of plants and animals as being historically connected to a people or place (most likely, both), recipes too can be historical and people- or place-based. Some might still be relevant to modern cooks, but with others we've no idea. Not everyone will take up the challenge to cook traditional recipes like Crow bison cattail stew, blue crab and Choppee okra stew, or carpetbag steak stuffed with Apalachicola oysters, but dishes like these show us how plants and animals of a particular food nation were once paired and enjoyed together. It's a fascinating business to look back at old recipes, like many of those in this book, to see how much has changed (and how hard it is to imagine cramming the pockets of a pierced steak with oysters, eating a fuzzy-headed reed, or stuffing a moose heart). But then, tastes do change, and they just might go backward as well as forward. Could it be that backward is the new forward in the food world? Stranger things have happened.

When the RAFT partners first met, the acronym stood for Rescuing America's Food Traditions. But after a day spent talking and tasting some of the remarkable foods that would eventually board the raft, we decided that maybe *rescuing* wasn't the right word, after all. It sounded to us as if "rescued" foods might be relegated to a shelf, museum pieces dedicated to a dead and gone past, whereas we wanted more for these foods than some static preservation.

The word *renewing* implied more of the energy and life we hoped for—the idea that these uniquely American foods, so nearly forgotten, might well be made new again and brought back to life as a part of our lives. Food by food, this is now happening. RAFT gives us a great food adventure to embark on—really no less than discovering ourselves through foods that we didn't even know were, in some way, ours. And what an amazing adventure this is!

Deborah Madison

INTRODUCTION

We live, eat, tend the land, and shape the flow of its waters during a remarkable moment in American history. Perhaps with more insight than ever before, we can recognize and celebrate the remarkable diversity of foods unique to American places and savor their unparalleled flavors. Simultaneously, we have finally begun to fathom just how many plants and animals historically used as food by our ancestors have been lost from our landscapes, seascapes, rivers, lakes, and springs. And yet, if the food diversity of this continent has been historically depleted by human agency, is it not possible to restore some of those foods to our fields and tables and to celebrate their roles in our cultures once again?

Those two poles—one of celebration, the other of sorrow—are what this book's chain of stories is stretched between. To renew America's food traditions, we must take stock of what we have squandered just as much as we must endeavor to take pleasure in the edible species and associated foodways that are already back on the road to recovery. By *foodways,* we mean the entire chain of cultural practices, from the praying for and the sowing of seeds or the casting of nets to the cleaning, storing, preparation, serving, and storytelling surrounding our most cherished foods.

The Renewing America's Food Traditions (RAFT) collaborative was founded in 2004 on the premise that chefs, gourmands, consumers, and others in the "food chain" can play positive roles in the conservation, restoration, and celebration of the food traditions unique to the North American continent. The seven founding organizations—the Center for Sustainable Environments, Slow Food USA, American Livestock Breeds Conservancy, Chefs Collaborative, Native Seeds/SEARCH, Cultural Conservancy, and Seed Savers Exchange—had already been catalysts in the conservation of heirloom vegetables and fruits, grains and beans, livestock and poultry, fish and shellfish, and foraged plants and wild game, as well as in the protection of traditional hunting, fishing, farming, and gathering grounds.

We also believed that others should be welcomed to share their experiences in collaborative conservation with us. Our circle has grown as we have reached out and listened to groups as varied as Ecotrust, the Traditional Native American Farmers' Association, the Southern Foodways Alliance, Vermont Fresh Network, the New Mexico Acequia Association, Bon Appetít Management Company, the American Grassfed Association, and the Arizona-Sonora Desert Museum. Formally or informally, these groups have become our second tier of partners.

Despite our initial, shared successes, we must humbly concede that many of America's most unique and delicious foods have nevertheless fallen into neglect. So have certain of the centuries-old cultural and culinary traditions associated with them. Some of the ancient fruit-bearing trees still stand on the edges of our villages and barrios, but they have been largely forgotten by some of the communities that had once carefully tended them. Other species, such as leatherback sea turtles and Colorado pikeminnows, are, in fact, on the verge of extinction, **and we do not recommend eating them at any time in the near future, until biologists affirm that they are fully recovered.** And yet all of us feel confident that if more Americans are once again exposed to the rich stories and recipes associated with these foods, they will be inspired to help return these plants and animals to their habitats and, ultimately, to our tables, where they can become part of our blessings and feasts once again. This process is what our Slow Food colleagues call *eater-based conservation.*

And so the RAFT collaborative began to develop the first-ever comprehensive list of food species and varieties unique to the North American continent. (Ironically, many countries poorer than the United States, Mexico, and Canada—from Italy and Ethiopia to South Korea—have already completed such inventories of food biodiversity, while ours is still in its infancy in North America.) We were particularly interested in foods that have had place-based, multicultural traditions linked to them for a half century or more. Drawing on the wealth of knowledge that exists among farmers, fishers, foragers, food historians, and folklorists, we have assembled inventories of the foods unique to each ecoregion of North America and noted the indigenous and immigrant cultural communities in which they have been grown.

Once these regional inventories of historic foods were compiled, we worked with conservation biologists, activists, and government agencies to determine which foods were truly at risk of being lost, either ecologically or culturally. We now recognize that at least 1,060 food varieties unique to North America are threatened, endangered, or functionally extinct in the marketplaces of the United States, Canada, and northern Mexico. Unwilling to accept further losses, we then began a process in which we "raft" these endangered foods over to the Slow Food Ark of Taste, which identifies foods worthy of market recovery. This "Ark" attempts to honor the most delicious foods of our country, ones that retain the potential to be sustainably produced at a scale appropriate to the communities in which they originated. Once a food is placed on the Ark of Taste, we mobilize many talents to publicize impending threats to this cornucopia, so that the public at large understands the root causes of the loss of culinary diversity.

Finally, we have invested most of our time fostering collaborative conservation and promotion efforts that bring producers and consumers together to taste, touch, propagate, and celebrate these culinary wonders. Rather than treating these foods as quaint oddities suited to viewing only in historical museums—or worse, as mere abstractions—we want people to know them as living, evolving organisms. We want you to sense how deeply linked these foods are to the health, wealth, gustatory pleasure, and spiritual well-being of America's diverse communities. In that manner, perhaps, people of many colors and walks of life will feel motivated enough to keep them in our bays and streams, on our mountains and prairies, and in our root cellars and larders forever.

In short, RAFT participants aspire to the vision offered by Native American activist Winona LaDuke, who says that this work must ultimately be about more than just saving an heirloom vegetable. In fact, we are explicitly working toward renewing nothing less than the diverse, multicultural food traditions of the North American continent, accepting all of the social, technical, ethical, economic, and ecological challenges that task may entail.

A quarter century ago, some foods in this inventory were subject to efforts by a few nonprofits to ensure their biological conservation, that is, their survival as unique seeds, breeds, fish stocks, or game species. Such work is undoubtedly integral to the larger task of bringing these foods back into their traditional habitats, seasonal rituals, feasts, and culinary presentations. However, we no longer feel confident that their survival in seed banks, zoos, botanical gardens, or agricultural museums is enough.

We need to invest as much time, energy, and inspiration in assuring that the cultural fabric of our food-producing communities is neither neglected nor further degraded, because a traditional food is not merely a bunch of genes or nutritional chemicals.

The term *place-based food traditions* suggests a cohesive set of time-tried relationships among plants and animals, their favored habitats, and their attendant cultures, as well as their most creative, dedicated stewards. These relationships encompass homeland and hearth, extending from fish trap and field to oven and table. To qualify as *traditions*—however dynamic they may be—such relationships must have some modicum of continuity through time and must be rooted in particular places and particular cultural values. Implicit in the use of terms such as *heirloom vegetable* and *heritage breed* is the notion that these plants and animals have been part of certain cultural communities for generation after generation. RAFT participants have begun to gather from their own communities oral histories about how to harvest and cook these special foods. This kind of traditional agricultural and culinary knowledge has been passed on by story from one practitioner to the next, just as the seeds themselves have been passed from hand to hand through the ages.

But enough of such musings for the moment; let's get on to the celebration of the flavors, fragrances, colors, textures, and stories that this place-based food diversity brings into our lives.

A Menagerie for Our Memories, a Feast for Our Senses

North America has been blessed by an astonishing cornucopia of edible plants and animals, both wild and domesticated, most of which occur no place else on the face of Earth. As the five of us worked to compile the following "biographies" of uniquely American foods, we often took time to read each other's drafts and to comment on their contents. The prevailing response we offered one another was an impulsive, rather hedonistic one—to set our reading aside right then and there, to follow our urge *to go taste and see.* Merely reading about some of these foods as they were historically prepared made my own mouth water. I could not only visualize them as they might stand in their forests or fields, but, in some cases, I could smell and taste them, imagining scenes in which they were being carried forth at county fairs and village feasts.

It is a rather bizarre menagerie of swimmers and fliers, of rooters, roosters, and climbers, that has filled American bellies and minds over the centuries and millennia: eels and turtles, herring roe and passion fruit, drumming prairie chickens and gangly moose, devil's claw seeds and the sappy sugars pent up in the trunks and roots of the maple tree. Collectively, they tell America's story even more than do the battlefields, sports arenas, and town council chambers, for they are what we eat and what we dream about.

At the same time, I am amazed at how many of these plants and animals now have human faces associated with them. I can see Raymond Red Corn struggling to find a patch of land where he could grow his namesake, the Osage Red flint corn, to keep it available for his tribal ceremonies. I can imagine the delighted expression of a Louisiana slave named Antoine when his first graft of the Centennial pecan began to put out new leaves. I can hear the cheers of Gold Rush prospectors as an inspired chef in a California saloon made the first dish of Hangtown fry from Olympia oysters for one of their gang who had just struck it rich. And I can imagine the joy that Virginia nurseryman and fruit historian Tom Burford felt when he confirmed the rediscovery of the Harrison cider apple, an heirloom thought to have been lost many decades before.

Some of the food-producing organisms themselves have had names and faces that do not fade from our memories. I am haunted by a photo of Martha, the last passenger pigeon, for she was truly a rare bird. An Arkansas Black apple tree planted above Slide Rock near Sedona, Arizona, is known as the Heritage Tree and has had innumerable children climb its trunk and branches over the years. Burr Morris, who works sugarbushes in Vermont for their sweetness, calls one tree with a particularly voluptuous trunk his "Venus de Maple." Just as much as our heroes, outlaws, and clowns, these foods have become embedded in what William Carlos Williams called "the American grain," for they have become mythic in our collective subconscious.

In these stories of various traditional foods, I often hear the incantations from choirs of voices rising, voices that testify in the various styles of our ethnic communities: the Seminole, Shoshone, Mohegan, and Makah; Minorcans, Sonorans, Swahili-speaking South Africans, and Moors; Hutterites, Mennonites, and Ashkenazi Jews; Polynesian, Viking, English, French, Basque, and Spanish seafarers; Chinese, Irish, Cuban, and Arab refugees; Florida Crackers, Connecticut Yankees, N'awluns Creoles,

Bayou Cajuns, the Gullah from Daufuskie Island, and the Bonacker of Long Island's east end. Somehow their traditional foods always seem to contain more than mere calories, minerals, protein, and fiber. There is spirit, heritage, and even humor embedded in morsel after morsel.

Even when we listen to their earliest written accounts of the foods encountered in North America during the initial intermingling among Native Americans, Africans, Europeans, and Asians, we hear them giving praise to the sheer abundance and variety of foods found in one another's fields, orchards, stockyards, cellars, and kitchens. As Gaspar Pérez de Villagrá described in northern New Mexico in 1598:

[These peoples of America are] much inclined
To cultivate the earth and steward the same.
They harvest beans, corn, and squashes,
Melons and rich sloes of Castile,
And grapes in quantity throughout their landscape . . .
They harvest red wheat and garden fare
Such as lettuce and cabbage, green beans and peas,
Cilantro, carrots, turnips, garlic,
Onions, artichokes, radishes and cucumbers.
They have pleasing herds of turkeys
In abundance and fowl of Castile too,
In addition to sheep and cattle and goats.

If you presume that such food diversity could be found only along the rivers of New Mexico, then listen as Frederick Douglass describes a comparable diversity found on the plantations of Virginia:

Fish, flesh and fowl were here in profusion.
Chickens of all breeds, ducks of all kinds . . .
Guinea fowls, turkeys, geese, and peafowls . . .
Partridges, quails, pheasants, pigeons . . .
Beef, veal, mutton, and venison . . .

The teeming riches of the Chesapeake Bay,
Its rock perch, drums, crocus, trout,
Oysters, crabs and terrapin,
Were drawn hither to adorn the glittering table.
The dairy, too . . . poured its rich donations
Of fragrant cheese, golden butter, and delicious cream
To heighten the attractions of the gorgeous,
Unending rounds of feasting . . .
The tender asparagus, the crisp celery,
And the delicious cauliflower, eggplants, beets,
Lettuce, parsnips, peas, and French beans . . .
Radishes, cantaloupes, melons of all kinds;
And the fruits of all climes . . . here were gathered
Figs, raisins, almonds and grapes . . .
Wines and brandies . . . teas . . . coffee . . .
All conspiring to swell the tide of high life.

The sheer fecundity of American soils and the fluid abundance rushing through American waters astounded an Italian immigrant, Angelo Pellegrini, when he journeyed to the Pacific coast in the early twentieth century. Compared to the worn-out soils and depleted rivers of his birthplace, the forests, fields, and streams of North America seemed almost overendowed with edible plants, animals, and fungi at nearly every turn:

> During the first few months in America, I went to the forest every day and returned home laden with its precious fruit. There were nuts and berries in profusion. With my father I hunted grouse, pheasant, quail and rabbit. Here and there were abandoned homesteads with plum, pear and apple orchards. The reality was more fantastic than the dream . . . It seemed possible to live on the prodigal yields of the surrounding hills . . . And while we were gradually becoming naturalized and eagerly looking forward to citizenship, we were also naturalizing our cuisine.

And yet, as one who had known hunger as a child, Pellegrini was astounded that more Americans did not use the full range of foods that could be found at their back doorstep. Like other immigrants, he saw America as a land with

> tree trunks so large that several couples might dance below them without ever getting into one another's way; of wheat fields so vast that no fast train could traverse them in a single day; of meats and sweets so universally enjoyed that it was impossible to distinguish the rich from the poor. And of incredible waste! No American . . . ever eats an entire sandwich; he always throws away the fringe of the crust.

Pellegrini, much like ethnobotanist Melvin Gilmore, sought to make the most out of the natural endowments of North America, rather than being fixated by introducing more exotic species and importing more goods from distant lands. Gilmore put the dilemma bluntly when he wrote this prophetic warning to Americans in 1919:

> We shall make the best and most economical use of our land when our population shall become adjusted in habit to the natural conditions. The country cannot be wholly made over and adjusted to a people of foreign tastes. There are large tracts of land in America whose bounty is wasted because the plants that can be grown on them are not acceptable to our people. This is not because the plants are not useful and desirable but because their valuable properties are not known . . . The adjustment of American consumption to American conditions of production will bring about greater improvement in the conditions of life [here on this continent] than any other material agency.

Of course, not everyone agreed with Gilmore that the majority of uniquely American foods were useful and desirable. François-André Michaux—whom Napoleon first sent to the United States in 1784 and who returned to study its useful trees in 1802—suggested that the bulk of American lands be cleared of the nearly worthless lot that dominated the natural vegetation to make room for a few "superior" plants:

> I have endeavored . . . to impress on American farmers the advantage of preserving and multiplying some species and of destroying others . . . and in no country is selection more necessary than in North America.

Over the past two centuries, certain Americans have done exactly that, destroying many species to favor just a few. And now some of us deeply regret that our forefathers inadvertently heeded Michaux's words. Incidentally, it has been suggested that Michaux's reports on the relatively low economic value of the American flora and fauna prompted Napoleon to offer to sell some 828,000 square miles of this underappreciated continent to the United States in 1803 for just four cents per acre. We must begin to ask ourselves what we might have been eating—and how American biodiversity would be faring—if we had followed the Gilmore's rather than Michaux's advice.

The Causes of Culinary Impoverishment, the Case for Biocultural Conservation

You might wonder where our culinary cornucopia has gone when you enter any town or city strung out along an American interstate highway. The fast-food drive-ins and quick-marts you find there might offer you calories and convenience, but most of them epitomize the term *tasteless*. Most of them put on your plastic plates are out of just fifteen species or varieties of fried animal flesh, frozen vegetables, and highly processed cereals. They feature Angus beef from feedlots, factory-raised chicken, frozen cod, confinement-raised pork, hothouse-raised turkey, russet potatoes, genetically modified corn and soy, hybrid wheats and beer barleys, iceberg lettuce, hydroponically grown Big Boy tomatoes, industrial-strength coffee, cola nut syrup, and cane sugar. Much of what you get may taste oily or sweet, for it has been loaded up with saturated fats and fructose, fructose, fructose.

Statistics cannot tell the entire story, but, according to Dan Bussey, Americans grew and ate more than 15,000 named varieties of apples a century ago. Today, through

Dan's diligent searching, we might be lucky to find a few trees representing most of the 1,500 apple varieties remaining in North America. Gone are many of the myriad combinations of flavor, color, and texture once brought to us by the likes of Johnny Appleseed, Padre Kino, Archbishop Lamy, and the Burford brothers: tart, juicy, and yellow-green; dry, white, and winelike; syrupy with sugars; melting, with flesh streaked and blotched with crimson.

Perhaps the disappearance of heirloom apples is the easiest part of the story to trace. What has happened to the dozens of annual crop varieties found in the prehistoric ruins of the North American continent that have not been seen growing in any field since the founding of Jamestown, Plymouth Colony, Saint Augustine, and Santa Fe? Why are at least a third of the native fish remaining in our rivers, lakes, bays, and estuaries at risk of extinction, and why have dozens of others already sunk from sight?

When we ask historians, ecologists, and agricultural scientists just why that former wealth has so rapidly disappeared, they offer answers that recall the layers of an onion. As you peel off the papery skin, you can see the tremendous physical changes that have altered our soils, streams, oceans, aquifers, and atmosphere. Rivers have been dammed, inundating some ancient forests and cornfields, while starving others of the moisture they require. Wetlands and valleys have been leveled, filled, paved, or built on, increasing storm runoff and contamination entering our rivers, reservoirs, and estuaries. Forests have been logged, prairies plowed, and clam beds dredged.

Once you slice into the next rose-tinged layer, you glimpse the purely biological changes that have occurred—sometimes in tandem with the physical changes, at other times independent of them. Weeds, diseases, parasites, and plagues have been introduced from distant lands and waters and have outcompeted or consumed the natives. Genetically modified organisms (GMOs) have contaminated open-pollinated corn and free-living salmon. Algal blooms have caused red tides that overwhelm seagrass beds and slow the growth of quahog clams.

Further inside the onion, you find another layer that is hard to separate from the ones on either side of it: the disruption of ecological relationships among organisms, such as pollinators and flowering plants or predators and their prey. If nectar-feeding bats, bees, or butterflies become scarce, the wild or cultivated plants that they pollinate may inadvertently decline as well. If predators are killed off, as wolves and mountain lions have been in many places, certain herbivores like deer and elk proliferate to the point that they damage native vegetation.

The next layer you slice into is that of the genetic erosion caused by changes in land-use practices, dietary preferences, corporate interests, and legal constraints imposed by governments on farmers and ranchers. For example, when cereal producers are forced to grow just a single hybrid variety because breweries or mills demand a uniform product, other varieties are driven toward extinction.

Getting toward the deeply hued core of the onion is the loss of cultural and culinary traditions, factors that biologists tend to ignore at their own peril. Because traditional "digging-stick" harvesting practices for clams or camas roots actually favored the regeneration of those food resources, the cessation of such cultural traditions could have caused local declines in plant and animal populations. If resident cultures forget the multiple uses of a crop, selecting a certain sorghum exclusively for animal feed (as opposed to a versatile variety that also serves for pressing syrup, for shaping brooms, and for making porridges), then the loss of local knowledge accelerates genetic erosion. If a native language or immigrant dialect is lost from a community, the specific names that distinguish the varieties of beans may be lost along with it.

At the center of the onion is what Wendell Berry first recognized as the spiritual cause of the loss of our food diversity and the rural communities that formerly supported it. Following his lead, I have attempted to articulate this issue in my book, *Coming Home to Eat:*

> The real bottleneck to the revival of native, locally-grown foods is a cultural—or more precisely, a spiritual—dilemma. If we no longer believe that the earth is sacred, or that we are blessed by the bounty around us, or that we have a caretaking responsibility [for the whole of Creation] . . . then it does not really matter to most folks how much ecological and cultural damage is done by the way we eat. It does not matter whether we ever participate in the butchering of our own meat, the harvesting and grinding of our own grain, the foraging and drying of our own foods.

Many American foods tell us this story: Where stable rural cultures have lived on the land and tended certain waters for decades, if not centuries, these negative effects are held in check. Thus habitat heterogeneity and food diversity are more or less maintained. But where the stability of cultural communities has been disrupted—with high rates of in-migration and out-migration—there are also high rates of habitat loss, of farmland loss, and of loss of food diversity. Specifically, when parts of America have been "unsettled"—with traditional farmers and foragers moved off the land to make room for more highways, dams, and industrial developments—the cornucopia of wild and domesticated foods there has vanished from sight. It is not surprising that rapidly growing states such as California, Florida, Arizona, Georgia, and Texas have the most threatened and endangered foods, as does Louisiana, which has suffered massive out-migrations from its rural landscapes in the wake of Hurricanes Katrina and Rita.

We must ultimately deal with *all* of these root causes of diversity loss, but as rancher Gretel Ehrlich has urged us to do, we must at the same time tangibly work to save "the remaining living riches of this continent." The Renewing America's Food Traditions collaborative formed to initiate actions that can foster biocultural conservation strategies that in turn foster diversity from our farms, wildlands, and waters all the way to our tables, root cellars, and community feasts. Here's how.

A Manifesto for Renewing Place-Based Food Traditions through Biocultural Conservation

When the Renewing America's Food Traditions collaborative first came together, its founding organizations sought to find synergies and overlaps among their missions, as a means to broaden the "eater-based" conservation constituencies engaged in such work. Gradually, through discussion, debate, and the planning of on-ground pilot projects, these organizations articulated these synergies and began to model certain shared principles to guide their collective actions. The elucidation of those principles is still evolving, but one attempt at their expression is as follows:

Personal, familial, and community engagements with plants and animals, edible or otherwise, may be the surest means to keep us appreciative of their value, and to keep us alert to their vulnerabilities. When such engagement atrophies, the biological loss of species, varieties, stocks, seeds, or breeds traditionally used as food on this continent may accelerate, resulting in immeasurable cultural and culinary losses as well.

To reverse the trend toward ever-accelerating losses of diverse foods that are unique to this continent, we must simultaneously deal with root causes *and* effectively model collaborative conservation actions on the ground that engage food producers, resource managers, chefs, and eaters in achieving the following goals:

1. Recognizing which place-based foods are most at risk
2. Recovering their species, varieties, or populations
3. Restoring their habitats, in both wild and (agri-) cultural landscapes
4. Rescuing and passing on local, traditional knowledge about their stewardship and their culinary uses
5. Recuperating markets and local infrastructures to support their production and use
6. Rewarding the original stewards of these resources with market-based incentives, recognition of their "farmers' rights," and (cross-) cultural reinforcement
7. Reducing or altogether eliminating contamination, both chemical and genetic

This book is but one of many means we have used for identifying and publicizing the uniquely American foods most at risk of extinction and cultural loss. We have also collaborated with Bon Appetít Management Company in sponsoring a competition among its chefs to incorporate rare heirloom vegetables, heritage meats, and their stories into menus offered at restaurants based at colleges, museums, zoos, and botanical gardens. We have sponsored a series of American Traditions Picnics in great American places, from Puget Sound near Seattle to Shelburne Farms on the edge of Lake Champlain, near Burlington, Vermont. We have gathered food stories from folks like you, as they attend the Smithsonian Folklife Festival on the Mall in Washington, D.C., the Seed Savers Exchange Campout in Decorah, Iowa, and the Sitka Conservation Society's Saturday gathering of fishermen and hunters on Baranof

Island in Alaska. We have engaged hundreds of the best market gardeners in America in growing heirloom vegetables for local chefs and have gifted thousands of packets of heirloom seeds to Louisiana farmers who lost their own seed stores in the floods of Hurricanes Katrina and Rita.

Underlying much of this work is our community-based field research to discern which traditional foods may be at risk in each ecoregion or "food nation" across the continent. To give this "red list" a framework—to create a culinary geography—we have roughed out a map that circumscribes the various ecocultural regions as we recognize them at this point in time. We have named each ecocultural region or food nation for an iconic food species that may have functioned as a cultural and ecological keystone there over the centuries. In a similar effort to define the food geography of North America in prehistoric times, ethnobotanist Richard Ford first defined and circumscribed certain "agricultural complexes" with regional integrity in this manner:

> The concept of a prehistoric agricultural or crop complex implies a group of species with an apparent common geographic origin and mutual association within particular environmental parameters in which the complex is developed.

We have extended his concept of food *crops* shared within a particular region to cover wild plants, game, fish, shellfish, and livestock that form a shared nutritional base among the resident cultures found within an environmentally cohesive region. We have chosen the iconic food for each region out of several possible ecological and cultural keystone species, emphasizing those that have suffered historic or recent declines in use.

We have then selected a particular variety, population, or cultural tradition to emphasize the particular stories of certain charismatic elements of these keystone foods—sassafras leaves for gumbo filé, the American chestnuts of Alabama, range-fed bison, quahog clams of Great South Bay, blue crabs of Chesapeake Bay, sugar maples, Southern dent hominy corns, hand-harvested wild rice, El Guique chiles, the fall run of Chinook salmon, Minnesota moose, Nevada single-leafed pinyons, acorns of Englemann's oak. None of these thirteen iconic foods is as threatened as the other eighty species or varieties featured in the following stories, but they have suffered dramatic declines in their once unfathomable abundance. Of course, not every species or variety that has reached extinction was historically rare, of limited range, or few in population numbers. The extinction of the passenger pigeon and the decline of the American chestnut remind us that formerly abundant, even ubiquitous species can sometimes be quickly lost due to combinations of overharvesting, disease, and loss of habitat.

With regard to the other eighty species and varieties featured here, we have used rather consistent criteria to select them on the basis of their truly endangered status. In a general sense, we have followed criteria first articulated by Deborah Rabinowitz for plants and then quantitatively applied Georgina Mace's research on behalf of the World Conservation Union (IUCN) to take into account the narrow geographic range of a species or variety, the scarcity of viable populations capable of regeneration in the face of a changing environment, and the paucity of reproductive individuals within each population.

For wild plants and animals, we generally followed the NatureServe rankings of risk on the North American continent, paying closest attention to those species, subspecies, or stocks (such as salmon runs) that are found at fewer than fifteen sites or in a restricted geographic range, with small populations at each site. In a few cases, we have also included broader-ranging species that are now suffering widespread declines due to insect infestations, introduced diseases, catastrophic wildfires, floods, or droughts.

For cultivated fruits, vegetables, and cereals, we considered those most at risk to have a geographically or culturally restricted area of cultivation, where farming traditions appear to be disappearing and where few farmers remain in each community. This follows Karl Hammer's adoption of the IUCN criteria to accommodate domesticated plant species. However, we have also pioneered the use of seed bank and nursery catalogs to assess the rarity of cultivated plants. For this book, we have focused on those varieties that are available on a regular basis from no more than three commercial nurseries or seed catalogs.

For livestock breeds, we adapted the rankings formulated by the American Livestock Breeds Conservancy, focusing on critically endangered breeds represented by few herds or flocks and by small herd or flock sizes. Of course, such parameters used to assess rarity shift through time, so we will use the Slow Food USA website to periodically update the larger RAFT list.

Two last notes about the map in which these patterns of endangerment can be nested: As noted earlier, the regions with the most endangered foods include Gumbo and Chile Pepper Nations, which have the highest rates of in-migration and out-migration of humans. And yet we also see the loss of farmed foods in Maple Syrup and Clambake Nations, where there has been the gradual breakdown of place-based food traditions since World War II. Aside from offering us these preliminary insights, we see this map as an imaginative, dynamic participatory exercise in which you can help assess the vulnerability of the links between your community and its cultures, habitats, and traditional dietary mainstays. We do not wish to set definitive boundaries in space and time, as if such relationships were static. The map is not meant to pigeonhole any dietary tradition nor essentialize any culture; rather, it might help you visualize patterns that answer the following questions about the place in which you live and eat:

1. What food fragrances, textures, and tastes have pervaded your place of residence for the longest amount of time?
2. How does your contemporary community relate to the plants and animals that formerly offered themselves as such signature foods, in terms of knowing the character and consuming their calories (if at all) in this day and age?
3. How do you imagine your community's future in relation to those historic foods or others that have come to define the nature and culture(s) of your place?
4. What flavors do you want to ensure your grandchildren have a chance to experience?
5. How can you go about safeguarding that culinary opportunity on their behalf?

If the stories are like seeds set out for you to plant, let them grow into a garden that allows you to imagine a richer, tastier world, where the plants and animals that coexist with us have a safer, healthier home.

Further Readings

Berry, Wendell. *The Gift of Good Land.* San Francisco: North Point Press, 1981.

Bussey, Dan. *The Apple in America.* Madison, Wisconsin: privately printed five-volume draft, 2006.

Chinard, Gilbert. "Andre and Francois-Andre Michaux and Their Predecessors. An Essay on Early Botanical Exchanges between America and France." *Proceedings of the American Philosophical Society*, 101:4 (Aug. 16, 1957), 344–361.

Ford, Richard I. "Gardening and Farming before A.D. 1000: Patterns of Prehistoric Cultivation North of Mexico." *Journal of Ethnobiology,* 1 (1981), 6–27.

Gilmore, Melvin R. "Uses of Plants by the Indians of the Missouri River Region." *Bureau of American Ethnology Annual Reports,* 33:43 (1919), 154.

Hammer, Karl, and Korous Khoshbakht. "Toward a Red List for Crop Plant Species." *Genetic Resources and Crop Evolution,* 52:3 (2005), 249.

Hammer, Karl, H. Knüppfer, G. Laghetti, and P. Perrino. *Seeds from the Past: A Catalogue of Crop Germplasm in Southern Italy and Sicily.* Gatersleben, Germany: Academy of Science, 1992.

Michaux, François-André. *Histoire des abres forestiers de l'Amerique aeptentrionale, considers principalment aous les eapportes de leur usage dans les arts.* Paris, France: privately printed in eight volumes, 1810–1813.

Nabhan, Gary Paul. *Coming Home to Eat: The Pleasures and Politics of Local Foods.* New York: W.W. Norton, 2002.

Pellegrini, Angelo. *The Unprejudiced Palate.* San Francisco: North Point Press, 1984.

Rabinowitz, Deborah, S. Cairns, and T. Dillon. "Seven Forms of Rarity and the Frequency in the Floras of the British Isles." In Michael E. Soulé, ed., *Conservation Biology: The Science of Scarcity and Diversity,* pp. 182–204. Sunderland, Massachusetts: Sinauer Associates, 1986.

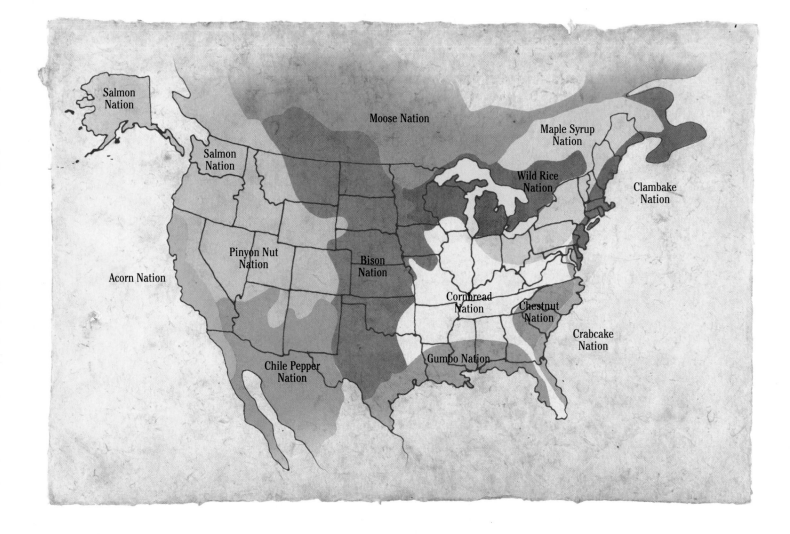

THE FOOD NATIONS OF NORTH AMERICA

What food passport do you carry? What landscape do you see in your mind when you close your eyes while eating a mouthful of food that makes you feel immediately *at home?*

Our sense of place and our sense of taste are intimately related. From a small barrier island off the coast of South Carolina to the pink sandstone canyons of Utah, the landscape of the United States is as varied as its cultures. The farmers' markets, fishmongers, and fruit vendors of each region across North America have their own distinctive calls, colors, and flavors. Our sense of place is determined as much by the food we see and taste as we walk the streets or drive the backroads of our home ground as it is by our postal address.

As we began the RAFT project to document the unique foods of this country, we wondered how we should structure our inquiries into the traditional foods unique to American landscapes and seascapes. Should we inventory them time period by time period or consult with culture after culture across the entire continent? What would our organizing principle be?

Of course, we realized that ecological regions, agricultural production zones, and culinary conventions cut across state and national boundaries. So do our organizations' concentrations of membership. But is there such a thing as an ecogastronomic region? Could those regions be mapped?

One morning a cartoonlike map appeared on a napkin while two of us were merely doodling before launching into our day's work. What if that hypothetical map of ecogastronomic regions was, as National Book Award–winning poet William Safford once said, "a story that *could* be true"?

Once the first draft had seen the light of day, we went out to test whether our hypothesis regarding the existence of "food nations" was true, false, or debatable. To our amazement, we found that several individuals and organizations had already pushed past conventional political boundaries to imagine a fresh geographic framework that had food and food traditions at its base.

We quickly realized that we were not at all the first Americans who had used the convention of calling various ecoregions of North America "food nations." For roughly a decade, Ecotrust and other organizations in the Pacific Northwest of the United States and Canada have referred to "Salmon Nation," a binational region of the watersheds in which various species of salmon have been ecologically, culturally, and spiritually significant. In fact, the imagining of a Salmon Nation had brought together previously unlikely partners who subsequently forged effective alliances to restore salmon streams, forests, and foodsheds in their region. Indigenous communities or "First Nations" of this ecoregion have referred to themselves as Salmon People in meetings and in their own publications for many decades. On reading their anthology, *First Fish, First Peoples: Salmon Tales from the Pacific North Rim,* former U.S. Poet Laureate Robert Hass exclaimed that such re-visioning "re-teaches us our own geography, leaps silver and fresh like the salmon, which is its subject."

Across the continent to the southeast of Salmon Nation, the Southern Foodways Alliance has hosted a series of food conferences and workshops in which African-, European-, and Native American historians and writers have explored their shared culinary traditions. Under the leadership of John T. Edge, they have published a series of books on their regional foodways titled *Cornbread Nation*. If only Ivory Tower scholars had embraced this label it would be one thing, but chefs like Hoppin' John Martin Taylor, humorists like Roy Blount Jr., and bluegrass artists like Tim O'Brien have also pledged allegiance to Cornbread Nation. O'Brien even penned a brilliant song named "Cornbread Nation," which became the title cut on one of his recent CDs.

There are other, similar examples of this ecoregional thinking, as well. Jane and Michael Stern authored a book titled *Chili Nation,* although it was a national survey of chile-based traditions rather than one focused more generally on all foods of the U.S. Southwest. Nevertheless, by using food nations as a framework for our projects, we are giving a knowing nod to some grassroots initiatives already taken by foodies, bioregionalists, and culinary folklorists.

The following descriptions briefly highlight some unique ecological, cultural, and culinary traits of each of these nations. While we expect the boundaries and names to change through time, we see this playful naming as an imaginative tool to help us all think about the relationships among food, place, and culture. By naming each ecoregion for a traditional food that has served as an ecological and cultural keystone there for centuries, if not millennia, we hope to encourage residents of that region to take particular pride in their iconic food and in all the other food species associated with it.

ABOUT RAFT'S FOUNDING PARTNERS

American Livestock Breeds Conservancy (www.albc-usa.org)
The ALBC was founded in 1977 and is headquartered in Pittsboro, North Carolina. The ALBC is dedicated to the conservation and promotion of endangered breeds of livestock and poultry. The conservancy monitors breed populations of ten traditional livestock species in the United States, identifies endangered breeds, documents breed performance, and promotes their use. The ALBC is the preeminent U.S. source for information on domestic animal genetic conservation and has long recognized that small-scale sustainable agriculture systems provide the ideal means to conserve many breeds that are regionally adapted and that have been selected for self-sufficiency.

Center for Sustainable Environments (home.nau.edu/environment)
The Center for Sustainable Environments (CSE) was established at Northern Arizona University (NAU) to serve as an umbrella organization for interdisciplinary environmental collaborations and community outreach in the culturally diverse Intermountain West. In particular, the CSE promotes the linkages between biodiversity and agricultural conservation, especially working to retain traditional ecological knowledge associated with place-based cultures. The center has hosted the Canyon Country Fresh Network of farmers, ranchers, and chefs in the Grand Canyon region and has facilitated the Northern Arizona Food and Agriculture Council. It has a successful track record of working with several tribes on the renewal of their food systems; for example, the CSE facilitated the largest seed repatriation in history to benefit the Hopi tribe and spearheaded the effort to form a Slow Food Presidium for Navajo-Churro sheep among Diné sheepherders. Dr. Gary Nabhan, the center's outgoing director, is also the founder and facilitator of the RAFT project.

Chefs Collaborative (www.chefscollaborative.org)

The Chefs Collaborative is a national network of more than 1,000 members of the food community who promote sustainable cuisine by celebrating the joys of local, seasonal, and artisanal cooking. Since 1993, the collaborative has held successful tastings and briefings on a variety of issues, including sustainable seafood solutions; grassfed, free-range meat production; GMOs; and animal welfare and safety. The collaborative provides its members with the tools to run both economically and environmentally sustainable food-service businesses.

Cultural Conservancy (www.nativeland.org)

This Native American nonprofit organization is dedicated to the preservation and revitalization of indigenous cultures and their ancestral lands, storytelling, and harvesting traditions. The Cultural Conservancy's Storyscape media project focuses on the protection of storehouses of traditional knowledge surrounding nutrition, resource use, farming, foraging, and time-tested sustainable land management practices. The conservancy strives to preserve and renew this endangered knowledge through ethnographic recordings and by providing technical assistance for tribes to protect their own cultural legacies.

Native Seeds/SEARCH (www.nativeseeds.org)

Native Seeds/SEARCH is a nonprofit conservation organization based in Tucson, Arizona. NS/S works to conserve, distribute, and document the adapted and diverse varieties of agricultural seed, their wild relatives, and the role these seeds play in cultures of the American Southwest and northwest Mexico. Founded in 1983, NS/S now safeguards 2,000 varieties of desert-adapted agricultural crops. In addition, NS/S promotes the use of these ancient crops and their wild relatives by distributing seeds to traditional communities and to gardeners worldwide. Some 350 varieties grown at the NS/S Conservation Farm in Patagonia, Arizona, are currently available.

Seed Savers Exchange (www.seedsavers.org)

The Seed Savers Exchange, founded in 1975 by Kent and Diane Whealy, is the single most effective food-crop conservation nonprofit in history. The SSE's Heritage Farm in Decorah, Iowa, permanently maintains and displays 24,000 heirloom vegetable varieties, 700 pre-1900 apples, 200 hardy grapes, and herds of extremely rare Ancient White Park cattle. Since 1981, the SSE's *Garden Seed Inventory* (now in its sixth edition) and similar publications have tracked the availability of all nonhybrid vegetables, fruits, nuts, and berries in the United States. Through its yearbook, the SSE annually offers its members network access to 12,000 varieties of heirloom vegetables—almost twice as many nonhybrid varieties as are offered by the entire U.S. mail-order garden seed industry. The Seed Savers Exchange and Heritage Farm have provided the models for organizations and projects in more than thirty countries.

Slow Food USA (www.slowfoodusa.org)

Slow Food USA is a nonprofit organization that supports a biodiverse, sustainable food supply; local producers; and heritage foodways. Founded in 1986 in Italy to protect the pleasures of the table from the homogenization of modern fast food and fast life, Slow Food has grown to encompass a worldwide membership of 80,000 members in one hundred countries. With 170 *convivia* (chapters) emerging in the United States since 2000, Slow Food USA organizes projects including the Ark of Taste and Presidia, which identify and revitalize foods, farmers, and traditions that are at risk of extinction; Slow Food in Schools, which establishes garden-to-table projects that cultivate the senses and teach an ecological approach to food; and Slow Food Nation, a networking conference of 50,000 food producers, activists, and chefs from all fifty states.

CONTRIBUTORS

Gary Paul Nabhan, PhD, is the founder of the Renewing America's Food Traditions collaborative and editor of four regional monographs related to foods at risk in North America. He has also been among the founders of Native Seeds/SEARCH, the Forgotten Pollinators Campaign, the Migratory Pollinators Project, and the Ethnobiology and Conservation Team. Author or editor of some twenty books that have been translated into five languages, Nabhan has received the John Burroughs Medal for nature writing, a Lannan Literary Fellowship, and the Western States Book Award. For his conservation work, he has received a lifetime achievement award from the Society for Conservation Biology and a MacArthur "genius" grant. He raises Navajo-Churro sheep, heritage turkeys, and native crops in Arizona.

Ashley Rood was coauthor of the precursor of this volume, a RAFT book that was featured as one of the hundred top food stories by *Saveur* magazine in 2005. An environmental advocate and sustainable agriculture activist who works for Environmental Defense in San Francisco, California, Rood is a graduate of Northern Arizona University, where she coordinated a community-supported agriculture (CSA) project that still feeds some 170 families.

Anne Minard is an environmental journalist who has worked or freelanced for several newspapers, magazines, and radio programs in the West. Also a graduate of Northern Arizona University, Minard is the author of books and countless feature articles on science and nature. For the Center for Sustainable Environments, she has spearheaded an agritourism initiative in Arizona that links heritage food promotion to the visitation of great natural and cultural landscapes in that state.

Makalé Faber Cullen is a cultural anthropologist who directs the RAFT, Ark, and Presidia initiatives of Slow Food USA at its national headquarters in Brooklyn, New York. Prior to working with Slow Food, she developed in-school and public programs for City Lore and the Smithsonian's Festival of American Folklife.

Don Bixby, DVM, is the former executive director of the American Livestock Breeds Conservancy, which was honored with the Slow Food International Biodiversity Award during his tenure of leadership. He currently serves as the ALBC's technical programs director and representative to the RAFT collaborative. Coauthor of several books on the conservation of rare livestock breeds, Bixby has been an advisor to the USDA and to many nonprofit breed associations that are working to conserve America's genetic diversity of livestock. Don is one of the people most responsible for the revival of standard breeds of American heritage turkeys in the U.S. marketplace.

ACORN NATION

Stretching along the Pacific coast of northern Baja California and most of Alta California, Acorn Nation embraces the mountains, valleys, and coastal plains that share a Mediterranean climate. From prehistoric through early historic times, most of its peoples hunted, fished, and gathered plants, although many also tended perennial food plants through the use of fire, pruning, and digging-stick cultivation. Clam beds were also tended. The acorns of numerous species of oaks provided staple foodstuffs to many cultural communities, who used ingeniously designed baskets to leach them in streams. Early Spanish settlers introduced orchard fruits, annual crops, and livestock from the Mediterranean climates of the Old World. From the time of the California Gold Rush onward, numerous immigrant groups added to the culinary diversity of the region. Although more species are endangered in California by intense urban and agricultural development than in any other state on the mainland, few of these (other than fish) were historically used as food. Nevertheless, at least sixty-two foods are threatened or endangered in Acorn Nation and the waters adjacent to it.

Mission Grape

Although no domesticated grapes were grown in California prior to 1795, the state is now renowned for its world-class wines, attracting over 19 million visitors to its wine country in 2006. These oenophiles usually come to taste the nuanced flavors of California's Pinot Noir, Cabernet, and old-vine Zinfandel. Yet few people—even the most experienced of vintners—know that the foundation of California viticulture rests on the vines of the Mission grape. Luckily, you can still taste this history—best enjoyed as a glass of sweet Angelica (see below)—thanks to the diligence of a small handful of family winemakers on the rolling hills of Acorn Nation's Central Coast, where locals are struggling to ensure that the history of the Mission grape is preserved.

The Mission grape was first introduced into the present-day United States by a Franciscan, Padre García, around 1660, when he brought black Mission grapes to El Paso in what is now Texas. It did not arrive on Acorn Nation's Central Coast until other Franciscan friars brought it there at the end of the eighteenth century. Slips from its vines were planted alongside the many missions built all along the west coast of Baja and Alta California. According to recent DNA testing conducted by the Centro Nacional de Biotecnología in Madrid, these imported vines came directly from the Spanish variety known as Listan Prieto. The Franciscan padres planted the Listan Prieto grape slips around each mission, ostensibly to make wine for the altar as well as for the table. The padres not only introduced this new genetic material of wine grapes to California but also taught the Spanish and Italian practices of cultivating and processing wine.

The Mission grape thrived in the hot summers of California, producing its loose hanging clusters of reddish-purple grapes in abundance. As new settlers began to arrive in California, and the vineyard tradition eventually moved away from the missions thanks to cuttings taken from their Mission grapevines. Yet the Mission grape was regarded as a utilitarian grape—good for sacramental use and cookery, yet not deeply flavorful or sophisticated except when it was made into sweet wine. New immigrants to California began to introduce wine grapes from other parts of the world: the Pinots, the Cabernets, and the Zinfandels, all with their intensely complex flavors. And soon the Mission grape, which once covered at least 11,000 acres in California, was almost completely forgotten.

Today there are fewer than 500 acres of Mission grapes preserved in a handful of small family-owned vineyards. Many of these vineyards have been home to the Mission grape since the early 1800s. Septuagenarian Rocco Malvini produces his Malvadino Mission wine just as his father did in California's gold country at his Com'e Bella winery. Ken Deaver of Deaver Vineyards maintains eight acres of Mission grapes that his great-grandfather planted in the 1850s. You'll find Mission grape vines from the early 1900s at Nine Gables Winery.

One winemaker has turned her treasured happenstance, a three-acre, old-vine Mission grape vineyard, into a gorgeous artisanal product. Gypsy Canyon Winery proprietor Deborah Hall handcrafts a single barrel of Angelica, a fortified sweet wine, each year following the recipe of the Mission padres. Deborah began winemaking as a novice, embracing the wine traditions of her newfound home in the Santa Rita fields. Working with a vineyard developer, Deborah dove into wine growing, clearing the land to make way for Pinot grapes. But an old hillside covered in sagebrush offered a surprise—vine after vine appeared as the sagebrush was cleared away, until they found a full three acres of old vines that had been neglected for more than seventy years. As Deborah recalls, "I knew I would never be able to grow these kinds of vines in my lifetime—beautiful, old, gnarled vines." So Deborah nursed the venerable vines back to health, and they produced succulent fruit—fruit that was at first mistakenly identified as old Zinfandel and was sold as such for two years.

But as Deborah began to study winemaking, she decided to send the grapes to be tested at UC Davis, discovering that instead of old-vine Zinfandels she had a piece of California history: the Mission grape. However, the Mission grape, a mystery to most winemakers, did not have any buyers. With a vineyard full of Mission grapes ready to be harvested, Deborah turned to her love of history to find a new way of marketing this unique grape. The Mission Archives Library at Santa Barbara Mission preserves a treasure trove of historical documentation from the mission days. Deborah uncovered correspondence between padres dating back to the 1700s. It detailed how to grow the Mission grapes and how to make wines, from dry reds and whites to the sweet Angelica.

Inspired by these archives, Deborah determined to make her Angelica according to historically correct prescriptions. She uses a recipe for this sweet, forti-

Photo by Dimitris Zorbas

Photo by Dimitris Zorbas

fied wine pieced together from the padres' correspondence. The Angelica is packaged in a handblown bottle made of recycled glass, with a handmade paper label and a seal made from beeswax harvested on her land—history in a bottle.

Deborah's Mission grape vineyard, Dona Marcelina Vineyard, named after California's first woman wine grower, is one of the last vineyards of old-vine Mission grapes (vines older than one hundred years); there are an estimated ten acres left in California. During Prohibition, many of these old vines were ripped out; the sagebrush that hid Deborah's Mission grapes for decades was probably planted to protect the vines from destruction by Prohibitionists. But the Mission grape is once again gaining ground. Through cuttings from the Dona Marcelina Vineyard, Mission grapevines are being planted throughout the old missions in California. The Huerta Project, led by horticulturalist Jerry Sortomme, is dedicated to reviving an entire garden full of original plants found at the Santa Barbara Mission from Mission olives, pears, and to, of course, the precious Mission grape—preserving the roots of California's rich history and agricultural bounty.

Sadly, when Sonoma Grapevines, Inc., was purchased by Vintage Nurseries, the only commercial source of red Mission grape slips fell out of availability, so that only the Foundation Plant Materials Service at the University of California at Davis now maintains clones for distribution.

The following two simple but elegant recipes are adapted from *Encarnación's Kitchen*, the first cookbook written by a Hispanic woman in the United States, circa 1890s.

Further Readings

Dunmire, William M. *Gardens of New Spain: How Mediterranean Plants and Foods Changed America.* Austin: University of Texas Press, 2004.

Iverson, Eve. "Wine at the California Missions." California Mission Studies Association website. Accessed July 5, 2007, from www.ca-missions .org/iversen.html.

Pinedo, Encarnación. *Encarnación's Kitchen: Mexican Recipes from Nineteenth-Century California.* Berkeley: University of California Press, 2003.

MERMELADA DE UVA DE LA MISIÓN (MISSION GRAPE MARMALADE)

1 pound Mission grapes
1 pound sugar
juice of one Washington navel orange

Place the ripened Mission grapes in a glass bowl and remove their skins and seeds. Place their pulp in a cooking pot over medium-low heat and slowly add the sugar, stirring with a wooden spoon. Add the juice of an orange and continue to cook and stir until the marmalade thickens. When very thick on the wooden spoon, remove from the flame, let cool, and pour into presterilized jars.

PONCHE DE VINO DE LA MISIÓN (MISSION WINE PUNCH)

2 cinnamon sticks
2 whole cloves
2 (daidai) sour oranges, peeled and pulped
3 tablespoons grated peel (zest) of one of the sour oranges
2 quarts Angelica wine from Mission grapes
6 tablespoons sugar

In a large jug, soak the two cinnamon sticks, the cloves, and the sour orange pulp and zest in the Angelica wine. In the morning, strain the wine, spices, and pulp through a colander into a saucepan. Place the saucepan over low heat and gradually stir in the sugar. As soon as this punch reaches the boiling point, remove it from the fire, pour into a heat-resistant pitcher, and serve.

California Mission Olive

It is a sight to behold: the sprawling, split-trunked, gnarled canopy of one of the earliest olive trees in North America, planted along the first stone irrigation canal in Baja California by Padre Juan de Ugarte around 1699. Amazingly, it still stands—and produces asymmetric, ovoid, freestone olives—within a four-minute walk from the altar of Misión San Francisco Xavier in Baja California Sur. Within a century of its planting, cuttings from this precursor of the California Mission olive had arrived in Alta California. Harvested from the gnarled brown branches of trees planted 220 years ago by Jesuits or by later Franciscan missionaries, the California Mission variety of olive is now unique to the United States and to adjacent Baja California. Filled with the flavors of California's sun and soil, these olives are unlike most other types, whose bitterness mellows only with ripening. Both the green (unripe) and black (ripe) California Mission table olives are mild and rich in oil, 22 percent of which can be pressed out of the fruit. Depending on their degree of ripeness, the oil made from early harvests can have a mild grassy taste, while later harvests yield a rich buttery taste.

When Spain became interested in settling northern California, it used the church as a vehicle. Missions were established to overtake the cultures and economies of the Miwok, Esselen, Wappo, Kashaya, and nearly fifty other native communities residing in the region. Once the chapel and private quarters of the missions were built, vegetable gardens and orchards were cultivated. Because olive trees took upward of five years to yield their first fruits, they were a priority to plant. The padres from the Mediterranean could hardly imagine life without olives, or at least without the oil that they burned as candles during Lent and on certain feast days. The oil not only was used for burning but was essential for cooking, healing wounds, and lubricating machinery, just as it had been in Europe for over 4,000 years.

Spain's missions made strong contributions to California's landscape, culture, and cuisine, and at one time the Mission olive accounted for over half of the state's yield of table olives. Today, fewer than 30,000 acres of America's only unique olive variety remain, and much of that acreage is in the pathway of urban development. Only one commercial nursery, Pacific Tree Farms in Chula Vista, regularly offers propagation material for planting.

In 1998 a group of community members interested in their local history formed the Mission Olive Preservation, Restoration, and Education Project (MOPREP). The organization's volunteers research the history of the California Mission olive trees, locating and authenticating original groves and artifacts. They also coordinate horticultural care, replanting, and olive harvests from trees located at the twenty-one California missions. There are now a handful of missions with working orchards and two retail distributors of California Mission olive oil.

While there are some terrific historic recipes featuring Mission olives to be found in Bess Cleveland's *California Mission Recipes,* we have adapted one from Chez Panisse's Alice Waters that, in our version, pairs Mission olives with another rare fruit, the Meyer lemon.

David Cavagnaro

Further Readings

Barranco-Navarro, Diego, et al. *World Catalogue of Olive Varieties.* Madrid: International Olive Oil Council, 2000.

Cleveland, Bess Anderson. *California Mission Recipes.* Rutland, Vermont: Charles E. Tuttle, 1965.

Mission Olive Preservation, Restoration and Education Project (MOPREP) website, from www.missionolive.org.

Waters, Alice, Alan Tangren, and Fritz Streiff. *Chez Panisse Fruit.* New York: HarperCollins, 2002.

Webb, Edith. "Agriculture in the Days of the California Padres." *The Americas* 4:3 (1948): 325–344.

David Cavagnaro

Sierra Beauty Apple

One of the few great heirloom apples to emerge from Acorn Nation, Sierra Beauty was first discovered around 1890 growing in the Sierra Nevada. It is derived from a seedling apple, one presumably found as a remnant of miners' movements following the California Gold Rush, for it next appeared in mining camps above the town of Chico in Butte County in 1923. Although handled by a few regional nurseries for a number of decades, it disappeared for a while, only to be rediscovered further toward the coast in 1980 still being grown in the Gowan family orchard near Philo, in Mendocino County. Only three major heirloom nurseries—Orchard Lane, Trees of Antiquity, and Greenmantle—continue to offer this unique heirloom for propagation, while three smaller California nurseries—L. E. Cooke, David Wilson, and Garcia River—offer it primarily to Acorn Nation growers. It remains critically threatened as a commercial variety, one that is suitable for table use and that deserves much more widespread appreciation and distribution.

Bumper crops of blocky but handsome Sierra Beauty apples are produced on vigorous, hardy, upright trees every other year, with a few apples found within their open canopies on off-bearing years. The large, handsome apples themselves are round to slightly conical, with tough, thick skin roughened by netlike veins. As the Sierra Beauty slowly ripens, its skin color deepens from a pale yellow-green to a wash of pinks, a blush of scarlets, and a riot of crimson streaks. The yellowish flesh has a brisk, sprightly flavor, with an astonishingly crisp texture. The Fruit Guys claim that "the Sierra Beauty will wake up your mouth with a resounding snap, a light crisp texture, and a gentle floral finish on the palate." It has a pleasant tartness when eaten fresh but is also used in purees, pies, butters, and sauces. Alice Waters at Berkeley's Chez Panisse restaurant has featured the Sierra Beauty in both tarts and crostatas on her menus over the years.

The following recipe is adapted from one offered by Gowan's Oak Tree, an orchard of award-winning California heirloom apples, which seasonally features the Sierra Beauty for use by restaurant chefs and home cooks in northern California.

CAROL'S SIERRA BEAUTY APPLE PIE

5–6 ripe Sierra Beauty apples, peeled and cored
¾–1 cup turbinado sugar, depending on the sweetness of the crop
3 tablespoons unbleached whole-wheat flour
3 teaspoons freshly ground cinnamon bark
two 9-inch pie shells for a double-crust pie
2 tablespoons unsalted butter
3 tablespoons cream or half-and-half

Slice the apples and place them in a mixing bowl. Add the sugar, flour, and cinnamon, then mix them with the slices until all surfaces of the apples are fully coated. Place a bottom crust in the pie pan and prick the surface with the tines of a fork. Pour the apple mixture onto the bottom piecrust. Cut the butter into small pieces and place them atop the coated apple slices, then place the second piecrust upside-down over the filling and crimp together the edges of the top and bottom crusts until the apple mixture is sealed inside. Cut decorative patterns for the vents in the upper crust. With a pastry brush, coat the upper crust with cream, then sprinkle the moist surface with sugar. Place the pie into a preheated 450-degree oven and bake for 10 minutes, then turn the heat down to 350 and continue baking for 50 minutes. Remove from oven, cut into eight slices, and serve warm.

David Karp

Further Readings

Bussey, Dan. *The Apple in America*. Madison, Wisconsin: privately printed five-volume draft, 2006.

The Fruit Guys website. Accessed February 15, 2007, at www.thefruitguys.com.

Waters, Alice, Alan Tangren, and Fritz Streiff. *Chez Pannise Fruit*. New York: HarperCollins, 2002.

Whealy, Kent. *Fruit, Nut and Berry Inventory*, 3rd ed. Decorah, Iowa: Seed Savers Exchange, 2001.

A valley in the Sierra Nevada.

Santa Maria Pinquito Bean

Santa Maria barbecue—a mainstay of California's culinary heritage—would not be complete without a side of garlic-infused Santa Maria *pinquito* beans as a salad or a hot casserole. A pea-sized pink bean similar to a pinto, the Santa Maria *pinquito* is grown almost exclusively on the Central Coast of Acorn Nation. To truly enjoy the garlic-infused smoky flavor of Santa Maria–style *pinquito* beans, you must make the journey to this beautiful place.

Begin with a Saturday-morning stroll down Broadway and Main in Santa Maria, where you'll be nearly overwhelmed by the smell of burning red oak. Barbecue stands line the streets, serving up simple Santa Maria–style barbecue made by small, family-owned businesses or as the occasional church fund-raiser. You won't find dry rubs, smokers, or heavily guarded secret sauces in Santa Maria—just a simple tri-tip steak, grilled over native coastal red oak wood, seasoned with garlic, salt, and pepper, then slathered with salsa and served with a side salad and a slice of French bread with sweet butter. And of course don't forget the slow-cooked Santa Maria *pinquito* beans.

For a more formal experience, head out to Far Western Ranch, owned by one of Santa Maria's founding Swiss-Italian families, the Minettis, or the Hitching Post. These restaurants have been serving up Santa Maria–style barbecue for over fifty years. If you can't make the trip to Santa Maria, one of the Minetti daughters, Susie Righetti, offers *pinquito* beans and Santa Maria–style seasonings through her specialty foods company, Susie Q.

As legend tells it, this tradition of Santa Maria barbecue dates back to the nineteenth-century ranchero days on California's Central Coast. Large families would gather each spring to brand the new calves, and a barbecue under the shade of the oak

David Cavagnaro

trees capped the day's hard labors. When Swiss-Italian farmers settled in Santa Maria to grow beans for the U.S. government, they may have brought the *pinquito* bean along with them. It is quite unlike any other bean from the American Southwest, so it probably came to Acorn Nation by boat rather than by overland route across the desert. Even though no one knows quite how this little pink bean arrived on the Central Coast of Acorn Nation, it thrives there during the hot summers and is always prolific. In fact, it is so climatically adapted to the heat-and-fog interplay of the valley that it is rarely grown anywhere else. Its seeds are offered by very few garden seed catalogs, and so mail-order bags of beans from Santa Maria businesses are the best means to share in this tradition.

New World heirloom bean champion Steve Sando, of Rancho Gordo, began offering the Santa Maria *pinquito* bean after customers requested it by name. After experiencing this California classic cuisine—Santa Maria–style barbecue with all of its trimmings—you'll be pining to taste it again. The following recipe for bean salad comes from the Far Western Tavern near Santa Maria, via the California Farm Bureau Federation.

SANTA MARIA PINQUITO BEAN SALAD

½ pound Santa Maria *pinquito* beans
2 green scallions
1 small red onion
1 bell pepper or Fresno jalapeño pepper
⅓ cup Mission olive oil
⅛ cup red wine vinegar
juice of 1½ lemons
1 tablespoon minced fresh cilantro leaves
¼ teaspoon sea salt
¼ teaspoon freshly ground black pepper
1 teaspoon oven-roasted Sonoran garlic

Soak the *pinquito* beans in a bowl overnight. Drain the water, and place the beans in a cooking pot with fresh water. Boil uncovered for 1½ hours or until tender but firm. Meanwhile, grill the scallions, onion, and pepper until slightly caramelized or charred on the outside, then dice. (Choose either a jalapeño or a bell pepper, depending on your tolerance for heat.) Drain the beans and place them in a large glass mixing bowl, and combine with olive oil, vinegar, lemon juice, diced vegetables, and cilantro. Season to taste with salt, pepper, and roasted garlic. Chill for several hours, then toss with spoons just prior to serving.

Santa Maria Valley style barbecue. Courtesy Santa Maria Valley Chamber of Commerce

Further Readings

Gullo, Jim. "Savoring the West: Santa Maria Steaks Its Claim," 2003. Accessed March 15, 2007, from www.viamagazine.com/top_stories/articles/santa_maria03.as.

Parsons, Russ. "Finally, the Tri-Tip of His Dreams." *Los Angeles Times,* June 29, 2005.

White Abalone

Tucked within its mother-of-pearl shell, the white abalone is a delectable marine snail native to a small stretch of the Pacific coast off Acorn Nation. It is the deliciously delicate white meat of this mollusk that has placed its survival in peril. For centuries it was perhaps the least-known abalone of the eight species that occur along the Pacific coast of North America, for it prefers the deepest waters, dwelling on ledges and boulders sixty to two hundred feet below sea level.

This kept it out of reach of the earliest abalone divers of the coastal Chumash and Gabrieleño peoples, so that the populations of this mollusk grew to 4,000,000 individuals during late prehistoric times. That was good for the mollusks living in these magnificent oval-shaped shells, for they must mate with another abalone of the opposite sex who lives within a yard's distance, or else the thousands of eggs and sperm released into the salty waters will not produce larvae.

Being rather stationary creatures, they need to live in high densities to regenerate.

Unfortunately, their populations began to dramatically diminish when Japanese immigrants familiar with other abalone reached the California coast in the 1890s. A pioneering entrepreneur named Otosaburo Noda observed an untouched bounty of abalone species south of Carmel, which prompted him to summon one of Japan's greatest marine biologists, Gennosuke Kodani, to check it out. In 1896, Kodani completed such a thorough reconnaissance of abalone beds out from the coast of Acorn Nation that

Workers and white abalone at the Pierce Brothers wholesaler at Morro Bay, California, circa 1933. California Views: The Pat Hathaway Photo Collection, Monterey, California

investors became willing to recruit and grubstake some of the finest "hard-hat" divers from the Chiba Prefecture near Tokyo. Within a decade's time, they were bringing in hundreds of kilos of abalone meat per day to cube, mince, and can for international export. These Japanese immigrants dominated the California abalone industry until the start of World War II, at which time many were placed in government "relocation" (i.e., internment) camps.

During and immediately after World War II, few European-Americans were willing to attempt the dangerous dives down to the cold depths that the white abalone favors. By that time, however, the white abalone already had gained a mythic reputation because of its sweet, uniquely flavored meat. So when improved scuba-diving equipment became affordable in California beach towns in the late 1950s, commercial harvesters gradually accelerated their activities around the relatively pristine abalone beds. Soon, as much as 450 pounds of abalone meat per day was being hauled up and delivered by a single skiff full of scuba divers. In one year alone, 1972, divers took over 140,000 pounds of white abalone, virtually emptying the beds on deeper reefs. The commercial harvest flourished for less than a decade, but white abalone became the rage in seafood restaurants along the West Coast. By 1977, the populations had been hit so hard that the diver's extra search time to bring in each additional abalone caused its price to soar. By 1985, a few persistent commercial divers had cleaned out the last remaining aggregations of white abalone, gaining an average of $1,000 per landing. They did not know it then, but over 95 percent of all white abalone ever eaten in the world had been consumed within a period of just nine years.

The commercial fishery for white abalone was forced to close after 1995, when only one hundred live individuals could be found by all commercial divers in the United States. In Channel Island habitats where this species was once abundant, less than one live white abalone remained per 12,000 square yards by the time their harvesting was made illegal. However, clandestine diving activity may still be diminishing these remnant populations, given that black-market prices among a few unscrupulous restaurateurs reach as high as $85 per pound.

Further Readings

Davis, Gary E. "White Abalone: Going, Going, Gone?" *Natural Resource Year in Review, 1998.* National Park Service Publication D-1346. Available at www2.nature.nps.gov/TearInReview/yir/yir98/chapter02pg2.html.

Hemp, Michael Kenneth. *Cannery Row: The History of John Steinbeck's Old Ocean View Avenue.* Carmel, California: The History Company, 2002.

Karpov, Konstantin. "White Abalone—An Extinct Possibility?" 1998. Available at www.psmfc.org/recfin/pub/kelp/no6/WHITEAB.htm.

Lafferty, Kevin D. "White Abalone Restoration," 2004. U.S. Geological Survey, Western Ecological Research Center. Available at www.werc.usgs.gov/coastal/abalone.html.

Neumann, Melissa. "Recovery Planning for the White Abalone." *Endangered Species Bulletin* 28:4 (2003): 20–21.

Sarvis, Shirley. *Crab & Abalone: West Coast Ways with Fish & Shellfish.* Indianapolis, Indiana: Bobbs-Merrill Company, 1968.

The species was federally listed as an endangered species in 2000, when it was estimated that fewer than 1,000 mature individuals remained in American waters, with an unknown quantity surviving continued diving pressure off the coast of Baja California. At that time, fisheries biologists realized that placing size limits on abalone catches would never be enough; they warned that unless foolproof protection of remnant beds was combined with aggressive attempts to recover these populations, this mollusk would be driven into extinction.

Fortunately, a private/public partnership known as the White Abalone Restoration Consortium began extensive abalone breeding programs in 2001, with the hope of reintroducing breeding stock back into the species' historic habitats. Until such reintroductions prove to be successful and the federal government delists white abalone as a protected species, wild ones remain off-limits for human consumption. Nevertheless, other species of abalone are being successfully farmed, and their delicious meat is an acceptable consumer choice. Although it is unlikely that wild populations of white abalone and some

POP ERNST'S CANNERY ROW ABALONE STEAKS

6 farm-raised California red abalone steaks
2 teaspoons Mission olive oil
3 tablespoons unsalted butter
½ tablespoon sea salt
¼ teaspoon black peppercorns, freshly cracked

Trim off the dark portions of the farm-raised red abalone steaks, as you would with scallops. Cut each steak across the grain into slices $3/8$ inch thick and then pound them with a wooden mallet until they are velvety and limp. Place them in a hot skillet drizzled with olive oil and fast-fry them, flipping them in the skillet after 15 seconds so that they are quickly fried on each side—fast enough to barely make them sizzle.

Next, wipe the fried steaks with a damp cloth and clean the skillet. Place them in the same skillet with sizzling hot butter, cooking for 30 seconds on the first side and 20 seconds on the other. Sprinkle with sea salt and fresh-cracked black peppercorns. Serve with lemon slices.

of its rarer relatives will recover in such numbers during our lifetimes to allow commercial harvesting once again, at least the species will be brought back from the brink of extinction.

The recipe preparation above became a standard on Cannery Row in Monterey, California—home to John Steinbeck and Doc Ricketts—thanks to an abalone gourmet named Pop Ernst. Today, the Monterrey Abalone Company bases itself near Doc and Steinbeck's old haunts, sustainably farming red abalone of excellent quality that reach one-quarter pound live weights per shell. It is one of several shellfish farming firms that has brought California red abalone back to our tables without further depleting these species.

Leatherback Sea Turtles

They are ancient giants, the largest marine reptiles in the world. The leatherback sea turtles that have reached the Pacific coast of Acorn and Chile Pepper Nations have tipped the scales at 2,000 pounds. For millennia they have roamed the high seas of the Pacific for the most part of each year, only to come landward in the spring, touching down on the shores of bays and lagoons of the Californias and adjacent Sonora state. There, some of the females have occasionally nested, while others have been lured in by the songs of indigenous peoples who traditionally offered them water and food for four days before releasing them again to the wild. The Seri Indians of the Sonoran coast and the islands of the Gulf of California still consider them the most sacred of all animals and classify them as a kind of human being long ago transformed, still retaining the human capacity to shed tears.

The leatherbacks' little tear ducts and gigantic body size are not their only defining characteristics. Their massive, rather rubbery, ribbed carapace is shaped unlike that of any other sea turtle. Charcoal green in color and ridged lengthwise with seven rays, the leatherback's distinctive carapace is reflected in

the Spanish name used for this turtle in the North Pacific, *siete filos*. Elsewhere in Latin America the leatherback is known as the *baula* or *laúd* ("lute-shaped"). Oddly, these giants feed on some of the smallest invertebrates in the Pacific, sea gooseberries and jellyfish. Unlike other sea turtles of the Pacific, which are so intolerant of the cold that they are rarely seen north of San Diego, leatherbacks are well insulated enough to travel as far north as the ice floes of the Arctic Circle. They can also dive to deeper levels off the coastal shelf than any other marine reptile—turtle, crocodile, iguana, or sea snake.

Although there is a taboo against eating leatherbacks among some tribes, some of the first immigrant populations arriving to California had no qualms about consuming the flesh of these giants. In 1871, "the largest turtle we ever saw" was brought into the Horton House restaurant in San Diego on the backs of four Chinese immigrants. A *San Diego Herald* reporter admitted that "we had turtle steak for dinner and it was good." Sixteen years later, the *Chicago Tribune* reported that in California, "turtle soup is as abundant as bread and butter."

That same year (1887), the *San Diego Herald* offered the following report from a small fishing village edging San Diego Bay:

Mr. W. A. Cabral of Roseville caught a turtle weighing 1,200 pounds while fishing on the kelp beds of Point Loma on 1 June . . . It was caught on an ordinary-sized fishing hook, and in endeavoring to pull the turtle into the boat, the fisherman was almost drawn overboard. The monster fish was exhibited for several days at Jorre's Wharf before going the way of all sea turtles—toward the tureen.

Exactly sixty years later to the week in the very same bay, the same newspaper reported a similar incident:

An 890-pound turtle with a shell 7½ feet long towed a 25-foot cabin cruiser 5 miles through Catalina Channel before it died of a broken back and exhaustion, four Long Beach fishermen reported. The leatherback turtle, [now]

rare in waters this far north, collided with the cruiser, and the impact tore off the boat's rudder and cracked the turtle's shell . . . the crew gaffed the turtle, roped it with an anchor line, then fashioned a makeshift rudder as the turtle headed toward harbor.

By the time that leatherback died hauling a cabin cruiser into harbor in 1967, most turtle biologists had already recognized that its species was the most endangered of all marine reptiles. It has been protected as an endangered species by the U.S. government now for over a quarter century and is considered to be endangered globally by the World Conservation Union. Nevertheless, commercial fishermen pursuing swordfish in the Humboldt Current off Peru and Chile are still allowed to kill a disproportionate number of all leatherbacks in the Pacific. As a result, the number of females nesting on the Pacific coast of the Americas in recent years has dwindled down to less than one-hundredth of those available in the 1980s, with fewer than 500 individuals nesting some years.

Recently, a dedicated cadre of turtle biologists and activists from western Mexico has labored hard to protect the nesting beaches of that country, which formerly hosted more egg-laying leatherback mothers than all other American countries combined. In recent years, leatherbacks have begun once again to lay eggs on the Pacific coast of Baja California, where biologists protect their nests on the beach or incubate them in labs when perils on land appear insurmountable; any hatchlings are allowed to paddle their way down the beach and into the surf. There they will meet other perils, but some leatherbacks will survive against all odds. Fortunately, there are concerted efforts to reduce these perils, undertaken by a number of grassroots conservation groups in Baja California, California, and Sonora—including the Seri Indian youth who were honored on World Oceans Day in 2006. Although leatherbacks remain critically endangered throughout the northern Pacific and are predicted to be extinct within two decades if nothing is done, there is at least a critical mass of conservationists working toward bringing them back from the brink of extinction.

Further Readings

Felger, Richard S., Wallace J. Nichols, and Jeffrey A. Seminoff. "Sea Turtles in Northwestern Mexico: Conservation, Ethnobiology, and Desperation." In Jean-Luc E. Catron, Gerardo Ceballos, and Richard S. Felger, eds., *Biodiversity, Ecosystems, and Conservation in Northern Mexico*, pp. 405–424. New York: Oxford University Press, 2005.

Nabhan, Gary Paul. *Singing the Turtles to Sea: The Comcáac (Seri) Art and Science of Reptiles.* Berkeley: University of California Press, 2003.

Sarti, Laura M., Scott A. Eckert, N. T. Garcia, and A. R. Barragán. "Decline of the World's Largest Nesting Assemblage of Leatherback Turtles." *Marine Turtle Newsletter* 74 (1996): 2–5.

Spotila, James. "Worldwide Population Decline of *Dermochelys coricea*: Are Leatherbacks Going Extinct?" *Chelonian Conservation and Biology* 2:2 (1996): 209–222.

Stinson, M. L. "Biology of Sea Turtles in San Diego Bay, California, and in the Northeastern Pacific Ocean."Master's Thesis: San Diego State University, 1984.

Thelander, Carl G., ed. *Life on the Edge: A Guide to California's Endangered Natural Resources.* Santa Cruz, California: BioSystems Books, in collaboration with Heyday Books, 1994.

Instead of offering a historic regional recipe for leatherback steak or soup, we wish to note that leatherbacks are not intentionally harpooned or eaten by the Seri Indians. However, on the rare occasion that a leatherback is encountered while it is dying or when it has recently become dead, it is said to offer its flesh to the human community for a ritual communion. Historically, the Seri fishermen who shared this sacrament had to close their eyes during this communal feast, or they would go blind. Visions often came to those who participated in leatherback ceremonies, who would later dream that turtles were speaking to them and serving as spiritual guides. However, the last full-fledged leatherback ceremony occurred among the Seri in 1981, when sightings of this species were far more frequent than they are today.

Acorns of Engelmann's Oak

The most endangered of all oak trees in Acorn Nation, Engelmann's *(Quercus engelmannii)* is also one that can live the longest: Individual trees that still exist were born more than three centuries ago, some before Spanish missionaries reached the coast of Alta California. It can be a stately tree, with angular limbs and an open, rounded canopy cresting forty feet above the stony ground. It drops its leathery, muted blue-green leaves during months of drought and produces its inch-long, oval-cylindrical acorns in the fall, prior to the beginning of the gentle winter rains.

As Pomo storyteller and basket maker Julia Parker recalls for the many tribes of Acorn Nation, "When the acorns do come, there are dances and songs. We take from the earth, we give to the earth, we say thank you." For centuries, these acorns were the mainstay of the Digueño and Luiseño peoples in what is now called San Diego County, California. Family members would work together to gather, shell, grind, leach, and store acorn flour in granaries for year-round use. Their reddish-beige acorn porridge was cooked over an oak-wood fire, in an earthen vessel that often sweetened the mix by removing any remaining bitter tannins. Acorn stews, cakes, and gruels were eaten with venison or other game. The camps had the smoky scents of oak wood in the air, and the flesh of deer, bear, and sheep had the flavors and calories of acorns embedded in them.

Although rare today, it is worth remembering that during ancient Pleistocene times, Engelmann's oak savannas and woodlands covered a rather large swath of Baja and Alta California as well as Arizona. As the climate changed, that range dwindled, and in recent decades, as Southern California has become a suburban blur, the oak habitats have been diminished even further. The sites where Engelmann's oak once thrived are now found under the pavement of Pasadena and Pomona; on the rangelands outside

Stephen Francis Photography.

David Cavagnaro

of San Diego and Riverside, the soil has become so compacted that little regeneration has occurred over the last seventy-five years. The two remaining refugia of any size that support Engelmann's oak are the woodlands of Black Mountain in central San Diego County and the savannas of the Santa Rosa Plateau in Riverside County. With the spread of sudden oak death throughout California, the future of Engelmann's oak and its kin currently looks grim.

The following recipe for acorn burritos is a family heirloom of Amalia Ruiz Clark, an elderly Hispanic woman who recorded the foods eaten during her childhood in the Southwest in a folio called *Special Mexican Recipes;* it was later included in Carolyn Niethammer's collection, *The Tumbleweed Gourmet,* and is adapted here for the acorns of the Engelmann's oak, which require leaching.

ENGELMANN'S OAK ACORN BURRITOS

1 cup Engelmann's oak acorns, shelled, leached, and ground (see directions)
6 small flour tortillas
1½ cups melted butter
1 cup brown sugar or grated *piloncillo,* dried cones of brown sugar called *panocha de piloncillo*
3 tablespoons Mission olive oil

Crack the acorn shells with a hammer and pick out their meats. Next, place the acorn meats in the inner pot of a double-pot spaghetti cooker and fill the outer pot with water. Bring the pot to a boil; to leach out the tannins, continue boiling for 2½ hours, changing the water every 15 minutes. Grind the acorn meats in a blender or with a mortar and pestle until the meats are fine grained.

Brush the flour tortillas with melted butter, sprinkle on brown sugar, and spoon in several teaspoons of ground acorns, depending on how much the tortilla can hold. Roll up the tortillas to make cylindrical burritos; fasten the ends with toothpicks should they tend to unroll. Deep-fry in hot olive oil until golden. Drain on paper towels, and then cut in half to make 12 servings.

Further Readings

Hedges, Ken. *San Ysabel Ethnobotany*. Ethnic Technology Notes 20. San Diego: San Diego Museum of Man, 1986.

Moerman, Daniel. *Native American Ethnobotany.* Portland, Oregon: Timber Press, 1998.

Niethammer, Carolyn J. *The Tumbleweed Gourmet: Cooking with Wild Southwestern Plants.* Tucson: University of Arizona Press, 1987.

Pavlik, Bruce M., Pamela C. Musick, Sharon Johnson, and Marjorie Popper. *Oaks of California.* Los Olivos, California: Cachuma Press, 1991.

BISON NATION

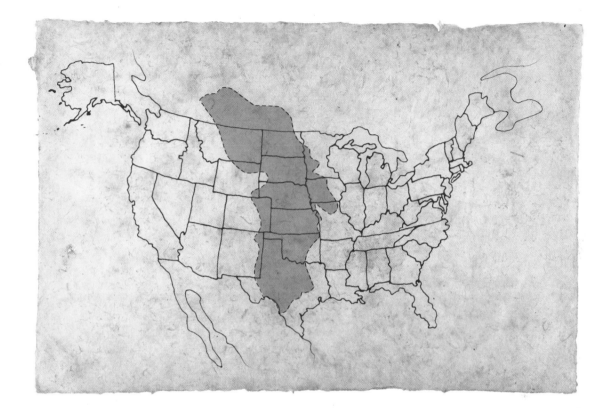

Encompassing all of the short-grass plains and most of the tall-grass prairies in the honey-colored heartland of North America, Bison Nation has been historically enriched by fertile soils, dozens of wild edible seeds and roots, sizable herds of game, and the farming of annual crops such as corn, sunflowers, beans, and squashes. Bison literally shaped the landscape by their wallows, grazing, and interactions with fires and floods. Later, when bison declined and immigrants began to plow extensive tracts for wheat, corn, and soy production, diversity and water quality dramatically declined, and game birds like Atwater's prairie chicken also grew scarce. Recently, out-migration from rural communities to metro areas in other regions has further disrupted land-based traditions. As a result, some forty-seven traditional foods are currently threatened or endangered in Bison Nation. Nevertheless, Bison Nation today harbors some of the most vibrant local-foods initiatives anywhere on the continent, which support the production of many heirloom vegetables and heritage livestock breeds.

Free-Ranging American Bison

Bison—the American "buffalo"—are the largest free-ranging species in North America to have survived the mass extinctions that occurred around the time of the last Ice Age, 10,000 to 13,000 years ago. Since that time, bison herds have served as an ecological keystone by shaping prairie habitats and as a cultural keystone by being prominently featured in Plains Indian subsistence and cosmology. Creating hundreds of thousands of buffalo wallows rich in nutrients and moisture, they generated favorable habitats for prairie turnips, American groundnuts, onions, and prairie chickens used as food by numerous hunting and gathering cultures. These cultures did not merely rely on bison and their ecological associates for food but coevolved with them, integrating them into their shelter, clothing, stories, songs, and ceremonies. Bison have become their symbol of tenacity, enduring all sorts of weather and rough terrain to ensure that grassland habitats remain their domain.

As tough and adaptable as they are, though, plains bison didn't fare too well after a critical mass of hunters and cattlemen arrived in Bison Nation during the nineteenth century to carve up the abundance they found there. Debate still rages about whether human hunters, livestock diseases, habitat fragmentation, or climate has been the most important factor in the animal's dramatic decline. Regardless of the ultimate answer, it's a fact that as many as 40,000,000 bison once roamed free from the central highlands of Mexico to northern Canada before the species almost crashed to extinction more than a hundred years ago. Some United States government officials clearly encouraged the extermination of the plains bison as a means to break the backs of native cultures. As Columbus Delano, Secretary of Interior under President Grant, wrote in 1873, "I would not seriously regret the total disappearance of the buffalo from our western prairies, in its effect upon the Indians, regarding it as a means of hastening their sense of dependence upon the products of the soil and their own labors."

The credit for their survival goes to a few cattle ranchers, including the famous Charles Jesse "Buffalo" Jones, a man who spent some of his last days among the vastly diminished population of bison on the edge of the Grand Canyon. Jones and his cohorts captured some of the country's last remaining bison and maintained them in captive herds. But they also saddled the animals with a hidden legacy: cattle genes.

Most of the continent's modern bison herds are the descendants of accidental crosses or the result of failed experiments in the early twentieth century to produce "cattelo" or "beefalo." These experiments failed in the sense that they didn't produce hardier beef cows, as ranchers like Jones and others had hoped. But other consequences lingered, in the sense that the cattle genes had already become embedded in most commercial bison herds. Many of the bison that are now raised for meat production depend on supplemental feed or on feedlot fattening for at least a portion of the year, just as most beef cattle in the marketplace do.

Recently, however, some enthusiasts have envisioned a larger, more ecological and genetically robust future for the American bison. They propose efforts toward the genetic recovery of bison, using multiple, genetically pure, and healthy herds of bison that are now on federal lands at places such as Wind Cave and Yellowstone as sources of genes for other herds. These purer strains of bison thrive in a few national parks, particularly in the West, and on ranches that encompass a mix of private and public lands. The same enthusiasts call for phasing out all feedlot finishing of bison and placing them permanently in larger landscapes where they can range more freely and resume their historic role as an ecological keystone species. Some of the thirty-one tribes that form the Intertribal Bison Coooperative have already embraced this vision, releasing bison back onto their reservations' wild lands.

James Derr, a wildlife geneticist out of Texas A&M University, has done extensive research on the nation's public buffalo herds, which has revealed the extensive hybridization that has taken place in bison. Derr points out that the presence of cattle genes is actually quite low in many herds, so he advocates consuming bison as a healthy alternative to beef if for no other reason than it promotes the preservation of the species and what remains of its native ecosystems, the Great Plains of Bison Nation.

"With trivial amounts of cattle genetics that are segregating in a herd, you are still predominantly eating North American bison," Derr says. "They're

Sara Roahen

going to have in general the healthy attributes of bison that are not hybrids."

In their 2007 nomination of bison for the Slow Food Ark of Taste, Matt Jones and Rebecca Pasquariello point out that bison meat contains as many omega-3 fatty acids per serving as salmon and three to six times the amount of omega-3s as grain-fed animals. Bison meat also harbors the highest-known levels of the fat-blocker and anticarcinogen known as conjugated linoleic acid, or CLA. Evidence is emerging that CLA has the potential to reduce the risk of cancer, obesity, diabetes, and a number of immune disorders. Previous research has shown that cooked bison meat is low in fat and sodium and high in protein and is a good source of selenium, thiamin, and vitamins B_6 and B_{12}. Bison's high concentrations of selenium, a natural trace element that acts as a mood elevator, have led Jones and Pasquariello to dub the meat of this free-ranging wildlife species "the original happy meal." Both Slow Food USA and Slow Food Canada have begun to collaborate with producers of grass-fed bison to promote their exceptional meat products, and the RAFT collaborative played a key role in a recent gathering of scientists and ranchers considering the ecological future of the bison in North American landscapes.

The following historic recipe is adapted from Crow ethnobotanist and storyteller Alma Hogan Snell.

Further Readings

Danz, Harold. *Of Bison and Man.* Denver: University of Colorado Press, 1997.

Driskell, J. A., X. Yuan, D. W. Giraud, and M. J. Marchello. "Concentrations of Selected Vitamins and Selenium in Bison Cuts." *Journal of Animal Science* 75 (1997): 2950–2954.

Halbert, Natalie D., Peter J. P. Gogan, Ronald Hiebert, and James N. Derr. "Where the Buffalo Roam: The Role of History and Genetics in the Conservation of Bison on U.S. Federal Lands." *Park Science* 24 (2007): 2.

Jones, Matt, and Rebecca Pasquariello. "North American Plains Bison Nomination to Slow Food USA Ark of Taste." 2007. Accessed July 12, 2007, from www.slowfoodusa.org.

McClenahan, Jayne M., Fayrene L. Hamouz, Budi Setiawan, Martin J. Marchello, and Judy A. Driskell. "Sensory Evaluation of Broiled and Grilled Bison Patties by Trained Panelists." *Journal of Food Quality* 24 (2002): 283–289.

Nabhan, Gary Paul. "Bison as a Food Source: Linking the Recovery of Free-Ranging Bison to Habitat Restoration and Diversified Food Production in Bison Nation." In Kent H. Redford and Eva Fearn, eds., *Ecological Future of Bison in North America: A Report from a Multi-Stakeholder, Transboundary Meeting,* pp. 19–20. Bronx, New York: Wildlife Conservation Society Working Paper Number 30, 2007.

Snell, Alma Hogan. *A Taste of Heritage: Crow Indian Recipes and Herbal Medicines.* Lincoln: University of Nebraska Press, 2006.

Arikara Yellow Bean

From North Dakota to Monticello, from the pages of Oscar Will's revolutionary seed catalog to the *Seed Savers Exchange Yearbook*—the travels of the Arikara Yellow bean are a remarkable example of the profound stories that live within the heirloom beans of Bison Nation.

The Arikara Yellow bean is linked to the story not only of a particular people but of a poignant place as well. Look at a map of Fort Berthold Reservation and what you find is disconcerting: The most distinguishing feature is what appears to be a large ink spot dividing the land into small, fractured pieces. This ink spot is Lake Sakakawea, the third-largest reservoir in the United States. The small fractured pieces are all that remain from the Fort Berthold Reservation near Bismarck, North Dakota, now home to the Arikara—a home they share with their sister tribes the Mandan and the Hidatsa. Garrison Dam, the fifth dam on the Missouri River, in 1956 flooded the rich agricultural lands that had once sustained the Arikara people. It drowned much of the heirloom crops that they had cultivated over centuries and adapted to withstand the harsh climate of the northern Plains, leaving the tribes and their lifeways on the brink of extinction.

It was along the banks of the Missouri River that the Arikara Yellow bean was first documented, over 200 years ago, on Lewis and Clark's journey of botanical discovery. The small, yellow dried beans sustained the explorers during the impossibly cold winter at Fort Mandan in 1805. The dried bean eventually made its way to Thomas Jefferson, the visionary president behind Lewis and Clark, nestled in boats brimming with botanical and ethnological treasures from this momentous voyage. The Arikara Yellow bean became a favorite in Jefferson's gardens at Monticello, where he described it as a "forward bean" that produced earlier than most other dried beans. This adaptation had probably allowed it to survive the short growing season of the northern Plains.

Primarily an agricultural tribe, the Arikara grew corn, beans, squash, and melons that thrived in the climate of North Dakota. Only in the rarest of circum-

This Edward Curtis photograph depicts an Arikara corn ceremony.

stances would the Arikara take to hunting bison on their own. The Arikara also traded their agricultural bounty with neighboring tribes. In the case of the Sioux, this was a trade for peace. This peaceful coexistence proved short lived, however, and the Arikara were forced to share their land with the Mandan and the Hidatsa, forming a bond with these tribes that survives today.

In the early 1900s, two prominent garden aficionados, Oscar Will and his son George, took an interest in the advanced agricultural skills of the northern Plains tribes. The heirloom grains and vegetables of the Hidatsa, Arikara, and Mandan became a mainstay of the Oscar Will & Company seed catalog. Avid students of Native American agriculture, both Oscar and George knew that farmers among these tribes were particularly adept at seed selection and growing practices. The pair relied on gifts from local tribes to expand the inventory of adapted seeds offered in the Oscar Will catalog. This catalog, which distributed such seeds in the Plains states and prairie provinces for more than a half century, kept Native American heirlooms like the Arikara Yellow bean from going extinct in the face of relocation and systematic oppression of Native American tribes throughout the Midwest. Non-Indian gardeners have gradually returned some of these seeds to descendants of their original stewards, who now reside in the little remaining upland habitats of the Fort Berthold Reservation.

The Arikara had already been struggling to maintain their self-sustaining agricultural ways through the mid-1950s, when the Army Corps of Engineers built Garrison Dam, flooding the Arikara's best agricultural and timberlands. The Arikara tribe then lost a quarter of its reservation, and its community was completely fractured by the reservoir. Some families' lands were split by the reservoir, then isolated by a lack of accessible roads. Garrison Dam was built to ensure flood control for North Dakota's urban areas and to provide water for its arable lands. Yet more than fifty years after its construction, this dam has done little to provide either irrigation or flood control. Instead, the Army Corps of Engineers has faced litigation from environmental advocacy groups for its

destruction to the Missouri River watershed. The National Trust for Historic Preservation has named the Missouri River one of the most endangered historical places in North America.

Fortunately, the Seed Savers Exchange has picked up where Oscar Will's historic catalog left off, maintaining and distributing the endangered Arikara Yellow bean along with other heirloom crops of the three sister tribes. The Slow Food Ark of Taste is also preserving and maintaining the largely obscured history nestled in this bean seed. The succotash recipe at right, adapted from the culinary work of Beverly Cox, reminds us that the American-English term *succotash* comes from the Narragansett word *msickquatash*.

Further Readings

Cox, Beverly, and Martin Jacobs. *Spirit of the Harvest: North American Indian Cooking.* New York: Stewart, Tabori and Chang, 1991.

Hedrick, U. P. *Beans of New York.* Vegetables of New York 1, part 2. Albany, New York: J. B. Lyon Company, 1931.

Nabhan, Gary Paul. "Harvest Time: Northern Plains Agricultural Change." In *Enduring Seeds: Native American Agriculture and Wild Plant Conservation.* San Francisco: North Point Press, 1989.

Schneider, Fred. "Oscar H. Will: North Dakota's Pioneer Seedman." *Seed Savers 2002 Summer Edition.* Decorah, Iowa: Seed Savers Exchange.

Watson, Benjamin. *Taylor's Guide to Heirloom Vegetables.* Boston: Houghton Mifflin, 1996.

Will, George F. "Indian Harvesting." *North Dakota and South Dakota Horticulture* 20:9 (1947): 131.

Will, George F., and George H. Hyde. *Corn among the Indians of the Upper Missouri.* St. Louis, Missouri: William Harvey Miner Company, 1917.

Wilson, Gilbert A. *Buffalo Bird Woman's Garden: Agriculture of the Hidatsa Indians.* St. Paul: Minnesota Historical Society Press, 1987.

David Cavagnaro

SUCCOTASH WITH ARIKARA YELLOW BEANS

4 ears Mandan Clay red corn kernels, shelled and soaked with ash into hominy
4 cups Arikara Yellow beans, soaked overnight and parboiled
1 cup diced Arikara Hubbard squash
¼ cup butter
salt and pepper to taste
1⅓ cups of minced ramps (wild leeks, *Allium tricoccum*)
1 green bell pepper, minced
1 red bell pepper, minced

Place the corn, beans, and squash in a large kettle and cover with water. Add the butter, salt, and pepper and bring to a boil over high heat. Reduce heat to medium-low, then simmer for 10 more minutes. Stir in the ramps and peppers and simmer 10 more minutes, or until beans, corn, and squash are tender. Remove the lid and cook over high heat for 4 more minutes, until the liquid is reduced to a thick gravy consistency. Serve in six warm bowls.

Hutterite Soup Bean

The Hutterite soup bean is many things. It's a delicacy. It's a mystery. And it may not be a bean of Hutterite cultural origin at all. But by all accounts, it's worth preserving.

For decades, cryptic descriptions of this bean in seed catalogs have suggested that it was a staple of the Hutterite colonists, which they brought with them when they escaped religious persecution in Austria by coming to North America in the mid-1700s. There are problems with these assertions. For starters, scholarly works on the Hutterite people have them coming to North America a century later than the bean, and

from Austria, not Russia. Furthermore, their agriculture has typically revolved around wheat, barley, rye, oats, hay, and a few vegetables. A recent search of archives revealed that nowhere in the historic literature is there a specific mention of Hutterite beans.

Tony Waldner is the gardener at the Forest River Hutterite Colony in North Dakota, the place that Seed Savers Exchange once suggested as the original source of the bean now grown by heirloom vegetable enthusiasts. Waldner was taken by surprise by this contention because he had never previously heard of the Hutterite soup bean. "We do have soup; we

just use white lima beans," he said. "To tell you the truth, I'm going to order them myself and see what they are."

William Woys Weaver is a food historian who has written extensively on heirloom foods. He believes the bean is a Russian selection of Coco Jaune de la Chine, otherwise known in nineteenth-century seed catalogs as China Yellow. That bean's distinctive, plump seeds have been described as ranging from a creamy white or tan color to pale green, with a charcoal ring around the hilum, or "eye." Weaver said the original strain was actually lemon yellow, "and this may indicate some crossing with a white variety sometime in the past, perhaps to improve its qualities as a soup bean." He supposes the Hutterites

David Cavagnaro

could have indeed brought the bean with them to Canada and the Dakotas, but even this is in some doubt. In any case, China Yellow had been widely known among American and Canadian growers since the 1820s. And the Hutterite soup bean that may or may not have descended from it still makes a soup unlike any other bean. Catalog descriptions consistently rave about the delicious, creamy chowder it yields in a little under an hour of cooking time.

The bean soup is what sold Alan Kapuler, a cofounder of Peace Seeds now living in Corvallis, Oregon, on the Hutterite bean and heirloom foods in general. In fact, the bean deserves some of the credit, Kapuler says, for the fact that we still have many of our heirloom seed conservation outlets at all. He said he was snowbound for a time in the 1960s and was forced to raid his food stores. "We went through half a dozen beans, and when we cooked the Hutterite I understood why it was an heirloom seed. It made the base of a thick, creamy soup very quickly. None of the other beans did that." Soon after that revelation, Kapuler and his friends started an early heirloom seed company and called it Stone Broke Hippie Seeds. Later, as the popularity of the enterprise grew, they changed the name to Peace Seeds. He says many of the other original grassroots seed companies—including Synergy Seeds, Seeds Blum, SourcePoint Seeds, and Seeds of Change—were either started by his colleagues or followed this example.

The Hutterite bean has recently shown a dip in availability, with only three known sources in 1991, according to the Seed Savers Exchange *Garden Seed Inventory*. But by 2004, the number of outlets had rebounded to eleven. Nevertheless, it remains possible to purchase only small quantities of its seeds, thus heirloom conservationists remain concerned about its status.

Patti Qua runs a business called the Beanery in Exeter, Maine, where she raises Hutterite soup beans for a nearby distributor called Fedco Seeds. She says that this the Hutterite bean has become a regular ingredient in a friend's bean soup as well her own sweet potato curry dish and curry-bean soup, featured in the recipe below. She's a longtime fan of its delicate, buttery flavor. In the garden, the small Hutterite bean bush finishes early and generates a high yield.

PATTI QUA'S HUTTERITE BEAN AND SWEET POTATO SOUP

1½ cups Hutterite beans, rinsed and picked over
2 tablespoons dried vegetable flakes
1 large carrot, shredded
1 celery stalk, diced
3 large garlic cloves (skin on)
1–2 tablespoons olive oil
2 sweet potatoes, cut into ¾-inch cubes
½ teaspoon orange curry powder
2 tablespoons crumbled seaweed (dulse; optional)
1 cup half-and-half
salt and freshly ground black pepper to taste

Combine the beans and 2 quarts of water and boil for 2 minutes. Remove from the heat and let sit for 1 hour before draining. Add the vegetable flakes, a fresh 2 quarts of water, the shredded carrot, and the celery. Simmer uncovered. Meanwhile, coat the garlic cloves in olive oil. Place them on a piece of aluminum foil and roast them at 375 degrees F for 15 minutes, or until the edges turn brown. Cool the garlic cloves, remove the skins, and add them to the pot. Simmer the contents about 2 hours total. Add the sweet potatoes to the pot along with the orange curry powder and, if you like, crumbled seaweed. Simmer 1 hour more. The beans should be fairly soft after cooking, adding viscosity to the soup.

Remove the soup from the heat. Take approximately half the contents of the pot and puree or beat with an electric blender (use a deep bowl, as the mix will be hot). Return the mixture to the pot and add the half-and-half. Add salt and pepper to taste. More milk or water may be added to make a thinner soup.

Further Readings

Bennett, John W. *Hutterite Brethren: The Agricultural Economy and Social Organization of a Communal People*. Stanford, California: Stanford University Press, 1967.

Hostetler, John A. *Hutterite Society*. Baltimore: The Johns Hopkins University Press, 1974.

Seed Savers Exchange. "Hutterite Soup Bean." *Seed Savers 2007 Catalog*. Decorah, Iowa: Seed Savers Exchange, 2007.

Slow Food USA. Ark of Taste; Hutterite soup bean. Available at www.slowfoodusa.org/ark/hutterite_soup_bean.html.

Sow Organic Seeds. "Hutterite Bean." 2000. Available at www.organicseed.com.

Whealy, Kent, and Joanne Thuente. *Garden Seed Inventory*, 5th ed. Decorah, Iowa: Seed Savers Exchange, 2004.

Osage Red Flint Corn

At one time not too long ago, all of the surviving seed stock for Osage Red flint corn was down to just three ears and a few kernels in an old Mason jar. And yet the purples, pinks, and rosy reds that appeared among the eight to fourteen rows of those ears could not be forgotten. The Red Corn family of the Osage Nation of Oklahoma asked for help in renewing their ancient seed and, by doing so, kept this flint corn alive as one of the most versatile crops ever to be grown in Bison Nation.

The corn's lineage can be traced back to families of Native American farmers camped at Fort Osage in Missouri in 1805. From that time on, the seven- to nine-inch ears of flinty kernels were passed down hand to hand, season after season, by the family known as the Red Corns of Pawhuska, Oklahoma.

When she was ninety-one years of age, Waltena Red Corn, widow of Raymond Red Corn Sr., put it as simply and elegantly as possible: "What we have is what my husband's ancestors had."

Waltena learned how to keep the seed pure, how to pick the ripening ears at dawn, and how to boil and dry the corn in the traditional manner from Raymond's aunt Mary Whitehorn, an Osage elder: "We saved the seed through her guidance. Aunt Mary Whitehorn would lease a place close to the airport where we could plant the corn away from other varieties."

Nonetheless, as she and her husband got older they could not continue their own plantings every year, even though they were needed for use in the *I-lon-schka,* a seasonal ceremony in which the Osage dance for the bounty given to them by the Creator. Their seed stock dwindled down to less than a half pound of kernels, and not all of those were necessarily viable. Recognizing that if their corn was biologically on the brink of extinction their traditions could not be properly maintained, Waltena reached out for help. She found an agronomist at Oklahoma State University who was willing to help her replenish their seed stock, returning the harvest to the Red Corn family.

When Raymond Senior died in 2003, Waltena encouraged her son Raymond Junior to answer the challenge of maintaining this family and tribal legacy. Raymond Junior found two farmers in Missouri who helped him with growouts in areas where the seed could remain uncontaminated by GMOs and other hybrid corn varieties. The Missouri farmers marveled at the vigor of the ten-foot-tall stalks and the vividness of the crimson colors in the

David Cavagnaro

Fort Osage in the 1950s. Osage Red flint corn has been traced to Native American farmers living near the fort in 1805. Gerald Massie; courtesy Missouri State Archives

leaves. Gradually, they helped the Red Corn family accumulate enough seed to feel that Osage Red flint was safe from extinction and ready for tasting by others through cottage-industry production of traditional hominy products.

The Red Corns go out at dawn to harvest the ears of red, purple, and pink flints when they are still in the milk stage. They then blanch the entire ears in water set to boil in a large cast-iron kettle. When the ears have been fully saturated, they are lifted out of the kettle and spread out over a layer of freshly picked corn husks. There, they are left to cool and dry. Next, a heavy metal spoon is used to strip the kernels off the cob, so that they fall onto sheets where they can be gathered up and placed in baskets or bowls.

While the seed of this corn has been conserved by only one nonprofit, the Sand Hill Preservation Center, the production of this corn in Osage fields has not remained secure from year to year. The dried hominy has been marketed in recent years under the Ha-Pah-Shu-Tse brand by Raymond Junior's daughter, but quantities were too low to make it available in the spring of 2007. Nevertheless, as she has testified to her customers, "for the last sixty years, my father, Raymond Red Corn Jr., has kept our namesake Osage

corn viable by planting backyard patches for use by our family during the Osage ceremonial dances. It has taken years to build stock of this ancient variety to commercial quantities."

In turn, her customers have responded by bearing witness to the uniqueness of their Osage Red flint, describing it as "meaty," "rosy," and "full of corn flavor not found in current varieties."

The following recipe for a Bison Nation stew or chowder featuring Osage Red flint corn and Cherokee Trail of Tears beans is adapted from directions for preparing a hominy and bean soup set down by Fernando and Marlene Divina.

Further Readings

Divina, Fernando and Marlene. *Foods of the Americas: Native Recipes and Traditions.* Berkeley, California: Ten Speed Press, 2004.

Red Corn Native Foods/Ha-Pah-Shu-Tse. 2007. Available at www.cookingpost.com.

Rich, Doug. "Preserving Corn Harvest Traditions." *High Plains Journal*, 2006. Available at www.hpj.com/archives/2006/Octo6/Oct16/preservingcornharvesttradit.cfm.

BISON NATION HOMINY AND BEAN CHOWDER

2 cups Cherokee Trail of Tears dried beans
1 cup dried hominy from Osage Red flint corn (see instructions for making hominy on page 209)
½ cup peeled and chopped prairie turnips *(Psorelea hypogaea)*
½ cup peeled and cracked American (prairie) groundnuts *(Apios americana)*
6 tablespoons finely chopped bison jerky (optional)
3–4 ramps or green onions, white parts minced
3 wild celery stalks, minced
4 cups cream or vegetable stock
1 teaspoon sea salt

Place the beans in a bowl, cover them with water, and let them soak overnight. In the morning, drain and discard the water as well as any shriveled-up beans. In a large, heavy saucepan, combine the beans and the dried corn and bring to a rolling boil. After 2 minutes of boiling, reduce the heat and use a slotted spoon to skim off any remaining impurities. Let the beans and corn simmer for a half hour, stirring often. Add more water if necessary, so that the beans and corn remain covered. Next, add the prairie turnips and groundnuts, as well as the chopped pieces of bison jerky. Simmer for another half hour, then add the ramps, celery, cream or vegetable stock, and sea salt. Simmer the entire mixture until the beans, corn, turnips, and groundnuts are all tender without being mushy, a condition that may be achieved in as little as another half hour or as much as an hour. Remove the saucepan from the fire and ladle the chowder into warm bowls to serve immediately.

Sibley (Pike's Peak) Squash

"The champion," writes heirloom vegetable enthusiast Amy Goldman of the banana squash group, "has to be the Sibley, or Pike's Peak, which surpasses even Blue Banana in sweetness, texture and flavor . . ." It is one of the progeny of the brown-seeded, mild-flavored, brilliantly colored *maxima* squashes first introduced from the Andes to Marblehead, Massachusetts, around 1798; for although Native Americans had prehistorically grown other species of *askutasquash,* this species did not get north of the West Indies until after the American Revolution. Over the following century, however, *maxima* squashes took the U.S. marketplace by storm, as Fearing Burr's celebration of "hubbardy" squashes from 1863 affirms.

The smooth-skinned, bluish-gray Sibley apparently emerged as a distinct variety somewhere in the Missouri River watershed of Bison Nation in the 1830s, about the same time that kindred varieties were first found among Arikara and Winnebago Indian gardens. It was likely named for the town of Sibley, Iowa, not even thirty miles as the crow flies from the Mighty Missouri. In 1887, an elderly woman who gardened near Van Diman, Iowa, claimed to have first grown it in Missouri a half century earlier. That same year, Hiram Sibley and Company of Rochester, New York, first offered Sibley to the national audience of gardeners, who soon became as impressed by it as its local fans around Van Diman had been. When Sibley's dry, buff-orange flesh was first eaten by James J. H. Gregory—the man who introduced Hubbard squashes into the American seed trade—he had but one word for it: "magnificent."

Sibley promoters soon found the perfect climatic and soil conditions for its production below Pike's Peak, where mountain streams from the Rockies flow out on the Great Plains. There on the western edges of Bison Nation, Sibley became the highly esteemed standard for all squashes, just as Rocky Ford became for melons. As Amy Goldman has noted, it has "rare

David Cavagnaro

Pike's Peak, Colorado. The climate near the base of the mountain is perfect for growing Sibley squash.

edible qualities, being dry[-fleshed], with a rich delicate flavor peculiarly its own."

And yet most banana-like squashes such as Sibley have gradually been dropped from commercial seed catalogs, perhaps because pumpkins with rounder shapes and smaller sizes have come into vogue. Today, seeds of the Sibley are regularly available only from J. L. Hudson, Seedsman, of California; the Prize Seeds website; and the Seed Savers Exchange. Recently boarded onto the Slow Food Ark of Taste in the United States, perhaps it will have a comeback among gardeners who are eager to taste the best of heirloom vegetables. The following recipe for a pumpkin pie is adapted from one shared by the German immigrants who established the Amana Colonies in central Iowa in the 1850s and 1860s, about the time Sibley became legendary in Iowa. But we have also included an elegant recipe adapted from Crow Indian food historian Alma Hogan Snell's instructions for baked squash.

AMANA COLONIES' KÜRBIS PASTETE

2 cups cooked, strained, and pureed Sibley squash
1 cup turbinado sugar or sorghum syrup
4 egg yolks
3 cups milk
1 cup sour cream
2 tablespoons maple syrup
1 teaspoon freshly ground cinnamon
¼ teaspoon each freshly ground mace and nutmeg
⅛ teaspoon ground ginger
4 egg whites, beaten into stiff peaks
piecrust for two 9-inch pie shells

Preheat the oven to 450 degrees F. In a glass mixing bowl, combine the squash puree with the sugar or sorghum syrup, egg yolks, milk, sour cream, maple syrup, cinnamon, and other spices. Mix well with a whisk and then gently fold in the stiffly beaten egg whites. Pour the mixture into two 9-inch handmade pie shells and place them in the oven for 10 minutes before reducing the heat to 325 degrees F. Bake the two pies at that temperature for another 45 minutes or until a fork inserted into the puree comes out clean. Serve topped with freshly whipped cream that had a tablespoon of maple syrup mixed into it before it was beaten.

BAKED COOGOOEHSA, CROW INDIAN STYLE

½ mature Sibley squash, cut into slices about an inch thick
¼ cup water
¼ cup brown sugar
1 yellow onion, washed but not peeled

Place the Sibley squash slices in the bottom of a roasting pan and cover with just enough water to prevent scorching. Sprinkle brown sugar onto the slices and then place the whole unpeeled onion in the midst of them. Place the roasting pan in an oven preheated to 300 degrees F and cook until tender when tested with an inserted fork. Remove the onion skin, slice the onion, and mix the baked, reddened slices in with the squash slices. Serves 10 to 12 people.

Further Readings

Burr, Fearing Jr. *The Field and Garden Vegetables of America*. Boston: Crosby and Nichols, 1863.

Goldman, Amy. *The Compleat Squash: A Passionate Grower's Guide*. New York: Artisan Books/Workman Publishing, 2004.

Gregory, James J. H. *Squashes: How to Grow Them*. New York: Orange Judd, 1867.

Ladies Auxiliary of the Homestead Welfare Club. *A Collection of Traditional Amana Colony Recipes*. Homestead, Iowa: Homestead Welfare Club, 1948.

Snell, Alma Hogan. *A Taste of Heritage: Crow Indian Recipes and Herbal Medicines*. Lincoln: University of Nebraska Press, 2006.

Tapley, William T., Walter D. Enzie, and Glen P. Van Eselstine. "The Cucurbits." *The Vegetables of New York 1, part 4*. Albany: J. B. Lyon, 1937.

Weaver, William Woys. *Heirloom Vegetable Gardening*. New York: Henry Holt, 1997.

Silver Fox Rabbit

The Silver Fox rabbit is among the first three truly American breeds of domesticated hares, and perhaps it is the rarest as well. It was developed in North Canton, Ohio, by Walter B. Garland, who bred it from Checkered Giants, a landrace from Germany. Garland crossed the Checkered Giants with either Champagne d'Argent or English Silver rabbits, but the exact parentage has been obscured by time. The American Rabbit Breeding Association first recognized it as a distinct breed in 1925, approving its presentation in competitions under the name of the American Heavyweight Silver. That name never really stuck, so in 1971 the ARBA judges formally recognized the breed under its current name, the Silver Fox.

Not all rabbits have been bred for their culinary qualities, but the Silver Fox has been regularly praised for the high-quality flavor and fine texture of its meat, as well as for its deep loins, which are ideal for grilling. The does reach ten to twelve pounds, while the bucks range from nine to eleven pounds at maturity, dressing out at about two-thirds of their live weight. Although their coats range from blue to black, all individuals of the Silver Fox breed have the distinctive trait of long silvery hairs, which stand up when they are brushed. Thus, they are as much a show animal as a meat animal.

Silver Fox rabbits have never been abundant, but today the global population stands at less than 500 individuals. Because there are only fifty annual registrations of newborn bunnies, the American Livestock Breeds Conservancy considers them to be critically endangered. Recently, however, Slow Food members in Marin County, California, have taken up the cause to support conservation efforts for this breed. In addition, a breed association based in Iowa has done much to popularize Silver Fox rabbits among serious breeders, many of whom are also based in Iowa.

The following historic recipe is adapted from two cookbooks from the Community of True Inspiration, better known as the Amana Society, which has farmed some 26,000 acres of land in central Iowa since 1854. Their religious movement began in 1714 in the province of Hesse near Frankfurt, Germany, and spread to the United States and Canada around 1842.

Jeannette Beranger; courtesy American Livestock Breeds Conservancy

GEKOCHTE HASEN (SKILLET-STEWED SILVER FOX RABBIT)

1 Silver Fox rabbit, dressed and washed
4 tablespoons unsalted butter
6 medium-sized white onions, sliced
1 tablespoon minced parsley
1½ cups water
1 teaspoon sea salt
⅛ teaspoon freshly ground black pepper
½ bay leaf
a few peppercorns
1 teaspoon apple cider vinegar
3 tablespoons rhubarb wine

Debone and cut the rabbit meat into serving-size pieces. In a heavy iron skillet, layer pieces of boned rabbit meat to cover the bottom. Add half the butter, all of the onion slices, and the minced parsley, then sauté until the meat is deep brown and the onions are translucent. Add the water, salt, pepper, bay leaf, and peppercorns. Cook slowly over low heat for at least 30 minutes or until the meat is tender. Add the vinegar, rhubarb wine, and remaining butter and cook 2 minutes longer. When done, thicken a gravy from the remaining juices mixed with cornstarch or finely milled cornmeal. Serves 4.

Further Readings

Goree, Sue Roemig, and Joanne Asala, eds. *German Recipes: Old World Specialities and Photography from the Amana Colonies*. Amana, Iowa: privately printed, 2002.

Ladies Auxiliary of the Homestead Welfare Club. *A Collection of Traditional Amish Colony Recipes*. Homestead, Iowa: Homestead Welfare Club, 1948.

Hidatsa Sunflower

One of the few crops native to North America that has become a major commodity internationally, the annual sunflower *(Helianthus annuus)* was apparently domesticated in the Mississippi River Valley and was prehistorically traded westward beyond the Great Plains. There, the tribes of the Upper Missouri—including the Hidatsa, Mandan, and Arikara—developed hardy varieties that were later taken to eastern Europe, where they were further selected for their oil-bearing seeds. Although sunflowers first reached Europe in 1510, these later introductions from the Upper Missouri were among the first whose seeds were pressed into oil, which was burnt as Lenten candles. The original heirlooms grown by the Missouri tribes had seedlike "achenes" that were striped, streaked, or solid red, white, or black; they were produced on seedheads that measured up to a foot across, atop stalks that grew eight to twelve feet high.

A variety named Hidatsa Number 1 has striped seeds that are now available to the general public through two small seed catalogs mailed out of Port Townsend, Washington. Its seeds were so important culturally to Hidatsa farmers a century ago that the full moon rising in early April was known among them as the Sunflower Planting Moon. Planted early, these sunflowers were among the last of the Hidatsa crops to be harvested from their floodplain gardens along the Missouri River. Once the seeds were harvested, they were toasted and ground, to be shaped later into oily cakes or mixed with parched corn, boiled beans, and rehydrated squash to make a delicious stew. The oily seed meal was also mixed with cornmeal, juneberries, kidney tallow, and sugar into a pemmican-like ball called *mah-pi*. Well into the 1980s, Hidatsa elder Vera Bracklin continued to make *mah-pi* with her mother-in-law's flour corn and sunflower varieties.

Unfortunately, the introduction of Mammoth Russian and other improved cultivars of sunflowers by the 1920s lured most native farmers away from growing their own distinctive varieties; worse yet, the Mammoth Russians outcrossed with native sunflowers in nearby gardens, genetically contaminating them. Of some thirty tribes that still grew

David Cavagnaro

their own distinctive sunflower heirlooms in the 1940s, only six continued with these traditions into the 1980s. Even though more than 3,000,000 acres of sunflowers have been cultivated in the United States and Canada in recent years, fewer than fifty acres of these are likely to be of the original native varieties. They are clearly endangered in Bison Nation and deserve to be recovered in ways that directly benefit the Mandan, Hidatsa, and Arikara.

The following recipe for Hidatsa sunflower/wild rice pilaf echoes the four-vegetable recipe offered by Maxi'diwiac, or Buffalo Bird Woman, to historian Gilbert Wilson a century ago.

HIDATSA SUNFLOWER/WILD RICE PILAF

1 cup Hidatsa sunflower seeds (achenes)
2 tablespoons unsalted butter
¼ teaspoon salt
1 teaspoon thyme, bushmint, or bee balm
   (*Monarda fistulosa*)
5 ramps (wild leeks) or 1 white onion
1 yellow bell pepper
¼ cup juneberries, cranberries, or blueberries
6 tablespoons sunflower oil
2½ cups hand-harvested river or lake wild rice
   (*manoomin*), rinsed in three changes of water
4½ cups chicken (or prairie chicken) broth

In a skillet over medium-high heat, toast and toss the sunflower seeds with butter, salt, and thyme or another herb for 5 minutes. Set the seeds aside and use the same skillet to sauté the chopped onion, pepper, and berries in sunflower oil. After stirring them for 10 minutes over low heat, add the wild rice and the chicken broth. Bring to a boil, cover, then cook over low heat for 40 minutes. Next, preheat the oven to 350 degrees F. Transfer the rice to an ovenproof casserole dish and add the toasted, herb-covered sunflower seeds. Place the casserole dish in the oven, cover, and bake for half an hour or until all the broth is absorbed. Serves 8.

Further Readings

Myers, Robert L., and Harry C. Minor. *Sunflower: An American Native.* Columbia: University of Missouri Extension Service, 1993. Available at http://extension.missouri.edu/xplor/agguides/crops/g04290.htm.

Nabhan, Gary Paul. "Harvest Time: Northern Plains Agricultural Change." In *Enduring Seeds: Native American Agriculture and Wild Plant Conservation.* San Francisco: North Point Press, 1989.

Wilson, Gilbert. *Buffalo Bird Woman's Garden: Agriculture of the Hidatsa Indians.* Minneapolis: Borealis Books, 1917.

CHESTNUT NATION

Centered on the Blue Ridge Mountains, including the southern Appalachian plateau and the piedmont above the coastal plains of the Southeast, Chestnut Nation remains rich in small farmsteads and culinary celebrations. The American chestnut formerly dominated the wild food crops gleaned from the forests, but it was nearly driven into extinction by an introduced chestnut blight. Today, remnant and (perhaps) resistant chestnut trees are inspiring efforts at chestnut reintroduction and forest restoration. This region is rich in heirloom fruit trees and vegetables, heritage livestock breeds, and small game. The traditions of Cherokee wildcrafters and Scots-Irish woodspeople have shaped the subsistence traditions of this region. Its living heritage of fishing, farming, and foraging folklore is widely celebrated in story and song. However, the metro areas of Washington, D.C., and Atlanta, Georgia, at either end of this region have a ripple effect of second-home developments that are now changing the predominantly rural character of Chestnut Nation. At least seventy-four of its traditional foods are now threatened or endangered.

American Chestnuts of Pine Mountain, Georgia

Although as many as four billion American chestnut trees *(Castanea dentata)* may have been wiped out by the blight that was introduced from Asia to eastern forests in 1904, a scattering of trees have survived to this day in isolated locations from Maine and Ohio to Alabama and Georgia. The recent discoveries of an entire stand of healthy chestnuts near President Franklin Delano Roosevelt's Little White House at Pine Mountain, Georgia, and an 85-foot "mother tree" in Talladega National Forest have generated optimism that genes for immunity to blight may exist in the upland forests of Chestnut Nation.

This may be the most hopeful news about chestnuts in over a century, given that this once ubiquitous species was weakened by disease and stripped from forests across 200,000,000 acres from the Gulf of Mexico northward to the Canadian border. It remains difficult to imagine how a nut-bearing tree than once provided a quarter of all canopy cover and foodstuffs in eastern temperate forests could have fallen so quickly. In 1612, two centuries before its fall from grace, Captain John Smith had declared that among Native Americans in Virginia, boiled chestnuts made "both broth and bread for their chief men at their greatest feasts."

Prior to the decimation of American chestnut trees, their nuts had been relished for millennia, being eaten raw or pounded, boiled, and mixed with cornmeal to form doughy bread. The velvety brown nuts were tucked into prickly green burrs that littered the ground in piles under trees that reached heights of one hundred feet and had trunks with girths of six feet in diameter. A single tree could produce as many as 6,000 nuts and reliably yielded such a harvest year after year. When Napoleon commissioned François-André Michaux to report to him on the value of American trees, he described American chestnuts as being "smaller but sweeter than the wild chestnut of Europe, and sold at 3 dollars a bushel in the markets of New York, Philadelphia and Baltimore."

From Cherokee hunters to Scots-Irish dirt farmers, the chestnut was seen as the most democratic of all American foods, for it was equally accessible and delectable to the rich and the poor. As the leaves of the chestnut trees turned color in autumn, hundreds of thousands of Americans could be seen scrambling below their canopies, gathering up the burr-covered nuts by the bushel and carrying them back to camp-fires and kitchens for roasting, pounding, baking, or stuffing into turkeys. Naturalist Henry David Thoreau was one such Chestnut Democrat, as this passage from *Walden* clearly indicates:

> When chestnuts were ripe I laid up half a bushel for winter. It was very exciting at that season to roam the then boundless chestnut woods . . . with a bag on my shoulder, and a stick to open burs in my hand . . . amid the rustling of the leaves and the loud reproofs of the red squirrels and the jays, whose half-consumed nuts I sometimes stole . . . These nuts, as far as they went, were a good substitute for bread.

At the same time, the chestnut's hardwood lumber and bark tannins were just as widely used as its nuts.

The prickly burr of the American chestnut is hard on the hands. Here, several burrs balance precariously. Courtesy American Chestnut Foundation

It is no overstatement to assert that from prehistoric times through the entire nineteenth century, the chestnut was America's most versatile and valued forest tree, accompanying both natives and immigrants literally in the cradle and grave, as material for both their cribs and their coffins.

This was to change all too quickly when a shipment of ornamental chestnuts from the Orient arrived at the port of New York City in the 1890s, destined for a nursery of trees to be sold for urban landscaping. Then in 1904, Herman Menkle began to notice that there were large cankers forming on American chestnut trees planted around the Bronx Zoo, and all of these trees had begun to die. They had been infected with a canker-forming bark disease from Asia, one for which the vast majority of chestnuts native to North America had no immunity.

Like the passenger pigeon, the American chestnut went from being one of the common organisms on the continent to the brink of extinction. By 1938, nearly every native tree of nut-bearing age from Maine to Alabama had died; populations of the wild turkeys that once depended on their nut crop declined as well. No wonder Robert Frost asked the question he posed in this 1930 poem, "Evil Tendencies Cancel":

Further Reading

Carson, Dale. *New Native American Cooking.* New York: Random House, 1996.

Frost, Robert. "Evil Tendencies Cancel." In *The Poetry of Robert Frost: The Complete Poems,* edited by Edward Connery Lathem. New York: Owl Books/Henry Holt Publishing, 2002. (Originally published in 1930.)

Janson, H. Frederic. *Pomona's Harvest: An Illustrated Chronicle of Antiquarian Fruit Literature.* Portland, Oregon: Timber Press, 1996.

Minor, Elliott. "Rare American Chestnut Trees Discovered." *Washington Post,* May 10, 2006. Feature for the Associated Press. Available at www.washingtonpost.com.

Rosengarten, Frederic Jr. *The Book of Exotic Nuts.* New York: Walker and Company, 1984.

Thoreau, Henry David. *Walden, or a Life in the Woods.* Boston: Ticknor and Fields, 1854.

Will the blight end the chestnut?
The farmers rather guess not.
It keeps smoldering at the roots
and sending up new shoots
Till another parasite
Shall come to end the blight.

Nevertheless, the American public did not exactly sit still and fatalistically accept the decline of the chestnut as they did the extinction of the passenger pigeon. Land-grant university researchers began to cross the few known remaining American chestnuts outside their native range with fungus-resistant Chinese and Japanese chestnuts. Then, in 1983, Dr. Charles Burnham founded the American Chestnut Foundation to restore this hallmark tree to its native range. The foundation developed a backcross breeding program that used the fungus-resistant hybrids already created to cross with more typical American chestnuts until trees were produced that are over 90 percent American genetically but immune to the blight. The foundation's many state chapters have begun transplanting these trees to forests where their ancestors once grew.

As important, perhaps, is the role the foundation has played in raising public awareness that there

Dr. Fred Hebard, scientist with The American Chestnut Foundation demonstrates one step in the process of pollinating an American chestnut tree. Courtesy American Chestnut Foundation

At the beginning of the 20th century American chestnut trees the size of this one in Great Smoky Mountains National Park were common in the eastern half of the United States. Courtesy Great Smoky Mountain National Park

might still be nonsusceptible trees hidden in the forests, encouraging hikers and foresters to document their presence. Around Earth Day in 2004, a biologist with the Georgia Department of Natural Resources stumbled upon some spiny burrs while hiking along a dry, rocky ridge on Pine Mountain near Warm Springs, Georgia. When he looked up to see what trees they had fallen from, Nathan Klaus discovered a half-dozen perfectly healthy chestnut trees, one of them forty feet tall. These few trees represent the southernmost survivors of this native species that have been found capable of maturing to flower and fruit without being damaged by the canker-forming fungus. Klaus was elated by his discovery but curious as to why these particular trees survived:

> There's something about this place that has allowed them to endure the blight. It's either that these trees are [genetically] able to resist the blight, which is unlikely, or Pine Mountain has something unique that is giving these trees resistance.

One potential clue comes from another recently discovered survivor, an eighty-five-foot-tall American chestnut found in Talladega National Forest in Alabama. After timber scouts discovered this tree in 2004, forest geneticists determined that one of its maternal ancestors was not a chestnut but a chinquapin, a related burr-bearing nut of Chestnut Nation that is immune to the chestnut blight. It may well be that natural hybrids of American chestnuts and chinquapins already have the resistance that Burnham and others are attempting to gain through their meticulous backcrossing program.

In any case, David Keehen of the American Chestnut Foundation was correct when he called the Pine Mountain stand "a terrific find. A [single] tree of this size is one in a million."

That forty-foot tree grows not too far from a cabin that was built for President Franklin Delano Roosevelt, where he took refuge to recover from his own devastating disease, polio. Known as the Little White House at Warm Springs, an hour outside of Atlanta, it became Roosevelt's sanctuary after he was stricken with the polio virus in 1921. While the chestnut trees now growing within walking distance of the Little White House were not alive during Roosevelt's residency on Pine Mountain, their ancestors were no doubt of nut-producing age at that time. It has prompted Nathan Klaus to suggest that FDR himself may have been nourished by those chestnuts while undergoing treatments to recover his own immunity: "FDR may well have roasted some chestnuts on the fire at Christmas, or enjoyed their blooms in the spring." Perhaps he even savored a soup such as this at one time.

AMERICAN CHESTNUT– BUTTERNUT SQUASH SOUP

2 tablespoons butter
1 large onion, chopped
1 stalk celery, chopped
1 carrot, chopped
3 pounds butternut squash, peeled, seeded, and cut in chunks
½ pound shelled chestnuts
4 cups chicken broth
1 teaspoon ground ginger
1 cup Nickajack apple juice or cider
1½ cups cream
salt and freshly ground pepper to taste

In a 4-quart saucepan, melt the butter and add the chopped onion, celery, and carrot. When these are wilted, not browned, add the squash and chestnuts. Pour in the chicken broth and bring to a boil. Cover, reduce the heat, and simmer for 35 to 40 minutes, then add the ginger. Remove the soup from the heat and puree it all in a blender along with the apple juice or cider. Add the cream, salt, and pepper. Reheat and serve in warmed bowls. Serves 6 to 8.

Jack's Copperclad Jerusalem Artichoke

Perhaps the only vegetable native to North America that has achieved worldwide acclaim, the Jerusalem artichoke is more appreciated overseas than in its center of origin in south-central Canada and the midwestern United States. Its estrangement from its homeland is perhaps best indicated by the fact that this *openauk* or "Canada potato" is now called Jerusalem artichoke, even though it is neither an artichoke nor native to Jerusalem. Worse yet, in the last half century, hundreds of heirloom varieties that were carefully selected by American family farmers and gardeners for their distinctive flavors, textures, and hardiness have been all but replaced by the sunchoke, a single sterile hybrid made between sunflowers and Jerusalem artichokes.

Remnant wild populations can be found in forty-four states and seven Canadian provinces, but within that range, the historic heirloom cultivars such as Jack's Copperclad have grown increasingly rare. This variety has plump but knobby tubers whose skins are colored a lovely dark copper or rose-purple. The tubers themselves have an excellent, subtly sweet flavor and are found at the base of ten-foot stalks that bear aboveground a bright display of sunflowers. Jack's Copperclad is commercially available only from Horus Botanicals in Salem, Arkansas, and is endangered. Many other heirlooms of the same ilk are literally lost within the rural-suburban continuum, no longer known by their historic names nor celebrated for their unique qualities.

And yet this perennial tuber-bearing sunflower (*Helianthus tuberosus*) was once one of the most widely used root vegetables in North America, whether wild-harvested or intentionally cultivated in fields and gardens. At least fifteen tribes boiled or roasted the tubers, sometimes eating them whole but other times mixing them with acorn meal to fry into cakes. We can assume that some prehistoric tribes intentionally transplanted and tended the tubers, for Samuel de Champlain saw them growing in Native American gardens at Mallebarre on Nauset Harbor in Massachusetts on July 21, 1605. Botanist Asa Gray discerned that the Jerusalem artichoke originated west of the Mississippi watershed and that it was probably carried and transplanted eastward through Native American trade. However, most indigenous harvesters within its natural range had no need to intentionally plant it because their practice of "digging-stick cultivation" enhanced the productivity of each tuber patch. Over time, there may even have been selection for larger tubers or different shapes or flavors. Various "wild" populations of Jerusalem artichokes have been reported to tolerate freezing temperatures, waterlogging, acidity, alkalinity,

David Cavagnaro

different photoperiods, sand, shade, lateritic soils, virus, bacteria, or weeds.

One of the first written reports about this root vegetable came from Thomas Hariot, during the second expedition to establish the first "English plantation" on Roanoke Island in 1585:

> Openauk are a kind of roots of round forme, some of the bignes of walnuts, some far greater, which are found in moist & marish ground growing many together one by another in ropes, or as thogh they were fastened with a string. Being boiled or sodden they are a very good meate.

By 1605, the explorer Samuel de Champlain had enjoyed their flavor frequently enough to want to send some of the tubers back from Canada to his native France. It may be that he had already gathered or described this plant in Massachusetts as well, for a book published in 1609 mentions that this vegetable was known in France even before Champlain had initiated his exploration of Canada. Among the French, the vegetable that Champlain likened to an artichoke became known as *topinambour*—a country bumpkin—while the English settling north of the St. Lawrence River claimed it as the Canada potato.

Exactly when and how the term *Jerusalem* became added to this artichoke's name remains a mystery. One explanation is that once this root became a staple food for the Pilgrims, they praised it as the new food that would nourish a "new Jerusalem." Alternative explanations are that "Jerusalem" is simply a mispronunciation of the Italian word for sunflower, *girasol,* or of the Dutch place-name *Ter-Heusen,* a farm village in Holland where many of these tubers were planted. In any case, the Jerusalem artichoke or topinambour has met with three centuries of acclaim in Europe, and many of the most widely propagated cultivars come from there. The 1833 edition of Gerard's *Herball* underscores how prolific this plant was in the eyes of the Europeans:

> This wonderfull increasing plant hath growing up from one root, one, sometimes two, three or more round green rough hairy straked stalks, commonly about twelve foot

David Cavagnaro

high, sometimes sixteene foot high or higher . . . producing from the increase of one root, thirty, forty, or fifty in number or more.

Back in the United States, it was at least appreciated as a survival food, as this April 9, 1805, entry from the journals of Meriwether Lewis indicates:

> When we halted for dinner [Sacagawea] busied herself in serching for the wild artichokes . . . this operation she performed by penetrating the earth with a sharp stick about some small collections of drift wood. Her labour soon proved successful, and she procurrd a good quantity of these roots.

And yet other American observers gave the plant decidedly mixed reviews. In 1681, Reverend John Banister of Virginia was already discounting its value in his *Natural History,* claiming that "the Batatas Canadensis, or Jerusalem Artichokes are little esteemed of here, yet it is sometimes used to brew with when corn is scarce." In 1768, Miller wrote this disparaging note in *The Gardeners Dictionary:* "The Jerusalem Artichokes . . . are very subject to trouble the belly by their windy quality, which hath brought them almost in decline."

John Goodyer, who had pioneered their cultivation by English-speaking farmers in the 1600s, was more to the point: "In my judgement, which way soever they be drest and eaten they stir up and cause a filthie loathesome stinking winde with the bodie, thereby causing the belly to bee much pained and tormented, and are a meat more fit for swine, than men."

The source of that "windiness" may also be the tubers' greatest asset for modern consumers, for it is due to the slow release of inulin, a complex polysaccharide they contain. Slowly digested and broken down into fructose and other carbohydrates, inulin serves to protect those who suffer from diabetes from dramatic changes in blood sugar levels and from pancreatic stress.

Fortunately, the Jerusalem artichoke still had a few champions, including none other than George Washington and Thomas Jefferson. In a May 2, 1817, letter to an agricultural magazine editor, Tristan Dalton, Jefferson favored this native tuber (or introduced varieties of the same) as a winter feed for livestock: "With respect to field culture of vegetables for cattle, instead of the carrot and potato recommended by yourself, and the magazine, and the beet by others, we find the Jerusalem artichoke best for winter."

During the decades immediately following Jefferson's promotion of it, a good number of varieties of the Jerusalem artichoke were selected, and these revived interest in the vegetable among chefs. In the 1847 cookbook *The Carolina Housewife,* there are instructions for pickling this kind of artichoke, and much the same recipe has persisted in the Carolinas to this day. In his 1865 classic, *Field and Garden Vegetables of America,* Fearing Burr noted at least four exceptionally flavorful varieties that had been developed by backyard plant selection:

> For a long period there was but a single variety cultivated, or even known. Recent experiments in the use of seeds as a means of propagation have developed new kinds, varying greatly in their size, form, and color, possessing little of the watery and insipid character of the heretofore grown Jerusalem Artichoke, and nearly or quite equaling the potato in flavor and excellence.

From the early nineteenth through the early twentieth century, American gardeners and horticulturists selected and named over 1,300 forms, heirloom stocks, and unusual strains of the Jerusalem artichokes. Only 200 of these heirlooms have survived into the twenty-first century, and most of them are now available to the public only on a limited basis from experimental farms, botanical gardens, and germplasm repositories. Aside from the sterile hybrid sunchoke, which can be propagated vegetatively only by replanting tubers, there are only ten cultivars of the Jerusalem artichoke that have persisted to any extent in garden catalogs of the United States and Canada: Boston Red, Dwarf Sunray, French White Improved, Fuseau, Golden Nugget, Jack's Copperclad, Jerusalem White, Mammoth French White, Mulles Rose, Stampede, Sutton's New White, and Veitch's Improved Long White. Three are of particular interest as American heirlooms: the Boston Red, which has large knobby tubers with rose-red skin; Jack's Copperclad, which has dark coppery purple, excellent-tasting tubers; and the Mulles Rose, which has large white tubers with rose-purple-fleshed eyes. All of these may now be considered endangered because of the predominance of sterile hybrid sunchokes in the marketplace.

The recipe included here is adapted from Joseph Earl Dabney's fine collection, *Smokehouse Ham, Spoon Bread, and Scuppernong Wine.*

SOUTH CAROLINA CHOW-CHOW WITH JACK'S COPPERCLAD ARTICHOKES

1 gallon Jack's Copperclad Jerusalem artichokes
1 cup sea salt
1 quart (4 large) green tomatoes, coarsely chopped
6 large red bell peppers
6 large green bell peppers
1 large rib pale green celery
1 quart (8 medium) Vidalia onions
2 quarts apple cider vinegar
½ cup bleached wheat flour
3 tablespoons turmeric
6 cups turbinado sugar
½ cup dry mustard
5 tablespoons mustard seed
2 tablespoons dill seed
2 tablespoons celery seed

Scrub the artichokes with a brush to remove any spots. Place them in a large glass bowl and cover them with cold water mixed with ¼ cup salt. Refrigerate overnight. The next morning, mince the tomatoes, peppers, celery, and onions, then cover them with water and the remaining ¾ cup salt in a second large bowl. Drain the artichokes, rinse them in cold water, then chop them coarsely. Drain the salt water from the minced vegetables but reserve this liquid.

Next, pour the apple cider vinegar into a large saucepan and combine the flour, turmeric, and sugar with the vinegar. Beat this mix with a whisk, then add the dry mustard and the mustard, dill, and celery seeds. Bring this mixture to a boil. Add the vegetables and bring all the ingredients back to a boil. Cook only 1 minute, stirring vigorously so as not to let anything stick to the pan. Finally, add the chopped artichokes and stir them in, but don't let them cook any further. Pour the reserved liquid from the vegetables over the artichokes. Spoon the artichokes and liquid into hot, clean pint jars, filling them up to a quarter inch from the top. Seal at once. Yields 12 pints.

Further Reading

Ammundsen, C. Rene. "Jerusalem Artichoke." In the "Homestead and Garden" category of the "This and That" website. Accessed April 22, 2007, from www.fogwhistle.ca/thisandthat/artichoke.htm.

Boswell, Victor. R. *Studies of the Culture and Certain Varieties of the Jerusalem Artichoke.* Washington, D.C.: U.S. Department of Agriculture, 1936.

Burr, Fearing Jr. *Field and Garden Vegetables of America.* Boston: J. E. Tilton, 1865.

Champlain, Samuel D. *The Voyages of Samuel de Champlain, 1604–1616.* New York: Simon and Schuster, 1922.

Dabney, Joseph E. *Smokehouse Ham, Spoon Bread, and Scuppernong Wine: The Folklore and Art of Southern Appalachian Cooking.* Nashville: Cumberland House Publishing, 1998.

Gray, Asa. *Manual of the Botany of the Northern United States.* New York: Ivison, Blakeman and Company, 1890.

Hariot, Thomas. *1588 Narrative of the First English Plantation of Virginia.* London: B. Quatrich, 1893 (reprint).

Miller, Phillip. *The Gardener's Dictionary.* London: privately printed, 1768.

Moulton, Gary E., ed. *The Definitive Journals of the Lewis and Clark Expedition.* Lincoln: University of Nebraska Press, 2002.

Rutledge, Sarah. *The Carolina Housewife, or House and Home, by a Lady of Charleston.* Charleston, South Carolina: W. R. Babcock, 1847. Reprinted in Columbia: University of South Carolina Press, 1969.

Shoemaker, D. N. *The Jerusalem Artichoke as a Crop Plant.* USDA Technical Bulletin no. 33. Washington, D.C.: U.S. Government Printing Office, 1927.

Waters, L., D. Davis, J. Riehle, and M. Weins. *Jerusalem Artichoke Trials.* St. Paul: Department of Horticulture, University of Minnesota, 1981.

Guinea Hog

With a stout, compact body, upright ears, a curly tail, and a black coat, the Guinea hog might at first glance seem to be your average American pig. Instead, it should be regarded as an American original, one whose ancestors three centuries ago accompanied West African slaves to Appalachia, where the African Guinea stock picked up genes from English pigs.

Around 1804, Thomas Jefferson and his Virginia neighbors obtained rose-tinged black hogs from Africa via the Canary Islands. While these introductions were at first called Red Guineas, the subsequent crosses with Appalachian English pigs, Essex pigs, and West African Dwarfs tended to retain black coats. Both Red and Black Guineas spread to farms up and down the Appalachian Trail, where they were variously called Yard Pigs, Pineywoods Guinea Hogs, Forest Pigs, and Acorn Eaters. Indeed, they did consume various acorns, hickories, and chestnuts from the forests of Chestnut Nation, but they would also grub out and eat rodents, roots, and snakes. The Guineas fed largely on acorns and other nuts were found to be excellent producers of pork, ham, and lard. But they also provided additional benefits to homesteads and small farms by virtue of their capac-ity to control pests, graze rough ground, till the soil, and root out perennial weeds.

Guinea boars may seem small when judged by modern standards, for they seldom weigh much more than 200 pounds at maturity, rendering a carcass weight of meat and fat in the range of 50 to 100 pounds. They can subsist as free-ranging foragers in forests, orchards, and fields but are docile enough to keep on table scraps in a barnyard as well. Indeed, Guineas were a common fixture on homesteads throughout the Appalachian corridor of Chestnut Nation well into the 1880s, when improved breeds began to capture the American farmer's imagination. The small but sturdy Guinea fell from grace along with most other multipurpose livestock, for their size

Guinea Hog piglets on Cascade Meadow Farm. Cascade Meadow Farm

Courtesy American Livestock Breeds Conservancy

ranges and foraging capacities were tangential to where the hog industry was headed.

For most of the twentieth century, Guineas remained critically rare, if not on the brink of extinction. Then, in 1991, the American Guinea Hog Association was incorporated and now includes members who steward more than fifteen herds. Heeding its motto of being "dedicated to the preservation of an American original," the association keeps a registry that now includes more than 200 breeding pigs. Although they remain critically endangered, they have been boarded onto the Slow Food Ark of Taste and are attracting more and more attention each year.

The following recipe combines an old method for roasting pork ribs in biscuit dough and ashes with Moonlite Dip barbecue sauce first used in the 1960s by Pappy Bosley. Pappy used it for both barbecued mutton and pork at the Moonlite Bar-B-Q Inn in

Further Readings

Christman, Carolyn J., D. Phillip Sponenberg, and Donald E. Bixby. *A Rare Breeds Album of American Livestock.* Pittsboro, North Carolina: American Livestock Breeds Conservancy, 1997.

Dohner, Janet Vorwald. *The Encyclopedia of Historic and Endangered Livestock and Poultry Breeds.* New Haven, Connecticut: Yale University Press, 2001.

Elie, Lolis Eric. *Smokestack Lightning: Adventures in the Heart of Barbecue Country.* Berkeley, California: Ten Speed Press, 2005.

Spivey, Diane M. *The Peppers, Cracklings, and Knots of Wool Cookbook: The Global Migration of African Cuisine.* Albany, New York: State University of Albany Press, 1999.

Owensboro, Kentucky, the self-proclaimed "Bar-B-Que Capitol of the World." As barbecue historian and journalist Lolis Eric Elie has wryly noted on his visit to the Land of Burgoo, Pork and Mutton Bar-B-Q,

They allow Protestants to barbecue in Owensboro, but they don't encourage it. The first recorded barbecue here was in 1834 at a gathering of Baptists. But in this [last] century the Catholics have taken over and people are disinclined to wait for the Protestants to catch up. For the Protestants, barbecue is a secular undertaking, but for the papists it is a calling of a higher order.

GUINEA HOG RIBS IN BISCUIT DOUGH AND ASHES, WITH MOONLITE DIP

For ribs in ashes and biscuit dough:
1 slab Guinea hog ribs
1 teaspoon sea salt
1 tablespoon freshly ground black peppercorns
½ cup dry rub (see below)
4 cups biscuit dough
1 cup Moonlite Dip barbecue sauce (see below)

In a barbecue pit or fireplace, start a good bed of coals from hickory wood 2 hours in advance of roasting. Once the coals are red-hot, season the Guinea hog ribs in a large bowl with salt, pepper, and a dry rub, covering their entire surface. Next, pack the moist biscuit dough against the ribs, until there is a 1½-inch-thick coating on all sides. Place the dough-coated ribs right onto the ashes and coals left from the hickory wood and let them slowly roast over the coals for 12 hours. Remove them from the pit, discard the now-blackened biscuit dough, and present the ribs on a platter next to a bowl of Moonlite Dip sauce. Serves 2 Catholics or 3 Protestants.

Dry rub:
2 tablespoons celery salt
2 tablespoons garlic salt
4 tablespoons sea salt
3 tablespoons Tabasco pepper sauce
2 tablespoons paprika
2 tablespoons ground white pepper
2 tablespoons brown sugar

½ teaspoon roasted and ground cumin seeds
½ teaspoon ground coriander seeds
1 teaspoon dry mustard

Sift all ingredients together and store in a glass jar that holds a cup or more of contents and has a tight-fitting lid. Take out ½ cup per roasting and rub into the ribs before adding the biscuit dough.

Moonlite Dip barbecue sauce:
(This is a minor adaptation of the recipe formerly used in the early days of the Moonlite Bar-B-Q Inn in Owensboro, Kentucky, recorded for posterity by Pappy Bosley and Lolis Eric Elie.)

1 gallon spring water
1⅔ cups Worcestershire sauce
2½ tablespoons freshly ground black peppercorns
⅓ cup brown sugar
1 teaspoon allspice
1 teaspoon onion salt
1 teaspoon minced garlic cloves
2 tablespoons salt
2 tablespoons lemon juice
1⅔ cups apple cider vinegar

Mix all ingredients together in a large pot, bring to a boil, then transfer (when cooled) to a gallon jug.

Carolina Northern Flying Squirrel

The Carolina northern flying squirrel is an endangered animal of the boreal forests of Chestnut Nation and one that was formerly used as a game food by Native American and immigrant hunters alike. Once widespread in the Appalachian Mountains of North Carolina and eastern Tennessee, it is now known only from five isolated localities in these two states, all in places where coniferous and hardwood forests intermingle. It appears that the squirrel's habitat and range have been shrinking since the last Ice Age, but human impacts have accelerated this process.

A foot-long glider that seldom weighs more than a half pound, this squirrel has dense, silky fur; a broad, flattened tail; and a thin but fuzzy membrane extending between the wrist and the ankle that aids it in "flying" fifteen to sixty feet—rarely as much as 120 feet—between the upper branches of trees. While the backs of adults can be gray, brown, or tan, the young have slate-gray backs and undersides that are whiter than those of their parents. They consume mushrooms, lichens, flowers, buds, seeds, nuts, insects, and bird eggs, caching some of their food in cavities within trees just as other squirrels tend to do. Their capacity to sniff out truffles is renowned.

Because northern flying squirrels are so dependent on the old-growth hardwoods and conifers found together on rugged mountain islands along the Appalachian corridor, they are increasingly vulnerable to the climatic changes that are progressively diminishing the area of such habitat. They are also particularly vulnerable to predators and parasites in fragmented forests surrounded by human developments. Logging, ski developments, and certain forms of winter recreation are having further impact on their favored forested habitats. Today, it would be difficult to trap more than six squirrels a season in a forested area the size of one to two football fields. Both the Carolina and the Virginia subspecies are now protected by state and federal governments.

Although both are endangered today, the Virginia and Carolina subspecies of northern flying squirrels were for many decades trapped and then eaten by residents of Appalachia. Until three or four decades ago, the mildly gamy, pleasing, pinkish flesh of the many species of squirrels in Chestnut Nation was highly prized as a bush meat. Dozens of recipes specifically written for squirrel can be found in historic cookbooks, but squirrel was also substituted for domestic rabbit or chicken in favorite stews whenever the latter were unavailable. Two of the legendary squirrel dishes of Chestnut Nation are burgoo and Brunswick stew, both of which were historically made with flying squirrel. Variations of both stews can be found from Illinois, Kentucky, and Missouri through Virginia, the Carolinas, Tennessee, and Louisiana. To this day, a Burgoo Festival is celebrated every year in Utica, Illinois. And one rather spicy Kentucky version of burgoo is still regularly featured at George's Bar-B-Q in Owensboro, Kentucky.

The roots of the term *burgoo* for game-and-vegetable stews have been subject to raging debates among culinary historians. Some suggest that the term is derived from the Arabic *burghul* and was first used in the Western world in reference to Turkish pilafs, stews, and porridges that were made from cracked wheat and served to international sailors on British whalers in the 1700s. Whatever its etymology, the word appears to have been in use within Chestnut Nation by the 1840s, where it was applied to fire-thickened stews consisting of hominy (instead of wheat), game, and vegetables tossed into large pots

Melissa McGaw, courtesy North Carolina Wildlife Resources Commission

Further Readings

Geffen, Alice M., and Carole Berglie. *Food Festival: The Ultimate Guidebook to America's Best Regional Food Celebrations.* New York: Pantheon Books, 1986.

Stern, Jane, and Michael Stern. *Goodfood.* New York: Alfred Knopf, 1983.

U.S. Fish and Wildlife Service. "Endangered and Threatened Wildlife and Plants: Determination of Endangered Status for Two Kinds of Northern Flying Squirrel." *Federal Register* 50:128 (1985): 26999–27002.

Weigl, Peter D. "The Northern Flying Squirrel *(Glaucomys sabrinus):* A Conservation Challenge." *Journal of Mammalogy* 88:4 (2007): 897–907.

that were simmered on open wood fires. Some historians suggest that the term *burgoo* was first applied to the savory blackbird stews of the Mississippi River watershed by a Frenchman, chef Gus Jaubert; indeed blackbird-based jambalayas are still prepared in northern Louisiana among Cajun hunters. Jaubert served as a cook for the cavalry troops under General John Hunt Morgan during the Civil War and later settled in Lexington, Kentucky. In any case, the tradition of making burgoos at barbecues and in hunting camps caught on in Kentucky and in southern Illinois, and by 1900, J. T. Looney of Lexington had begun to promote them as a regional specialty.

KENTUCKY BURGOO WITH SQUIRREL

2 pounds squirrel meat (flying squirrel now prohibited)
2 tablespoons sunflower oil
6 cups spring water
1 cup white hominy
1½ cups white lima or butter beans
2 stalks celery, chopped
1 cup minced ramps (wild leeks)
1 bay leaf
1 cup sliced Alice Elliot okra
1 orange bell pepper, diced
2 cups diced Amish paste tomatoes
1 cup potatoes, diced
1 cup fresh shoepeg corn kernels
1 tablespoon salt
½ teaspoon freshly ground black pepper
½ teaspoon cayenne chile powder
½ teaspoon Tabasco pepper sauce
1 teaspoon Worcestershire sauce

Two days prior to a barbecue or picnic, clean 3 or 4 squirrels to obtain 2 pounds of meat on the bone. Rub the meat with salt and pepper and broil the cleaned but whole squirrels for 40 minutes. Debone and cut into 1-inch cubes of meat. Next, heat the oil in the bottom of a 2- to 3-gallon stew pot suited to placing on an open wood fire. Place the cubes of squirrel meat in the hot oil and brown them all in a matter of 4 minutes, turning the cubes frequently. Add the 6 cups of spring water to the pot and toss in the hominy, lima beans, potatoes, celery, ramps, and bay leaf. Simmer for an hour, then skim off the grease. Add the okra, bell pepper, tomatoes, shoepeg corn kernels, salt, pepper, cayenne, and Tabasco and Worcestershire sauces. Bring the stew back to a boil, then reduce its heat until it keeps a steady, gentle boil for another hour. The mixture will get exceedingly thick and try to stick to the bottom of the pot. Stir the sticky mass away from the pot as frequently as you are able, but let it continue to thicken into a rib-sticking mass for 1 more hour. Cut the heat when you go to bed and cover until the next day. Twenty minutes before the picnic, set the pot to simmer once more, then scoop the stew up into wooden bowls and serve with johnnycakes, whiskey, and water.

CHILE PEPPER NATION

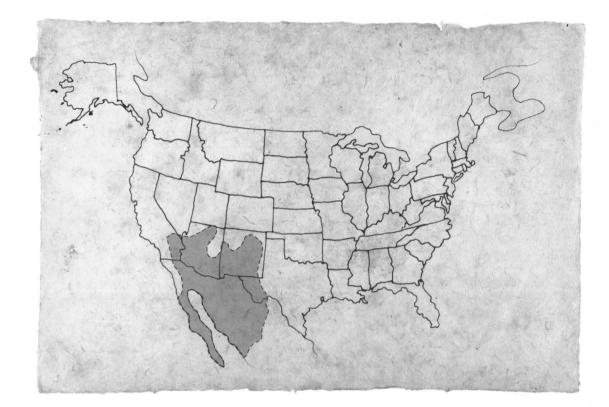

The hottest, driest food nation on the continent, Chile Pepper Nation is also the spiciest. This region stretches from the southern reaches of the Colorado Plateau or Painted Desert down through the Sonoran, Chihuahuan, and Mohave deserts, encompassing the intervening semiarid uplands as well. It has the oldest extant agricultural traditions of any region north of the Tropic of Cancer, with 4,000-year-old corn remains having been found near Tucson, Hopi, and Zuni. This binational region also has the greatest surviving linguistic diversity of native peoples of any region and the largest populations of Native American language speakers. Hispanic, Arab, and Basque farming and herding traditions blended with indigenous ones here more than three centuries ago, resulting in a bewildering diversity of heirloom vegetables, corns, and beans. The region is also rich in wild edible cacti and legumes but has lost most of its fish, as dams and groundwater pumping destroyed most of its riverside habitats and freshwater springs.

Rapid urbanization since World War II has fragmented farm and ranch lands and usurped most of their waters. As a result, at least 174 traditional foods are now threatened or endangered in Chile Pepper Nation.

El Guique New Mexican Chile Pepper

If an heirloom chile variety can have a human face to it, the face of the El Guique chile from northern New Mexico is that of Pete Casados. This Hispanic heirloom is so strongly associated with Pete and his wife Juanita that it is sometimes called the "Casados Native" chile as well. Like the Chimayó chile grown in the highlands of the same "Rio Arriba" watershed, El Guique is one of the few authentic remnants of northern New Mexico chiles to remain uncontaminated by more recently developed hybrid cultivars.

El Guique is named for a little Hispanic farming village across the Rio Grande from San Juan Pueblo, on the back road between Santa Fe and Taos. There, for decades, Pete and Juanita Casados have grown thousands of pounds of blue corn, white corn for *chicos,* and El Guique chiles in their irrigated fields along the fertile floodplain of the Rio Grande. Pete grew up in El Guique, and Juanita in nearby Chamita; for more than a half century, they have farmed and marketed historic Southwestern foods together through a partnership called Dos Ves, Inc. For many decades, it was one of the few reliable commercial suppliers of place-based heritage foods in all of Chile Pepper Nation. The first journalists who raised Southwestern foods to national and even international attention inevitably featured the tireless work of Pete and Juanita; when writers for magazines like *Food and Wine, Gourmet,* and *Women's Day* wanted to know how New Mexican chile grew and what it tasted like, they went to the Casados farm.

The medium-hot chile pod of El Guique is four to five inches long and at least an inch wide and has relatively thin flesh. However, when still green, it is slightly fleshier and sweeter than other New Mexican chiles, making it ideal for stuffing as a chile relleno. As it matures, the pod becomes more pendant, turning from its bright green to a brilliant red in a matter of weeks. The El Guique pepper plant matures rather rapidly, seldom reaching two feet tall before it begins to produce flowers and fruit.

Although heirloom "landraces" of New Mexican chiles have both Hispanic and Native American culinary traditions associated with them, no archaeologist or historian has thus far been able to definitively determine when they were first grown in the state. And yet, as Eric Votava once noted, "These landraces are the direct descendants of chile brought to New Mexico from Mexico. In essence they are a living link to 400 years of New Mexico history."

By the beginning of nineteenth century, chiles had become an essential ingredient in New Mexican cuisine, which is definitively different from both Tex-Mex cuisine to the east and Sonoran cuisine to the west. Unfortunately, the distinctiveness of these landraces in New Mexico chiles is now at risk. New Mexico State University scientists Paul Bosland and Eric Votava have estimated that as much as 21 percent of the New Mexican heirloom landraces have already been contaminated by gene flow from improved cultivars. Because of such risks, all of the remaining "pure" heirloom chiles of New Mexico have been boarded onto the Slow Food Ark of Taste, and each needs to be grown in isolation to maintain its authenticity.

The following recipe is part of a widespread tradition in northern New Mexico and Chihuahua, Mexico, of marinating pork in a *chile caribe* sauce, a custom that first appeared in Chile Pepper Nation at about the time of the Spanish-American War and the Mexican Revolution. According to Hispanic historian Estevan Arrellano, *caribe* is derived from the Spanish term for the Carib Indians, and it implies powerfully wild qualities. Pork is not much produced or consumed elsewhere in Chile Pepper Nation, perhaps because of the early influence of Crypto-Jews and Crypto-Moslems there who still observe their ancient religious taboos. By the Mexican Revolution, however, these influences had waned in northern New Mexico, and *carne adovada* became a hit.

CARNE ADOVADA CON CHILES EL GUIQUE

1½ cups crushed dried red El Guique New Mexican chiles, seeds included
4 cloves Sonoran or New Mexican garlic, minced
3 teaspoons dried Sonoran oregano
2 tablespoons ground coriander seeds
1 white onion, diced
1½ cups water
½ cup chicken broth
2 tablespoons honey
2 pounds pork or *javelina* (white-lipped peccary), cut into strips or cubed

In a glass mixing bowl, prepare a *caribe* sauce by combining the crushed El Guique chiles, garlic, oregano, coriander, onion, water, broth, and honey. Mix well and set aside to thicken. Next, place the pork in a glass pan and brush the *caribe* sauce on both sides, then pour the remaining sauce over the pork. Marinate the pork in the sauce overnight in the refrigerator. The next day, place the marinated pork in a 300-degree F oven and bake it in the glass pan, uncovered, for 2 hours. If it is not very tender and starting to fall apart at that time, lower the heat to 250 degrees F and bake for 20 more minutes, adding a little water if necessary. Serve in tortillas as a burrito or turn into a stuffing for enchiladas or sopapillas.

Further Readings

Cuvelier, Monique. "Saving the Native New Mexican Chiles." Accessed April 20, 2007, from www.fiery-foods.com/dave/landrace.asp.

Votava, Eric J., Jit B. Baral, and Paul. W. Bosland. "Diversity of Chile (*Capsicum annuum* L. var. *annuum* L.) Landraces from New Mexico, Colorado and Mexico." *Economic Botany* 59:1 (2005): 8–17.

The fertile floodplain of the Rio Grande near San Juan Pueblo. William L. Graf

Chapalote Popcorn

Chapalote popcorn is by far the most ancient type of maize to be grown in what is now the United States, arriving in Chile Pepper Nation more than 4,100 years ago. For years, nearly every student of archaeology who studied the origins of agriculture knew something of *chapalote,* for it was deemed to be among the first cultivated landraces of maize in Mexico, and its tiny cobs had been found in a famous site known as Bat Cave in central New Mexico as well.

When you hold one of its eight-inch cobs in your hand and its smoky, coffee-colored kernels glisten like amber, *chapalote* seems like no other corn you have ever seen. It has twelve to fourteen rows of small, tannish brown kernels; a third of them are flinty, but the rest are more like the ornamental popcorn kernels featured around the time of Halloween. Once the kernels are shucked from the cigar-shaped cobs and toasted, they can be ground into a sweet, powdery meal that is excellent for *pinole,* America's first trail food.

While it is still grown in a few lowland subtropical villages on the flanks of the Sierra Madre Occidental, *chapalote* was somehow extirpated from the U.S. Southwest many decades or even centuries ago.

Using seeds collected for a gene bank, field archaeologists in the late 1970s reintroduced it into cultivation near Alamogordo, New Mexico. It became almost legendary in some circles, and groups of botanists and archaeologists sought out other relictual sources of seed still maintained by indigenous and mestizo farmers in northwestern Mexico. These have since been maintained by Native Seeds/SEARCH and periodically grown in the United States with some success.

If only because it is North America's oldest surviving maize variety, *chapalote* should be grown in every schoolyard on the continent for use in interpreting our agricultural heritage. Yet this ancient corn should not remain merely an intellectual abstraction, for its delicious flinty meal deserves to be found on our tables and in our mouths once again. The following preparation is traditional among the Yoemem or Yaqui people of Mexico and Arizona.

David Cavagnaro

Further Readings

Echeverría, María Esther, and Luz Elena Arroyo. *Recetario de Maíz.* Cocina Indígena y Popular 10. Mexico City: Consejo Nacional para la Cultura y las Artes, 2000.

Pennington, Campbell W. *The Tepehuan of Chihuahua: Their Material Culture*. Salt Lake City: University of Utah Press, 1969.

BATARETE DE LOS YAQUIS

1 cup water
1¼ pounds brown sugar *(panocha de piloncillo)*
2 cups *pinole* ground from *chapalote* corn kernels
⅓ pound *asadero* cheese, grated

In a kettle over a wood fire, bring the water to a boil and dissolve the brown sugar in it. When it forms a light syrup, move it off the heat. When it is cool, mix in the *chapalote pinole,* stirring vigorously. Top with grated cheese and serve on little dishes.

Black Sphinx Date

Occurring only in the desert oases of Chile Pepper Nation, this endangered heirloom was discovered as a chance seedling below Hayani date cuttings that had been introduced to experimental plantations in the Sonoran Desert of central Arizona. That single Black Sphinx seedling was discovered by Roy Franklin in 1928, at the Sphinx Ranch plantation on West Glenwood Avenue in Phoenix, where some twenty-three date varieties had been brought from Arabia in 1917. The plantation owners, Brophy and McChesney, propagated it by crown separation, and by 1931 they were tending 156 Black Sphinx date palms on their ranch. The Black Sphinx soon became one of the two most highly prized and expensive varieties in Arizona, and by 1993 there were between 6,000 and 8,000 Black Sphinx palms in the state, 98 percent of them in the Arcadia neighborhood below Camelback Mountain in Metro Phoenix.

The palms of this variety reach more than thirty feet in height, so that professional tree climbers must be enlisted to hand-pollinate them. They produce a soft, plump date that is slightly ovoid and rather large. Its thin skin deepens from a carmine to a chocolate brown when ripe. Its deep amber flesh is buttery soft, almost syrupy, but mild in flavor.

In *Chez Panisse Fruits,* Alice Waters writes that "its fruits have fragile, brown-black skins and rich, sweet, flavorful flesh." Early on, the Black Sphinx was appreciated only locally, for its skin was so delicate that it spoiled under extended storage and shipping. Like desert manna, it could be used fresh for only a few weeks each year. However, Frank Brophy once put a few in the hands of President Dwight D. Eisenhower, who is said to have relished them. Once air shipping became possible, the Black Sphinx date became featured as one of the all-time favorite dessert fruits at restaurants like Chez Panisse in Berkeley and in several specialty date markets.

The Black Sphinx would have remained poorly cared for and erratically distributed were it not for a man named Harry Polk, who rekindled interest in its exceptional flavor and texture. Polk tended virtually all the trees that grew in the remaining historic grove in the Arcadia district on the south side of

Black Sphinx date palms survive in the midst of metro Phoenix, along the boulevards of the Arcadia neighborhood below Camelback Mountain. Gary Paul Nabhan

Black Sphinx (mostly *bisr*-stage) at Four Apostles Ranch, Bermuda Dunes. David Karp

Further Readings

Albert, D. W., and R. H. Hilgeman. *Date Growing in Arizona.* University of Arizona Agricultural Experiment Station Bulletin 149. Tucson: University of Arizona Agricultural Experiment Station, 1935.

Nabhan, G. P., and Kanin Josef Routson. *Southwest Regis-Tree, 2006.* Available at www.nativeseeds. org.

Salloum, Habeeb, and James Peters. *From the Lands of Figs and Olives.* New York: Interlink Press, 2002.

Waters, Alice, Alan Tangren, and Fritz Streiff. *Chez Panisse Fruit.* San Francisco: HarperCollins, 2002.

Camelback Mountain and distributed them through the Arizona Date Gardens. Only a few other Black Sphinx palms have survived elsewhere, like those at Ehrlich's Date Gardens in Yuma. Already, land-use changes in the Arcadia neighborhood are eliminating some of the oldest remaining Black Sphinx palms, and its propagation by crown separation is so difficult that it seldom proves successful. They are extremely rare in commerce today and are offered only by the Black Sphinx Date Ranch of Scottsdale, Arizona. If someone does not step up to continue Polk's work, they will become even more critically endangered.

The following recipe is adapted from Arab-Canadian food writer Habeeb Salloum, who suggests that Phoenician traders carried both dates and their recipes from the Fertile Crescent to North Africa to Spain, where they entered western European cuisine around A.D. 711. By 1765, some dates had arrived in northern Mexico with exiled Moors and Jews, who took them to California and Arizona. There, the Black Sphinx is but one of several varieties that barely survives today. Fortunately, a new wave of immigration from Arabian countries to Chile Pepper Nation over the last two decades is creating a renewed demand for dates such as the Black Sphinx.

BLACK SPHINX DATE FRUIT CUP

4 cups rose water or orange blossom water
2 cups Black Sphinx dates
⅓ cup turbinado sugar
½ cup sultana or Mission raisins, washed
3 whole cardamom pods
6 whole cloves
2 tablespoons lemon juice
½ cup whipping cream
2½ teaspoons slivered California almonds, toasted

Place the rose water or orange blossom water in a saucepan and bring it to a boil. Add the dates and simmer them for 5 minutes. With a slotted spoon, remove the dates from the saucepan, while reserving the cooking water. Let the dates cool, peel and pit them, then set aside.

Next, bring the reserved water back to a boil, slowly adding the sugar and stirring until it dissolves. Stir in the raisins, dates, cardamom pods, and cloves, simmering for another 15 minutes. Add the lemon juice and simmer 5 more minutes. Then remove the cloves and cardamom pods and remove the pan from the heat. Once cool, spoon this mixture into fruit cups. Whip the cream and spoon it over the fruit. Sprinkle the toasted slivered almonds on top of the whipped cream. Serves 5.

Masked Bobwhite Quail

The endangered subspecies of bobwhite quail found in Chile Pepper Nation is far removed from its closest kin, but it offers one of the most improbable links between food and conservation ever recorded. As David Brown has noted, "No bird of the Southwest has stimulated as much anxiety as the masked bobwhite." Unlike the white-throated bobwhite populations to the east of Arizona, the males of this "masked" subspecies have dark chestnut or cinnamon-red breasts and black throats and heads. They, like their eastern kin, have been grilled around campfires by Native Americans and others for millennia. These game birds were historically hunted in the desert grassland valleys and level plains that stretch from Tucson southward to Hermosillo, the capitol of Sonora, Mexico.

The presence of a bobwhite quail in the Arizona bush was first reported by Eliot Coues in 1864, but no scientist got this bird in hand until 1884, when a hunter named Andrews offered Herbert Brown two masked bobwhites he had bagged on the grasslands below the Baboquivari Mountains. That same year, Brown first described this distinctive game bird in *Forest and Stream,* but an eastern scientist named Robert Ridgway doubted that a bobwhite could be found that far west and complained that Brown had misidentified a Mearn's quail. Even though Brown presented additional masked bobwhites and was vindicated, the new subspecies was eventually named for Ridgway, the man who had denied their existence!

Not long after its presence in Arizona and distinctive identity were at last accepted, the bird disappeared due to a series of droughts that hit Chile Pepper Nation. The last specimens of masked bobwhites native to the United States were collected in 1896, but Arizona populations were never again encountered after 1899, when the second prolonged drought in a decade devastated their habitats. In 1904, Herbert Brown—the very man who had first described this species—conceded that "for the past several years [the bobwhite] has been safeguarded by law in this territory [of Arizona], but unfortunately there are none left to protect."

What caused the masked bobwhite to suddenly vanish? Biologist John Alcock has suggested that "the cause of its remarkably rapid disappearance has been traced with reasonable certainty to the stupendous overgrazing that took place in the 1880s and 1890s . . . The million plus cows in Arizona before the turn of the century quite literally ate the quail out of house and home." The unprecedented droughts of the 1890s served as the trigger for their demise, but there was little hope for any quail recovery while overgrazing persisted and desert shrubs invaded habitats once covered by grass. Fortunately, some birds still hung on, albeit precariously, just south of

iStockphoto

the U.S./Mexico border, enough for pioneering southwestern ornithologist Stokely Ligon to capture them for release in New Mexico and Arizona in the 1930s. They barely survived until another drought hit in the 1950s, and none were seen in the wild on either side of the border over the following fifteen years. By 1960, the masked bobwhite quail was considered extinct, not only in the United States, but in the wilds of Mexico as well.

Then came the sighting of a minor miracle—their resurrection—in a small Mexican restaurant in Magdalena, Sonora. At Restaurant Tecolote, this very bird was offered as lunch to Jim and Seymour Levy in the 1964, when the chef had no chicken for the enchiladas they had requested. Seymour Levy had already been involved in their captive breeding, so

Further Readings

Alcock, John. *The Masked Bobwhite Rides Again.* Tucson: University of Arizona Press, 1993.

Bonta, Marcia. "Arizona's Passenger Pigeon," 2000. Available at http://marciabonta.wordpress.com/tag/birds/masked-bobwhite/.

Brown, David. E. *Arizona Game Birds.* Tucson: University of Arizona Press, 1989.

Brown, David. E., and D. H. Ellis. *Masked Bobwhite Recovery Plan.* Alburquerque, New Mexico: U.S. Fish and Wildlife Service, 1984.

Brown, Herbert. "Conditions Governing Bird Life in Arizona." *Auk* 17 (1900): 31–34.

Brown, Herbert. 1904. "Masked Bobwhite (*Colinus ridgwayi*)." *Auk* 21 (1904): 209–213.

"Quail a la Millbrook presented by the Millbrook Inn." Bed and Breakfasts Inns Online, n.d. Available at www.bbonline.com/millbrookvt-recipe1.html.

"Roasted Quail with Andouille Sausage and Pecan Cornbread Stuffing." Snowbird Mountain Lodge, Robbinsville, North Carolina, Specialty Recipe, n.d. Available at www.virtualcities.com/ons/nc/a/ncab9013.htm.

he fortunately recognized the pricelessness of the chef's offer. Together with wildlife biologist Steve Gallizioti, the Levy brothers found the birds living on the nearby Rancho Carrizo, owned by Don Pedro Camou, confirming that the masked bobwhite was down but not yet out. They brought up enough birds from Mexico to reestablish the masked bobwhite's presence in the United States.

When the bird was first listed as legally protected in the United States in 1974, the Fish and Wildlife Service began to collaborate with Mexican biologists and ranchers on its recovery in both countries, releasing thousands of birds from hatchlings with sterilized foster male parents taken from Texas populations. These reintroductions had modest success in the 1970s, with seventy-four males surviving through 1979, but then another round of drought hit the Southwest. By 1983, only a few male masked bobwhites were left in the degraded habitat into which they had been placed, prompting the Fish and Wildlife Service to purchase the Buenos Aires Ranch as a refuge for the birds for $8.9 million, adding other

ranches later on. And yet the masked bobwhite has still not gotten out of trouble since this investment was made—barely sixty calling males have survived from year to year, and the Buenos Aires Wildlife Refuge biologists heard not a single calling male in 2006.

The refuge has now closed down its captive breeding and reintroduction program located on the border, so that the only captive breeding done from now on will be in zoos. This game bird remains one of the most endangered animals in Chile Pepper Nation and may not ever be available as a food again in the United States, moving nature writer Marcia Bonta to call the masked bobwhite "Arizona's passenger pigeon."

The following recipe for bobwhite quail is therefore not offered as an enticement to hunt or to eat this subspecies but as a reminder of its loss. It is loosely adapted from stuffed quail recipes from the Millbrook Inn in Waitsfield, Vermont, and from Snowbird Mountain Lodge in Robbinsville, North Carolina.

ROASTED BOBWHITE QUAIL WITH MESCAL, SAUSAGE, AND CORNBREAD STUFFING

2 cups day-old cornbread
¼ cup olive oil
¾ pound andouille sausage (or chorizo), diced
½ cup chopped I'itoi onions or other shallots
3 stalks celery, chopped
1 cup chopped, toasted pecans
¼ teaspoon dried cayenne or Tabasco pepper
¼ teaspoon sea salt
¼ teaspoon freshly ground black pepper
1½ cups chicken stock
12 whole bobwhite quail
½ cup mescal bacanora
1 cup white wine
1 cup chopped porcini mushrooms (or morels, if in season)

Crumble the day-old cornbread into a glass mixing bowl. In a hot skillet, drizzle in the olive oil, then sauté the sausage, onions, celery, toasted pecans, and seasonings. When the onions are browned, pour the contents of the skillet into the mixing bowl with the cornbread and mix well to combine. Add the chicken stock to the stuffing in stages, 2 to 3 tablespoons at a time, until the moistened cornbread holds all other ingredients

together; you may not need all the chicken stock to accomplish this. Before it turns mushy, taste the stuffing for texture and seasoning; add more seasoning if necessary.

Next, wash each quail and pat it dry. Fill the body cavity of each bird with just enough stuffing to make it plump but not to tear its meat. Fold the legs of each quail crossways and tuck the ends of the legs beneath the stuffing-filled cavity to secure them. Baste each bird in a little olive oil and place them breast-side-down in a pan over a medium-low flame, browning the breasts. Turn them over and brown as much as possible on each side. Next, pour a few tablespoons of mescal over the quail and ignite it, letting the flames burn out on their own. Add the white wine and the chopped mushrooms to the pan and simmer for 10 minutes.

Finally, place the stuffed quails, breast-side-up in a baking dish, spoon the wine and mushrooms over them, and roast uncovered in a 350-degree F oven for 15 to 20 minutes. Place 2 quail on a plate and spoon the liquid and the mushrooms over each bird. Serves 6.

Wild Tomatillo of the Continental Divide

Variously known as the wild husk tomato, Zuni tomatillo, Tarahumara tomatillo, or *miltomate de las sierras,* this small ground cherry has a distinctively sweet flavor and succulent texture unlike other more acrid, pulpy tomatillos. It has been found along the continental divide between the Gulf of Mexico and the Gulf of California, from the Colorado Plateau southward along the cordilleras of the Sierra Madre Occidental. It typically grows as a weed among Tarahumara and Tepehuan fields in the Sierras but also appears to have been semicultivated by some Pueblo, Navajo, and Hispanic gardeners of northern New Mexico. Its culinary use in the region may go back centuries, if not millennia. Eight-hundred-year-old seeds of tomatillos have been found in Yellow Jacket Ruin by the staff of the Crow Canyon Archaeological Center in southwestern Colorado.

The Spanish terms *tomate* and *tomatillo* are both derived from the Nahuatl word *tomatl,* which was commonly used throughout the Aztec empire. This term generically refers to any edible globose fruit or berry that has many seeds and somewhat watery or juicy flesh. The term *jitomate*—or *tomate* for short—refers to fully domesticated, usually larger, "true" tomatoes. In contrast, the term *miltomate* is still used for ground cherries that are harvested from cornfields or *milpas.* These are typically semivining plants that sprawl across plowed ground, maturing at about the same time that intentionally sown crops are ready for the harvest. Still widespread in the Sierra Madre of Mexico, this wild subspecies of the Mexican tomatillo is now found north of the border only in one or two counties of the United States, in and around Puebloan gardens.

Fortunately, its seeds have been made available to North American gardeners via Native Seeds/SEARCH of the southwestern United States, Argental Heritage Seeds of Canada, and the Chile Woman website. In addition, there are several related species and varieties still in use in North America, including the Cape gooseberry and Aunt Molly's ground cherry; Aunt Molly's is a Polish heirloom that, like this wild tomatillo, has been boarded onto the Slow Food Ark of Taste.

Courtesy Native Seeds/SEARCH

One of the long-term caretakers and traditional harvesters of this wild vegetable was the late Chester Gaspar of Ojo Caliente, New Mexico, who was also one of several legendary Native American musicians to play in jazz and big bands. After harvesting the fruit and removing the sticky, Chinese-lantern-like husk from the pale green tomatoes, Mr. Gaspar roasted them in an oven, then blended them with garlic, onion, chile peppers, and cilantro to make a zesty, tart, but somewhat sweet hot sauce. The following recipe—adapted from Rita Edaakie's Zuni recipe and as well as one from Rick and Deann Bayless's Frontera Grill—would make Mr. Gaspar feel right at home.

Courtesy Native Seeds/SEARCH

Further Readings

Bayless, Rick, JeanMarie Brownson, and Deann Groen Bayless. *Salsas That Cook*. New York: Simon and Schuster/Fireside Books, 1998.

Edaakie, Rita. *Idonapshe: Let's Eat Traditional Zuni Foods*. Zuni, New Mexico: A:shiwi A:wan Museum and Heritage Center, 1999.

Hudson, W. D. Jr. "Relationships of Domesticated and Wild *Physalis philadelphica*." In William G. D'Arcy, ed., *Solanaceae: Biology and Systematics*, pp. 416–433. New York: Columbia University Press, 1986.

Hudson, W. D. Jr. "The Relationships of Wild and Domesticated Tomato, Physalis philadelphica Lamarck (Solanaceae)." Master's thesis, Indiana University, 1983.

Montes Hernandez, Salvador, and J. R. Aguirre Rivera. "Tomatillos." In J. E. Hernándo Bermejo and J. León, eds., *Neglected Crops: 1492 from a Different Perspective*, pp. 117–122. Plant Production and Protection Series No. 26. Rome: FAO, 1994.

Murray, Shawn S., and Nicole D. Jackman-Craig. "Archaeobotanical Remains." In Kristin A. Kuckelman, ed., *The Archaeology of Yellow Jacket Pueblo: Excavations at a Large Community Center in Southwestern Colorado*, pp. 1–68. Dolores, Colorado: Crow Canyon Archaeological Center, 2003. Accessed May 23, 2007, from www.crowcanyon.org/yellowjacket.

K'OLA K'YALK'OSENNE (ROASTED TOMATILLO SALSA)

3 pounds wild tomatillos, husked and rinsed
12 to 15 fresh serrano chile peppers, stems removed
2 medium-sized white Bermuda onions, sliced
9 Sonoran softneck garlic cloves
1 cup chopped cilantro or coriander leaves
3 teaspoons dried Sonoran oregano leaves
1 tablespoon salt
1 tablespoon prickly pear syrup
1½ cups water

Set your oven to broil and place the whole tomatillos and serrano chiles on a baking sheet. Set the sheet 4 inches below the broiler and let the chiles and tomatillos roast until they are softened and charred sooty black in a few places per fruit. In less than 5 minutes the skins of the chiles should split, while the tomatillos should turn from pale to dark olive green, signaling that it is time to reduce the heat to 425 degrees F. Flip them over with tongs and roast their other sides just 4 minutes more, then remove the baking sheet from the oven and let cool. Next, separate the onion slices into rings and place them together with slices of garlic cloves on another baking sheet. Place in the oven and stir every few minutes until they have been roasted for a total of 15 minutes and have turned a deep lustrous brown. Remove them from the oven and set them aside to cool. Next, place the onions, garlic, and serrano peppers into a food processor and pulse-chop them until they are finely diced. Use a wooden spatula to scoop the diced mixture into a glass bowl. Without washing the processor, add the roasted tomatillos to it and chop them into a coarse puree. Use the spatula to scoop them from the processor into the glass bowl and mix them in with the onions, garlic, and chiles. Add a little water to smooth out the mixture and then sprinkle the finely chopped cilantro and oregano on top. Add the salt and prickly pear syrup, then a little more water, until you can whip the mixture into a smooth puree with the spatula. The 6 cups of salsa can be refrigerated for later use, and a few drops of lemon juice will rejuvenate its zestiness. As it thickens, the salsa can also be used as a "tomatillo paste"—which the Zuni call *k'ets'ido'kya k'yalk'osenne*—to baste steaks or to serve as a dip for onion slices or tortilla chips.

Ny'pa (Palmer's Saltgrass)

In 1922, not too long before the complete damming and taming of the Colorado River, naturalist Aldo Leopold found a paradise of green lagoons on that river's delta, just south of the Mexican border with California and Arizona. Seven decades earlier—in the very midst of those green lagoons—Mexican mapmaker Jacobo Blanco had described "lands bathed by tides . . . covered with saltgrass [that] forms prairies extending beyond eyesight." It took another three decades for scientists to determine just what type of saltgrass formed those prairies between the delta's lagoons. When they did, they estimated that a perennial grass called *Distichlis palmeri* was covering some 20,000 acres of the Colorado River delta and producing tons of edible seed. To the astonishment of scientists, that seed was being harvested, threshed, and stored as if it were wild rice, feeding some 20,000 to 50,000 Cucupá who lived along the Colorado. Indeed, Edward Palmer, the pioneering ethnobotanist who first witnessed the harvest of the grass now associated with his name,

found Cucupá who considered the *ny'pa* grain to be one of their most important staples.

Unfortunately, the remarkable productivity of the Colorado River delta—and of this nutritious cereal found nowhere else in the world—was soon to wither for lack of water. The Colorado River was dammed not once but several times, in several places, starving the delta of the nutrient-rich floodwaters derived from snowmelt in the Rockies. Left high and dry was the little foot-tall saltgrass that formerly ranged from the lower Colorado River southward to the northern islands of the Gulf of California. Ethnobotanist Richard Felger documented that many populations of the grass went extinct for lack of the fresh water required for germinating new plants; indeed, for decades, Felger and other scientists believed that the entire species had gone extinct. While the delta prairies shrunk in size, so did the Cucupá tribe. By the 1970s, fewer than 5,000 Cucupá survived the poverty found on their small reservations in Somerton, Arizona, and El Mayor, Baja California, where they

Edward Palmer, the pioneering ethnobotanist who first witnessed the harvest of the grass now associated with his name. Smithsonian Institution Archives, Record Unit 95, image # SIA2008-2445

suffered some of the highest incidences of diabetes and malnutrition of any people on the planet.

Ironically, it was at this low point in saltgrass survival and Cucupá well-being that two scientists discovered that the saltgrass called *ny'pa* or *inbahj* by Cucupá elders was not extinct at all. In 1979, Nicholas Yensen and Miguel Fontes rediscovered remnant stands of saltgrass on the delta that had all the characteristics first described by Palmer: stiff, grayish-green leaves a foot in length that are covered by a salty exude that looks like gray whiskers; flower stalks up to three feet tall; and tear-shaped cereal grains two inches long that are ready for harvest around the time of the summer solstice. Arizonan Nicholas Yensen and his Sonoran wife, Susana Bojórquez, took it upon themselves to save this grass from inevitable extinction, but they ultimately went far beyond that. They also sought to rescue the cultural traditions that went with the grain and revive its use in the modern world. With the help of delta historian Anita Williams and

Courtesy Anita Alvarez de Williams

Grains of ny'pa were last collected and threshed by Nicholas Yensen and his wife Susana Bojorquez de Yensen in Baja, California. Courtesy Anita Alvarez de Williams

Cucupá elder Juan Garcia Aldama, they learned that the Cucupá had continued to harvest their beloved *ny'pa* up through the 1950s, even though the delta had nearly dried up by then. Cucupá women would raft out into tidal marshes or wade through the shallow waters on mud flats to cut the seed-bearing stalks with knives and throw them into their baskets for drying. They would also glean unthreshed seeds from windrows that would be heaved up onto the shores of lagoons and beaches of the Gulf during tidal bores. They would carry basketloads of the seed back to Yuma, Somerton, and San Luis to dry and thresh by stomping on them. Within the same two-week harvest time, they would store the precious grain in huge baskets of arrowweed that they would place atop their *ramadas* and cabin roofs so that neither floods nor rodents could reach them. The harvest was accompanied by singing, social dancing, the playing of traditional games, and feasting on *ny'pa* cakes and *atoles,* as well as wild game and fish.

The *ny'pa* grain was typically ground on a metate into a coarse flour, which was sometimes mixed with hot water on the spot and drunk as a nutritious *atole.* But the whole grain was also added to mullet stews or to posoles made with chopped and boiled meat from wild game. The flour, mixed with water, salt, and leavening agents, was shaped by hand into thick tortillas or cakes that were toasted or grilled directly over hot coals of mesquite firewood, imbuing them with a smoky aftertaste.

Having learned how *ny'pa* was traditionally harvested and prepared, Nick and Susana dedicated

Further Readings

Felger, Richard Stephen. "Living Resources at the Center of the Sonoran Desert: Regional Uses of Plants and Animals by Native Americans." In Richard Stephen Felger and Bill Broyles, eds., *Dry Borders: Great Nature Reserves of the Sonoran Desert*, pp. 147–192. Salt Lake City: University of Utah Press, 2006.

Leopold, Aldo. "Green Lagoons." In *A Sand County Almanac, with Essays on Conservation from Round River.* New York: Oxford University Press, 1966.

Niethammer, Carolyn J. *The Tumbleweed Gourmet: Cooking with Wild Southwestern Plants.* Tucson: University of Arizona Press, 1987.

Williams, Anita Alvarez. "Sing the River." In Richard Stephen Felger and Bill Broyles, eds., *Dry Borders: Great Nature Reserves of the Sonoran Desert,* pp. 99–116. Salt Lake City: University of Utah Press, 2006.

Yensen, Nicholas P. *Halophyte DataBase: Salt Tolerant Plants and Their Uses.* Riverside, California: USDA-ARS U.S. Salinity Laboratory and NyPa International, 2006.

Yensen, Susana Bojórquez de, and Charles W. Weber. "Composition of *Distichlis palmeri* Grain, a Saltgrass." *Journal of Food Science* 51 (1986): 1089–1090.

the next thirty years of their lives to promoting this halophyte, or salt-tolerant plant. They learned that it could survive in hypersaline marshlands where salt concentrations reached 50,000 parts per million, conditions far more briny than any other cereal crop could tolerate. They collected over ninety different seed samples from the wild and compared their nutritional contents. They found that *ny'pa* grains are gluten free, high in fiber, and balanced in their amino acid content. Toasted, the grain tastes like nuts; baked into biscuits or bread, it compares favorably to whole wheat. They selected certain seed strains, propagated them on Cucupá lands, and helped to market *ny'pa* on both sides of the United States/Mexico border, hoping that their efforts would eventually benefit the original stewards of its wild stands.

Tragically, only 4 percent of the Colorado River flows that floated Aldo Leopold's canoe now cross the border and make it into the delta. The river's water is overallocated, and much of the former habitat for Palmer's saltgrass is now choked with invasive salt cedar or tamarisk. Some conservationists guess that only 2,000 acres of habitat suitable for saltgrass has stayed free of invasive weeds. Just as tragic are the premature deaths of both Nicholas and Susana Bojórquez de Yensen, a few months apart from one another in 2006, before their lifework was completed.

Although rediscovered and still surviving, Palmer's saltgrass remains listed among the most endangered cereal grains on the entire planet in terms of the loss of its traditional uses. The recipe on the preceding page was developed by Susana Bojórquez de Yensen in the mid-1980s and shared with her friend, Carolyn Niethammer.

Courtesy Anita Alvarez de Williams

Santo Domingo Casaba Melon

Casabas are sweet winter melons with firm, juicy flesh that seldom exudes the overpowering fragrance that other melons do. If melon fruits could talk or even sing, the Santo Domingo casaba melon might join the Grateful Dead in their chorus of "What a long, strange trip it's been." They began their journey in the fertile bottomlands of the Gediz watershed in Turkey thousands of years ago. When the great Middle Eastern chef and musician Ziryab left the Abbasid court in Baghdad for the Ummayad court in Córdoba, Spain, he likely brought the seeds of this Middle Eastern melon along with him. Casaba melons were thriving in Moorish Spain by 1492. That was not merely the year that Columbus began his voyages westward but also the one in which the Moorish Islamic farmer became a *persona non grata* on the Iberian peninsula. Both the expelled Moors and their favorite melon seeds left the Iberian shores to reappear in what historian William Dunmire calls "the gardens of New Spain."

By 1530, melons were planted in the gardens of Puebla, Mexico, and by 1598 they had made their way up to what is now called New Mexico. Archaeologists have even contended that Old World melons and watermelons were passed northward from Mexico City through intertribal trade routes, so that they had in fact arrived in Chile Pepper Nation several years before the conquistadors themselves made an appearance.

The Santo Domingo Pueblo, not far from Santa Fe, New Mexico, is one of several ethnic communities that have traded their prized casaba melon seeds back and forth with one another for decades, if not

Courtesy Native Seeds/SEARCH

centuries. Theirs is a basketball-sized honeydew casaba. The skin is slightly wrinkled and blotched, but the pale green flesh is aromatic and juicy. Well adapted to high deserts, this sweet, tasty melon has been grown traditionally by Hispanic and Native American farmers in their *acequia*-irrigated gardens along the Rio Grande, from Española in the north to Alameda in the south. It is a good keeper, yet its seeds have been distributed through just three small seed catalogs over the last few decades. It appears to be endangered in the sense that some of the agricultural lands once planted by Santo Domingo Pueblo have been inundated by a reservoir or overtaken by invasive floodplain-loving weeds. Fortunately, a Seed Sovereignty initiative among the Rio Grande pueblos and their Hispanic neighbors is keeping gardeners alert to possible threats looming in their watershed.

The following preparation is adapted from a delicious recipe elaborated by James Beard Award–winning chef-photographer Lois Ellen Frank, who resides not far from Santo Domingo Pueblo.

Further Readings

Dunmire, William W. *The Gardens of New Spain: How Mediterranean Plants and Foods Changed America.* Austin: University of Texas Press, 2004.

Frank, Lois Ellen. *Foods of the Southwest Indian Nations.* Berkeley, California: Ten Speed Press, 2002.

Goldman, Amy. *Melons for the Passionate Grower.* New York: Artisan, 2002.

SANTO DOMINGO CASABA MELON SALAD WITH PRICKLY PEAR SYRUP

1 ripened Santo Domingo casaba melon
¼ large, yellow-meated watermelon
10 fresh Indian cling peaches
1 tender young prickly pear cactus pad
¾ cup prickly pear syrup
½ cup mint leaves for garnish

On a cutting board, chop the casaba in half. Scoop out the seeds and fibers from both the casaba and the watermelon. Scoop out their meat in 1-inch balls and place in a large decorative bowl. Slice the peaches into strips and add to the melons. Slice the trimmed cactus pad into similar strips, but blanch them in salty water, simmering in a saucepan for 2 minutes. Drain and rinse them, then add the strips to the melons as well. Toss all these fruit balls and strips together, drizzle prickly pear syrup over them, and garnish the edges of the mounded-up fruit in the bowl with clusters of mint leaves. Serves 10 to 12.

Courtesy Native Seeds/SEARCH

Pueblo Red Dye Amaranth

First domesticated in tropical Mexico as early as 2000 B.C., grain amaranths made their way into the present-day United States in prehistoric times, where they hybridized with local wild species. They were traded northward and then widely grown in Chile Pepper Nation by the time Spanish conquistadors tried to put an end to the ritualistic mixing of human blood and amaranth seeds in native rituals. And yet the Spanish did not entirely cleanse the American landscape of this multipurpose crop: It persisted several more centuries in the recesses of the northern Sierra Madre and, across the border, in the pueblos and rancherías of Chile Pepper Nation. There, two cultivated species have persisted in terraced gardens and fields, producing a small poppable grain; tender, spinachlike leaves; and, in some cases, red dyes used in coloring corn breads such as piki wafers.

The red dye amaranth of the Pueblo peoples is the heirloom variety most distinct from its kin in Mexico. Every part of the plant, also known as *komo* or Hopi dye amaranth, carries reddish-purple pigmentation from anthocyanins, the same type of chemical compounds that we see in fall foliage. These pigments imbue a deep scarlet hue to the flowers, seeds, seedlings, bracts, stalks, and roots of the amaranth and to the corn-based foods that are intentionally colored with them.

While *komo* plants can reach up to six feet in height, they are often found sprawling across the sandy soils of gardens tended by Hopi, Tewa, Navajo, and Towa cultivators. Once ranging across the lower Colorado Plateau into the Rio Grande as well as the Colorado River watersheds, this distinctive amaranth is now largely restricted to the Hopi and Navajo around Tuba City, Arizona. Unlike other heirloom varieties "revived" by the Rodale Amaranth Project of the 1970s, there has as yet been no commercial cultivation of this amaranth as a foodstuff, and only five or six nurseries and catalogs occasionally offer its seeds to gardeners.

The uniqueness of this particular plant may be due to centuries of natural hybridization with a wild amaranth of the Colorado Plateau that also frequents Hopi and Navajo gardens. Its drooping, heavily seeded flower stalk is no longer much used to tint piki bread; its black seeds are hardly popped anymore either. However, its fresh leaves have a nutty flavor and delicate texture, best braised or sautéed like spinach or used fresh as a colorful garnish in tossed salads. Although one of five current seed outlets for this variety, Native Seeds/SEARCH is the only one that has distributed and repatriated this variety back to the Hopi Tribal Cultural Preservation Office, to individual Hopi farmers, and to the Healing Garden tended by Hopi and Navajo youth. However, a drought that has raged over the last decade has dramatically reduced the number of traditional fields and gardens planted. The grain remains biologically and culturally endangered. The following recipe comes from south of the border, where grain amaranths are known as *huatle*. It continues to be served in a summer ritual in the Sierra Madre in honor of the planet Venus, the morning star believed to promote the growth of amaranth and other native crops.

Further Readings

Nabhan, Gary Paul. "Amaranth Cultivation in Northwest Mexico and the U.S. Southwest." In *Second Amaranth Conference Proceedings*, pp. 129–133. Emmaus, Pennsylvania: Rodale Press, 1979.

Rayas Aldana, Josefina. *Recetario Exótico de Sinaloa*. Cocina Indígena y Popular. Mexico City: Consejo Nacional para la Cultura y las Artes, 2004.

Sauer, Jonathan D. "Amaranths as Dye Plants among the Pueblo Peoples." *Southwest Journal of Anthropology* 6 (1950): 412–416.

Sauer, Jonathan D. "The Grain Amaranths: A Survey of Their History and Classification." *Annals of the Missouri Botanical Garden* 37 (1950): 561–632.

Watson, Benjamin. *Taylor's Guide to Heirloom Vegetables*. Boston: Houghton Mifflin, 1996.

HUATLE EN CHILE VERDE (PUEBLO RED DYE AMARANTH WITH GREEN CHILES)

2 tablespoons sunflower oil

2 I'itoi's onions, chopped

½ cup water

¼ cup premixed masa harina flour made from purple corn

3 green ancho chile pods, chopped and deseeded

1 large handful Pueblo red dye amaranth greens

¼ teaspoon sea salt

Warm the oil in a skillet. Place the chopped onions in the skillet and fry until they are caramelized. Add the water to the skillet and break up the ball of corn masa, then whip it into the water with a wooden spoon until it makes a thick liquid. Add the chopped chiles, amaranth greens, and salt, mixing until you have a spicy greens soup of about the same consistency as seaweed in miso.

Courtesy Native Seeds/SEARCH

David Cavagnaro

Sonoran Pronghorn Antelope

All eyes and legs, the pronghorn antelope has unique characteristics, a distinct genetic heritage, and a fairly specific set of needs that's not being met in a large portion of its range. Often mistakenly called "American antelope," the pronghorn is actually the sole surviving member of its own family, the Antiocapridae. Pronghorn are exceptional runners, clocking speeds of up to sixty miles per hour. Their eyes are disproportionally large for their bodies and can detect motion up to four miles away. Yet pronghorn haven't adapted well to modern realities. Because they don't jump over obstacles, they tend to become trapped by fences within the grasslands where most of them live. This character trait can turn even snowstorms into fatal events. And for the ever-expanding coyote populations, pronghorn fawns are easy prey.

Of five subspecies of pronghorn in the United States, the Sonoran pronghorn of Chile Pepper Nation is the most imperiled. Historically, Sonoran pronghorn lived in southern Arizona, from Tucson clear to Yuma, and into the northern part of Sonora, Mexico. They were once reported as far west as California's Imperial Valley. Within the past several years, though, estimates have put the number of Sonoran pronghorn at fewer than two hundred individuals.

The viability of Sonoran pronghorn populations took a major hit from the decade-long drought that began around 1995; by 2002, the Arizona population had plummeted from about 130 to an estimated twenty-one. Spurred partly by a lawsuit that charged insufficient actions, the U.S. Fish and Wildlife Service has recently pieced together money and help from other federal agencies, including the Marine Corps, Air Force, National Guard, National Park Service, and Bureau of Land Management. As of 2007, the U.S. population had rebounded to just over one hundred individuals.

Mike Coffeen, Sonoran pronghorn recovery team leader for the U.S. Fish and Wildlife Service in the Cabeza Prieta National Wildlife Refuge, said he doesn't often think about eating the beleaguered animals—but he knows that past desert inhabitants certainly had to. There are well-established records of both the Tohono O'odham and the Hia-ceḍ O'odham (or Sand Papago) occasionally hunting these herbivores and cremating their bones, just as they did for the sacred bighorn sheep.

Coffeen, like many people knowledgeable about pronghorn, says the animals are curious, to their own detriment, for they reputedly can be lured in for an easy hunt simply by waving a brightly colored flag. But a writer from the early part of the twentieth century, Jack O'Connor, disputes that claim. "I waved flags until I had cramps," he wrote in his 1939 book, *Game in the Desert*. "I camped in bushes until ants and flies almost ate me alive." The pronghorn gathered several hundred yards away, he recalled: "They stared at me fixedly by the hour and wondered what the hell I was up to, but their curiosity never got the better of their discretion."

It may be that the ease of shooting pronghorn didn't get tested much, as its meat tends to be both dry and extremely lean. "Indians and mountain men held that their meat was not nourishing and that a man could not keep in good shape on antelope venison alone," O'Connor wrote. Despite O'Connor's protests, many Native American hunters west of the Mississippi found roasted or jerked pronghorn meat satisfying. Still, indirect effects of the settling of the Chile Pepper Nation—more than any recent poaching—have taken their toll. Besides the fences, cattle grazing has changed pronghorn habitat by altering the plants that grow there. The Gila River has been largely dewatered in much of the range of the Sonoran pronghorn. Yet despite these strikes against Sonoran pronghorn, Coffeen and his partners are energetic in their efforts to save them. He said the goal for a self-sustaining population is up to three hundred animals, at which size the pronghorn could theoretically sustain itself for five hundred years.

In presenting the following recipe, we encourage readers not to hunt the Sonoran pronghorn species, but to focus their attention on plains populations that have already recovered with enough individuals to sustain a managed hunt. The adapted recipe comes from Darcy Williamson's *Cooking with Spirit*.

PIT-ROASTED PLAINS PRONGHORN

1 whole pronghorn antelope, freshly killed and gutted

Dig an earthen pit 2 feet wide and 2 feet deep, then line it with cobblestones. Once the pit is lined, build a fire of willow, mesquite, or sage, and keep adding wood to the pit until there is a steady supply of red-hot coals. Remove the coals and stones with a shovel, then line the pit with the freshly skinned pronghorn hide, hair-side down. Place 2- to 3-inch-long chunks of antelope meat on the hide, and fold the flesh side of the skin over the meat. Place the coals and stones recently removed from the pit on top of the hide, then cover the pit with branches and dirt. Five to 6 hours later, reopen the pit, unfold the hide, and distribute the pit-roasted meat.

Further Readings

Blue Planet Biomes. "Sonoran Pronghorn Antelope." 2002. http://www.blueplanetbiomes.org/sonoran_pronghorn_antelope.htm.

O'Connor, Jack. 1939. *Game in the Desert*. New York: Derrydale Press, Inc.

Pima County. "Sonoran Pronghorn Antelope." Sonoran Desert Conservation Plan Species Fact Sheets. 2006. http://www.co.pima.az.us/cmo/sdcp/species/fsheets/sp.html.

Rotstein, Arthur H. "Captive Breeding Plan Working for Pronghorn." *Tucson Citizen* (Associated Press), May 14, 2007.

Williamson, Darcy, and Lisa Railsback. *Cooking with Spirit: North American Indian Food and Fact*. Bend, Oregon: Maverick Publications, 1987.

Alan D. Wilson, naturespicsonline.com

Sonoran White Pomegranate

Once known as "the seeded apple" that Adam and Eve reputedly shared in the Garden of Eden, the pomegranate made its way from the Holy Lands to Spain with the fall of the Ummayad Empire in Damascus around A.D. 740. The Ummayad survivors transplanted the very same trees from their palatial gardens in Damascus to the Alhambra in Andalusia sometime after A.D. 756. Seven hundred and fifty years later, Crypto-Jews and Moorish Moslems fleeing the Spanish Inquisition carried them to the New World. Pomegranates were seen in Hispaniola by 1520, in the southern reaches of Chile Pepper Nation by 1687, and in Acorn Nation along the California coast by 1795. In short, one of the great fruits of the Old World deserts found a new home very early on in the deserts of the New World.

An "albino"-fleshed pomegranate emerged out of the stretch of Chile Pepper Nation historically known as Pimeria Alta, and this pale fruit is still savored in that region today. Also known as the Papago or O'odham pomegranate, it is propagated for distribution by only one commercial outlet, Catalina Heights Nursery in Tucson, Arizona. Although it is featured at a few public arboretums like the Desert Botanical Gardens in Phoenix, it is critically endangered both north and south of the U.S./Mexico border.

The Sonoran White pomegranate grows on a thicket-forming shrub that is tolerant of both saline and alkaline soils. The skin of the fruit is a pale, lustrous fire-engine red and does not crack as deeply and as frequently as the skin of other pomegranate varieties exposed to the desert heat. The sweet, sharply flavored juice seldom stains one's hands as much as the juices of other varieties do. The glistening masses of seeds inside range from pale pink to creamy white. Ethnobiologist Amadeo Rea has noted that its importance among the indigenous cultures of Chile Pepper Nation is not merely culinary but extends to other artistic traditions as well:

In addition to supplying a delicious fruit, [these] pomegranate shrubs bear quite attractive flowers in the spring. The entire bud or calyx is scarlet. This bursts open at the tip, producing a Star of David that appears as if sharply cut from thick red leather. Indeed, these are the buds that inspire the so-called squash blossoms of Southwestern Indian silversmiths, a pattern that came by way of Hispanic Moors.

Rea wistfully noted that living fences of pomegranates were still planted "on virtually every rancho" in the Gila River Indian Community of the Akimel O'odham in 1975, but "today they are far fewer." Like their desert cousins to the south, the Tohono O'odham, the Gila River (Pima) residents call the fruit *galnáayo,* a loan word from the Spanish *granada.* Pomegranate hedges were once prevalent in southern California and Georgia as well; in fact, this Old World introduction once went feral in the wild savannas of Georgia. In Arizona and southern California, it persists around historic Hispanic missions such as Tumacacori and once inhabited springs such as Quitobaquito, but it has been pulled up to make room for asphalt and concrete at many other sites.

Further Readings

Anonymous. *Dining with the Desert Museum: Favorite Recipes from the Arizona-Sonora Desert Museum.* Tucson: Arizona-Sonora Desert Museum Press, 2005.

Dunmire, William W. *Gardens of New Spain: How Mediterranean Plants and Foods Changed America.* Austin: University of Texas Press, 2004.

Mariani, John F. *The Dictionary of American Food & Drink.* New York: Ticknor & Fields, 1983.

Rea, Amadeo M. *At the Desert's Green Edge: An Ethnobotany of the Gila River Pima.* Tucson: University of Arizona Press, 1997.

Rivera, Guadalupe, and Marie-Pierre Cole. *Las Fiestas de Frida y Diego: Recuerdos y Recetas.* Mexico City: Promexa, 1994.

Until the late 1990s, it seemed as though pomegranates were in steady decline throughout North America. But then a handful of nutritional scientists, marketing entrepreneurs, and health food enthusiasts placed capes on the shoulders of the bumpy, crimson-skinned pomegranate and inducted it into the "superfood" hall of fame. Drinking its antioxidant-rich juices became widely heralded as means to reduce bad cholesterol, slow the aging process, and control blood pressure. Uniquely shaped bottles filled with ruby-colored juice soon appeared on grocery store shelves covered with bold "elixir of life" claims. A determined marketing campaign has captivated the press and seduced consumers who were looking for a quick new fix to their health problems. Ironically, all this recent attention to an anciently used fruit that is native to Iran belies the thousand-year-old agricultural, culinary, social, and medical history of the pomegranate. It has always been just as delicious—and just as worthy of conserving—as it is today. It remains a unique jewel in the crown of fruits adorning America's historic orchards and hedgerows.

The following recipe, made famous in the film *Like Water for Chocolate,* is a Sonoran Desert–adapted version of *chiles en nogada.*

CHILES EN NOGADA CON GRANADAS BLANCAS

8 fire-roasted green poblano or Patagonia chiles, peeled, deseeded, and deveined

For the picadillo del pollo (chicken hash)
2 cups prebaked, shredded chicken meat
2 I'itoi's onions, minced
1 clove Sonoran red garlic, minced
2 tablespoons Sonoran manzanillo olive oil
1 carrot, shredded
1 cup Papago peas
1 cup *calabacitas* ("baby squashes" or tender, young cushaw squashes), chopped
1 cup *papitas gueras* (spring potatoes), boiled and chopped
¼ cup slivered almonds
¼ cup Mission grape raisins
1 cup chicken stock
1 teaspoon sugar
1 small sprig parsley
1 teaspoon dried Sonoran oregano
⅛ teaspoon freshly ground cinnamon
salt and pepper to taste

In a large skillet, sauté the shredded chicken, onion, and garlic in the olive oil over medium heat. Sequentially add the other vegetables, then the potatoes, nuts, raisins, chicken stock, sugar, and herbs and spices and simmer for 15 minutes, until all the liquids are absorbed. Next, using a small teaspoon, stuff the chiles with the *picadillo* and arrange as a sunburst on a serving platter.

For the salsa nogada and pomegranate seed garnish
1 cup Santa Cruz Valley pecans or Arizona walnuts
1 tablespoon brown sugar
6 tablespoons dryish Riesling wine
½ cup fine dry bread crumbs
1 tablespoon fig vinegar
1 cup light cream
¾ cup Sonoran white pomegranate seeds

In a blender or food processor, puree the nuts. Then soak the nuts in brown sugar and wine in a glass mixing bowl. Add the bread crumbs, mix, and let stand in the bowl for 15 minutes. Add the fig vinegar and the light cream and mix until the salsa is thin enough to pour over the chiles. Finally, garnish each chile with several tablespoons of Sonoran white pomegranate seeds. Serves 4 to 6.

Jesús Manuel García

Totoaba

Now listed as endangered in both the United States and Mexico, the totoaba is a fish that spawns on the Colorado River delta and reaches six feet in length and 250 pounds as a maximum weight. After centuries of being fished for subsistence use by the Yaqui, Seri, and Cucupá peoples of the Gulf of California, the totoaba began to be commercially exploited in 1910; within sixty years, its fishery had to be closed because it was considered "commercially extinct" for lack of sufficient numbers to support a sustainable harvest. Despite being officially protected by both the Mexican and U.S. governments, thousands of mature totoaba have continued to be lost to poachers and hundreds of thousands incidentally killed when hauled onto the decks of shrimp trawlers as bycatch. The history of totoaba depletion is a history of indigenous fishermen being exploited to provide tonnages of delicious fish at cheap prices to Chinese and American consumers.

The totoaba was endemic to the northern and central Gulf of California and to the adjacent Colorado River delta before dams disrupted its migration. It is the largest fish in a family best known for its species of corvina, and the females tend to be larger, with far more breast meat than the males. Totoaba meat was once praised for its flavor and texture by chefs from California through Texas, while the air bladder or *buché* of the female totoaba was considered a vitamin-rich delicacy that was aggressively sought after by the Chinese. The commercial demand for totoaba began in northern Mexico around 1910 and by 1925 had spread northward to the rest of Chile Pepper Nation.

And yet there is an older, richer history of cultural connections to the totoaba that has been obscured by the tragic boom-and-bust exploitation that occurred between 1910 and 1970. The Seri Indians, who call totoaba *zixcám cacöla*, "the Big Fish," had songs, stories, feasts, and dances dedicated to the totoaba. The Seri believe that black brants—one of migratory waterfowl that winter on the Colorado River delta—are magically transformed in totoaba when they dive into the water there. The term *totoaba* comes from the Yaqui words *totoli* (bird) and *buaua* (insatiable eater). The Cucupá, who now live in Arizona, Baja California, and Sonora, also have an ancient and intricate connection to the totoaba. Fortunately, Mexican hatchery efforts in and near the Colorado River Delta and Upper Gulf Biosphere Reserve have begun to replenish totoaba populations.

The following recipe is adapted from the Seri, a group that has inhabited the Sonoran coast for centuries. The Seris excel at fishing, whether using harpoons, nets, or baskets *(coritas)* made from dried branches. In the Seris' festivities, the totoaba rests on a bed of sticks, roasting slowly over an open fire to seal in the juices.

Further Readings

Bahre, Conrad J., Luis Bourillón, and Jorge Torre. "The Seri and Commercial Totoaba Fishing (1930–1965)." *Journal of the Southwest* 42:3 (2000): 559–575.

Chute, G. R. "Seen Kow, a Regal Soup-Stock." *California Fish and Game Bulletin* 16 (1930): 23–35.

Flanagan, C. A., and John R. Henrickson. "Observations on the Commercial Fishery and Reproductive Biology of the Totoaba, *Cynoscion macdonaldi,* in the Northern Gulf of California." *Fishery Bulletin* 74 (1976): 531–535.

Quintana, Patricia. *Cuisine of the Water Gods: The Authentic Seafood and Vegetable Cookery of Mexico.* New York: Simon and Schuster, 1994.

TOTOABA FRITA (FRIED TOTOABA)

6 totoaba filets (½ pound each)
7 cloves Sonoran garlic
8 black peppercorns
3 limes, juiced
sea salt
¾ cup flour
3 cups olive oil

Garnish
1 head romaine lettuce, shredded
½ cup white wine vinegar
½ teaspoon sea salt
2 peppercorns, finely ground with a mortar and pestle
6 tablespoons olive oil
4 black peppercorns, coarsely cracked
12 lime wedges

Place the fish in a shallow glass dish. In a blender or food processor, puree four of the garlic cloves (reserve the three largest for later use) and the peppercorns; mix with lime juice and season with sea salt to taste. Spread this mixture over the fish. Marinate for 10 minutes at room temperature, then refrigerate for a half hour to an hour.

Place the flour in a shallow bowl. Dip the fish into the flour, coating both sides well. Heat the olive oil in a deep casserole, a large skillet, or a wok. Add the remaining three garlic cloves and cook them until golden brown. Remove the cloves from the pan and discard. Next, fry the fish in batches until they are fully crisp on both sides, which usually takes about 5 minutes. Keep the fish warm in the oven, while preparing the platter on which to serve them.

Cover a serving platter with the shredded romaine lettuce as a bed for the fish filets. Mix together the vinegar, salt, pepper, and olive oil, then shake the mixture up in a jar. Sprinkle the vinaigrette over the fish, then garnish with cracked peppercorns and lime wedges. Serve with chiltepin salsa on the side.

Conservation biologists in Ensenada, Baja California, observe totoaba as part of their captive breeding program. © SeaPics.com

CLAMBAKE NATION

Including most of the Atlantic seaboard and adjacent islands north of the Chesapeake Bay, Clambake Nation retains a curious mix of maritime and farming traditions of the "Swamp Yankees." Yet while outsiders may assume that Clambake Nation's s culinary traditions are exclusively Yankee, there are in fact many native and immigrant traditions hidden within that regional umbrella. The region is rich in shellfish, fish, fruits, berries, and root vegetables. Unfortunately, contamination from its many riverside factories and mills tragically brought to an end the widespread use of many of its fish and aquatic plants. Well over one hundred of its traditional foods are now threatened or endangered. The quahog may be its signature shellfish, but other clams, oysters, scallops, and lobsters round out the regional bouillabaisse. Fortunately, the citizens of Clambake Nation have pioneered the large-scale ecological restoration of rivers, bays, beaches, and coastal waters, so that many historically important food species are now being recovered.

Quahogs of Great South Bay

There are many different styles of clambakes among the fishing communities along the Atlantic seaboard, including the Wampanoag *(appanaug)* tradition of steaming quahog clams, lobsters, mussels, and bluefish on smoldering beds of rockweed (an intertidal seaweed). In Mrs. Lincoln's 1884 *Boston Cooking School Cook Book,* even women of that Victorian era were encouraged to "go wild" in their impromptu hunt for the quahogs, seaweeds, and tidepool rocks required for a good clambake:

> If you wish to have genuine fun, and to know what an appetite one can have for the bivalves, make up a pleasant party and dig for the clams yourselves. A short thick dress, shade hat, rubber boots,—or, better still, no boots at all, if you can bring your mind to the comfort of bare feet,—a small garden trowel, a fork, and a basket, and you are ready.

The clam of choice for such events is the Northern Quahog (pronounced *ko-hog*), one of the largest hardshell clam species of the Atlantic seaboard and the one that has a distinctively bluish inner shell. Its name comes from the Narragansett Indian term *poquauhock.* The Narragansetts, who lived in what is now the state of Delaware, and the Lenape of Long Island made blue-and-white shell beads that were strung together and used as wampum, a currency that was traded among many tribes. The relative absence of quahog remains in prehistoric middens (trash heaps) at feasting sites suggests that, for centuries, the shells were as carefully utilized as the clam meats themselves and were therefore not thrown out along with oyster shells, crab claws, fish bones, and other seafood refuse.

The Northern Quahog as a species is still widespread and even increasing in abundance within some bays along the coast of Clambake Nation. But a quahog tragedy has occurred in the last three decades in two bays located south of Long Island: Great South Bay and Barnegat Bay, which lies along the New Jersey shore about halfway between midtown Manhattan and Cape May. Perhaps this tragedy has been felt most poignantly in Great South Bay, nestled as it is up against the southern shore of Long Island, within sight of New York City's skyscrapers. To fathom the magnitude of this tragedy, though, we must step back and imagine the quahog fishery as it was during its heyday.

For decades, if not centuries, some 50,000 acres of clam beds in Great South Bay provided over half of all quahogs eaten in Clambake Nation. The shallow waters of the bay were periodically refreshed by those of the Atlantic Ocean passing through the Fire Island inlet, and the bay provided an ideal location for producing thick, white-meated quahogs of exceptional flavor, just as they produced the world-famous Blue Point oysters. The primacy of Great South Bay for clam production in the United States persisted through the first few years following World War II. During that era, thousands of men called handrakers used their muscle power to push bullrakes through the sediments on the bay's bottom to uncover quahogs, which they then picked up with tongs. Each handraker might harvest an average of ten bushels of large quahogs per day, in addition to gleaning his share of smaller cherrystone and littleneck clams. The annual quahog harvest, although somewhat variable, was measured in the hundreds of thousands of bushels from Great South Bay alone.

Claming off the ice in Great South Bay. Long Island Maritime Museum

Then, in the early 1950s, several conditions began to change around Great South Bay: Runoff from construction sites muddied the waters; chemical contamination from factory drainage pipes polluted them; and more frequent red and brown tides caused by microscopic organisms contaminated the bay's shellfish. At the same time, another group of quahoggers appeared on the scene, and they used boats to drag metal-toothed dredges across the clam beds, outcompeting the handrakers for most of the available quahogs and leaving considerable damage in their wake. In less than a decade, the quahog yield from Great South Bay plummeted, going from 50 percent of the nation's production to under 20 percent by 1954. By the time that dredging was legally restricted to certain areas, hundreds of handrakers had been left without work.

There was a brief resurgence of quahog production in Great South Bay in the 1970s, when the Fire Island inlet was dredged to allow more water flow into the clam beds, just as the Environmental Protection Agency began cracking down on polluters. For a few years, hundreds of handrakers returned to the bay, with improved designs for their bullrakes, and once again they brought home harvests of five to ten bushels per day. The Great South Bay temporarily regained its status as the premier quahog fishery in the country. However, by 1980, this second golden era was over as well.

Since 1999, fewer than fifty men have continued to rake up quahogs from the Great South Bay, and fewer still ever go home with more than two bushels of clams per day. Most are now harvesting only about six bushels of thin, discolored quahogs per week, far less than a single day's harvest fifty years ago. There are several causes for this decline, but current harvesting pressure is probably not one of them. Curiously, blue crab predation of quahogs has dramatically increased.

Most damaging, however, have been the effects of increased urban runoff, which since the 1980s have included diminished water quality, increasing turbidity, and the frequency of red, green, and brown tides. These tides have been associated with algal blooms in both Great South Bay and Barnegat Bay in most years

NOAA Estuarine Research Reserve Collection

since 1985. Quahog yields in these two bays are now only 1 to 3 percent of their former maximum yield. As New Jersey marine ecologist Clyde MacKenzie and his colleagues have concluded, "Dense blooms . . . force the quahogs to cease feeding and also crowd out the algae that quahogs normally use for food . . . The blooms have been devastating to quahog stock [which] have become relatively scarce . . . the fishery has declined sharply."

Fortunately, other bays along the coast of Clambake Nation have not suffered such declines. Between pollution cleanups, harvesting quotas agreed on between quahoggers and government agencies, and hatchery-based aquaculture initiatives, healthy quahogs are still available in the marketplace.

The following recipe is adapted from Chef Earl Mills Jr., a member of the Mashpee Wampanoag tribe, and comes from his fine Cape Cod restaurant, the Flume.

Further Readings

Ely, Eleanor. "Quahog." Rhode Island Sea Grant Fact Sheet P1223. Accessed June 20, 2007, from www .seagrant.gso.uri.edu/factsheets/fsquahog.html.

Kurlansky, Mark. *The Big Oyster: History on the Half Shell*. New York: Ballantine Books, 2006.

Lincoln, D. A. *Boston Cooking School Cook Book*. Boston: Roberts Brothers, 1884.

MacKenzie, Clyde L. Jr., Allan Morrison, David L. Taylor, Victor G. Burrell Jr., William S. Arnold, and Armando T. Wakida-Kusunoki. "Quahogs in Eastern North America I: Biology, Ecology, and Historic Uses." *Marine Fisheries Review*, Spring 2002.

Mills, Earl Sr., and Betty Sheen. *Cape Cod Wampanoag Cookbook: Wampanoag Indian Recipes, Images & Lore*. Santa Fe, New Mexico: Clear Light Publishers, 2001.

Peters, Russel. *Clambake: A Wampanoag Tradition*. Minneapolis: Lerner Publications/First Avenue Editions, 1992.

MASHPEE WAMPANOAG QUAHOG CHOWDER

18 medium quahogs, providing 2 cups meat and 2½ cups juice
¼ pound of salt pork
1 medium onion, minced
9 tablespoons margarine
1½ teaspoons sea salt
2 Green Mountain potatoes, peeled and diced
10 tablespoons unbleached flour
1 teaspoon freshly ground black pepper
1 cup or more light cream

Shuck the quahogs, making sure to save their juice as well as the clam meat. Rinse the meat well and then set aside. Place a sieve over a saucepan and drain the clam juice through it, filtering out any shell pieces and grit. Coarsely chop the quahogs on a cutting board and then mix them back with the juice in a glass mixing bowl.

Next, cut the salt pork into small pieces. In a skillet, sauté the pork, then drain away the excess fat. Add the minced onion, 1 tablespoon of the margarine, and half of the sea salt to the rendered salt pork and heat until the onions are translucent. Remove the skillet from the heat and set aside to cool.

In a saucepan, place the diced potatoes, the remaining salt, and a little water, then boil until the potatoes are soft. Drain off the salt water and set the potatoes aside. Place the same pan over low heat and make a roux from the flour and the remaining 8 tablespoons of margarine. Set it aside as well.

Combine the quahogs and their juice and the onion mixture over medium-high heat in a larger cooking pot, stirring often with a wooden spoon while the mixture is simmering. Add the roux, stirring as the chowder thickens. Toss in the potatoes and the black pepper, using the spoon to fold them into the chowder.

Just before serving, add the cream and gently simmer the full chowder until you are ready to serve. Grind some more black pepper over it, then ladle it into heated bowls. Serve with oyster crackers, sweet pickles, or slices of artisanal bread. Serves 6 to 8.

Berry Berry American Cranberry

Selected by Albert Berry in 1883 from the wild bogs of Martha's Vineyard, the Berry berry has been cultivated almost entirely within twenty-five miles of where American cranberry cultivation began around 1816. Of course, wild harvesting of this uniquely American fruit had already been going on for centuries, as both Native Americans and immigrants in Clambake Nation used the fruit as food, dye, and medicine.

In 1672, John Josselyn noted that the Mashpee Wampanoag families of Martha's Vineyard made several recipes with local cranberries: "The Indians and English use them much, boiling them with sugar for Sauce to eat with meat; and it is a delicate Sauce, especially with Roasted Mutton. Some make tarts with them as with Gooseberries."

In the early 1800s, however, the Mashpee tribe living on Martha's Vineyard at Gay Head had to petition the Massachusetts state legislature to guarantee their access to cranberry bogs "handed down to us by our Fathers," to ensure that the berries reached "the hands of the most Indigent of the Women and Children of our tribe who gather the Most of the Berries and which to them is a Staple means of support through the winter."

It is not surprising, then, that Yankees attempted to avoid competition with the Mashpee in the wild bogs of common lands by cultivating selected cranberries on their private lands. Around 1810, a serendipitous occurrence led to the initial cultivation of American cranberries.

It all began while Revolutionary War veteran Henry Hall was clearing brush on a sandy knoll overlooking a wild cranberry bog on the edge of his homestead in Dennis, Massachusetts. He noticed over the following months that his brush clearing had exposed the sand of the knoll to the winds, and that wherever the sand piled up against the cranberry vines, they produced larger berries the next season. In 1816, Hall uprooted some sod containing berry vines that he had nicknamed "Grandpa's blues" and transplanted them under a layer of sand in a clay-bottomed marsh. Hall confirmed that "sanding" the vines did renew them, so that they produced not only larger berries but higher yields as well. Within a decade, Hall was sending barrels of his surplus berries off to Long Island to be consumed there by the curious gourmets of New York City. Although Hall's sanding practice was soon adopted by his neighbors who also had bogs on Cape

Cranberry Day at the town bogs in Lobsterville, Martha's Vineyard, Massachusetts, circa 1930. The Wampanoag tribe owns the land on this side of Menemsha Harbor, and every fall they still observe this ritual in the small bogs that remain. Courtesy Martha's Vineyard Museum

Cod, their berry yields merely offered them some modest, supplemental income prior to the Civil War.

All that changed when Yankees came home from that war, weary or wounded but victorious. The economies of whaling, fishing, and shipbuilding had all suffered serious declines, so much so that seafaring men from Cape Cod and Martha's Vineyard began looking for income inland, rather than out in the ocean. By that time, cranberry sales to the eastern seaboard's burgeoning cities had become so lucrative that they even lured well-established Yankee sea captains away from whaling and shipping, as this rhyme by "Captain Bill" attests:

There's nothing to me in foreign lands
Like the stuff that grows in Cape Cod sands;
There's nothing in sailing the foreign seas
Equal to getting down on your knees
And pulling the pizen ivy out;

I guess I knew what I was about
When I put by my chart and glass
And took to growing cranberry sass."

Albert Berry got into the business after the war, and his discerning eye discovered a dark red berry with a waxy bloom that ripened around midseason on Martha's Vineyard. This berry was nearly round in shape, with its flower-side end slightly furrowed. Its vines were relatively vigorous, and its berries set on the tallest, most upright branches, making for easy picking. His neighbors on the Vineyard dryly referred to his prize as "Berry's berry," so much so that the "cran" dropped out of its name. His berries were plump enough that it took only fifty-five to sixty-five of them to fill a cup, half the number of other selections of that era.

Berry berries were mildly sour as well as sweet, and their thin skins popped when slightly heated,

offering a wonderful texture and aroma. However, the skins were so thin that the berries did not take to long-term storage or long-distance transport. Like some hundred other native selections from wild bogs made during the first century and a half of American cranberry cultivation, their place in the bogs was gradually usurped by just four selections, and, more recently, by some seven improved cultivars. For most of the last century, four out of every five plants in commercial cranberry acreage belonged to just four selections: Early black, Howes, McFarlin, and Searles. While these tough-skinned selections all predate the Berry berry in popularity, the "big four" alone simply cannot capture the incredible range in color, texture, and flavor found within the highly variable American cranberry species, *Vaccinium macrocarpon.* Sadly, the Berry berry is no longer commercially available from any mail-order nursery.

While the Berry berry may be in demise, the cranberry industry around its birthing grounds remains healthy. Cranberries remain the leading food crop harvested in coastal Massachusetts, accounting for about a third of the world's production. In recent years, cranberries have offered their farmers in Clambake Nation well over $100 million in annual revenues.

The following recipe is adapted from one Grandmother Mulligan of Cape Cod, whose granddaughter, Ann MacDonald-Rey, continued to bake these Irish scones at the Tea Shoppe at Mashpee Commons. It was further adapted by Virginia Spargo MacDonald and Earl Mills, a Wampanoag chief and chef. In fact, the Wampanoag community is said to have hosted the first Thanksgiving feast. And if you have ever wondered or worried whether cranberries were actually served at that feast—for it appears that turkeys were *not*—you can relax. In the best-known account of that cross-cultural partaking of the autumn harvest, Roger Williams noted that the Pilgrims and their Wampanoag hosts "ate plentiful of the strawberries that grew abundantly in the place." Williams must have been referring to the wild American cranberry that autumn, for strawberries are a rather perishable crop of the spring.

Further Readings

Anonymous. "From a Small, Native Fruit to a Multi-Million Dollar Industry." Conservation New England website. Accessed June 17, 2007, from http://efg.cs.umb.edu/conne/marsha/cranintro.html.

Eck, Paul. *The American Cranberry*. New Brunswick, New Jersey: Rutgers University Press, 1990.

Forristal, Linda. "The Holiday Berry." *Wise Traditions in Food, Farming and the Healing Arts*, Winter 2002. Accessed April 20, 2007, from http://westonaprice.org/motherland/cranberry.html.

Hall, C. J. "I Put by My Chart and Glass, Took to Raising Cranberry Sass." *Cranberries, the National Cranberry Magazine* 17:7 (1952): 10–16.

Josselyn, John. *New-England's Rarities Discovered*. Boston: Massachusetts Historical Society, 1972.

Kavasch, Barrie. *Native Harvests: Recipes and Botanicals of the American Indian.* New York: Random House, 1979.

Mills, Earl Sr., and Betty Breen. *Cape Cod Wampanoag Cookbook.* Santa Fe, New Mexico: Clear Light Publishers, 2001.

Thomas, Joseph D. *Cranberry Harvest: A History of Cranberry Growing in Massachusetts.* New Bedford, Massachusetts: Spinner Publications, 1990.

CAPE COD CRANBERRY SCONES

4 cups unbleached wheat flour
½ teaspoon baking powder
⅜ cup sugar
½ pound cold unsalted butter
2 eggs
1 cup heavy cream
1 tablespoon vanilla extract
1½ cups cranberries, chopped
½ cup shelled walnuts or chestnuts, chopped
granulated sugar

Preheat the oven to 350 degrees F. In a glass mixing bowl, combine the flour, baking powder, and sugar. Cut the butter into the mixture and stir it in coarsely. In a separate smaller bowl, combine the eggs, cream, and vanilla, then pour them into the first bowl. Mix them until all the dry ingredients are moistened. Add the finely chopped cranberries and nuts. On a greased baking sheet, drop 3-ounce scoops of batter and shape into scones. Sprinkle the tops with granulated sugar. Bake for 20 to 25 minutes.

Bronx Seedless Grape

To embrace the delectable heritage of the Bronx Seedless grape, we must trace its route from the East Coast to the West over a matter of some eighty years. Let's start in 1925, in the Bronx borough of New York City. The native American Concord, a tough-skinned purple fruit loaded with seeds, was crossed with the leading table grape of the times, the Thompson Seedless—one praised by some for being tender, sweet, and mild. All bets were on the new grape, especially if it could combine the almost cartoonishly grapy flavor of the Concord with the texture of the Thompson Seedless. In 1931, after six years of careful attention and selection, the Bronx Seedless arrived on stage. Green with a sunset pink blush, this medium-sized, round grape has a floral bouquet and a honeylike taste that melts on the tongue—characteristics that quickly earned it a prized nickname, "the Rolls Royce of table grapes."

The admirable traits of the Bronx Seedless were brought together in one grape by Dr. Arlow Stout of the New York Botanical Gardens, in partnership with the New York State Agricultural Experiment Station in Geneva, New York. Stout had earlier hybridized three grapes—Goff, Iona, and Sultania—then gradually selected their progeny for flavor. As such, the Bronx Seedless and Stout's other selections are wonderful examples of the kind of slow, not-for-profit plant breeding that developed many of the finest fruits and vegetables that once stocked our farmers' markets and corner grocery stores. Bred for taste and texture more than for high production, uniformity, and the ability to withstand long-distance shipping, the Bronx Seedless is what some might call a twentieth-century anachronism. The texture of the Bronx Seedless is both a blessing and a curse, for its juicy flesh and extremely thin skin make it prone to cracking under high summer heat or the most ordinary of afternoon rains. No wonder it has had a difficult time holding its own in a dog-eat-dog world focused on transportability more than taste. For the American table grape industry—the third largest in the world and one that was built on long-distance shipping—the fragility of the Bronx Seedless seemed to have doomed it to commercial failure.

Lon Rombough

Dr. Arlow Stout of the New York Botanical Gardens. The LuEster T. Mertz Library, New York Botanical Gardens

BREAD AND BRONX SEEDLESS GRAPE SALAD

2½ cups Bronx Seedless grapes, halved
½ cup stone-pressed walnut oil
1 cup shelled walnuts
3 tablespoons sherry vinegar (made by Orleans method)
freshly cracked black pepper to taste
6–8 slices sourdough bread, lightly toasted

In a bowl, combine the grapes, walnut oil, walnuts, and vinegar and season with pepper. Cut or tear the toasted bread into bite-sized pieces. Place half the bread pieces in a wide, shallow bowl. Spoon on half of the grape mixture. Layer the remaining bread on top and then the remaining grape mixture. Cover and refrigerate for half an hour. The grape juices will soak into the bread much like tomato juices do in *panzanella* (a Tuscan bread and summer vegetable salad). Serves 4.

Fortunately, two of the farmers in Acorn Nation who were committed to growing *flavorful* food adopted the Bronx Seedless, transplanting it from the Atlantic to the Pacific coast. They were in no way intimidated by the industry's profit-driven dismissal of the Bronx Seedless. And today they are allowing a new generation of intrepid shoppers to experience this Rolls Royce of table grapes.

"I started growing them because they're just so good to eat," says John Legier of Legier Ranches in Escalon, California. "If I followed what the industry was doing, I'd select only the thickest-skinned grapes that hold a shape and a profit but with no aroma, no flavor, no juice. But that's not why I grow food. It's got to taste good. Otherwise, what's the point?"

Long before our contemporary chefs developed the New American cuisine, farmers and horticulturists were the custodians of taste, walking their orchards, vineyards, and vegetable fields, sampling fruits and saving seeds from the most cleverly delicious tree, bush, or vine. For a farmer to grow a Bronx Seedless grape is to reclaim that custodial role, repositioning farmers as the guardians of flavor and their family-owned farms as the sanctuaries of quality. "And you know," John continues, "growing for flavor isn't a bad economic decision. I don't struggle to get customers. Despite split skins and loose berries that fall off the bunch, the moment people put a Bronx Seedless in their mouth they just want to know where they can get more. I never lack for a customer."

Although the Bronx Seedless is now available from only two nurseries on the continent—Lon Rombough and Weeks Berry Nursery, both in Oregon—the current revival of interest in its table qualities may help it squeak through hard times. The Bronx Seedless grape is among the most luscious table grapes grown anywhere and is best eaten fresh, for it loses its flavor when cooked.

The accompanying recipe is adapted from Chef Laurent Manrique of the Aqua Restaurant in San Francisco, California.

Further Readings

Duggan, Tara. "Table Grapes That Are a Cut Above." *San Francisco Chronicle*, August 31, 2005. Accessed March 16, 2007, from http://sfgate.com/cgi-bin/article.cgi?f=/c/a/2005/08/31/FDGPLED6EQ1.DTL&hw=alfieri&sn=001&sc=1000.

Reisch, Bruce I. "The 'Bronx Seedless' Grape: An Early Success from the Cornell-Geneva and New York Botanical Garden Grape Breeding Project," n.d. Accessed March 14, 2007, from www.nysaes.cornell.edu/hort/faculty/reisch/bronx.html.

Rombough, Lon J. *The Grape Grower: A Guide to Organic Viticulture.* White River Junction, Vermont: Chelsea Green Publishing, 2002.

Slate, George L., John Watson, and John Einset. *Grape Varieties Introduced by the New York State Agricultural Experiment Station 1928–1961.* Ithaca, New York: Cornell University Press, 1962.

Gaspé Flint Corn

Gaspé flint corn can be seen as the miniature maize of the Micmacs or as the fastest-growing historic corn on the North Atlantic shores, where it matures in just forty-five to sixty days. Jacques Cartier apparently observed fields of it at the same time that he named Quebec's northeasternmost peninsula Gaspé in 1534. This ancient, eight-rowed yellow and white maize was undoubtedly much more widespread in Clambake Nation at one time, no doubt being grown in mounds within many Iroquois gardens as well. This, like other flint corns of the northeastern shores of North America, diverged from the earliest corns to come into the region less than five hundred years ago and then finely adapted to the climatic constraints of the peninsula.

Although the plants tassel out at just two feet in height and the ears barely reach four inches in length, this corn can be grown further north than any other attempted in the St. Lawrence River watershed, well into what is now New York State. The most prized collection of this flint corn came from Mr. Landrey's Nouvel West residence in the eastern Quebec township of Bonaventure; it appears his family may have obtained this heirloom soon after their immigration to Bonaventure in 1684. Unfortunately, few seed samples of this historic flint corn have survived even in governmental seed banks, none are available commercially, and only a few gardeners still maintain this important heirloom in Clambake Nation.

The following recipe is adapted from ones that go back before the time of the first Thanksgiving. It is referred to by the Six Nations as Three Sisters Soup, in recognition of those three pillars of Native American agriculture: beans, squash, and corn.

THREE SISTERS SOUP

2 tablespoons olive oil
2 onions, chopped
2 leeks, chopped
3 cloves garlic, minced
1 quart tomatoes, chopped
2 green peppers, chopped
4 carrots, sliced
4 potatoes, diced
2 cups presoaked Gaspé flint corn kernels
2 cups green beans, cut into 1-inch pieces
2 summer squash, diced
3 tablespoons minced fresh basil
3 tablespoons minced fresh parsley
1 teaspoon minced hot pepper or ¼ teaspoon dried cayenne pepper
salt and freshly ground black pepper to taste

In a large saucepan, sauté in oil the onions, leeks, and garlic over medium heat until they begin to brown. Add the tomatoes and peppers and cook for a minute over high heat. Reduce the heat to a simmer and add the carrots, potatoes, and corn kernels; then add water to achieve the desired thickness of the soup. Bring to full boil, cover, and turn the heat down to medium-low. Simmer slowly for 2 hours. Add the green beans, summer squash, and herbs and spices during last 20 minutes of cooking.

David Cavagnaro

Further Readings

Kuleshov, N. N. "World's Diversity of Phenotypes of Maize." *Journal of the American Society of Agronomy*, 25 (1933): 688–700.

Mt. Pleasant, Jane. "The Science behind the Three Sisters Mound System: An Agronomic Assessment of an Indigenous Agricultural System in the Northeast." In Bruce F. Benz, Robert H. Tykot, and John. E. Staller, eds., *Histories of Maize*, 529–537. Burlington, Massachusetts: Academic Press, 2006.

Tuscarora School. "Tuscarora Cooking." www.nw.wnyric.org/tuscarora/tuscaroraschool/cooking.htm.

Harrison Cider Apple

Nearly lost forever from American tables, the Harrison cider apple has recently been resurrected in an attempt to rejuvenate its long and luscious collaboration with Maple Syrup Nation's makers of hard cider. The earliest written record of this long-stemmed apple being found among the Harrison family of Essex County, New Jersey, dates from 1803. When Samuel Harrison was eighty-four years old, he testified how, six years before his own birth, his father had begun a nursery with some apple sprouts obtained from a Mr. Osborne in the nearby town of South Orange. Around the time of Samuel's birth, these sprouts were transplanted out into an orchard, where he grew up with them. By the time he was a teenager in the 1730s, fifteen or twenty of these trees had begun to bear fruit by late October. Although his father called them Long Stem or Osborne apples, by Samuel's era they had become better known in Essex County as Harrison cider apples, a name that has stuck. In fact, the variety was one of Maple Syrup Nation's premier cider apples for more than a century, with ten barrels of its firm, dry fruit yielding a single barrel of hard cider. When Prohibition forced hard ciders out of the marketplace, the cultivation of the Harrison fell out of fashion.

Many believed it had disappeared altogether, until the great apple historian and nurseryman Tom Burford rediscovered the Harrison in the 1980s. Although it has been made commercially available again in recent years by Cider Hill Nursery and Orchard Lane Growers, it is still critically endangered.

A small to medium-sized apple that tends toward an ovate or oblong shape, the Harrison has both skin and flesh that are very yellow. Although it may at first seem rather tough and dry, the flesh of a Harrison has a complex subacid flavor that it carries through into a richly colored hard cider with great body. In 1817, the great pomologist William Coxe claimed that "as [it is] the more vinous, rich, and highly-flavoured liquor, I prefer the Harrison to the [Hewes or Virginia] crab cider. This preference may depend on the peculiarity of taste. The two liquors may in some degree be compared to the still and sparkling Champagne, both of which have their exclusive admirers."

Although a wonderful and classic hard cider can be made by balancing the juices of Harrison and Graniwinkle heirloom apples, the following recipe calls for using the two apples to make a boiled sweet cider syrupto be added to baked beans. For both hard and boiled sweet cider recipes, we are indebted to Ben Watson's historic accounts and contemporary adaptations. The baked bean recipe is adapted from Dale Carson of the Abenaki community of Clambake Nation.

Fruit expert Tom Burford (at right) stands next to a box of Harrison apples at an orchard in central Virginia. Burford is credited with rediscovering the Harrison, which was long thought extinct. Charlotte Shelton/Vintage Virginia Apples

Further Readings

Bussey, Dan. *The Apple in America*. Madison, Wisconsin: privately printed five-volume draft, 2006.

Carson, Dale. *New Native American Cooking*. New York: Random House, 1996.

Coxe, William A. *A View of the Cultivated Fruit Trees*. Rockton, Ontario, Canada: Pomona Books, 1976. (Originally published in 1817.)

Whealy, Kent. *Fruit, Nut and Berry Inventory*, 3rd ed. Decorah, Iowa: Seed Savers Exchange, 2001.

Benjamin Watson

BOILED HARRISON-GRANIWINKLE CIDER IN BAKED BEANS

2½ cups sweet cider pressed from Harrison apples
2½ cups sweet cider pressed from Graniwinkle apples
1 tablespoon freshly ground cinnamon bark
1 pound dried Quaker or Jacob's Cattle beans
4 cups water
1 medium-sized white onion, diced
1 tablespoon sunflower oil
½ cup maple syrup
1 teaspoon dry mustard
1 teaspoon powdered ginger
1 bunch green scallions, finely diced

After sweating, grinding, and pressing separate batches of the Harrison and Graniwinkle apples into cider, pour a total of 5 cups of fresh sweet cider into a heavy-duty, nonreactive kettle. Bring to a boil, then reduce the heat and slowly simmer the cider until it is reduced to 2 cups, keeping vigilant watch so that it doesn't scorch. Add the cinnamon and set aside to cool. Meanwhile, bring a large pot of beans and water to boil, reduce the heat, and simmer for 2 hours until almost tender. Drain the beans, but retain 2 cups of their cooking liquid. Preheat the oven to 350 degrees F. While the oven is heating, take a skillet and sauté the diced onions in sunflower oil for 5 to 7 minutes or until translucent. Add the sautéed onions to the pot of beans. Next, pour the boiled cider, maple syrup, and bean liquid back into the bean pot, adding the mustard and ginger as well. Transfer the mixture to a 2-quart crock suitable for baking and cover. Place in the oven and bake for 2 hours, occasionally adding more water if necessary. Finally, uncover the crock and bake an additional 30 minutes or until all the liquid is absorbed by the beans. Let stand for 2 more minutes before garnishing with finely chopped scallions, then serve warm.

Meech's Prolific Quince

From their very arrival in the Caribbean around 1520 and in North America around 1649, quinces took on the role of underdogs, so that even the best varieties were always treated as if they were second choices to apples, peaches, or pears. As Liberty Hyde Bailey lamented of the second-class status of the quince, "Few fruit played a more important part of ancient history than the quince, and yet there is hardly a fruit . . . that in recent years has received less attention."

The quince did take root in New Jersey along the shores of Clambake Nation, in Virginia along the shores of Crabcake Nation, and in northern New Mexico along the rivers of Chile Pepper Nation. And yet North America did not realize its best quince until some three and a half centuries after this fruit species' introduction to the continent. That was about the time Reverend W. W. Meech began to promote the particular pear-shaped fruit that grew from a seedling he had rescued in the New Jersey countryside. The seedling had traits that suggest its kinship to other "orange quinces"; in fact, Meech first introduced it as the Pear-Shaped Orange Quince in 1883. Meech's coinage never really stuck as an official name, so after decades of his "converts" simply calling it "Meech's quince," the good reverend finally conceded that the name "Meech's Prolific" would distinguish his selection for posterity.

Meech's Prolific has now had more than a century of dispersal out from Clambake Nation to other orchards across the continent, but its stronghold has always been New Jersey, New York, Pennsylvania, and Connecticut. By the 1740s, Peter Kalm noted that quinces were "everywhere" among the German settlers of Pennsylvania. But a century later, as refrigeration reduced the need for fruits that were "good keepers," the quince fell out of fashion in many circles; only Hidden Springs Nursery in Tennessee still regularly offers cuttings of Meech's Prolific to the American public. It is now better known in western Europe than in its homeland; it has become a popular garden variety in the Netherlands and in the British Isles.

This pear-shaped quince has bright orange-yellow fine-textured skin; the deeply fragrant fruit grow to eighteen ounces in size on large, slow-growing trees that bear heavily year after year. As one nurseryman from Curve, Tennessee, noted of Meech's Prolific in 1890, "Its flesh has the most delightful fragrance and delicious flavor, as well as a tenderness of pulp that makes it ideal for marmalades." In fact, the word *marmalade* comes from the Portuguese word *marmela,* meaning quince. Nurserymen are not its only fans; one chef stood amazed that it "cooks as tender as a peach."

At a quince evaluation for the Slow Food USA Ark of Taste, tasters found Meech's among the most aromatic varieties, with a delightful fragrance reminiscent of apples, flowers, and vanilla. The quick-cooked fruit slices were soft, sweet, and nicely crisp, with a clear, bright color and a complex flavor that mingles the piney tartness of tropical fruits like pineapple and mango with caramel and pear notes.

As John Parkinson conceded, "There is no fruit growing in this Land that is of so many excellent uses." Traditionally it was stewed; baked; boiled down into a thick, cheeselike compote; or transformed into chutneylike relishes and wines.

The following recipe for clarifying quinces was brought back into light by the publication of *Sauerkraut Yankees,* a celebration of the foodways of the Pennsylvania Dutch by William Woys Weaver.

WIE MER GWITTE EIMACHT (CLARIFIED QUINCES)

6 Meech's Prolific quinces
turbinado sugar
¾ cup water

Select six firm but ripened quinces and pare them, cutting them lengthwise into several pieces. In a large kettle, cover them with water and boil them until they are uniformly softened but not quite mushy. Strain them through a food mill and return them to the pot, then boil them until they begin to clarify. Reduce the heat, add a pound of sugar for each pound of quinces, and augment the liquids by adding about ¾ cup of additional water. Increase the heat until the syrupy liquid is clarified once more. Place the remaining solids of the quinces in large-mouth jars and pour the clarified liquid over them. Place towels over the jars and let them stand covered for 2 days. On the third morning, pour off the syrup and set it in another kettle over the fire. Once it begins to boil, cook it for 15 minutes or more, adding any remaining quince solids to thicken the syrup. Cool the contents of the kettle, use a slotted wooden spoon to retrieve the remaining chunks of quince, place them in jars, and pour the syrup over them. Seal and store for later use as a dessert or as an ingredient in marmalades or candy.

Further Readings

Burr, Fearing. *Field and Garden Vegetables in America.* Chillicothe, Illinois: American Botanical Booksellers, 1994.

Hatch, Peter J. *The Fruits and Fruit Trees of Monticello: Thomas Jefferson and the Origins of American Horticulture.* Charlottesville: University Press of Virginia, 1998.

Meech, William W. *Quince Culture: An Illustrated Hand-Book for the Propagation and Cultivation of the Quince, With Descriptions of Its Varieties, Insect Enemies, Diseases, and Their Remedies.* New York: Orange Judd, 1888.

Parkinson, John. *Paradisi in Sole Paradisus Terrestris.* London: private printing, 1629.

Weaver, William Woys. *Sauerkraut Yankees: Pennsylvania Dutch Foods & Foodways.* Mechanicsburg, Pennsylvania: Stackpole Books, 2002.

David Karp

Milking Devon Cattle

First brought by the Pilgrims to the coastal hay meadows of Clambake Nation in 1623, Devon cattle had gradually developed as a distinctive breed on the southwestern peninsula of England over the three or four centuries prior to the colonization of America. With ruby-red hides and black-tipped ivory horns, Devons have been called the quintessential triple-purpose breed. They provide a creamy milk; a flavorful, fine-textured meat; and, as draft oxen, fossil-fuel-free traction. In the British Isles, they have long been considered a fast, unflaggingly diligent draft animal, keeping up a pace of six miles an hour while pulling wagons. Once they arrived in North America, they became the draft oxen of choice for many farmers, pulling covered wagons all the way across the Oregon Trail. And yet their hardiness and capacity to thrive on rough forage made them particularly valuable in the coastlands surrounding Plymouth Plantation. Since 1900, they have rarely been raised beyond the range of Clambake Nation.

Over the last century, however, Devon herds were gradually phased out of this landscape as another multipurpose breed, the Shorthorn, ascended in popularity. By 1950, multipurpose breeds could not get any respect in the cattle industry, and Devons found themselves on the verge of extinction. Some of the remaining breeders decided to abandon the traditional selection of Devons as a multipurpose breed and cull out any animals from their herds that could not produce beef in a manner competitive with other meat breeds. As this "new" Beef Devon population diverged from the original gene pool, a few breeders held on tenaciously to the goal of a multipurpose breed. The populations still maintained for milk, meat, and traction became known as the American Milking Devon, a breed that is now unique to the United States. Ironically, it may be the closest remaining population to the original cattle of the western English counties of Devonshire, Cornwall, Somerset, and Dorset.

Once the Beef Devon diverged from them, the breeding stock of Milking Devon cattle dwindled in number for several decades. By its darkest days in the 1970s, fewer than one hundred individuals remained. Fortunately, there was someone on the scene who had both the foresight and the organizational skills to bring together the last few dairymen and teamsters with Milking Devon stock. John Wheelock of Colchester, Vermont, had his own herd, but he also understood that a breeder's association was urgently needed to guide the exchange of bulls and, ultimately, ensure the recovery of the breed. His efforts also inspired and informed the creation of the first livestock conservation organization in North America, which is known today as the American Livestock Breeds Conservancy.

After bottoming out with fewer than ninety milk cows in existence thirty-five years ago, the breed was put on the conservancy's critical list and was later boarded onto the Slow Food Ark of Taste. Fortunately, Milking Devon populations have recovered, and herd sizes are again increasing, with current herds in Clambake and Maple Syrup Nations including more than 400 individuals. They have become a favorite exhibition animal at historic farms such as Old Sturbridge Village, not only because of their fine appearance but because of their perseverance. Milking Devon cows average a little over 1,000 pounds in weight, have well-formed udders, and are one of several breeds that produce a milk rich enough to be made into a clotted topping known as Devonshire cream. Devonshire cream is traditionally ladled onto scones or fresh fruit.

DEVONSHIRE CREAM

2 cups clotted cream from Milking Devon cattle

2 tablespoons powdered sugar

1 tablespoon pure vanilla extract

After milking the cows, let their milk stand in a bucket for a few hours so that the cream rises to the top. Skim it off and pour it into a metal pan that can be floated in a larger vessel of constantly boiling water. This process should proceed until the cream is scalded enough to form a slight crust with a buttery consistency, while the rest of the liquid thickens into a rich yellow clotted cream, so thick that it does not require any whipping. Place this clotted cream and its crust in a glass bowl, mix in the powdered sugar and vanilla, and then let it sit in the refrigerator for 2 hours. When ready, scoop it onto cranberry scones (see the Berry berry cranberry scone recipe on page 113) or combine it with fresh berries.

Further Readings

American Milking Devon Cattle Association website, 2007. Available at www.milkingdevons.org.

Christman, Carolyn J., D. Phillip Sponenberg, and Donald E. Bixby. *A Rare Breeds Album of American Livestock*. Pittsboro, North Carolina: American Livestock Breeds Conservancy, 1997.

The bull is Wiseacre Farm Rufus 10325, about 6 years old. While not quite typical of Devons today, he is likely more representative of what the breed looked like 100 years ago. The heifer is about 20 months old. As females approach their full life span of twenty years or so (longevity being another superior trait of the breed) their horns will have grown long and upright into the shape of a lyre. Stephen Bibula

Narragansett Turkey

Named for Narragansett Bay in Rhode Island, where it was first developed by early colonists, this rare standard breed of heritage turkey emerged from crosses between the wild turkeys of eastern America and already domesticated turkey breeds such as the Norfolk Black. The Norfolk Black is one of the breeds derived from the Mexican turkey landraces that were first brought to Europe in the sixteenth century and that then returned to the Americas in the first century following colonization. The Narragansett breed is legendary for its stunning beauty, with black metallic plumage on its breast and back, banded black and gray tail feathers tipped with white, and toes and shanks that turn a deep salmon. The wattles on the face and throat typically have a rich red hue.

And yet its colorful feathers are not the only reason that the Narragansett has been so highly esteemed throughout most of American history. It is larger and hardier than most common farmyard turkeys, with mature toms weighing in at thirty-three pounds and hens at around eighteen pounds. In its Clambake Nation homeland of Rhode Island and Connecticut, it can survive without much supplemental feed, subsisting on grasshoppers, crickets, and other insects that would otherwise damage farmers' crops. The Narragansett was therefore kept in large flocks that foraged through fields and orchards. According to the December 1872 issue of *The Poultry World,* at that time it was not uncommon to find on a single farm a flock of some one or two hundred Narragansetts, whose population was sustained year after year by a dozen or so breeding hens. The rest went off to market, with young toms dressing out at fourteen pounds and six-month-old toms reaching twenty-eight pounds by Thanksgiving time.

One of the few species of tended fowl originating in the Americas, the turkey was first domesticated in Mexico more than 2,000 years ago. Although there were already wild subspecies of the turkey in North

Courtesy American Livestock Breeds Conservancy

America by the time the first farmers harvested their crops there, the domesticated turkey was introduced in prehistoric times from Mexico into what is now the U.S. Southwest. It not only proliferated as a multipurpose farm animal but also garnered considerable ceremonial and symbolic significance. Multicolored petroglyphs of domestic turkeys still adorn the sandstone walls of canyons in the U.S. Southwest, near prehistoric Pueblo ruins where turkey bones and mummified turkey carcasses have been excavated.

Soon after the Spanish reached Mexico, domesticated turkeys were taken both to Europe and to regions of the North American continent, where some heritage breeds crossed with the local wild subspecies, diversifying the gene pool. Eight to ten American standard breeds have been recognized over the last century and a half, with the characteristics codified by the American Poultry Association's (formerly) annual publication, *Standard of Perfection*. The Narragansett was first admitted to the *Standard of Perfection* roster in 1874, although by that time it was already a widely recognized breed. In fact, it became the foundation for the historic turkey industry in Clambake and Maple Syrup Nations, where it remained prominent into the early twentieth century. And yet by the end of that same century, it had been all but replaced by modern breeds of white turkeys, with only sixty-six hens and twenty-eight toms of Narragansetts comprising the entire gene pool for the breed by 1999.

Since then, the Narragansett has garnered considerable interest among producers, consumers, and chefs as one of several standard breeds of heritage turkeys that have suddenly received a flurry of media attention. Through a collaboration that was spearheaded by the American Livestock Breeds Conservancy with the help of Slow Food USA, dozens of producers have been enlisted to produce these standard turkeys for Thanksgiving feasts once again. The breed is listed on the Slow Food USA Ark of Taste, which has helped to bolster its revival along with that of other standard breeds such as the Bronze, Black Spanish, Bourbon Red, and Slate.

For a traditional recipe used in Clambake Nation during the time this breed was in its heyday, we have adapted one that appears to have been popular in the mid-1800s. It features another Native American food that was then popular along the mid-Atlantic coast, the Jerusalem artichoke (see page 71). It was included in Mrs. B. C. Howard's (1873) edition of *Fifty Years in a Maryland Kitchen.*

Further Readings

Chrisman, J., and Robert O. Hawes. *Birds of a Feather: Saving Rare Turkeys from Extinction.* Pittsboro, North Carolina: American Livestock Breeds Conservancy, 1999.

Dohner, Janet Vorwald. *The Encyclopedia of Historic and Endangered Livestock and Poultry Breeds.* New Haven, Connecticut: Yale University Press, 2001.

Howard, B. C. *Fifty Years in a Maryland Kitchen.* Baltimore: Turnball Brothers, 1873.

Nabhan, Gary Paul. *Enduring Seeds: Native American Agriculture and Wild Plant Conservation.* Berkeley, California: North Point Press, 1989.

Smith, Andrew F. *The Turkey: An American Story.* Champaign-Urbana: University of Illinois Press, 2006.

ROAST NARRAGANSETT TURKEY WITH JERUSALEM ARTICHOKES

1 small Narragansett turkey, plucked (typically 12 to 18 pounds)
2 tablespoons sea salt
1 teaspoon freshly ground black pepper
1 tablespoon dried marjoram or sweet basil leaves
¼ cup finely chopped flat-leaved parsley
½ cup whole-wheat bread crumbs
1 tablespoon unsalted Jersey cow butter
¼ cup coarsely chopped Golden Yellow celery stalks
2 tablespoons minced celery tops
1 small white Egyptian Walking onion, chopped
2 tablespoons lard
1 quart Jerusalem artichokes, washed and peeled

Several days before roasting, wash a small to medium-sized Narragansett turkey until it is clean, then rub its skin all over with salt; rub the cavities of the bird with salt, pepper, sweet basil or marjoram, and some of the finely chopped parsley. Stuff the cavities with a mix of bread crumbs, a lump of butter mixed with salt and pepper, the rest of the chopped parsley, and half of the chopped celery and onion. Set aside, sealed in a plastic bag, for 2 days in a refrigerator.

On the day of the feast, place some lard in a Dutch oven until it melts and is boiling, then brown the turkey in this grease, turning the bird from one side to the next until all sides are equally browned. Pour off all the grease from the Dutch oven and then pour a quart of boiling water into the oven until the bird is entirely covered, with at least an inch of water above its highest crest. Add the rest of the chopped onion, the celery tops, and the celery stalks, the latter tied with string into a compact bunch. Begin cooking all these ingredients in the Dutch oven about one and a half hours before serving, slowly stewing them, ladling the juices over the bird. About 40 minutes into the cooking in the Dutch oven, pour a quart of washed and peeled tubers of Jerusalem artichokes around the turkey, and occasionally ladle juices over them as well.

Rubel Northern Highbush Blueberry

The blueberry is one of the few fruits that North America has contributed to the global food economy, and Rubel was among the first highbush blueberries selected from native stock of Clambake Nation, for it was taken directly from the wilds of the New Jersey Pine Barrens. Botanist Frederick Coville named this small-fruited but vigorous bush, but while admitting that the name Rubel follows the German spelling of the Russian coin, he wryly added these comments:

> The name of the blueberry variety, Rubel, however, is of neither German nor Russian derivation. The man who discovered this bush was Rube Leek. But Rube did not seem an expressive name for a berry that was blue and beautiful, and Leek was suggestive of a flavor that the berry did not possess. Rubel was a compromise, made up of Mr. Leek's first name and the initial of his last . . .

As one nurseryman has noted, "Rubel is living proof that older is oftentimes better . . . [for] this heritage blueberry has continued to be popular . . . because of its uniformly small fruit, dark color, and intense flavor." Despite nine additional decades of intensive selection of blueberry cultivars, Rubel was recently found to have nearly twice the antioxidant levels as most other blueberries, so that consumers who formerly neglected it are suddenly flocking to the Rubel as a means to prevent cancer, lower cholesterol levels, and improve eyesight. Its intense flavor, firmness, cold hardiness, virus resistance, and ease of harvest are among its many other assets.

Yet despite these superlative qualities, Rubel is far less available today than at any time over the last century; in fact, there are forty blueberry cultivars other than Rubel that are offered by more nurseries. Just two nurseries in McMannville, Tennessee; another two in Michigan; and one in Oregon offer propagation materials of this sturdy, upright bush, which reaches a height of six feet once it matures. Older plants tend to decline in productivity, unless occasionally reinvigorated by fire, as Robert Frost reminds us in his poem "Blueberries":

> Why, there hasn't been time for the bushes to grow.
> That's always the way with the blueberries, though:
> There may not have been a ghost of a sign
> Of them anywhere under the shade of a pine,
> But get the pine out of the way, you may burn
> The pasture all over until not a fern
> Or grass-blade is left, not to mention a stick,
> And presto, they're up all around you as thick
> And hard to explain as a conjurer's trick.
>
> It must be on charcoal they fatten the fruit
> I taste in them sometimes the flavor of soot
> . . .

For centuries, Native Americans regularly burned blueberry glades as means of enhancing berry production and eliminating the competing woody vegetation that oftentimes blocked their access to the best stands. Some of the best blueberry recipes come to us directly from Native American chefs, such as this *attitaash* adapted from Abenaki tribal member Dale Carson.

ATTITAASH (BLUEBERRY CONSERVE)

1 quart freshly picked Rubel blueberries
½ cup water
4 cups turbinado sugar
1 Meyer lemon with peel intact, seeded and sliced paper thin
½ cup shelled black walnuts, toasted and chopped
½ teaspoon freshly ground cinnamon or sassafras bark

Place the berries in a large, nonreactive saucepan, cover with water, and cook over medium heat for 5 minutes or until they are tender. Reduce the heat and add the sugar, lemon slices, black walnuts, and ground sassafras or cinnamon. Simmer this mixture, stirring frequently with a wooden spoon to prevent burning. In a matter of 15 minutes or so, the conserve should thicken sufficiently to necessitate removing it from the heat. Let it cool slightly and then spoon the conserve into sterilized jars and seal with paraffin. Yields roughly 1 quart of conserve as a final product.

Further Readings

Carson, Dale. *New Native American Cooking*. New York: Random House, 1996.

Coville, Frederick V. "Improving the Wild Blueberry." *USDA Yearbook of Agriculture*. Washington, D.C.: U.S. Government Printing Office, 1937.

Frost, Robert. "Blueberries." In *North of Boston*. New York: Henry Holt and Company, 1915.

Reich, Lee. *Uncommon Fruits for Every Garden*. Portland, Oregon: Timber Press, 2004.

Whealy, Kent, and Joanne Thuente. *Fruit, Berry and Nut Inventory*, 3rd ed. Decorah, Iowa: Seed Savers Exchange, 2001.

David Karp

Waldoboro Green Neck "Turnip"

According to legend, the Waldoboro Green Neck is derived from rutabagas that washed ashore at Muscongus Bay along the Maine coast of Clambake Nation. On February 10, 1886, a 250-foot-long steamer christened the *Cambridge* became enveloped in foglike "sea smoke" off the shores of Friendship and ran aground on Old Man Ledge. It broke in two and then slowly sank over the following week. Once the word got out that the *Cambridge* was going under, fishermen and farmers from miles around rowed or sailed out to salvage her cargo, including this turniplike rutabaga, Thompson's Million Dollar melon, and Charlie Murphy's pole beans. From then on, the Green Neck has been kept safe and sound in the gardens around Waldoboro.

It may well be, though, that the Green Neck had been grown in parts of Maine since the 1780s, for there are records of the French introducing a similar turnip or rutabaga to farms along the Bay of Fundy a century earlier than the shipwreck of the *Cambridge*. It too was large, nonwoody, and knobby, with several knotted side roots. Such rutabagas, with yellow flesh and pale green skin, were introduced to what is now the United States as early as 1630. The Waldoboro itself can be the size of a watermelon, as Ron and Peggy Coulette have demonstrated to astounded judges at the Windsor Fair, where their prize-winning roots have weighed in at twenty-five pounds: "The biggest plant—without trying to stretch the leaves out—measures five feet across the top of the leaves . . . It's sweet and good eating all the way through." In fact, the entire plant has such a high sugar content that it was fed like candy—leaves, stems, roots, and all—to the teams of oxen working at Maine's many lumber mills. Carman Clark contends that "Waldoboro turnips are so delicious that folks who've gagged at the sight, smell, or mention of this vegetable eat them with pleasure and ask for more."

By all accounts, this is a rutabaga that is shrouded in stories, ones that are still gathered and spun around the Heirloom Seed Project Greenhouse in the village of Waldoboro, not far from Camden, Maine. The stories and the seeds of the Waldoboro Green Neck that now circulate among heirloom gardeners are likely to have been passed through Neil Lash, a teacher at Medomak Valley High School. For two decades, Lash has codirected the school's program in practical botany and horticulture. Lash and his colleague Jon Thurston have mailed seeds from the many heirloom treasures in the greenhouse—including the Waldoboro Green Neck—to some thirty-seven states in the United States and to another six countries. Nevertheless, only one commercial seed catalog, Horus Botanicals, has picked up the Waldoboro Green Neck to offer it for sale. This rutabaga remains endangered by most objective standards, although Lash, Thurston, Clark, the Coulettes, and others in Maine have ensured that its stories will not be forgotten.

In Maine, some claim that soaking the Waldoboro Green Necks in saltwater makes them especially flavorful and allows them to serve as a fitting complement to moose meat. Elements of the following recipe for North Woods stew, which may use either moose flank meat or venison, hearken back to the pages of an 1857 cookbook, the name of which has been lost. It is loosely adapted from recipes handed down by Pete Byrnes and A. J. McClane in the pages of *Sports Afield* magazine.

The steamship *Cambridge*, which ran aground off the Maine coast in 1886, was the only Boston-Bangor liner ever lost in service. Local tradition says that part of the salvaged cargo included the vegetable now known as the **Waldoboro Green Neck turnip.** Photo reproduced from John M. Richardson, *Steamboat Lore of the Penobscot* (Augusta, ME: Kennebec Journal Print Shop, 1941). Courtesy Neil Lash, Medomak Valley High School.

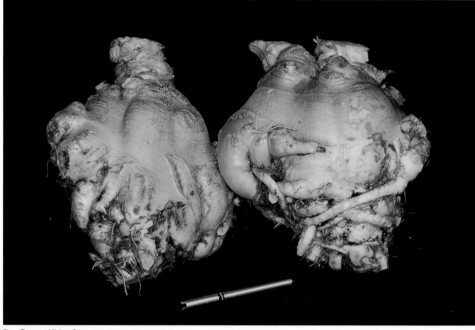
Shaun Turner and Kelsea Gunn

Further Readings

Ascrizzi, Lynn. "Giant Turnip Has Roots in Waldoboro History." *The Morning Sentinel* (Waterville, Maine), October 3–4, 1992.

Clark, A. Carman. "Down East Garden Ways." *The Camden Herald* (Maine), January 21,1993.

Colbert, Mike. "Saving Seeds from Extinction." *The Lincoln County News* (Maine), June 15, 2005.

Gold, Donna. "Maine School Salvages Historic Seeds." *Boston Globe,* April 29, 2001.

MOOSE AND WALDOBORO GREEN NECK RUTABAGA STEW

1 pound fresh moose flank, cut into thin pieces

3 cups Waldoboro Green Neck rutabaga, diced into 1-inch chunks

4 tablespoons sea salt

4 tablespoons unsalted butter

1 tablespoon currant jelly

¼ cup unbleached whole-wheat flour

6 Scarlet Keeper carrots, peeled and diced

3 Waldoboro Gold Jerusalem artichokes, diced

½ teaspoon freshly ground black pepper

¼ teaspoon freshly ground cinnamon bark

Place the moose flank slices in a saucepan, with enough water to just cover them. Let them stew, simmering, for 2 hours. In another saucepan, place the diced rutabagas, 2 tablespoons of sea salt, and water and let them soak 2 hours as well. When the meat is well stewed, strain the liquid from the saucepan into a skillet; add the butter, currant jelly, and flour; and then stir the mixture to make a light-colored gravy. Drain the diced rutabagas, and then add them, the carrots, and the Jerusalem artichokes to the saucepan. Boil in the covered saucepan for 30 to 45 minutes, until the vegetables are tender. Add the moose meat back in, season with the additional salt, pepper, and cinnamon, and reduce the heat. Simmer for 5 minutes more and then serve hot in bowls.

Boston Marrow Squash

In 1866, seedsman Benjamin Bliss referred to this autumnal marrow squash as "the most popular in the Boston market," due to its "deep-orange, finely-grained and excellent-flavored flesh." A year later, squash expert James J. H. Gregory of Marblehead, Massachusetts, sang the praises of this and other soft-stemmed, Hubbard-like squashes, noting that their ancestors had been brought to North America in the 1700s by whalers who found them in Argentine harbor towns or sailors who found them while trading in the West Indies. This marrow squash was first made available to the public in 1831, when John M. Ives of Salem, Massachusetts, put its mature fruit on exhibit at Faneuil Hall in Boston. Ives claimed that this squash had among its ancestors some seeds brought to Buffalo, New York, by Native Americans arriving from the west. How these indigenous farmers had received the seeds of a South American cucurbit so soon after its arrival in North America is anybody's guess.

Unlike most true Hubbards, the Boston Marrow has a red-hued rind that ranges in color from salmon pink to orange. By late summer or early fall, eight-to nine-pound pointed fruits have set on vines that often reach fifteen feet in length, especially when intercropped with corn and beans. These fruits are ovately shaped and like true Hubbards are somewhat top-heavy, but they have eggshell-thin skin that can be rough—almost pebbly—to the touch. Their seeds are white and look rather inflated. As Bliss noted in 1866, they keep well through the winter and "will boil as dry as a potato."

William Woys Weaver suggests that in the cool, short summers of Clambake and Maple Syrup Nations, "this squash is among the very best . . . For the lovers of pumpkin pie, this is indeed a first-class squash." Despite at least fifteen decades of popularity in North America, seeds of the Boston Marrow are increasingly hard to come by. The variety can be considered endangered at this point in time—now that Fox Hollow Seed Company has closed up shop, D. Landreth Seed and Meyer Seed International, both of Baltimore, are the only remaining commercial sources making its seeds available to the gardening public.

The following recipe for stewed pumpkin or squash as a "New England standing dish" was first recorded by John Josselyn on his voyages to New England in the 1600s. It is followed by an adaptation of the Plimoth Plantation's version. Josselyn's version goes like this:

Further Readings

Bliss, Benjamin K. *Bliss Spring Catalogue and Amateur's Guide to the Flower and Kitchen Garden*, 12th ed. Springfield, Massachusetts: B. K. Bliss, Seedsman and Florist.

Bowles, Elie Shannon, and Dorothy S. Towles. 1947 (2000). *Secrets of New England Cooking.* Mineola, New York: Dover Editions.

Goldman, Amy. *The Compleat Squash: A Passionate Grower's Guide.* New York: Artisan Books, 2004.

Gregory, James J. H. *Squashes: How to Grow Them.* New York: Orange Judd. 1867.

Hornblower, Malabar. *The Plimoth Plantation New England Cookery Book.* Boston: The Harvard Common Press, 1990.

Lindholdt, Paul J., ed. *John Josselyn, Colonial Traveler: A Critical Edition of Two Voyages to New England.* Hanover, New Hampshire: University Press of New England, 1998.

Plimoth Plantation. "Recipes." http://www.plimoth.org/kids/recipes.php.

Weaver, William Woys. *Heirloom Vegetable Gardening.* New York: Henry Holt. 1997.

THE ANCIENT NEW ENGLAND STANDING DISH

". . . the Housewives manner is to slice them when ripe, and cut them into dice, and so fill a pot with them of two or three Gallons, and stew them upon a gentle fire a whole day, and as they sink, they fill again with fresh Pompions, not putting any liquor to them; and when it is stew'd enough, it will look like bak'd Apples; this they Dish, putting Butter to it, and a little Vinegar, (with some Spice, as Ginger, &c.) which makes it tart like an Apple, and so serve it up to be eaten with Fish or Flesh: It provokes Urine extreamly and is very windy."

STANDING DISH OF STEWED BOSTON MARROW "POMPION"

4 cups stewed Boston Marrow pumpkin, roughly mashed
3 tablespoons butter
2 to 3 teaspoons apple cider vinegar
1 to 2 teaspoons ground ginger
½ teaspoon salt
1 teaspoon maple syrup (optional)

In a saucepan over medium heat, stir and heat all the ingredients together. Adjust seasonings to taste, and serve hot.

David Cavagnaro

Gloria Mundi Apple

One of the great baking apples of Clambake and Maple Syrup nations, the Gloria Mundi is also among the largest ever to be grown in America, with one prize-winning specimen in 1860 reaching three and a half pounds. Also called the Mammoth, the Melon, and the Ox, it was first recorded near Red Hook, New York, in 1803, where it was apparently found in the orchards of German immigrants. It became well established in Long Island and elsewhere in eastern New York before it spread to New Jersey and adjacent Pennsylvania by the beginning of the nineteenth century.

The Gloria Mundi is always large and somewhat round, with truncate ends, but its sides are unequal. The skin is greenish yellow, but as it matures it gains a bronze blush. The crisp, coarse, tender flesh is tinged with yellowish greens or whites, and its flavor is both tartly subacid and bittersweet. When baked, the flesh turns to a dark gold and sweetens.

It was one of the great "show" apples of county and state fairs throughout the nineteenth century, but because it is a shy bearer, it never made the transition to industrialized production. Over the last two decades, its availability for cultivation has been shouldered by as little as two or as many as five nurseries that specialize in heirloom fruits, but one of those has recently gone out of business.

This endangered apple is particularly delicious when baked, as demonstrated by this maple-imbued recipe adapted from Lucia Watson and Beth Dooley.

Further Readings

Bussey, Dan. *The Apple in America*. Madison, Wisconsin: privately printed five-volume draft, 2006.

Dooley, Beth, and Lucia Watson. *Savoring the Seasons of the Northern Heartland*. New York: Alfred A. Knopf, 1994.

Morgan, Joan, and Alison Richards. *The New Book of Apples*. London: Ebury Press/Random House, 1991.

Whealy, Kent, and Joanne Thuent. *Fruit, Nut and Berry Inventory*, 3rd ed. Decorah, Iowa: Seed Savers Exchange, 2001.

MAPLE-GLAZED GLORIA MUNDI APPLES

4 large Gloria Mundi apples
4 tablespoons maple syrup
4 tablespoons raisins made from Niagara grapes
4 tablespoons dried Governor Wood sour cherries
hard cider made from Harrison apples (see page 118)

Preheat the oven to 350 degrees F. Peel each apple just halfway down its sides and then partially core it, leaving the bottom half inch of the flesh uncored. Place the apples in a baking dish with the uncored, unpeeled sides down and fill each of the partially hollowed centers with a tablespoon of maple syrup, a tablespoon of raisins, and a tablespoon of dried cherries. Cover the bottom of the baking dish with ¼ inch of hard cider. Place the dish full of apples in the oven for 45 minutes or until the apples are tender but not mushy. Serve warm.

Benjamin Watson

CORNBREAD NATION

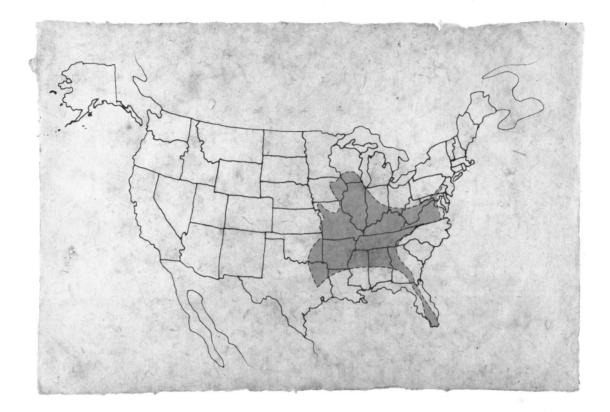

Encompassing most of the Mississippi River watershed north of the delta, Cornbread Nation now features a wonderful mingling of African and European food traditions along with remnants of indigenous traditions. The rich soils, wet climate, lush habitats, and place-based cultures of this region have generated an astonishing variety of heirloom vegetables and fruits, as well as heritage breeds. Its white corns are used for hominy, grits, spoonbreads, johnnycakes, and a myriad of other specialties. Pride in local and regional food traditions is rampant, producing seemingly endless variants of cornbread, barbecue, burgoo, and other stews. Nevertheless, rural out-migration has weakened many of Cornbread Nation's celebrated rural traditions, so that at least seventy-five of its traditional foods are now threatened or endangered.

Yellow Hickory King Dent Corn

The yellow and white strains of Hickory King may be the finest hominy corns that North Americans have ever known. They are eight-rowed, large-grained, small-cobbed landraces of the Old Southern Dents, a group of corns that came directly from Mexico into Cornbread Nation around A.D. 1500. Since that time, they have been selected to excel as roasting ears and as hominy, milled grits, and cornmeal. They serve so well for hominy because the skins of their kernels are effortlessly removed after they have been soaked in water mixed with wood ash or lye. The term *hominy*, incidentally, made its way into print by 1620 and is derived from terms in Algonquian languages for various corn products, including *rockahominie* (parched corn) and *tackhummin* (hulled corn).

It might seem odd to single out a *yellow* hominy corn to represent the Dixie traditions of Cornbread Nation because white corns tend to dominate the production of pones, hush puppies, and other cornbreads south of the Mason-Dixon line, while yellows hold favor to the north. Nevertheless, it has never been the case that yellow corns were excluded from the making of hoecakes, ashcakes, dodgers, muffins, and grits in the Deep South. In her authentic recipe for Tennessee muffins, published in 1837, Eliza Leslie begins her directions by telling her readers to "sift three pints of yellow Indian meal, and put one-half into a pan and scald it."

Food writer Celia Marks recalls from her Southern childhood that Hickory Kings were the corns that grew "as high as an elephant's eye," for the stalks often reach twelve feet in height, providing perfect support for pole beans. But the real attraction, according to Marks, is that the luster and texture of Hickory King kernels are incomparable:

> . . . pearly, shiny, satiny, full to bursting. If you sink your thumb into a kernel to test its freshness, it will pop and squirt the milky juice with the force of a spray gun. You *have to* eat this corn when it is fresh.

Yellow Hickory King has been grown in Cornbread and Chestnut Nations since before 1875. It produces two ears per stalk, each more tightly wrapped in the husk than most other varieties, which gives them a modicum of protection against corn earworm and pesky beetles. It also has some tolerance to southern leaf blight, the disease that otherwise devastated nearly a quarter of the U.S. corn crop in 1970. Continually grown in cornfield trials as a control crop since 1907, Hickory King has nevertheless declined in popularity in farmers' fields and in seed catalogs. Whereas six seed companies offered Yellow Hickory King in 1981, that number has now declined to one, Horus Botanicals, in Salem, Arkansas. In contrast, White Hickory King seed continues to be offered by more than eighteen commercial seed companies and nonprofit sources. Fortunately, the seeds of Yellow Hickory King can also still be purchased in half-pound bags in country stores in far western Kentucky. Nevertheless, this variety is now considered critically endangered.

The following recipe reminds us that spoonbreads and cornpones are likely derived from the woodfire-baked *suppones* or *suppawns*. John Egerton has called spoonbread "the lightest, richest, most delicious of all cornbread dishes, a veritable soufflé . . . an excellent companion to country ham and red-eye gravy."

Further Readings

Brown, William L. "Numbers and Distribution of Chromosome Knobs in United States Maize." *Genetics* 34 (1949): 524–534.

Egerton, John. *Southern Food: At Home, on the Road, in History*. Chapel Hill: University of North Carolina Press, 1993.

Fussell, Betty. *The Story of Corn.* New York: Alfred A. Knopf, 1994.

Hardeman, Nicholas P. *Shucks, Shocks, and Hominy Blocks: Corn as a Way of Life in Pioneer America.* Baton Rouge: Louisiana State University Press, 1981.

Leslie, Eliza. *Directions for Cookery in Its Various Branches.* Philadelphia: Carey and Hart, 1837.

Mariani, John F. *The Encyclopedia of American Food and Drink.* New York: Lebhar-Friedman Books, 1999.

Marks, Celia. "Where Corn Is as High as an Elephant's Eye." *Come into My Kitchen*, August 2000. Accessed June 16, 2007, from www.casa-chia.org/Cooking/CMAug00.html.

YELLOW HICKORY KING SUPPONE (SPOONBREAD) WITH ROASTED HICKORY NUTS

2 cups Yellow Hickory King cornmeal
4 cups water
2 teaspoons sea salt
2 cups whole, nonhomogenized milk
  (with the cream still mixed in)
8 tablespoons hickory nut meats,
  freshly roasted
4 eggs, beaten
4 tablespoons butter, softened

Preheat the oven to 400 degrees F. In a large, heavy saucepan, mix the Yellow Hickory King cornmeal into the water, adding the sea salt to dissolve as you briskly stir the mixture. Bring this batter to a boil, then reduce the heat and simmer for 5 minutes, stirring constantly as the porridge sputters and pops. Remove the saucepan from the heat and very slowly stir in the milk and then the chunks of roasted hickory nuts. Fold in the well-beaten eggs and the softened butter. Mix once again. Pour the batter into a preheated, pregreased baking dish, then place it in the oven to bake for 40 minutes, until golden brown on the top and firm in the middle. Serves 6 to 8 people straight from the dish, with slices of salt-cured country ham as a side dish.

David Cavagnaro

Tennessee Fainting (Myotonic) Goat

The recognition of the Tennessee Fainting goat as a distinctive American breed of livestock reaches back to the early 1880s, according to a reminiscence left by a Dr. H. H. Mayberry of Marshall County, Tennessee. Mayberry recalled how a farmhand from Nova Scotia named John Tinsley brought a buck or billy goat and three "nannies" (does) of this stiff-legged stock with him to the farm of J. M. Porter in central Tennessee. Tinsley briefly worked for Mayberry and eventually sold all four goats to him for the grand sum of thirty-six dollars but, within a year, was never seen again. However, Mayberry began to breed and sell kids from these "nervous goats" throughout Tennessee and Kentucky. In a matter of decades, their legendary progeny were seen far and wide across Cornbread Nation, where they were valued for their high reproductive rates, muscular conformation, and lack of any capacity to scale fences and escape. As their range expanded to Texas, Mississippi, and Alabama, so did the set of names by which they were hailed: Nervous goat, Epileptic goat, Texas Wooden Leg goat, Tennessee Mountain goat, Scared-Stiff goat, and Myotonic goat.

The peculiarity to which most of these names refer is the hallmark trait of this rare breed: a genetic disposition toward congenital myotonia, a recessive trait whose expression is triggered when the goats become startled. In essence, the muscle cells in their legs experience prolonged contractions, which cause them to become rigid and then keel over as if they were fainting. However, the stiffened or fallen goat never loses consciousness. Some simply have rigid limbs for a matter of seconds or minutes before they relax. However, others have been selected and bred for small size and heightened stiffness, for they are then used as novelties featured at "fainting performances."

Further Readings

Christman, Carolyn, J., Phillip Sponenberg, and Donald E. Bixby. *A Rare Breeds Album of American Livestock.* Pittsboro, North Carolina: American Livestock Breeds Conservancy, 1997.

Dohner, Janet Vorwald. *The Encyclopedia of Historic and Endangered Livestock and Poultry Breeds.* New Haven, Connecticut: Yale University Press, 2001.

International Fainting Goat Association website. Accessed June 14, 2007, at www.faintinggoat.com.

Jenkins, Marie M. *Goats, Sheep, and How They Live.* New York: Holiday House, 1978.

Mitcham, Stephanie, and Allison Mitcham. *Meat Goats: Their History, Management and Diseases.* Sumner, Iowa: Crane Creek Publications, 2000.

Myotonic Goat Registry website. Accessed June 16, 2007, at www.myotonicgoatregistry.net.

Parker, Cherry, and Frances Bradsher. *Hand-Me-Down Cookbook.* Durham, North Carolina: Moore Publishing Company, 1969.

Phillip Sponenburg; courtesy American Livestock Breeds Conservancy

All have loins and rear quarters that are thick with muscle tissue, which makes excellent meat.

Although they have scientifically studied this breed since 1904, physiologists continue to unravel how their stocky muscularity is linked to their propensity toward myotonia. Some scientists have hoped that their genetics and physiology might shed light on a similar human affliction known as Thomsen disease, which affects four out of every 100,000 people on the planet.

Putting their novelty and scientific value aside for a moment, Tennessee Fainting goats are almost always alert, good-natured producers of excellent, lean meat. They are, however, a heterogeneous lot, coming in all size classes and colors. They can weigh as little as thirty pounds at maturity or as much as 250 pounds. Their ears are medium sized and sit nearly horizontal from the sides of the head, as do their variably shaped horns. Most display short, smooth coats of varying colors, although some grow shaggy, skirted coats of abundant cashmere in the winter. The does or nannies often bear multicolored kids as twins or triplets every six months. To feed such a brood, the nannies are prodigious in their production of milk.

A fainting goat on R Fainting Farm in Mobile, Alabama. Photographer Sharon Reeves of R Fainting Farm

Although there are several organizations that keep breed registries for fainting or wooden-leg goats, there are fewer than a thousand individuals registered per year in the United States and Canada. The popularity of crossbreeding them with pygmy goats concerns some geneticists because the gene pool of purebreds has not been measurably expanded for some time. They are listed as rare in both Canada and the United States; and rather than merely being treated as a curiosity, they deserve more attention as a historically important meat animal well suited to Cornbread Nation.

The following Fourth of July barbecue recipe is adapted from one passed on by George Pilkinton of McNairy County, Tennessee, some fifty miles west of where the breed was first recognized. The original recipe and commentary by George were included in the collection known as the *Hand-Me-Down Cookbook*. George maintained that the secret to preparing fresh-tasting chevon (goat meat) is in keeping the hide from ever touching the meat of a young buck or doe; he hung the carcass in a cool place for at least a day before quartering it for ease of handling.

TENNESSEE FAINTING GOAT BARBECUE

1 30-pound goat, dressed to provide 15 pounds of chevon
18 Roma paste tomatoes, chopped and simmered into a thick paste
1 pint Scuppernong wine or wine vinegar
3 teaspoons ground cayenne pepper or Tabasco sauce
2 cloves garlic, roasted and minced
4 tablespoons sea salt
2 tablespoons turbinado sugar or sorghum syrup

Dig an 18-inch-deep pit in relatively soft ground and shape the diameter of its opening so that it can hold the meat in a wire rack. Several hours before the barbecue, build a bed of glowing coals by burning red or white oak in a hot fire; just before adding the meat, top the coals with presoaked hickory chips. As the fire is burning down and beginning to smoke with the hickory chips, take a small glass bowl and mix together the the tomato paste, wine, cayenne powder or Tabasco sauce, minced garlic, sea salt, and sugar or molasses. Stir thoroughly, using less wine or vinegar for a thicker basting sauce.

Next, place the quartered meat in the wire rack just above half the coals; keep the other half on the side to add to the core area to keep it from cooling down. Place a bent sheet of tin over the meat without touching it, especially if rain threatens the barbecue. While the quarters are roasting, use a brush to baste each of them with the barbecue sauce every 30 minutes for 4 to 5 hours, or until the meat falls off the bone. Serves 20 to 30 Tennesseans, depending upon how much Scuppernong wine and persimmon beer they have already imbibed.

Early Golden Persimmon

Early on, American persimmons were given a bad rap by Virginian William Strachey, who in 1612 accused the unripe fruit of being "harsh and choakie, and furre in a man's mouth like allam." Perhaps his tirade only ensures more fruit for those of us who know how to choose fully ripened persimmons, which may well have the most sensuous texture and luscious taste of anything ever put here on earth. The Cherokee, Rappahannock, Comanche, and Seminole certainly knew how to select wild persimmons when they were so ripe that their astringency and clawing tannins were at their lowest levels of potency. The traditional peoples of Cornbread and Gumbo Nations not only ate the fruit fresh but whipped it into a custardlike pudding or baked it and then fermented its pulp in hot springwater, brewing it up into a mild beer.

These golden orange, one- to two-inch fruits grow on beautifully symmetrical trees with rounded crowns. A northern, early-ripening race of wild persimmon trees favors deep, rich, somewhat sandy soils from the Atlantic coast of Clambake and Maple Syrup Nations all the way west across Cornbread Nation. A southerly race, with woollier leaves and larger fruits, reaches from the Floridian coast of Gumbo Nation all the way to Kansas, in the heart of Bison Nation.

Curiously, the cultivation and selection of American persimmons did not take hold until the 1880s, when the precursor of the Early Golden was found on a farm outside Alton, Illinois. A large, self-fertile fruit that ripens early in October, the Early Golden is sweet and flavorful, and some are even seedless. Its fruits are typically thick-skinned, with good keeping quality if you can refrain from eating them all immediately. It was historically one of the persimmon varieties grown by Hoosiers in a cottage industry that canned the pulp for national distribution. But even though the progeny of Early Golden remain popular among persimmon producers, this original cultivar seems to have fallen on hard times. It appears that only four nurseries carry it with any frequency anymore, including Nolin River Nut Tree Nursery in Upton, Kentucky; Raintree Nursery in Morton Washington; and Tripple Brook Farm in Southampton, Massachusetts. The following recipe for persimmon pudding, recorded by Beverly Cox, was offered by Lola Lively Burgess, a Choctaw woman who moved from Cornbread Nation to live with her Cherokee husband in Chestnut Nation, not far from Cherokee, North Carolina.

Courtesy Raintree Nursery

Further Readings

Cox, Beverly, and Martin Jacobs. *Spirit of the Harvest: North American Indian Cooking.* New York: Stewart, Tabori & Chang, 1991.

Moerman, Daniel. *Native American Ethnobotany.* Portland, Oregon: Timber Press, 1998.

Reich, Lee. *Uncommon Fruits for Every Garden.* Portland, Oregon: Timber Press, 2004.

Strachey, William. *The Historie of Travaile into Virginia Brittanica.* London: Louis B. Wright and Virginias Freund, 1953. (Originally published in 1612.)

Whealy, Kent, and Joanne Thuente. *Fruit, Nut and Berry Inventory*, 3rd ed. Decorah, Iowa: Seed Savers Exchange, 2001.

CHOCTAW PERSIMMON PUDDING

8 to 12 ripe persimmons (to yield 2 cups pulp)
2 eggs, beaten
1¼ cups fresh buttermilk
2 cups turbinado sugar
¼ cup butter
2 cups unbleached flour
2 drops vanilla extract
½ cup heavy cream, whipped

Over a small bowl, scoop the fresh persimmon pulp from its skin. Discard the seeds and puree the pulp by pressing it through a food mill or colander or putting it in a blender. Set aside and preheat the oven to 375 degrees F. In a larger mixing bowl, combine the beaten eggs with the buttermilk, turbinado sugar, butter, flour, vanilla, and persimmon pulp. Mix thoroughly until this batter is evenly colored. Pour the batter into a shallow 9 × 13 baking dish. Bake in the oven for 30 to 45 minutes or until the top turns an even, golden brown. Cut the persimmon pudding into diamond shapes and serve warm topped with the whipped cream. Serves 8.

Magnum Bonum Apple

This fine Southern apple, often called simply Bonum, originated in Davidson County, North Carolina, where a man named John Kenney (or Kinny) first grew it around 1828. It is thought to have grown as a seedling from the classic old Hall variety, which, according to apple historian Creighton Lee Calhoun, has disappeared from cultivation. (However, Big Horse Creek Farm in North Carolina claims that Hall may have been rediscovered in 2002 by Southern fruit explorer, Tom Brown.) In either case, some of Hall's good qualities may live on in the Magnum Bonum, which was first introduced by the nursery trade in 1856.

Blooming rather late, beginning in midseason, the fruit ripens on vigorous, upright, spreading trees in early September. The apples themselves are oblate and medium to large in size. Their yellow skin is smooth and tender but not easily bruised, and it is often covered with crimson stripes and large pale dots. The flesh can be white but is often stained pink next to the skin. It is firm yet fine textured, mildly subacid, juicy, and aromatic. A good keeper, the Magnum Bonum maintains its qualities in cold storage for up to four months. It is a very good dessert apple. It remains available from only three nurseries.

The following apple tart recipe has been adapted from Vintage Virginia Apples in North Garden, Virginia.

Ron Joyner/Big Horse Creek Farm

MAGNUM BONUM APPLE TART

For the flaky tart shell
2½ cups bleached whole-wheat flour
2 teaspoons sea salt
2 tablespoons sugar
¾ cup cold unsalted butter
3 cups solid vegetable shortening

In a mixing bowl, blend the flour, salt, sugar, chilled butter, and shortening. To this mixture, add ½ cup of ice water, then knead to make a soft dough that lightly holds itself together. Knead the dough two or three more times on a floured board, then divide the dough in half. Shape each half into a disk and then wrap it in plastic to store in the refrigerator until it is chilled. Remove from the refrigerator and roll each disk out onto the floured board until it fits into an 11-inch tart pan. Fit the shell into the pan and chill again. Line with foil and weigh down for several minutes while preheating the oven to 400 degrees F. Bake each shell for 20 to 25 minutes, then set aside to cool.

Tart puree filling
6 Magnum Bonum apples
¾ cup brown turbinado sugar
1 tablespoon bleached whole-wheat flour
1¼ teaspoons freshly ground cinnamon or
  sassafras bark
½ cup toasted bread crumbs
1 tablespoon Meyer lemon juice

While the shell is baking, peel, core, and cut each of the Magnum Bonum apples into 12 even wedges. In a mixing bowl, toss each apple wedge with the other ingredients. Spread on a baking pan with sides, such as a jelly roll pan, and bake in a 375-degree F oven for 20 minutes or until the apple slices are soft enough to mash. Put the apple wedges back into the mixing bowl and mash them with a potato masher or heavy spoon, leaving a few lumps, and then cool. Spoon this puree into the cooled tart shell and smooth the top. This amount of puree should fill the baked shell and come to just below the rim of the tart shell.

Apple topping
2 or 3 Magnum Bonum apples, peeled and cored
1 tablespoon Meyer lemon juice
2 tablespoons unsalted butter, melted
1 tablespoon brown turbinado sugar

Quarter the apples and cut them into slices ⅛ to ¼ inch thick. In a mixing bowl, toss them with the lemon juice and then drizzle half of the melted butter over them. Starting at the edge of the tart shell, arrange the apples in a circle atop the puree. Overlap the slices and continue, laying concentric circles until the tart puree is covered. Drizzle the remaining melted butter over the apples and then sprinkle the turbinado sugar over them as well. Bake the tarts at 375 degrees F for at least 30 minutes or until apples are tender. Serve chilled. Makes two 11-inch tarts.

Further Readings

Burford, Thomas. *Apples: A Catalog of International Varieties*. Monroe, Virginia: Privately published, 2004.

Bussey, Dan. *The Apple in America.* Madison, Wisconsin: privately printed five-volume draft, 2006.

Calhoun, Creighton Lee Jr. *Old Southern Apples.* Blacksburg, Virginia: McDonald & Woodward, 1995.

Whealy, Kent. *Fruit, Nut and Berry Inventory*, 3rd ed. Decorah, Iowa: Seed Savers Exchange, 2001.

Vintage Virginia Apples. "Apple Recipes." Accessed December 11, 2007, on www .vintagevirginiaapples.com/usingapples.htm.

Chickasaw Plum

The Chickasaw plum was among the first fruits to have been domesticated in North America. Nonetheless, its heirloom varieties are today poorly known, rare, difficult to identity, and labeled with a number of misleading names that obscure their primacy among the continent's great fruits. Fortunately, their true origins have recently been rediscovered, like a beautiful hardwood floor beneath layers of tacky linoleum. It is now clear that, in this case, all Americans owe not the Chickasaw but the Creek tribe a debt of gratitude for this mouthwatering plum.

"For their taste and cullour we call them cherries," wrote Jamestown colonist William Strachey about Chickasaw plums in 1608. His traveling companion Captain John Smith likened them to European hedge plums. Georgia gardener William White—who was among the first European settlers to realize their horticultural value—compared them to the Prince's Yellow Gage plum of Europe, noting that they are "either bright red or yellow [and] nearly free of astringency." And by 1890, the Forked Deer Nurseries of Tennessee marketed a Chickasaw plum that was "soft, juicy, of fine quality" under the alias of "Miner"; it had oblong, medium-sized fruit that were purplish red with a fine bloom.

At various places and times in the nineteenth and twentieth centuries, Miner—the very first heirloom selection—was touted under a plethora of other names, including Caddo Chief, Old Hickory, General Jackson, Hinckley, Townsend, and Dodd. Despite compelling evidence that this native plum species was prehistorically selected and cultivated by indigenous farmers of Cornbread Nation, most plant conservationists have naively treated "Chickasaw" plums as highly variable, unimproved fruits of a widespread species that was inherently *wild* rather than domesticated.

But let us crack the history books, go back to the sources, and set the record straight. One of the great historians of plums on this continent, Ulysses P. Hedrick, had already reassembled much of the true story of this plum when he set his pen to paper in 1911. The first clue to its origins had been scribbled down more than a century before Hedrick's own

writing, when William Bartram noted that he had witnessed Indians gathering and eating plums not in the forest, but in old orchardlike stands long ago planted by the Creek Confederacy.

"I never saw it wild in the forest," claimed Bartram in 1793, "but always in old deserted Indian plantations." With this tip, Hedrick inferred that, a century before his time, the first plum selection to be widely propagated by English settlers in Cornbread Nation had come directly from a Creek Indian plantation in Alabama. It was found at such a "plantation" along the Tallapoosa River by a Tennessee soldier, one who went by several names, including William Dodd. Dodd had been serving as a private in the mounted infantry of Captain Joe Calloway, although some have erroneously suggested that he rode under General Andrew Jackson in the civil war that broke out between two factions of the Creek Nation in 1813 and 1814. In any case, the First Regiment of East Tennessee Volunteer Militia regiment and some Cherokees did attack a group of Creek on the November 18, 1813, at the Hillabee villages, about twenty miles from Horseshoe

Bend on the Tallapoosa. As the Tennessee soldiers rode away from the Hillabees, one of them stumbled upon some large fruit bearing on the red, zigzagging branches of plum trees previously tended by the Creek, who had lost the battle.

Not only did the Creek lose the battle, but they lost their prized fruit as well, for a Tennessee soldier took the pits from the largest fruit he could find there and carried them on horseback to Knox County, Tennessee, where he meant to settle into civilian life. He built a cabin and planted the plums in 1814; within a matter of years, they were all the local rage. By that time, however, he had already uprooted himself as well as a few of the young trees from his hedge. After he'd gone, his Tennessee neighbors misremembered his name but did recall that he had ridden with Jackson. They simply began to refer to this special plum as "Old Hickory" or "General Jackson," unaware that the trees had Native American and not European roots to them.

It appears that this Tennessean moved up to Illinois in 1823, where he began to promote the same plums there as well. Once ensconced in the Midwest, he tried to honor one of the brave Indian soldiers who had fought alongside him in Alabama by call-

Edward W. Chester

Edward W. Chester

ing his transplanted saplings "Chickasaw Chief." The name didn't exactly take, for his new neighbors preferred to call the plums by English names such as "Townsend" and "Hinckley." And yet the name that has stuck with this selection more than any other in the nurseryman's literature is "Miner," named for a Mr. Miner who took the saplings up from Illinois to Lancaster, Wisconsin. The name even made it back to Tennessee, where Forked Deer Nurseries picked it up a few decades later. In 1890, Charles Downing obscured the trail even more by claiming that Miner was a cultivar that originated with a Mr. Miner from Lancaster, Pennsylvania, not Wisconsin. By the beginning of the nineteenth century, Miner had become

Further Readings

Bailey, Liberty Hyde. *Sketch of the Evolution of Our Native Fruits.* New York: MacMillan Company, 1898.

Bartram, William. *Travels through North and South Carolina, Georgia, East and West Florida, the Cherokee Country, the Extensive Territories of the Muscogulges or Creek Confederacy, and the Country of the Chactaws.* London: J. Johnson Publishers, 1794.

Downing, Charles. *The Fruits and Fruit Trees of America*, 2nd ed. New York: John Wiley and Sons, 1890.

Hatch, Peter J. *The Fruits and Fruit Trees of Monticello.* Charlottesville: University Press of Virginia, 1998.

Hedrick, Ulysses P. *The Plums of New York.* Albany, New York: J. B. Lyon, 1911.

National Park Service. *Park Species List, Flora.* Horseshoe Bend National Military Park. 2006. Available at www.nps.gov/hobe/naturescience/upload/parkflora.pdf.

Randolph, Mary. *The Virginia Housewife*, with historic notes and commentaries by Karen Hess. Columbia: University of South Carolina Press, 1984. (Originally published in 1819.)

Strachey, William. *The Historie of Travaile into Virginia Brittanica.* London: The Hakluyt Society, 1953. (Originally published in 1612.)

Sultzman, Lee. "Chickasaw History," 1999. Available at www.tolatsga.org/chick.html.

White, William. *Gardening for the South.* New York: B. F. Johnson Publishing, 1859.

Edward W. Chester

one of the most popular plums in the United States and was offered by nurseries from coast to coast.

As Peter Hatch has astutely observed, plums such as the Chickasaw, Potawatomi, and Ogeechee were adapted to conditions in which European cultivars failed miserably: The European transplants did well along the temperate coast of the mid-Atlantic, but "their inability to thrive in other parts of North America left an opening for the development and breeding of native plums."

Yet the misnamed fruit that Hedrick dryly gave "the distinction of being the first of the native plums to be named in America" ultimately lost not only its identity but its market niche as well. Of roughly a dozen named (or misnamed) selections of the native species known as the Chickasaw plum today, none are currently marketed as distinctive cultivars in nursery catalogs. Chickasaw plums are now available in retail trade only from the Forest Farm Nursery in Oregon, the Woodlanders in South Carolina, the

Sandusky Valley Nursery in Ohio, and the Nature Hills Nursery in Nebraska. In modern horticultural literature, they are treated more like thorny native shrubs suited to restoring wildlife habitats than as delectable fruit worthy of human consumption.

That is too bad, for as Liberty Hyde Bailey once noted, "the spotted, translucent fruit [contain] flesh which is soft, juicy, and more or less stringy." Such vinous, mildly acidic pulp is ideally suited to the making of tart, highly aromatic preserves and jellies.

While the nursery trade has apparently lost the Chickasaw plum selections that were widely propagated in the nineteenth century, the original source material for them may have survived, relatively unnoticed, back in its home ground along the Tallapoosa River. In 2004, field botanists collecting plants for a flora of the Horseshoe Bend National Military Park in Alabama found not one but seven species of wild plums and cherries surviving near the Creek's

Tohopeka village archaeological site; one of these they identified as the Chickasaw plum. However, the presence of other cross-compatible *Prunus* species around Horseshoe Bend raises the botanical question of whether the large fruits that the Tennessean removed from the site could have been "natural" hybrids of two native plum species. For at least a century, botanists have periodically complained that the traits of cultivated Chickasaw plum selections don't match well with those of the original description of the species *Prunus angustifolia.* Perhaps the Creek were more accomplished horticulturalists than anyone has given them credit for.

The following recipe for plums in brandy is adapted from the first full-blown American cookbook published in the United States, Mary Randolph's *The Virginia Housewife,* written in 1819.

CHICKASAW PLUMS IN WILD PLUM BRANDY OR BOURBON

1 pound Chickasaw plums, pitted
½ pound turbinado sugar
water, enough to cover the fruit in a pot
1 cup Wild Plum Brandy from Stringer's
　Orchard, or Kentucky bourbon

Select a little more than a pound of barely ripened, blemish-free plums, then wash them and remove their pits. Put them aside. In a cast-iron cooking pot combine the turbinado sugar and enough water as will cover the fruit once it is added. Boil the sugar in the pot until it is syrupy, skimming off any impurities. Reduce the heat and then add the plums, allowing them to stew in the syrup for 5 to 6 minutes. Next, ladle the fruit into a large serving dish to cool, draining off the syrup. Bring the syrup to a boil once more and then simmer until its volume is reduced by half. When the Chickasaw plums have fully cooled to room temperature, put them in widemouthed jars and cover them with equal amounts of the thickened syrup and plum brandy or Kentucky bourbon.

Nickajack Apple

Said to have originated where Cherokees lived along Nickajack Creek in Macon County, North Carolina, this heirloom apple likely dates back to the late 1700s. Silas McDowell of Franklin, North Carolina, first promoted it under the name of Nickajack in 1853, but this legendary apple has also been called Carolina Spice, Graham's Red Warrior, Spotted Buck, Summerour, Winter Horse, Winter Rose, and World's Wonder.

A Colonel Summerour of Lincoln County, North Carolina, once actively disseminated this variety throughout Chestnut and Cornbread Nations, for it was among the few available to him that had the ability to reproduce "true to type" from seed. (Apples in general almost never resemble their parents when grown from seed, because of extensive cross-pollination and natural hybridization.)

Nickajack apples grow on large, spreading, upright trees that bear well year after year, especially on the red clay soils of Virginia and the Carolinas. The trees have a peculiar trait to their wood, described by Downing in 1878: ". . . on branches two, three or four years old, there are woody knobs or warts of various sizes, which, when cut from the branch, are found to contain kernels entirely detached from the grain of the wood."

The large fruit has a rather rectangular shape, tapering to a truncate cone. Its glossy, greenish-yellow skin is thick and tough; it can be blushed, streaked, striped, or splashed with orange-reds and carmines as well as dotted with white lenticels. At maturity, the Nickajack apple carries a thin bloom that gives it a dull sheen. The crisp, creamy white flesh of a Nickajack is very firm and coarse-grained; as it ripens, its flavor changes from mildly subacid to unmistakably aromatic. A late ripener, it maintains good quality both for home kitchen use and for sales at farmers' markets over many months.

Unfortunately, it has been commercially available from less than a handful of nurseries, including Calhoun's, Edible Forest, Lawson's, and Orchard Lane.

Although many folks in Chestnut and Cornbread Nations prefer hard cider to sweet, this historic recipe for mulled sweet cider comes to us via William Woys Weaver's research from an early ethnic cookbook published around 1848.

Further Readings

Burford, Thomas. *Apples: A Catalog of International Varieties*. Monroe, Virginia: privately published, 2004.

Bussey, Dan. *The Apple in America*. Madison, Wisconsin: privately printed five-volume draft, 2006.

Weaver, William Woys. *The Sauerkraut Yankee: Pennsylvania Dutch Foods and Foodways.* Mechanicsburg, Pennsylvania: Stackpole Books, 2002.

Whealy, Kent, and Joanne Thuente. *Fruit, Nut and Berry Inventory*, 3rd ed. Decorah, Iowa: Seed Savers Exchange, 2001.

MULLED NICKAJACK APPLE CIDER

1 quart sweet cider made from Nickajack apples
12 cloves
6 eggs from free-ranging hens
1 cup sugar
2 teaspoons freshly grated nutmeg and mace

Pour a quart of cider into a large cooking pot, and toss in the cloves as you bring it to a boil. While it is approaching the boiling point, beat the eggs in a large jug, then pour the sugar into the jug and beat again. Just as the cider begins to boil, remove it from the heat and pour it over the beaten eggs and sugar. Cork the jug, and shake it until the sugar and eggs are absorbed into the cider. Pour this mulled cider back and forth between two jugs of the same size until a fine foam develops. Once the cider is prepared, pour it warm into mugs, and grate the nutmeg and mace over it.

Ron Joyner/Big Horse Creek Farm

Mulefoot Hog

Over the long haul, perhaps it is no great honor to be the rarest breed of swine in North America. Critically endangered, the Mulefoot hog survives as a breed with fewer than 150 purebred individuals being cared for today. That is a far cry from its status nearly a century ago, when, in 1910, some 235 breeders produced Mulefoot hogs in twenty-two different states. One thing is for certain, however: The reason for such a precipitous decline has nothing to do with the quality of the Mulefoot's pork, which is still considered some of the finest ever produced in America. For many decades, Mulefoots were legendary as the highest-quality "ham hogs" ever produced in Cornbread Nation, and they were fattened on acorns to hefty weights before being taken to be butchered, smoked, or salt cured.

The quality of its pork, as well as its build, suggests that this breed descended from the Spanish *pata negra* hogs that were first shipped to the Americas in the 1500s. Once introduced by Spanish explorers to the Gulf Coast or Mexico, the Mulefoot spread northward, making it as far north as the Ohio River Valley. Nevertheless, its history remained obscure until about 1900, when a resurgence of interest began to take place.

Many of the farmers who then sought out the Mulefoot were simply curious—as were Aristotle and Darwin before them—that any hogs could have solid, noncloven hooves like a mule. In fact, this single gene mutation occasionally crops up in a variety of breeds around the world, but the American Mulefoot lineage is the only one where this trait consistently appears along with other diagnostic characters. The Mulefoot's floppy ears are always pricked forward, and the vast majority of them have soft, solid black coats. Historically nicknamed the Ozark hog, the 250- to 400-pound sows have gentle dispositions and typically birth four to six piglets per litter, while the boars reach 400 to 600 pounds in less than two years after birth. They are truly hardy, for the herds survived for centuries under altogether wild conditions on the islands in the Mississippi River and its tributaries.

In 1910, this uniquely American heritage breed had already become so popular that the National Mulefoot Hog Record Association was established in Indianapolis, Indiana. At about this same time, they were introduced to Canada, but no herd book or pedigree records were maintained there. By 1912, however, when F. D. Coburn first described them in his classic *Swine in America,* Mulefoot hogs could be found in Arkansas, Missouri, Iowa, Indiana, and the remote farming valleys of the Southwest and adjacent Mexico. Yet in the years leading up to World War II, pork production in the United States began to shift toward just a few breeds that gained weight at astonishing rates, especially when they were corn-fed in pens. Breeds better adapted to free-range foraging fell by the wayside, and the Mulefoot was one of them.

Crystal, a mulefoot sow on Hillspring Farm in Blanchardville, Wisconsin. Mike Sula, *Chicago Reader*

Further Readings

American Livestock Breeds Conservancy. "Mulefoot Hog." www.albc-usa.org/cpl/mulefoot.html.

Christman, Carolyn J., D. Phillip Sponenberg, and Donald E. Bixby. *A Rare Breeds Album of American Livestock*. Pittsboro, North Carolina: American Livestock Breeds Conservancy, 1997.

Coburn, Foster Dwight. *Swine in America.* New York: Orange Judd, 1912.

Dohner, Janet Vorwild. *The Encyclopedia of Historic and Endangered Livestock and Poultry Breeds.* New Haven, Connecticut: Yale University Press, 2001.

Emsinger, M. Eugene. *Swine Science.* Danville, Illinois: Interstate Publishers, 2001.

Whealy, Kent, and Joanne Thuente. *Fruit, Nut and Berry Inventory*, 3rd ed. Decorah, Iowa: Seed Savers Exchange, 2001.

SMOKED AND BRAISED MULEFOOT HOG SHOULDER WITH SWEET PEPPERS, PROSCIUTTO, AND LACINATO KALE

1 2-pound pork shoulder roast, boned and netted (your butcher will do this for you)

¼ cup each salt and brown sugar, mixed with 2 tablespoons cracked black pepper

3 cups julienned sweet bell peppers, preferably of many colors

¼ cup very thinly sliced garlic cloves

1 large yellow onion, julienned

2 carrots, diced

2 stalks celery, diced

2 bay leaves

8 paper-thin slices prosciutto

8 large leaves Lacinato (a.k.a. Black Tuscan or "dinosaur") kale

2 quarts fresh chicken stock (or to cover), well seasoned

Two days in advance of the meal, rub the pork shoulder with the salt, brown sugar, and pepper, and refrigerate within a sealed plastic bag in a large pan overnight. One day in advance, slow-smoke the shoulder over hickory or cherry wood, at a temperature of 225 degrees F for 5 to 7 hours or until the crust is very dark and the internal temperature is about 160 degrees. Remove the roast from the heat, cool to room temperature, and refrigerate overnight.

On the feast day, mix the peppers, garlic, onions, carrots, celery, and bay leaves and place them in the bottom of a large, deep casserole or other ovenproof pan that is at least 5 inches deep. Preheat the oven to 350 degrees F and cut the pork into preferred portion size (roughly 6 to 9 ounces, depending on how hungry your guests will be). Wrap each piece of smoked pork roast with a slice of prosciutto and a leaf of kale. Place each piece seam-side down on the bed of vegetables in the casserole.

Next, add the chicken stock, enough to just cover the pork. Add a small amount of water or white wine if you're a little short of liquid. Cover the casserole tightly with a lid or with parchment and foil. Braise for 3 hours, then remove and allow to rest for 30 minutes. Serve over risotto or polenta. Makes 4 to 6 servings.

If there is a hero to this story, it is Mr. R. M. Holliday, who in 1964 gathered together Mulefoot stock from the last remaining breeders to establish what became the "conservation herd" from which all current hogs of this breed are descended. Mulefoots were not new to Mr. Holliday; during his boyhood, his kin and his neighbors put herds of this breed out on small islands not far from the muddy confluence of the Missouri and Mississippi rivers. There they foraged on their own throughout the summer before being rounded up in the fall, when some went off to slaughter. But as their numbers thinned and the last Mulefoot registry folded, Mr. Holliday had the foresight to create a herd large enough to stave off the probability of in-breeding. He made a sanctuary for all known Mulefoots remaining in the United States just above the Mississippi River, in Louisiana, Missouri, a farm town also famous for the heirloom fruits that have been shipped out by the Stark Brothers Nursery to all parts of the continent for well over a century.

Year after year for three decades, Mr. Holliday kept up a strong and consistent selection program to maintain a healthy Mulefoot herd. Then, in the fall of 1993, Mr. Holliday was contacted by Mark Fields, a seasoned conservationist of poultry breeds and heirloom seeds. Although at first wary of a stranger's interest in his hogs, Mr. Holliday agreed after several conversations to let Mark come over to see his Mulefoots. Mark's sincerity must have won Holliday's confidence, for the old man not only shared his oral history of the breed but agreed to sell a small breeding group of Mulefoots for the first time in seventeen years. Mark gained enough knowledge from Mr. Holliday to reactivate the Mulefoot hog registry for the first time in two decades. With the assistance of the American Livestock Breeds Conservancy and Seed Savers Exchange, Mark purchased additional stock from Mr. Holliday and located several growers in Iowa who were willing to periodically exchange boars and maintain pure, registered herds. Today, there is one large herd maintained by the Maveric Heritage Ranch, and more smaller-scale breeders are becoming engaged with Mulefoots every decade. Two breed associations—the American Mulefoot Hog Association and Registry run out of Tekonsha, Michigan, and the Mulefoot Pig Association of Strawberry Point, Iowa—have been collaborating with the American Livestock Breeds Conservancy to increase the numbers in this breed.

Chefs have already expressed their interest in paying worthy prices for Mulefoot pork once this breed has recovered to the point that its meat can be marketed on a regular basis once again. When the Mulefoot hog was nominated for the Slow Food Ark of Taste, Chef Kurt Friese of Devotay restaurant in Iowa City, Iowa, went "whole hog" and prepared the best pork that several judges had ever tasted. The recipe above was generously contributed by Chef Friese.

Southern Queen Yam

Perhaps the oldest and most unusual of all of America's "yams," the Southern Queen is a sweet potato with smooth, creamy skin and dry, snow-white flesh within. Variants of this same vegetatively propagated tuber also go by the names of Choker, White, Poplar Root, White Bunch, and Triumph. Like other sweet potatoes, they typically produce dark green leaves on pinkish-red stems that vigorously vine across the ground. The tubers themselves reach a foot in length and three inches in width, rendering a mashable flesh that is both sweet and dry. Carrotlike tuberous offshoots begin to accumulate under the leafy skirts of the mother plant in July, and the entire yield is typically ready for harvest around 100 to 120 days after planting.

Unlike true yams (genus *Dioscorea*), which hail from Africa, Asia, and Australia, sweet potatoes *(Ipomoea batatas)* are authentically American and may even have been grown in Gumbo Nation prehistorically, for de Soto found them being eaten in what we now call Louisiana and Georgia in 1540. Once in America, African slaves began to liken the newly found sweet potatoes to their yams back home; the word *yam* may be derived from the Senegalese *nyami*, the Vai *djambi,* or the Gullah term *njam.* European colonists were growing them in Virginia by 1648, and the term *yam* was first recorded in American print in 1676. In Cornbread and Gumbo Nations, the sweet tuber also became known as Carolina Potato, Dolley, Tuckahoc, or Hog Potato. The Southern Queen is undoubtedly one of the oldest cultivars in North America but has been called by so many names through place and time that its historic roots are difficult to trace.

As an American food, sweet potatoes have always retained a certain resilient popularity, for as Ralph Ellison wrote in *Invisible Man:* "Yes, and we'd loved them candied, or baked in a cobbler, deep-fat fried in a pocket of dough, or roasted with pork and glazed with the well-browned fat; had chewed them raw— yams and years ago."

Nevertheless, the ubiquity of the Southern Queen in Gumbo Nation may have peaked between 1865 and 1890, when Richard Fortscher's nursery in New Orleans listed it as its top pick among all yams and sweet potatoes of its era. Today, only the Sand Hill Preservation Center in Iowa offers this sweet potato under the name of Southern Queen, but six other mail-order catalogs may offer its variants under an assortment of aliases from time to time. The following recipe is adapted from Edna Lewis, who grew up in the small farming community of Freetown, Virginia.

Further Readings

Davidson, Alan. *The Oxford Companion to Food*. New York: Oxford University Press, 1999.

Ellison, Ralph. *Invisible Man*. New York: Random House, 1952.

Fortscher, Richard. *Almanac and Garden Manual for the Southern States*. New Orleans: George Muller Printer, 1890.

Lewis, Edna. 1988. *In Pursuit of Flavor*. Charlottesville: University Press of Virginia, 1988.

Maggon, C. A., and C. W. Culpepper. "A Study of Sweet Potato Varieties, with Special Reference to Their Canning Quality." *Technical Bulletin 1041.* Washington, D.C.: U.S. Department of Agriculture, 1922.

Mariani, John. *The Encyclopedia of American Food and Drink*. New York: Lebhar-Friedman Books, 1999.

BAKED SOUTHERN QUEEN YAMS FLAVORED WITH FRESH LEMON JUICE

3 medium Southern Queen yams (about 2½ pounds)

1 cup turbinado sugar

½ teaspoon freshly grated nutmeg

1 3-inch strip freshly grated Meyer lemon zest (the outer yellow portion of the peel)

¼ teaspoon sea salt

1½ cups water

3 tablespoons unsalted butter

2 tablespoons freshly squeezed Meyer lemon juice

Rinse the freshly harvested sweet potatoes under warm running water and then place them in a large pot of boiling water. Reduce the heat so that they simmer for about half an hour or until the sweet potatoes are tender but not mushy. After draining off the water, place them aside and let them cool in the pot for 15 minutes.

Next, take a large enamel saucepan and combine the sugar, nutmeg, lemon zest, and salt within it. Add the water, place on medium-low heat, and simmer for 10 minutes. Add the butter and, once it is melted, stir it into the syrupy mixture.

Next, stir in the lemon juice. Remove this syrup from direct heat but do not let it completely cool to room temperature.

Once the sweet potatoes are cool to the touch, peel them and then slice them into half-inch-thick rounds. Preheat the oven to 425 degrees F. Butter a shallow glass baking dish and lay the rounds in a single layer that covers the bottom of the dish. Stir the still-warm syrup with a wooden spoon, then pour it over the sweet potatoes. Bake the syrup-laden sweet potatoes for 30 minutes or until bubbling hot. Serve immediately.

David Cavagnaro

Tennessee Sweet Potato Cushaw Squash

Topped by a thick stem known as a corky peduncle, this teardrop-shaped squash packs ten to fifteen pounds of thick, dry, flavorful, fine-grained, bake-able flesh within it. Once the stringiness around the plump, glossy white seeds is removed, the flesh is nearly translucent, though tinged with a golden ocher hue. Its smooth, thick skin is wildly variable and can be the color of ivory, sienna, ruddy orange, or mustard yellow with dull green stripes. The name *cushaw* is usually reserved for squashes of the species *Curcurbita argyrosperma* and is derived from *coscushaw,* an Algonquian word historically used from the Carolinas through Virginia. It had made its way into print as an Americanized English term by 1580. Some claim that it is the same as the "Puritan squash" that descendants of the Pilgrims cultivated for centuries around Plymouth Colony. And yet this heirloom also traces its ancestry back to prehistoric eras in both Gumbo and Chile Pepper Nations.

The mainstream American culinary use of this squash, under its various aliases, was well established by 1847 but may have peaked soon after 1883, when W. Atlee Burpee first introduced it into commer-cial seed trade under the name of Tennessee Sweet Potato. Truck farmers relied heavily on this multipur-pose heirloom, reminding their clients that its flow-ers, immature fruits, and seeds were just as edible as the mature pear-shaped pumpkins themselves. In the subtropical climes of Gumbo Nation, cushaw plants have some place-based adaptations that may be valued even more than the flavor and texture of the squashes. Their stems have a measure of resis-tance against the pesky squash vine borer, for the vines easily root at the nodes. This adaptation allows most of the plant to survive even when one length of the vine becomes infested with larvae, withers, and dies. Few (if any) other squashes and pumpkins can claim this survival mechanism.

For such a hardy and versatile squash, it may seem surprising that its popularity has recently waned, so much so that Horus Botanicals and Seed Dreams may be the only two commercial seed catalogs that regularly offer it anymore. Due to this decline in the marketplace, it has recently been boarded onto the Slow Food Ark of Taste. Glenn Drowns of Sand Hill Preservation Center regularly ensures that its seed stock is replenished and shared with others through the Seed Savers Exchange. Fortunately, this cushaw can still be found at some roadside farmstands scattered along the rural routes running parallel to the Mississippi River, from southern Tennessee all the way to New Orleans. Within this stretch of Gumbo Nation, cushaw squashes keep so well with-out refrigeration that their pies remain traditional holiday fare from Thanksgiving to the New Year's holiday.

Well into the early spring, they are also used for another favorite cold-weather dish served at Southern plantations and Cajun and Cracker hunt-ing camps: Cushaw squash is simply baked as a side dish to go with grilled game, such as quail and venison. As Francis Chauvin told Lolis Eric Elie at the Red Stick Market in Baton Rouge, "My husband's mother was from Napoleonville. She would cook cushaw like a sweet potato dish during the holidays."

Sara Roahen

FRANCIS CHAUVIN'S CUSHAW PIE

1 Tennessee Sweet Potato cushaw, deseeded, cut into 2 to 4 pieces
¾ cup turbinado sugar
¼ teaspoon sea salt
1 tablespoon butter, melted
1 tablespoon pumpkin pie spice (a mixture of ground nutmeg, cloves, and cinnamon)
3 eggs from free-ranging chickens
1½ cups heavy whipping cream
1 unbaked deep-dish 10-inch pie crust

Bake the boatlike pieces of the cushaw on a metal pan in an oven set at 350 degrees F for 1½ hours or until tender when tested with a fork. Let cool for a few minutes and then peel off the thick skin and dispose of it. Next, mash the baked squash into a pulp, using either a food processor or a wooden bowl and mallet. In a mixing bowl, combine 1 heaping cupful of the cushaw pulp with the sugar, salt, melted butter, and pumpkin pie spices. Stir thoroughly until pureed. Add the eggs to the bowl and, with an electric mixer, beat the eggs into the puree. Do the same with the cream, until the consistency of this filling is smooth. Pour the pureed filling into an unbaked pie crust and then place the pie into an oven that has been preheated to 350 degrees F. Bake for an hour to an hour and a half or until the fill-ing has set up well enough that a toothpick inserted into it comes out clean.

Chauvin, who grew up as the daughter of a truck farmer in Lake Charles, has come to prefer Tennessee Sweet Potato cushaws for the thousands of pies she sells at Louisiana farmers' markets every year. To prepare pies of quality from the cushaw, Francis Chauvin cautions, "you don't boil them. If you boil them, they'll be full of water. You bake them."

David Cavagnaro

Further Readings

Angers, W. Thomas. *Cajun Cuisine.* Lafayette, Louisiana: Beau Bayou Publishing, 1985.

Elie, Lolis Eric. "Good Gourd Almighty: For This Pumpkin Pie Maker, Nothing Beats a Cushaw." *The Times-Picayune,* November 16, 2006. Accessed October 25, 2007, from www.nolacom/timespic/stories/index.ssf.

Goldman, Amy. *The Compleat Squash: A Passionate Grower's Guide.* New York: Artisan Books, 2004.

Mariani, John. *The Encyclopedia of American Food & Drink.* New York: Lebhar-Friedman Books, 1999.

Tapley, William T., Walter D. Enzie, and Glen P. Van Eseltine. "The Cucurbits." *The Vegetables of New York 1, part 4.* Albany: J. B. Lyon, 1937.

Whealy, Kent, and Joanne Thuente. *Garden Seed Inventory,* 6th ed. Decorah, Iowa: Seed Savers Exchange, 2004.

Honey Drip Cane Sorghum

Honey Drip sorghum is one of the few American foods originating in Africa that can be readily traced back to its cultural and geographic birthing grounds. It appears that it was brought from South Africa to North America in 1857 by an enigmatic English trader named Leonard Wray. Wray had ventured into Natal, the Zulu-speaking region that is now a province of South Africa, and had purchased seed of a number of distinctive varieties of "kaffir" or "imphee" sorghum. One variety, however, literally stood out above the rest, for it was the tallest and the sweetest of stalk; the Zulu called it *vimbischuapa*.

When Wray passed the Morocco-red seed on to another agricultural entrepreneur named Hedges, it was clear that he was astounded by its productivity: "This is the largest in size and the tallest of the whole [batch], while it is full of juice and very sweet . . . It grows to a height of ten to fifteen feet."

When they put the stalks into a rudimentary mill, 60 percent of the total weight of the stalks was expressed as juice. As Hedges later wrote, "The sugar it yielded was fully equal to the best cane sugar of the West Indies." By 1860, it was being used to press sorghum syrup, which remained an important sweetener throughout the latter half of the nineteenth century.

Hedges dubbed Wray's extraordinary find Honey Drip Sorgo, but as its production took root from South Carolina and Georgia to New Mexico and Texas, the makers of blackstrap molasses gave it other, more localized names. It became known as Texas Honey in the West and Honduran in the Midwest; a half-dozen other nicknames cropped up as well. By 1880, the USDA was actively promoting the late-maturing, stout stalks of this heirloom variety as the premier source of sorghum syrup in at least nine states in Gumbo, Cornbread, and Chile Pepper Nations. Over the following forty years, however, refined cane sugar from Florida, Cuba, and Central America became so accessible and cheap that the culinary use of sorghum syrup began to decline. Monkey rum—a distilled spirit made from sorghum syrup—has also become hard to find in the hills of the Carolinas.

It is therefore not surprising, as Kent Whealy of

Robert Soreng, USDA-NRCS PLANTS Database

Exhibition of pressing sorghum for syrup. Jeremiah C. Gettle/Baker Creek Farm

HONEY DRIP SORGHUM SYRUP CANDY

1 quart syrup made from Honey Drip cane sorghum
¼ pound brown sugar or Tupelo honey
½ pound unsalted butter
2 tablespoons freshly grated Meyer lemon zest (the outer yellow portion of the peel)

In a large cast-iron pot with a lid, bring the syrup to a boil and then add the brown sugar or tupelo honey. When those two ingredients are thoroughly blended into a thick syrup, add the butter. Boil for up to 1 hour, stirring constantly with a wooden spoon. Just before you take it off the heat, add the lemon zest. Quickly pour out onto a series of buttered enamel-covered plates. When slightly cooled, pick up small globs with a wooden spoon and then pull the mass lengthwise until it stretches into a strip and turns white.

It is therefore not surprising, as Kent Whealy of the Seed Savers Exchange recently lamented, that "this very old sweet sorghum has become quite rare." For most of the last two decades, only one mail-order seed catalog offered its red-hulled seeds to the public. Today, Baker Creek and Horus Botanicals in Arkansas are the only commercial suppliers, and only two Seed Savers Exchange members consistently sow it year after year.

As a corollary to the loss of great cane sorghum heirlooms, the tradition of making sorghum syrup has declined in the Midwest and South. As such, Slow Food USA has listed sorghum syrup on the Ark of Taste, recognizing that the artisanal tradition of pressing and boiling down cane sorghum sugars is not being passed on to younger generations. The following recipe for sorghum syrup candy comes from Rose P. Ravenel, who was born in 1850 and lived much of her life in the Carolina low country. She apparently learned how to prepare this particular treat from African-American women at Farmfield in St. Andrew's Parish in 1865.

Further Readings

Harrigan, Elizabeth Ravenel. *Charleston Recollections and Receipts: Rose P. Ravenel's Cookbook.* Columbia: University of South Carolina Press, 1983.

Hedges, I. A. *Sorgo, or the Northern Sugar Plant.* Cincinnati: Applegate and Company, 1863.

Mariani, John F. *The Encyclopedia of American Food and Drink.* New York: Lebhar-Friedman Books, 1999.

Whealy, Kent, and Joanne Thuente. *Garden Seed Inventory,* 6th ed. Decorah, Iowa: Seed Savers Exchange, 2004.

Vinall, H. N., J. C. Stephens, and J. H. Martin. "Identification, History and Distribution of Common Sorghum Varieties." *Technical Bulletin 506.* Washington, D.C.: U.S. Department of Agriculture, 1936.

CRABCAKE NATION

With its "vortex" situated in the tidal waters of the great Chesapeake Bay—the largest estuary on the East Coast—Crabcake Nation was formerly one of the most productive and diverse food-producing ecosystems in the Americas. Its watermen regularly harvested tons of crabs, bay clams, oysters, eels, and other fish from their skipjacks, pungies, and bug-eyed boats. Its chefs in crab houses, smokehouses, and oyster bars dowsed these seafoods with sauces conjured up from Old Bay seasonings, horseradish, molasses, fish peppers, and mace. The blue crab for which this nation is named provides sweet, delicious white meat for the signature dish, Maryland crabcakes. While blue crabs are in decline in many places, from Maryland clear down to Florida, they are increasing in other bays, functioning as an effective predator of immature clams and scallops. The watermen of Tangier Island and other fishing villages have recently taken the lead in community-based conservation efforts, but much remains to be done. Inland, this region is extremely rich in fruit tree varieties, African-derived grains and root crops, and fish. Nevertheless, more than 45 foods of the Crabcake Nation remain at risk.

Blue Crab of Chesapeake Bay

The first recipe for some concoction resembling a sautéed crabcake, a fried crab patty, or a crab coquette was published in 1685 and made its way to Crabcake Nation not long after that. It had first been put down on paper a quarter century earlier, in 1660, when a seventy-two-year-old chef named Robert May suggested to his readers that to fry crabs, one should:

> Take the meat out of the great claws being first boiled, flour and fry them and take the meat out of the body, strain half of it for sauce, and the other half to fry, and mix it with grated bread, almond paste, nutmeg, salt, and yolks of eggs, fry in clarified butter, being first dipped in batter, put in a spoonful at a time; then make sauce with wine-vinegar, butter, or juyce of orange, and grated nutmeg, beat up the butter thick, and put some of the meat that was strained into the sauce, warm it and put it in a clean dish, lay the meat on the sauce, slices of orange over all, and run it over with beaten butter, fryed parsley, round the dish brim, and the little legs round the meat.

Although the term *crabcake* did not reach print in America until 1930, it is clear that some chefs in Baltimore's crab joints, hackeries, and houses had been improvising around May's celebrated recipe for some time. In the years immediately following World War II, the crab houses on the shores of Chesapeake Bay had become world famous, and backyard crab feasts around Baltimore had a cult following. As Baltimore-born Chef John Shields recalls, the blue crabs of that era were legendary:

> Back in '48 all the crabs were at least ten inches across and heavy as horses . . . Your Uncle Elmer could pick a crab clean as a whistle with one hand, while drinking down a mug of beer with the other without taking a breath . . .

Crab and oyster houses scattered along the Bay shores and in nearby cities were once *the* places to be, from Maryland through Washington, D.C., and down through northeastern Virginia. Decades ago, the great American writer H. L. Mencken called the Bay "an immense protein factory," for its shallow waters harbored innumerable "prime blue crabs . . . with snow-white meat almost as firm as soap." The melting taste and texture of this crab meat is, by nearly all accounts, far better than any soap! It is buttery and satiny and sweet. Whether cracking open the cobalt-blue claws of males or the bright-orange claws of females, the historic residents of Crabcake Nation had much to celebrate and to savor.

Yet by the beginning of the new millennium, the signature seafood of Chesapeake Bay had definitely seen better days. Today, the blue crab population of Chesapeake Bay is only a quarter of what it was in 1990, and the *best* harvest in recent years was some 60 million pounds, one-fifth less than the long-running average. Perhaps more disconcerting is that while a few dozen boats used to haul in 75 to 100 million tons of crabs per year, today several hundred boats are struggling to rip a few tons of buried crabs out of the Bay's silty beds by dragging iron-toothed dredges across the estuary's floor. They collectively harvest far fewer crabs today, even though their search costs a hundred times more (economically and ecologically) than those crabbing operations did a half century ago.

"There are warning signs out there that the population is being over-fished," concludes scientist William

A watermen transfers his catch to a buyer on another boat at Tangier Island in 1951. Constance Stuart Larrabee, collection of Chesapeake Bay Maritime Museum

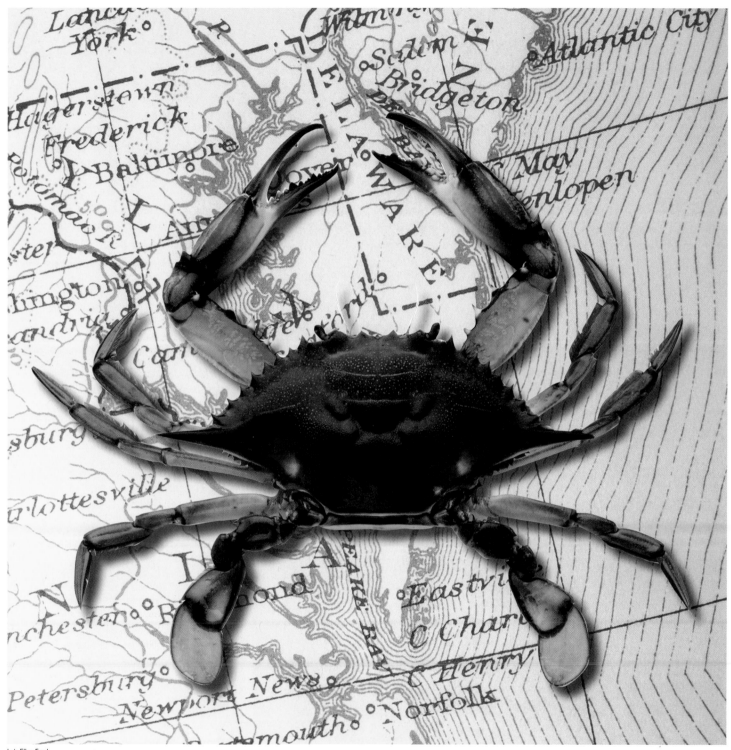

Lois Ellen Frank

The Chesapeake Bay

Goldsborough of the Chesapeake Bay Foundation, referring to the finding that in some years crabbers capture 92 percent of all legal-sized crabs available in the Bay waters. While overharvesting cannot be seen as the cause of declines in Delaware Bay one hundred miles to the north, signs of overharvesting are abundant as far south as Tampa Bay, Florida. In just five years—between 1999 and 2003—blue crab catches along the entire Atlantic coast of North America declined some 23 percent.

These declines have elicited expressions of both worry and frustration among seafood restaurant chefs and managers. Nicholas Cibel of the Dancing Crab in Washington, D.C., is one of those who, by 1995, was seeing the danger signs that indicated

Further Readings

Carson, Dale. *New Native American Cooking.* New York: Random House, 1996.

Forum on Religion and Ecology. "Christian Engaged Projects: Tangier Watermen's Stewardship for the Cheasapeake (TaSC)." Accessed October 24, 2007, from www.environment.harvard.edu/religion/religion/christianity/projects/tangier.html.

Kahn, Desmond M., and Thomas E. Heiser. "Abundance, Dynamics and Mortality of Delaware Bay Stock of Blue Crabs, *Callinectes sapidus.*" *Journal of Shellfisheries Research,* January 2005.

LaFray-Young, Joyce, Susan Shepard, and Laura DeSalvo. *The Underwater Gourmet.* St. Petersburg, Florida: LaFray Publishing, 1983.

Lipske, Michael. "Getting to Know You—Blue Crabs." *National Wildlife.* October–November, 1995. Accessed June 18, 2007, from www.nwf.org/nationalwildlife/article.cfm?issueID=50&articleID=633.

Mitrano, Erica. "Report Says Bay Health Grave, Declining." *Southern Maryland Newspapers,* June 8, 2007. Accessed June 18, 2007, from www.somdnews.com/stories/060807/rectop160125_32106.shtml.

Pittman, Craig. "Blue Crabs Melt Away." *St. Petersburg Times,* April 30, 2003. Accessed June 18, 2007, from www.sptimes.com/2003/04/20/TampaBay/Blue_crabs_melt_away.shtml.

Shields, John. *The Chesapeake Bay Cookbook: Rediscovering the Pleasures of a Great Regional Cuisine.* Berkeley, California: Aris Books, 1990.

supply could no longer meet demand: "Crab meat's out of control. I have to [charge] $40 a dozen just to break even. It's killing me. We're not making money, that's for sure. Not on crab, we're not."

Overharvesting, however, is not the only reason for blue crab declines in Chesapeake Bay and elsewhere. According to the 2006 Chesapeake Bay Health and Restoration Assessment, government agencies are lagging far behind in meeting their goals for improving water quality and clarity and for reducing toxins such as PCBs and mercury. For example, midchannel water clarity in the Bay has steadily declined over the last quarter century, and agencies that have a mandate to deal with this problem are reporting only 7 percent progress toward meeting their goals. The murkiness of the Bay's waters is due to algal blooms, which block the sunlight from reaching the seagrasses that blue crabs depend on for habitat and for food. Harmful algal blooms are now occurring year after year in the Bay, killing off the very seagrasses on which the blue crabs depend.

While efforts to restore seagrass beds and wetlands continue, they are in a race against time, because 70,000 new residents move into the Bay area each year, and runoff from their new homes and yards profoundly affects water quality in the Chesapeake Bay. These new residents should learn why their own land uses have contributed to what Tommy Leggett, a waterman from the Virginia side of Chesapeake, calls "the sorriest crab dredging season that I've known." In response to such declines, the traditional watermen themselves have begun to take action to ensure the survival of their livelihood; in 1998, fifty-six of them pledged to uphold a Waterman's Stewardship Covenant to take better care of the crabs as well as the Bay environments on which they depend.

The following elegant little crabcake recipe is a hybrid of a hand-me-down among the Wolchik family, which has run the Sea Grill for decades, and a Dale Carson version from further north.

BLUE CRABCAKE ALGONQUIAN

7–8 ounces lump blue crab meat, cartilage removed, steamed, and drained
2 tablespoons minced onion
¼ teaspoon dry mustard
¼ teaspoon paprika
1 teaspoon dry bread crumbs
dash of sea salt
dash of freshly ground black pepper
dash of Worcestershire sauce
2 tablespoons butter
1 ounce white wine

In a mixing bowl, use your hands to combine the steamed and drained crabmeat and all other ingredients except the butter and white wine. Form into small crabcakes and set aside. In a small skillet, melt the butter. Sauté the crabcakes over medium heat until browned and bubbly. Fluff up and turn over with a spatula without disturbing the lumps of crab, then brown on the other side. Next, remove the skillet from the heat and quickly pour the white wine around the edges of the crabcakes. While they are still sizzling and bubbling, serve in the skillet. Makes 4 small crabcakes.

Around the Chesapeake Bay, blue crabs are commonly steamed and served coated in Old Bay Seasoning. Curt Gibbs

Fish Pepper

This strikingly beautiful African-American heirloom from Maryland was first recognized for its multicolored foliage and flavorful fruit in the 1870s, when its sauces became all the rage in Chesapeake Bay's oyster and crab houses. As "Radish Bruce" once told the staff of Southern Exposure Seed Exchange, this is "a beautiful plant and a great pepper. The variegated leaves would look fabulous anywhere; grow a row in your vegetable garden, plant a cluster in with your flowers or herbs as well."

The variegated foliage that Radish Bruce speaks of is a unique green-and-white striping and swirling that brightens every Fish Pepper leaf on these two-foot-tall plants. The pendant two-inch-long peppers are just as colorful, for as they ripen their thin flesh changes from a creamy white with green stripes to an orange with brown stripes to a deep, glossy, almost robust red. But it is their delicious flavor, intermediate level of pungency, and versatility that have endeared Fish Peppers to so many chefs—from Baltimore to Philadelphia—over the last 140 years. The diminutive pepper seedlings could be transplanted out on the back porch of an oyster and crab house along the Bay in May, and even during the

hottest, wettest of summers, they would produce fruits within ninety days. Garden writer Jack Staub notes that Fish Peppers have become mythic in the Baltimore area:

> Interestingly, there was a local African American legend that held that in order for peppers to achieve their ultimate fieriness, one had to be in a fiery state as well. Therefore, the best Fish Peppers were said to be planted by those who were really angry. One supposes this made for all kinds of local fun.

The Fish Pepper's origins remain lost in the murkiness of American history. All that has been confirmed is that this African-American heirloom may have begun as an experiment or a chromosomal mutation of a common serrano pepper sometime during the 1870s. Seeds from the progeny of this first plant were passed from hand to hand until they landed with gardener Horace Pippin, who claimed that they originated in Baltimore. Soon they were being grown from Washington, D.C., northward to Philadelphia, almost always by African-American truck farmers

who supplied produce to the crab and oyster houses. Over time the Fish Pepper became a fixed variety, but it was never sold commercially. The creamy white Fish Peppers became a secret ingredient that chefs "hid away" in white sauces to give dishes like terrapin soup some unanticipated heat.

In the best of times around Chesapeake Bay, the Fish Pepper was traditionally used fresh in a wide range of shellfish, fish, and turtle cookery, but it was also kept to dry and crush for later use in stews, salsas, and fish sauces. Then, both contamination and chronic overharvesting began to take their toll on the Bay's fish and shellfish populations. By the mid-1950s, two diseases were inadvertently introduced with nonnative oysters to the estuaries along the Atlantic coast. Through the mid-1970s, despite declining numbers of shellfish, a few of the great crab and oyster houses maintained their loyal clientele in Bay-side locations like Nanticoke, in Wicomico County, Maryland.

As Dermo and MSX diseases spread through the Bay's oysters in the 1980s, Nanticoke's shellfish were among the first to be devastated. Soon, most of Maryland's oyster houses closed, and the few remaining ones began to source their oysters from elsewhere. With the decline of this great seafood tradition, the Fish Pepper tumbled from fame into obscurity.

Fortunately, just as Maryland's crab and oyster houses hit rock bottom, the craze for piquant peppers revved up. Over the last two decades, some thirteen different suppliers of chile seeds have offered the Fish Pepper at one time or another, but their stock is actually from a very few growers. Southern Exposure Seed Exchange, Cross Country Nurseries, and J. L. Hudson Seeds are among the most consistent carriers of this stunning heirloom.

H. Franklyn Hall, the famed chef of Boothby's Hotel in Philadelphia, was among the greatest promoters of the Fish Pepper. His 1901 classic, *300 Ways to Cook and Serve Shell Fish, Terrapin, Green Turtle,* claims that at one time this pepper was sold in fish markets right alongside terrapin and shellfish. The following recipe for piccalilli sauce is a long-standing favorite derived from B. C. Howard's 1881 classic, *Fifty Years in a Maryland Kitchen.*

David Cavagnaro

David Cavagnaro

Further Readings

Andrews, Jean. *Peppers: The Domesticated Capsicums.* Austin: University of Texas Press, 1984.

Hall, Harry Franklyn. *300 Ways to Cook and Serve Shell Fish, Terrapin, Green Turtle.* Philadelphia: Christian Banner Print, 1901.

Howard, B. C. *Fifty Years in a Maryland Kitchen: 403 Authentic Regional Recipes.* Philadelphia: J. P. Lippincott, 1881.

Staub, Jack E. *Seventy-Five Exciting Vegetables for Your Garden.* Layton, Utah: Gibbs Smith Imprints/Peregrine Smith Books, 2005.

Weaver, William Woys. *Heirloom Vegetable Gardening: A Master Gardener's Guide to Planting, Growing, Seed Saving, and Cultural History.* New York: Henry Holt, 1997.

Whealy, Kent, and Joanne Thuente. *Garden Seed Inventory*, 6th ed. Decorah, Iowa: Seed Savers Exchange, 2004.

MARYLAND PICCALILLI WITH FISH PEPPERS

1 or 2 ripe Fish Peppers, chopped
4 pounds Pink Brimmer tomatoes, minced
1 cup minced Doe Hill golden bell pepper
2 Vidalia onions, minced
1 cup sugar
¼ cup mustard seed
¼ teaspoon freshly ground black peppercorns
¼ teaspoon whole cloves
1½ teaspoons ground ginger
1 teaspoon turmeric
1 cup apple cider vinegar

In a large glass mixing bowl, combine the minced vegetables with the sugar, spices, and vinegar, then transfer them to a saucepan and add a scant ¼ cup of water to the pan. Cook over low heat for 30 minutes or until the tomatoes are tender. Pour into a quart jar and seal at once for later use. Makes 1 quart.

Choppee Okra

The hedonistic poet James Dickey offered fried okra his highest praise in his 1974 book, *Jericho:* "You talk of supping with the gods. You've just done it, for who but a god could have come up with the divine fact of okra?" Holding a special place in the line of these divine okras is Crabcake Nation's Choppee okra, an endangered heirloom variety named after the Native Americans who originally inhabited the Carolina coastlands of the Grand Strand.

The word *okra* is derived from the term *nkruma* of a West African dialect, but it was Americanized when this subtropical vegetable crossed the ocean in 1658. An African name for it, *ki ngombo,* was adulterated by Portuguese slave traders into *quingombo,* later shortened to *gumbo.* Since the mid-1800s, the Jacobs family has grown this dark green okra heirloom in Georgetown, South Carolina, just south of Myrtle Beach. The slender, smooth, spineless pods of this variety are somewhat similar to those of the variety Louisiana Green Velvet—they too are thick-walled, straight, and easy to pick—but the plants are not as large, seldom reaching five feet in height. Choppee okra has long been used in a Carolina *pilau* called "limping Susan," in Sea Island gumbos, in spicy

David Cavagnaro

Further Readings

Davidson, Alan. *The Oxford Companion to Food.* New York: Oxford University Press, 1999.

Dickey, James. *Jericho: The South Beheld.* Birmingham, Alabama: Oxmoor House, 1974.

Egerton, John. *Southern Food at Home, on the Road, in History.* Chapel Hill: University of North Carolina Press, 1993.

Mariani, John F. *The Encyclopedia of American Food and Drink.* New York: Lebhar-Friedman Books, 1999.

Robinson, Sallie Ann. *Gullah Home Cooking, the Dufuskie Way.* Chapel Hill: University of North Carolina Press, 2003.

Whealy, Kent, and Joanne Thuente. *Garden Seed Inventory,* 6th ed. Decorah, Iowa: Seed Savers Exchange, 2004.

pickle mixes, and as a skillet-fried vegetable coated in cornmeal.

Unfortunately, this coastal Carolina heirloom is available through only one seed catalog on the entire continent, Fedco Seeds in Maine. By that measure alone, it might be considered to be endangered. In addition, only one Seed Savers Exchange member, a Tennessee gardener, continues to offer its seeds to other seed savers.

This particular recipe comes from the Carolina shores some hundred miles south of Georgetown, on Daufuskie, where African-American Sea Islanders have conjured up an altogether colorful cuisine. It is adapted from the marvelous chef and storyteller of the Gullah culture, Sallie Ann Robinson, who grew up on Daufuskie Island but later moved to Savannah, Georgia.

David Cavagnaro

BROKEN CRAB AND CHOPPEE OKRA STEW

4 to 6 raw blue eating crabs
2 or 3 fatback bacon strips, preferably from an Ossabaw Island hog
1 medium Vidalia onion, cut into wedges
4 skinned and stewed Creole or Bonny Best tomatoes
1½ cups water
¼ teaspoon sea salt
¼ teaspoon freshly ground black pepper
2 cups chopped Choppee okra

Cooked separately:
2 cups Carolina Gold rice
4 cups chicken stock

Keep the live crabs in a bucket until you are ready to prepare the stew, then pour boiling water over them to reduce the probability of getting pinched by their claws. Clean them by removing the top shell and then the gills. Break their bodies in half and remove the meat, then do the same with the claws and back fins.

Fry the fatback bacon in a cast-iron skillet and then gradually add the chunks of crab meat, the onion wedges, the stewed tomatoes, and the water. Season with sea salt and pepper, then simmer in the skillet for 15 to 20 minutes. Add the chopped okra and bring the mixture to a boil. Slightly reduce the heat and simmer for another 15 minutes. Sample the stew to determine whether the okra is tender but the crab still firm. If not, continue to simmer and stir for another 5 minutes or until the deal is done. Serve over Carolina Gold rice that has been added to boiling chicken stock and then simmered until it is creamy. Serves 8.

White Maypop Passionfruit

Some say that the name *maypop* comes from the way the fruit pops in your mouth when its yellow-green skin is squeezed by your teeth; others say its name is an Anglicized loan word from the Algonquian *maracock* or Powhatan *mahcawq*. Around 1610, Jamestown colonists and chroniclers John Smith and William Strachey noticed its importance to the farming and foodways of Virginia's Algonquin, with Strachey observing that "in every field where the Indians plant that corn, [there] be cart-loads of them . . . [They] are the bigness of a green apple, and hath maine azurine or blue kernels, like as a pomegranat, a good summer cooling fruit."

Strachey's appraisal that cultivated maypop fruit of that time had "the bigness of a green apple" is curious because most wild maypops are no larger than a hen's egg, seldom reaching two inches in length. And yet archaeologists now suggest that the domestication of maypops in Crabcake and Cornbread Nations may have begun some 5,000 years ago, enough time to allow cultural selection for fruit size, texture, flavor, and color. The rare white-flowered maypop is the only extant cultivar of this species, but it was selected for its highly fragrant, nearly pungent, pale flowers more than for its fruit. It is a reminder, however, that native and nonnative gardeners alike have had ample opportunity to make selections from the gene pool of this highly variable species but that neglect, not opportunity, has characterized the American relationship with maypops over the last 200 years. As the populations of Native American farmers crashed in the century following European colonization, it is likely that numerous heirloom varieties of maypops were lost. Maypop's popularity has not yet recovered from the collateral damage of the colonial period.

In the wild thickets and waste places of America, however, the maypop species remains widespread, ranging from Pennsylvania and Nebraska in the north to Florida in the south. Its vines of three-lobed leaves run rampant along railroad tracks, climbing picket fences and draping themselves over old junked cars, chicken coops, and woodpiles. Among the Cherokee, the young shoots and leaves of maypop vines were picked, rinsed, mixed with other greens, and fried in grease as a potherb.

Yet Kristen Gremillion has confirmed that maypop fruit served as a real culinary mainstay for many

Photo by "Pollinator"; courtesy Wikimedia Commons

Further Readings

Gremillion, K. J. "The Development of a Mutualistic Relationship between Humans and Maypops (*Passiflora incarnata* L.) in the Southeastern United States." *Journal of Ethnobiology* 9:2 (1989): 135–138.

Hamel, Paul B., and Mary U. Chiltosky. *Cherokee Plants and Their Uses: A Four Hundred Year History.* Sylva, North Carolina: Herald Publishing, 1964.

Perry, Myra Jean. *Food Use of Wild Plants by Cherokee Indians.* Knoxville: University of Tennessee, 1975.

Reich, Lee. *Uncommon Fruits for Every Garden.* Portland, Oregon: Timber Press, 2004.

Strachey, William. *The Historie of Travaile into Virginia Brittanica.* London: Hakluyt Society, 1953. (Originally published in 1612.)

Williamson, Darcy, and Lisa Railsback. *Cooking with Spirit: North American Indian Food and Fact.* Bend, Oregon: Maverick Publications, 1987.

MAYPOP PASSIONFRUIT JELLY

4½ cups maypop juice and pulp (see below)
1 package pectin, or 1 cup dried and ground hawthorn berries
5 cups sugar

To obtain the fruit, check maypop trees for ripened fruits from late July through early October and freeze them. Once you are ready to make the jelly, thaw them and scoop out the pulp from their skins, retaining all juices. Place the pulp and juices in a saucepan or kettle and simmer for 10 minutes. Strain the juice and pulp through a colander into a large measuring cup to eliminate seeds and larger pieces of pulp. When you have 4½ cups of juicy pulp, pour it back into the saucepan and add the pectin or the ground-up hawthorn berries. Boil the mixture hard for a minute, then add the sugar and stir with a wooden spoon. After another minute of boiling, take off heat, skim off any impurities from the surface, pour the jelly into sterilized jars, and seal with paraffin. Makes enough to fill 8 to 10 pint jars.

Larry Allain @ USGS, National Wetlands Research Center

tribes in prehistoric and historic times. The fruit was crushed and the seeds sieved out of the pulp as the juice was caught and kept for later drinking. Maypop juice was the major social drink among the Cherokee of North Carolina and was readily offered to any visitors of the farming villages in Chestnut Nation. The fruit pulp and juice were mixed with cornmeal as well. The pleasant, subliminally tropical flavor of some maypops has been likened to that of apricots, while others have the passionfruit flavor familiar to many Americans as the signature taste of Hawaiian Punch. The somewhat acidic fruit pulp ranges in color from a creamy white to yellow-orange. Natives and immigrants alike have found the pulp to be excellent for jellies, juices, and marmalades.

While a number of American nurseries and seed catalogs offer wild, unimproved maypop vines, the white maypop passionfruit plant has typically been offered only by Woodlanders in South Carolina. However, members of NAFEX—the North American Fruit Explorers—have recently shown considerable interest in evaluating the variability of maypops in the wild and redomesticating them. It may well be worth their time to search abandoned historic villages and orchards that were long maintained by Native American horticulturalists to see whether any prehistoric selections have somehow survived.

The recipe at left for maypop passionfruit jelly comes from the experimentation done by Darcy Williamson and Lisa Railsback in the 1980s.

Zimmerman's Pawpaw

Way down yonder in the pawpaw patch, America's largest wild fruit still pleases most anyone who gets a chance to savor its powerfully aromatic flavors and creamy, custardlike pulp. In 1541, Hernando de Soto first reported Native Americans growing and eating pawpaws in the Mississippi Valley, and irrefutable evidence of prehistoric pawpaw use comes from archaeological remains in Arkansas, Kentucky, Ohio, and Wisconsin. Kin to the more tropical custard apples, soursops, cherimoyas, and guanabanas, the pawpaw *(Asimina triloba)* is a hardy tree adapted to temperate climates and to the fertile bottomland soils of river valleys.

While pawpaw consumption is strongest as a cultural phenomenon in Crabcake, Chestnut, and Cornbread Nations, wild and cultivated stands of pawpaws have been found in twenty-six U.S. states and in the Canadian province of Ontario as well. For centuries, rural Americans have found pawpaw shrubs in the underbrush by detecting the aroma of their ripened fruits. When the outer skin blackens around an oblong, seedy mass of pulp, the pawpaw offers up its most exquisite complex of flavors, which are most often likened to mango, pear, custard apple, and banana. The fruits in each stand seem to have their own distinctive taste, and the best stands were not only named but carefully guarded. Such place names are remembered in at least six states, and two counties are named for the pawpaw.

By 1784, the pawpaw was already receiving attention from pioneering horticulturists like Kentuckian John Filson, who wrote that "the pappa-tree does not grow to a great size [but] bears a fine fruit much like a cucumber in shape and size and tastes sweet." Thomas Jefferson took special pride in growing and distributing pawpaws to his guests from France and England, boasting that its fruit were as good as those of any European orchard crop. After Lewis and Clark returned from their expedition overland to the Pacific, Jefferson learned that, along the way, the pawpaw had saved them from starvation.

In 1916, the American Genetic Association decided to sponsor something that was then unprecedented in American horticultural history: It announced a contest through its *Journal of Heredity* offering cash awards for those who could find the very best pawpaws in the entire country. Seventy-five fruit samples were sent in to the judges, who also received more than 230 reports on the locations of large trees with superior fruit. The best fruit was judged to be one from the hills of Lawrence County, in southern Ohio, submitted by Mrs. Frank Ketter.

The contest did more than just discover the best wild fruits; it also stimulated scientific efforts to use these genetic materials to domesticate the native pawpaw and to hybridize it with other species. Legendary American plant explorer David Fairchild propagated Ketter's wild prize and other pawpaw seedlings from the contest's award-winning trees, evaluated them, and then selected the most promising ones for their horticultural and culinary qualities. In 1918, Fairchild passed on some of these selections as well as his encouragement to a young pawpaw enthusiast, Dr. George A. Zimmerman of Piketown, Pennsylvania, who deliberately crossed some with other species while continuing to select other natives for their superior qualities. Over more than two decades, Dr. Zimmerman assembled an astonishing collection of around seventy pawpaws at Fern Hill near Lingleston, Pennsylvania, which was later donated to the Blandy Experimental Farm of the University of Virginia.

From the time of the 1916 contest to the untimely death of Dr. Zimmerman in 1941, some fifty-six cultivars of the American pawpaw were developed by its enthusiasts, but then its cultivation began to fall out of fashion. Of the ten best pawpaw varieties from Zimmerman's era, only one, Taylor, has survived in the nursery trade. Only twenty of the seventy historic heirlooms remained when another man with a passion for pawpaws stepped up to the plate. Since 1975, plant geneticist Neal Peterson has revived the quest for the perfect pawpaw, riding backcountry roads to rediscover the original trees that were lauded by pawpaw pioneers. He found new seedlings and resprouted rootstocks but no older grafted trees surviving at Zimmerman's Fern Hill estate; then he hit the mother lode when he stumbled upon the original plantings at Blandy Experimental Farm: "Dr. Zimmerman's Blandy Farm collection survives apparently intact and contains fifty-six to sixty trees. The fruit of several have a very fine flavor, and a couple have exceptionally low seed content."

Plant geneticist Neal Peterson with pawpaws, 1992. Ray Jones

Kent Priestley; courtesy Slow Food USA

Since then, Neal Peterson has selected from seedlings found at Blandy Farm a cultivar he calls Rappahannock, with medium-sized fruits having firm yellow flesh and few seeds. It has a cheerfully sweet flavor with a pleasant, lingering aftertaste. Another enthusiast, George Slate, developed the cultivar named Zimmerman's from seed derived from Zimmerman's own collections, but it is available in the United States only from a single source, Dale Brooks in Decatur, Alabama. Another cultivar with large yellow fruit is named SAA-Zimmerman and was selected as a seedling by John Gordon from other seeds originating with the Pennsylvania doctor. Despite its exceptional qualities, the latter pawpaw named for Zimmerman is commercially available only from the John Gordon Nursery in Amherst, New York.

While there is considerable genetic diversity remaining in these three cultivars and some fifty other named varieties found in private orchards and university farms, only nineteen pawpaw varieties are still regularly promoted through the nursery trade. Despite the fruit's large geographic range, many superior wild stands of pawpaws have been plowed up and their habitats converted to fields of annual crops or to subdivisions. Worse yet, as Neal Peterson has witnessed, there has been a dramatic loss of traditional ecological knowledge about where remnant stands of superior pawpaws occur: "The pawpaw is not an endangered species, but the folks knowledgeable about the pawpaw are."

The following custard recipe is adapted from one in *Mountain Country Cooking,* compiled by Mark F. Sohn of Pikeville, Kentucky.

PAWPAW CUSTARD

1 cup pureed pulp from ripened
  Zimmerman's pawpaws
2 ounces grated, roasted coconut
1 cup cream or half-and-half
1 cup milk
3 fresh eggs from pasture-raised Dominique
  hens
4 ounces superfine sugar
1 teaspoon vanilla extract
 dash of salt

Preheat an oven to 325 degrees F. In a large glass bowl, mix the pureed pawpaw pulp with coconut, then add the cream, milk, eggs, sugar, vanilla, and salt. Beat this mixture until smooth, except for the bubbles that form while you're stirring. Pour the custard mixture into eight custard cups. Line the bottom of a large baking pan with a dish towel, then place the custard cups in the pan. Add boiling water to the pan until it rises two-thirds of the way up the sides of the cups. Bake for 45 minutes. Remove from the oven just before the custard is set in the center, or when a knife inserted near the edge of the custard comes out clean.

Further Readings

Anonymous. "The Best Pawpaws." *Journal of Heredity* 8:1 (1917): 21–33.

Anonymous. "Where Are the Best Pawpaws?" *Journal of Heredity* 7:7 (1916): 291–295.

Layne, D. R. "The Pawpaw [*Asimina triloba* L. (Dunal)]: A New Fruit Crop for Kentucky and the United States." *HortScience* 31 (1996): 777–784.

Peterson, R. N. "Pawpaw (*Asimina*)." In J. N. Moore and J. R. Balington, eds., *Genetic Resources of Temperate Fruit and Nut Crops.* Louvain, Belgium: International Society for Horticultural Science, 1991.

Pomper, Kirk W., Sheri B. Crabtree, Shawn P. Brown, Snake C. Jones, and Tera M. Bonney. "Assessment of Genetic Diversity of Pawpaw (*Asimina triloba*) Cultivars with Intersimple Sequence Repeat Markers." *Journal of the American Horticultural Society* 128: 4 (2003): 521–525.

Pomper, Kirk W., and Desmond R. Layne. "The North American Pawpaw: Botany and Horticulture." *Horticultural Reviews* 31 (2005): 349–364.

Sohn, Mark F. *Mountain Country Cooking: A Gathering of the Best Recipes from the Smokies to the Blue Ridge.* New York: St. Martin's Press, 1996.

Stevenson, Paul. "A Passion for the Pawpaw." *American Forests,* March–April, 1990.

Zimmerman, George A. "Hybrids of the American Pawpaw." *Journal of Heredity,* 13: 3 (1941): 83–91.

Ossabaw Island Hog

The Ossabaw Island hog is the kind of swine linked to the oldest European presence on the coast of Crabcake Nation, for it may well have landed on American soil just nine years after Ponce de Leon's first visit to Florida. Moreover, the Ossabaw Island hog just may be the closest surviving genetic stock to what Ibérico hogs were like in Spain at the time that Spanish explorers first tried to settle the North American coast. Like its European ancestors, it is a small, prick-eared, long-snouted, straight-tailed hog, one well suited for ranging free in wild habitats. In Spain, its kin are butchered and cured into the famous serrano hams known as *pata negra*. With dark purple to rosy red pork, an intense but nuanced aroma, and a lustrous texture, the meat of the Ossabaw Island hog still rouses the same sense of pleasure that it did more than four centuries ago, when homesick Spaniards roasted it on the barrier islands off the Georgia coast.

In his account of the origins of the Ossabaw Island hog, Peter Kaminsky hints at its long duration on the North American continent:

> How, exactly, Ossabaw's hogs came to be on the island is still not entirely clear . . . Nearly five hundred years ago—in 1526, to be exact—a Spaniard, Lucas Vasquez de Allyon, founded a

mission off the coast of Georgia. Historians agree that the site was either on Ossabaw or on the nearby islands of Saint Catherine's or Sapelo. Although the mission lasted less than a year, the pigs could well be descended from the farm animals of the short-lived priory.

By some accounts, Lucas Vasquéz de Allyon established the very first European settlement in North America and let Iberian pigs go feral on the barrier islands, where they might later be hunted. And yet, he was over 3,000 years too late to be the first human settler on the island, for Native Americans were using its resources as early as 2200 B.C. Incidentally, the name *Ossabaw* is derived from the Guale dialect of Creek, in which it means "place of the yaupon." Yaupon (descriptively named *Ilex vomitoria*) is a holly-leaved shrub that was historically used to make "black drink," a ceremonial beverage that triggered both vomiting and visions among many tribes residing in Crabcake and Gumbo Nations.

Of course, Ossabaw Island did not stay under the stewardship of either the Guale or the Spanish. Through the plantation era, the Morel family managed four farms on the island and no doubt hunted the hogs, if only to keep them from damaging crops in their fields. In the early 1900s, these farms were purchased by outsiders and used for game hunting. But since 1924, when Dr. Henry Norton Torrey and his wife, Nell Ford Torrey, purchased all of the private lands on the island, both the hogs and their habitats were given continuous protection by the Torreys and their descendants, who established the private Ossabaw Island Foundation in 1961. The island then became the first acquisition of the Heritage Trust Act of 1975, which protects the island, by legal contract, from overuse and development while restricting public access for purposes other than conservation research and education.

Since that time, a number of hogs have been moved to the mainland to establish public and

Further Readings

Christman, C. J., D. P. Sponenberg, and D. E. Bixby. *A Rare Breeds Album of American Livestock*. Pittsboro, North Carolina: American Livestock Breeds Conservancy, 1997.

Dohner, J. V. *The Encyclopedia of Historic and Endangered Livestock and Poultry Breeds*. New Haven, Connecticut: Yale University Press, 2001.

Kaminsky, P. *Pig Perfect*. New York: Hyperion Press, 2005.

University of Virginia Hospital Circle. *The Monticello Cook Book*. Richmond, Virginia: Deitz Press, 1950.

Wechsler, D. "Premium Pastured Pork 2004." Available at www.ssawg.org/deFelice.html.

Don Bixby; courtesy American Livestock Breeds Conservancy

Ossabaw Island, Georgia. Craig Dominey

private herds for conservation and research; they are featured at Mount Vernon and several other historic farms. However, it is currently not possible to import any more hogs directly from Ossabaw Island due to quarantine restrictions. With fewer than 200 descendants of these hogs now found in small breeding groups off the island, and no more than a thousand individuals remaining on the island, the Ossabaw Island hog's status is classified as critical by the American Livestock Breeds Conservancy, and it has been boarded onto the Slow Food Ark of Taste. There are, however, private producers, such as those at Caw Caw Creek Farm in Columbia, South Carolina, who are incorporating the production of Ossabaw Island hog descendants into their free-range, grass-fed pork production.

Because of their centuries of adaptation to a feast-or-famine environment, the physiology of Ossabaw Island hogs has shifted to promote the laying down of prodigious amounts of body fat. This has made the pigs the subject of intense medical research into diabetes and cardiac disease, but it also dictates the methods in which they are prepared for the table. Traditionally, these pigs have been roasted whole to render off the excess fat. The fat covering also enhances the keeping qualities of traditionally preserved country hams. The following recipe for preparing country-cured ham from Ossabaw hogs comes from the Crabcake Nation tradition, in which a ham is salt-cured, then smoked and hung for several months before being cooked. In this recipe, we feature the Ingleside directions for cooking the ham found in *The Monticello Cook Book* and then prepare a ham and lima bean soup.

OSSABAW HAM AND LIMA BEAN SOUP

Directions for preparing the country-cured ham
Remove the ham from hanging in a smoking shed, then wash and scrub it thoroughly. Place it in a large iron kettle, cover it with water, and bring the water just to the boiling point. Keep the water barely hot enough to stay at the boiling point and cook the ham until the meat is loosened from the bone while the skin is puffed and wrinkled. Reduce the heat but keep the ham in the kettle until the water around it has cooled. Remove the ham, skin it, sprinkle bread crumbs and brown sugar on its top, and stick it with cloves. Place it in a preheated 450-degree F oven and bake it until it is golden brown. Let it cool, then slice it wafer thin. Next, follow this recipe for preparing the soup:

1 pound dry Carolina lima beans (large)
6 cups chicken stock
4 Amish Paste tomatoes, diced
½ cup chopped Vidalia onions
½ cup chopped Martha Warde's celery
½ cup chopped White Parsley carrots
½ cup water
1 tablespoon chopped fresh thyme
¼ teaspoon freshly ground black pepper
3 cups baked Ossabaw ham, sliced then diced

In a large cooking pot, soak the Carolina lima beans overnight in 8 cups of water, then drain and rinse them the following morning. Place them back in the pot with the chicken stock, diced tomatoes, onions, celery, carrots, water, thyme, and pepper. Simmer for an hour, covered, until the beans are tender, then add the ham and cook for another half hour. Ladle 8 servings into warm bowls and serve with hush puppies or spoonbread (see page 136) and butter.

GUMBO NATION

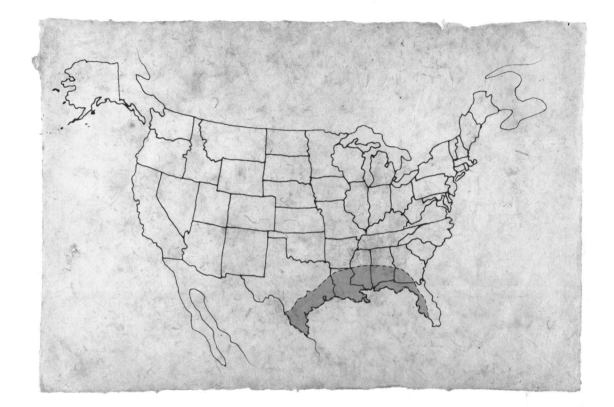

Nowhere else in North America do food, story, and song sublimely intertwine as they do in Gumbo Nation, the Gulf South region that stretches from east Texas past the Mississippi delta country and clear around to the Florida Keys. Fish, shellfish, turtles, and fowl have found a paradise here, although that paradise has recently been ravaged by the drilling of oil wells, the trawling of ocean bottoms, and the devastating floods generated by Hurricanes Katrina and Rita. Well over eighty traditional foods are now threatened or endangered in Gumbo Nation. Nevertheless, the indigenous, Cajun, Creole, and Cracker cultures of Gumbo Nation have always manifested great resilience, as their "White Boot Brigade" of shrimpers has recently demonstrated. They continue to forage for the sassafras leaves need for gumbo filé, to grow the okras needed for other gumbos, and to fish for crabs, shrimp, groupers, gators, and redfish. Their cuisines blend Native American, African, Caribbean, French, and Spanish influences in astonishing ways that have made them world famous.

Sassafras Leaves for Handmade Gumbo Filé

The roots and bark of *sasafrás*—long chewed by Native Americans for their medicinal and culinary qualities associated with the fragrant oil called safrole—were introduced in 1517 to Spanish colonists as they arrived in what we now call Gumbo Nation. By 1577, English speakers in the Virginia colonies were referring to *sassafras* in print, for it was among their first exports to Europe.

Ever since, the mittenlike leaves, bark, and roots of the widespread tree *Sassafras albidum* have been used by many native and immigrant cultures as a tonic and a flavoring for root beers, gums, soups, and soaps. But a more specific use of the ground leaves—as a thickener and flavoring known as gumbo filé—has remained much more geographically and culturally restricted in its traditional prep-

aration. Also known simply as filé, from a French word for "thread," this sassafras leaf powder has become internationally celebrated as an essential ingredient of the Cajun cuisine of rural Louisiana and the urban Creole cuisine of New Orleans. Its origin traces back to the Choctaw communities of Mississippi, Alabama, and Louisiana, but one of the few remaining practitioners of traditional sassafras processing for filé currently resides among Cajuns in Baton Rouge.

Sassafras itself is a distinctive American tree in

Sara Roahen

Lionel Key, Jr. Sara Roahen

Sara Roahen

the laurel family that ranges from Maine to Florida along the East Coast and from Illinois to Texas in the West. Although more like a shrub of wetland edges in the north, it achieves heights of up to ninety feet on the abandoned farmlands it shares with wild persimmons in Gumbo Nation. Its smooth, shiny green leaves typically have one side lobe, which makes them look like a mitten, but individual trees may also bear leaves that lack any lobes at all or that exhibit two or more. When fresh, the leaves have a lemony smell, with a slight aftertaste of thyme. But special hand-harvesting, drying, and processing into a fine powder transform them into a mucilaginous thickening agent with an altogether unique flavor.

When the leaves reach their peak in verdure and flavor, harvesters select the best ones from ancient gathering grounds known for their trees of exceptional potency. The harvesters carefully prune slender branches harboring clusters of leaves suitable for processing, then transport them home for rinsing, drying, and curing. The best filé is prepared from leaves that retain their verdure even after being dried, for which the stems as well as leaf veins are carefully removed. The remaining leaf matter is then pounded into a powder in a cypress-wood mortar with a wooden pestle. After grinding, the resulting powder is sifted through a hair sieve and then stored in a humidity-free jar.

Based in Baton Rouge, Lionel Key Jr. is one of the last practitioners through whom the traditional processing of handmade gumbo filé has survived to the present day. These traditions were passed on to him by his blind great-uncle—the late Joseph William Ricard—and Uncle Bill's widow, Aunt Sweet Ricard. As Uncle Bill taught him to do, Lionel still sustainably harvests sassafras leaves from Baton Rouge to Sunshine, Louisiana, though some of the stands he has pruned for years were damaged in 2005 by Hurricanes Katrina and Rita. Uncle Bill also taught Lionel exactly how to plunge a pecan-wood *mano* or maul into the hollowed center of cypress-stump metate to pulverize his dried sassafras leaves: "You got to hit the maul dead center to get the grind right, to pulverize the leaves fine . . . It's a real solid sound, like a home-run ball coming off a bat. The filé ends up much finer . . . "

Lionel's skills are not widely shared. For decades, harvesters of Choctaw descent would bring their filé to the French Market in New Orleans from Bayou Lacombe near Mandeville, Louisiana. Sales of prod-ucts from their traditions, however, appear to have declined in recent decades. In addition to Lionel Key's filé (sold under the name of Uncle Bill's Spices), there is also some authentic handmade gumbo filé processed for family use by the Houma Indians who live in the Point Coupe and West and East Feliciana parishes of Louisiana, but little of it is sold outside their communities. In contrast, there is more and more industrially processed gumbo filé being sold in the markets of New Orleans and Baton Rouge, much of it produced by electronic grinding machines that pulverize stems and veins as well as the leaves of poorly cured sassafras.

Properly used, gumbo filé is added as the very last ingredient to gumbos, shrimp or corn soups, potato stews, beans, and gravies. The Cajuns of Louisiana use the French verb *filer*, "to spin a thread," to describe the way its addition to hot liquids leaves a stringy texture in the liquids forming the base of their Acadian cuisine. The shrimp and crab gumbo recipe at left is from the bayous around Lafayette, Louisiana, where it has many local permutations. It is adapted from Hearn's 1885 *La Cuisine Creole* and W. Thomas Angiers's 1985 edition of *Cajun Cuisine.*

Further Readings

Angiers, W. Thomas. *Cajun Cuisine: Authentic Cajun Recipes from Louisiana's Bayou Country*. Lafayette, Louisiana: Beau Bayou Publishing Company, 1985.

Davidson, Alan. *The Oxford Companion to Food*. New York: Oxford University Press, 1999.

Edge, John T. *Southern Belly: The Ultimate Food Lover's Companion to the South.* Chapel Hill, North Carolina: Algonquin Books of Chapel Hill, 2007.

Egerton, John. *Southern Food: At Home, On the Road, In History*. Chapel Hill: University of North Carolina Press, 1993.

Hearn, Lafcadio. *La Cuisine Creole*. New York: Hill H. Coleman, 1885.

Southern Foodways Alliance. "New Orleans Eats: Lionel Key." An interview by Sara Roahen with Lionel Key Jr. Available at www.southernfoodways.com/oral_history/ neworleans_eats/key.shtml.

Centennial Pecan

Modern pecan culture began thanks to the handiwork of a Louisiana slave named Antoine, who successfully propagated the superior (and uniform) Centennial variety. He cut "whips," or scionwood, from trees he found on the east side of the Mississippi River and grafted them onto rootstocks that were located on the west side of the Big Muddy. The scions Antoine used came from a large, handsome tree with pendulous branches growing on the Anita Plantation in St. James Parish. Its owner, Amant Bourgeois, had noticed that its rather large pecan nuts were outstanding among all those that he harvested from his native trees; they had golden nut meat of delicate flavor and texture, held within oblong, bright gray-brown shells splashed with purple. Bourgeois encouraged a fruit and nut specialist, Dr. A. E. Colomb, to take cuttings from the tree for experimental propagation. His gesture of generosity was a fortunate one, for the original tree was later destroyed by floods during the devastating Anita Crevasse of 1890.

The Centennial was not yet out of the woods, however. Dr. Colomb nearly failed to keep the cuttings alive, for his own attempts at grafting them failed. Even though this accomplished scientist could not get his own grafts to set, Colomb had taught grafting techniques to the African slave Antoine, who in 1846 was adept enough to graft the Centennial scion onto the rootstock of sixteen trees at the Oak Alley Plantation. The plantation's owner, Telesphore J. Roman, allowed Antoine to plant them out in a pasture just fifty yards from the banks of the moody Mississippi. Antoine soon grafted another hundred cuttings onto other rootstock and carefully guarded these trees up through the end of the Civil War. They formed the beginnings of the cultivated pecan industry in Gumbo Nation, which now produces more than 2,000,000 pounds of domesticated nuts each year.

Just as Antoine's prizes began to bear nuts at the end of the war, Roman lost the plantation to Hubert Bonzano, who cut down many of the trees to make room for sugarcane. However, when his workers informed Bonzano that the nuts had been selling in New Orleans for $50 to $75 a barrel, he had a change of heart and spared the rest. He took them to the Centennial Exposition in Philadelphia, where they received the Best of Show honor on account of their "remarkable large size, tenderness of shell, and very special excellence."

The fame of these Centennial pecans grew, and by 1882 sales of their seedlings were actively being promoted by a New Orleans nursery. They were cultivated in formal plantations throughout Gumbo Nation, where selections of their progeny led to the development of perhaps hundreds of other cultivars. Sadly, Centennial itself was deemed "too tardy and shy in bearing" in an influential 1913 publication, so that its value was discounted and its stock retired from nursery propagation. Although old trees of Centennial may persist in the landscape and in genetic repositories, not a single commercial American nursery still offers this once-proud heirloom to the public.

Of course, native pecans and their relatives, the hickories, had been savored by Native American foragers for centuries prior to their domestication. We gain our word *pecan* from the Cree in the Algonquian language group, whose term *pakan* was first recorded in 1773. Of course, Northerners and Southerners now tend to accent different syllables when saying this name. The word *hickory* appears to have been derived from Powhatan in the same language family. First recorded in 1653, it originally referred to the creamy white liquid expressed from both pecans and hickories, *powcohickory.* French fur traders called them *nues du Illinois* because the Illinois tribe were among their primary suppliers of this delicious, highly storable foodstuff, used to thicken the broth of their venison stews and to add texture, flavor, and fragrance to their baked corn cakes.

And yet in 1529—well before the French ventured into the natural range of pecans—the Spanish explorer Cabeza de Vaca and his Moorish companion, Estevan el Moro, encountered wild pecans along the shores of the Gulf Coast of Gumbo Nation. Cabeza de Vaca later remembered that pecans kept his Native American hosts healthy and athletic, even though they were the "only subsistence for the people during a two-month period when no other foods were available." Word of the wonders of the pecan reached France in 1729 and England in 1773. Washington and Jefferson both recognized the utility of the pecan as food and as a source of hardwood. Both of them planted wild pecans and praised their flavors. By that time, the pecan praline was already being offered as a signature confection of New Orleans patisseries. Its culinary cousin, the pecan pie, is arguably the most famous of all authentically American desserts. The following recipe for pecan pie is adapted from several historic sources.

Further Readings

Manaster Jane. *The Pecan Tree.* Austin: University of Texas Press, 1994.

Rosengarten, Frederic. *The Book of Edible Nuts.* New York: Walker and Company, 1984.

Sewell Linck, Ernestine, and Joyce Gibson Roach. *Eats: A Folk History of Texas Foods.* Fort Worth: Texas Christian University Press, 1989.

Sparks, Darrell. *Pecan Cultivars.* Watkinsville, Georgia: Pecan Production Innovations, 1992.

Taylor, W. A. "Promising New Fruits." *Yearbook of Agriculture.* Washington, D.C.: U.S. Government Printing Office, 1904.

U.S. Department of Agriculture–Agricultural Research Service. "Pecan Breeding Program." http://extension-horticulture.tamu.edu/carya/.

CENTENNIAL PECAN PIE

3 eggs
1 cup sugar
1 cup white corn syrup
1 teaspoon vanilla extract
1 tablespoon liquid margarine
1 cup Centennial pecans
  (halves or pieces)

Beat the eggs with a whisk and incorporate the sugar, mixing until well blended. Stir in the remaining ingredients. Cook in unbaked 9-inch pie shell with a high fluted edge in a 350-degree F oven for 45 minutes.

Clay Field Peas

First brought from West African coastal communities to the West Indies in 1674 and to Georgia in 1734, this tropical legume provided African slaves with a sort of culinary solace, even though it did not actually accompany them on their way to Southern plantations in Gumbo Nation. These field peas, as well as their kin—Sea Island peas, crowder peas, cowpeas, and black-eyed peas—remain cherished ingredients in the soul food of both Cornbread and Gumbo Nations. There, they carry a mystical power and mythical capacity that brings good fortune to those who consume them. On New Year's Eve, the dry field peas are soaked so that they can be eaten the next day immediately after the children of the household are sent to hop around the table to "take up the good luck."

Speaking of hopping, field peas and crowder peas are called *pois à pigeon* in the French-speaking reaches of Louisiana and the Caribbean, and this term may have skipped a few syllables when it came into English around 1830 as *hoppin' John.* The term is now used for combinations of field peas with long-grain rice (which had arrived in the Carolinas by 1680) rather than for the peas alone. For the Gullah of South Carolina, hoppin' John is the sister dish to the *jambalaya au congri* of Creoles in New Orleans, the *Moros y Cristianos* served in Cuba, and the *gandul rojo y arroz* of Puerto Rico. To claim that this bean-and-grain combination enabled many of the poorest people of Gumbo Nation to survive and thrive is no hyperbole, but they also lived for its hearty, satisfying flavor, as storyteller Carson McCullers reminds us:

> Now Hopping-John was F. Jasmine's very favorite food. She had always warned them to wave a plate of rice and peas before her nose when she was in her coffin, to make certain there was no mistake; for if a breath of life was left in her, she would sit up and eat, but if she smelled the Hopping-John, and did not stir, then they could just nail down the coffin and be certain she was truly dead.

David Cavagnaro

This particular field pea, the Clay, is one of the older types that has adapted to the South. By the time the Civil War erupted, it was already an important staple in Gumbo and Crabcake Nations, and it is said to have fed many Rebel soldiers. The Clay field pea plant is a small bush that produces longish, narrow pods with tan, elongated, almost granular seeds. When these pea seeds are boiled, they impart a pronounced flavor to the rich, dark broth in their bean pot. Like other old heirloom varieties of field peas and Crowder peas, such as Whippoorwill and Blue Goose, the Clay is adaptable to a wide range of subtropical and wet temperate environments. Unfortunately, today it is available to the public only through the heirloom seed catalog of Baker Creek in Arkansas.

Further Readings

Egerton, John. *Southern Food: At Home, On the Road, In History*. Chapel Hill: University of North Carolina Press, 1997.

Fery, Richard L. "The Cowpea: Production, Utilization and Research in the United States." *Horticultural Reviews* 12 (1990): 197–222.

Hess, Karen. "Hoppin' John and Other Bean Pilaus of the African Xiaspora." In *The Carolina Rice Kitchen*, pp. 92–110. Columbia: University of South Carolina Press, 1992.

Mariani, John F. *The Encyclopedia of American Food and Drink*. New York: Lebhar-Friedman Books, 1999.

McCullers, Carson. *Member of the Wedding*. New York: Bantam, 1946.

Thorne, John. "Rice and Beans: The Itinerary of a Recipe." In John Thorne and Mathew Lewis Thorne, eds., *Serious Pig: An American Cook in Search of His Roots*. New York: North Point Press, 1996. (Essay originally published in 1981.)

HOPPIN' JOHN

2 tablespoons bacon grease or unsalted butter
1 pound smoked ham hock or diced salt pork
2 cups diced sweet Vidalia or Bermuda onions
2 garlic cloves, roasted then minced
1 pound dry Clay field peas, washed and sorted
2 quarts water
¼ teaspoon freshly ground black pepper
2 tablespoons dried red pods of tabasco or datil peppers, crushed
1 teaspoon sea salt
3 cups beef broth
1 sprig fresh thyme
3 cups Carolina Gold rice or other long-grained, nonaromatic rice
2 tablespoons chile-flavored vinegar or Tabasco sauce

In a Dutch oven that holds 4 to 5 quarts of liquid, heat the bacon grease or butter, then add the ham hock or diced salt pork, half of the onion, and all of the garlic. Sauté over medium heat for 10 minutes, or until the meat is browned, and then pour off the broth containing the excess fat to reserve for a later step. Add the freshly washed, shelled, and drained Clay peas, the water, and the black and red peppers. Bring the Dutch oven to a boil, cover, reduce the heat to low, and simmer the peas for an hour to an hour and a half. When the Clay peas are all tender, stir in a half teaspoon of the sea salt, remove from heat, and let them sit.

As the peas cool, in a medium-sized saucepan combine the 3 cups of beef broth and the last half teaspoon of salt as well as the thyme. Drizzle in some of the fatty broth that had been removed from the Dutch oven. Add all 3 cups of rice, cover, and simmer for about 20 minutes, until all the broth has been absorbed into the rice and it is tender and fluffy. Transfer the rice to a deep wooden serving bowl and dish out servings of it into smaller bowls or platters, spooning a nearly equal portion of the peas and meat onto it. Top each bowl or platter with 2 tablespoons of chopped sweet onions from the 1 cup you've reserved and drizzle onto them some of the hot pepper vinegar or Tabasco sauce.

Cotton Patch Goose

Up until the 1950s, the Cotton Patch goose was not merely eaten in Gumbo Nation but was also employed as a farmworker, weeding crabgrass from cotton patches and cornfields for its supper. While its eggs, meat, and feathers were all valued, its skill at pest and weed control encouraged Southern farmers to fully integrate this barnyard waterfowl into their farmstead management team. Particularly during the Great Depression era, such a multipurpose bird not only helped keep rural families fed but also reduced the amount of time they had to devote to weeding and hand-removing pests from their crops.

The Cotton Patch is a small to medium-sized breed as far as geese go, which helps it endure the hot, humid weather of Gumbo Nation summers. With an upright posture; a clean, wedge-shaped tail; a rounded head; and a dish-shaped beak, the Cotton Patch resembles the European Greyling goose in some characteristics. It is sexually dimorphic, with the ganders' plumage being white with an occasional brown wing feather, while the females have brownish-gray or white and brown plumage color. With light, elongated bodies, Cotton Patch geese have a remarkable ability to take flight and vault fences without a running start.

Their origins have been obscured by time, but it is believed that, like the Pilgrim landrace of geese,

Mark See; courtesy American Livestock Breeds Conservancy

the precursors of the Cotton Patch were brought from western Europe between 1640 and 1700, during the colonial period of American history. They share behaviors and markings with barnyard geese still found in Normandy and the Shetland Islands, but these breeds are not likely ancestors for the Cotton Patch. They were gradually adopted by homesteads and plantation owners in Arkansas, Texas, Mississippi, and Louisiana.

Tom T. Walker, a native of rural Arkansas born in 1927, remembers seeing Cotton Patch geese in the 1930s in Hempstead and Union counties, where these small, gentle geese wandered between the rows of cotton, hardly ever damaging the crops themselves. They saved him a lot of time hoeing, keeping down weeds that are now controlled by chemicals instead. He has joined the effort to flesh out the history and help conserve this rare bird:

This was a bird of early America. People picked up the feathers and down off live geese to make pillows, mattresses and comforters. The geese required no special food other than grass, and no shelter, and they suffered from no known poultry disease. They also provided eggs, meat and grease. This became an all-American bird.

Further Readings

American Livestock Breeds Conservancy. "Cotton Patch Goose." Accessed July 3, 2007, from www .albc-usa.org/cpl/waterfowl/cottonpatch.html.

Brown, Clarskon A., ed. *Sauce for the Goose: A New Orleans Cook Book.* New Orleans: Louisiana Pond Auxiliary of Blue Goose Internal, Number l, 1948.

James, Lamar. "The Hunt for 'Cotton Patch' Geese." *Delta Farm Press*, July 24, 2004. Accessed July 3, 2007, from www.deltafarmpress.com/news/040721.

Walker, Judy. "Heritage on the Hoof." *The Times-Picayune,* April 17, 2007. Accessed October 25, 2007, from www.nolacom/timespic/stories/index.ssf?.

That all-American bird is now represented on the face of our continent by fewer than one hundred individuals, and the breed is considered to be critically endangered. In 2007, the goose was placed on Slow Food's Ark of Taste, and one hopes this will bring more attention to this heritage goose and result in more breeders raising the bird for culinary and other purposes.

The following recipe combination is derived from a grassroots community cookbook, *Sauce for a Goose,* first published in New Orleans in 1948, just as the Cotton Patch began to suffer its decline.

STUFFED COTTON PATCH GOOSE IN ORANGE WINE SAUCE

1 10-pound (4- to 8-month-old) Cotton Patch goose, plucked and cleaned
2 tablespoons sea salt
1 tablespoon freshly ground black peppercorns

Preheat the oven to 350 degrees F. Place the whole goose in a large roasting pan. Rub its skin with salt and pepper.

In a glass mixing bowl, combine the following ingredients and insert this stuffing into the cavities of the Cotton Patch with a wooden spoon.

½ cup chopped goose liver
6 cups bread crumbs
6 Shockley apples, cored and diced
1 cup chopped celery stalks
½ cup muscadine raisins
½ teaspoon salt
½ cup butter
½ cup chopped Louisiana shallots
½ cup diced green pepper

⅛ teaspoon cloves
1 cup hot water or Scuppernong wine

Roast the goose for 2½ hours. Before the last half hour of cooking, remove the pan from the oven and drain away the grease from the pan for later use, reserving ½ cup to use in the basting mixture. When the reserved goose grease has cooled, whisk together all of the following ingredients in a large mixing bowl

½ cup goose grease, cooled
½ pound unsalted butter, melted
2 cups Louisiana orange wine or ¼ cup Cointreau and 1¾ cups Reisling
1 teaspoon Worcestershire sauce
5 drops Tabasco sauce
1 tablespoon grated orange zest

Return the goose to the oven for the final half hour of cooking, basting every 5 minutes with the tangy sauce.

Datil Chile Pepper

The golden, wrinkled pungent fruits of the datil chile pepper were hardly known outside the St. Augustine, Florida, vicinity until fifteen or so years ago. It is the only close kin to the fiery habanero chile that has historic roots, as well as some notoriety, in North America. Yet that notoriety came belatedly—almost too late to keep the datil's pepper pods afloat. Fortunately the "fiery foods craze" hit America by storm in the 1980s and has set datil pepper production on a lucrative path that may yet ensure this heirloom's survival.

To understand why this pepper has recently attracted so much attention, you may need to know only that it has a much richer, more nuanced flavor than do the habanero heirlooms of the same species. The datil ranks a bit lower on the pungency scale, so its flavors are not fully obscured by the flashes of fire coming out of your mouth! Nevertheless, the more interesting story to tell of the datil pepper lies in its deep history—one that features Taino-Arawak Indian seafarers of the Caribbean, Spanish and British colonists, and indentured laborers from Africa and Minorca. They all participated in a sort of culinary relay race that brought this chile safely ashore and into cultivation in Florida. Amazingly, a recipe for Minorcan pilau with datil peppers—one that may date as far back as 1768—has survived after being passed on orally from generation to generation until it was at last put to paper in 1968.

There is little doubt that the precursors of the datil pepper heirloom were grown among the Taino-Arawak Indians of Cuba and other islands of the Caribbean at the time that Columbus first described red peppers, on New Year's Day, 1493. The *chinense* chile peppers that were ancestors to habaneros and datils had come to the Caribbean from South America hundreds of years earlier. They had not, however, reached the Florida peninsula or the rest of North America at the time of Spanish arrival. However, within a century of Peter Martyr's first written account of Columbus finding peppers, the Taino-Arawak were trading spices, including peppers, with all the Europeans and Africans arriving in their midst. And yet it was not until after 1763, when Spain lost her territory in Florida to England, that the datil pepper's precursor finally found its way from Cuba to Florida.

In the wake of the Spanish abandonment of Florida, a Scottish speculator named Dr. Andrew Turnbull began an indigo dye plantation at New Smyrna, Florida. He immediately brought in through Cuba some 1,400 indentured laborers who hailed from the islands of Minorca and Corsica, as well as from Africa, Greece, and Italy. Someone among this ethnic mix had apparently brought chile seeds along with him or her from Cuba, but who it might have been remains unknown because over a third of Turnbull's laborers died within the first decade of making indigo there. Having had enough of Turnbull and his grisly dye business, the surviving Minorcans fled in 1776 to St. Augustine, Florida, where some of their offspring have resided ever since. One of their traditions has been the dooryard garden cultivation of datil chile peppers for use in a local dish called Minorcan pilau. As Betty Gooch Gaster recalled in 1968, "This is an authentic Minorcan recipe handed down for genera-

Courtesy dixiedatil.com

tions in my mother's family, who were among the early settlers in historic St. Augustine, Florida."

Fortunately, Mrs. Gaster's kin were not the only citizens of St. Augustine to save the seeds of datil peppers. By 1993, when chile historian Jean Andrews realized that the datil was a distinctive heirloom variety unrelated to any other pepper that was native to the North American continent, there were some forty local growers who were raising this pepper for hot-sauce processors in the St. Augustine area.

Because the pepper does not store or ship well, the consumption of fresh datil peppers has been largely restricted to this one area of Florida. While there are three seed catalogs that regularly supply datil seeds to chile aficionados across the country, these pepper plants are so well adapted to the St. Augustine climate and soils that gardeners who attempt to grow them elsewhere seldom achieve the same flavor, aroma, or yield. Nonetheless, it is a chile destined for gardens strewn along the shores of Gumbo Nation, as well as for the tables in multiethnic neighborhoods around St. Augustine.

Further Readings

Andrews, Jean. "A Botanical Mystery: The Elusive Trail of the Datil Pepper to St. Augustine." *Florida Historical Quarterly,* Fall 1995: 132–147,

Andrews, Jean. *The Pepper Trail: History & Recipes from Around the World.* Denton: University of North Texas Press, 1999.

Doggett, Carita. *Andrew Turnbull and the New Smyrna Colony of Florida.* Jacksonville, Florida: Drew Press, 1919.

Zanger, Mark A. *The American History Cookbook.* Westport, Connecticut: Greenwood Press, 2003.

MINORCAN PILAU WITH DATIL CHILE PEPPERS

1 5- to 6-pound hen
sea salt to taste
freshly ground black pepper to taste
4 stalks celery
2 onions, peeled
2 tablespoons oil
1 14-ounce can stewed tomatoes
1 tablespoon sugar
1 teaspoon fresh thyme
3 cups long-grained rice
3 cups chicken broth
1 fresh datil chile pepper

Cut up the hen into serving pieces, bony parts, gizzards, and all, except for the liver. Place them in a large pot with water, salt, and pepper and bring to a quick boil. Cut the celery into ½-inch pieces and cut one of the onions into quarters, adding them to the soup pot. Reduce the heat and allow them to simmer until the chicken meat is tender but not yet falling off the bone.

While the soup pot is simmering, halve the other onion, chop it up, and place it in a skillet with the oil. Sauté the onion until it is golden brown, then add the tomatoes, sugar, thyme, and some salt. Mash the stewed tomatoes into smaller pieces and stir frequently. Cook until these vegetables and their juices are bubbling, then reduce the heat and simmer until a thick broth forms. Dump this mixture into a glass bowl and mash it into a pulp. Add 2 tablespoons of water and put the mixture back into the skillet until the liquid is absorbed once again.

Place this pulpy mixture into a second soup pot, and add the rice, the chicken broth, and salt and pepper to taste. Place the pot on high heat and bring it to a boil. Stir the rice once and add the chicken from the other pot as a topping. Do not stir the pot again. Reduce the heat to low, cover the pot, and let it simmer for several minutes. Finally, halve the datil pepper, scrape out the seeds and veins, then uncover the pot and place the halves of the pepper atop the rice and chicken. Simmer for 20 more minutes, then cut the heat, remove the peppers, and dish out the pilau into bowls. (Reserve the pepper halves for chile aficionados or for unsuspecting visitors.) Serves 6.

Goliath Grouper

Weighing in at 800 pounds and living for as long as thirty-seven years, goliath groupers in the Gulf of Mexico and the Caribbean were once commonly served in the signature dish of Florida's cafés and bars, the grouper sandwich. During the early 1980s, consumption levels for this sandwich tripled within a matter of three years, as fishing boats newly equipped with long lines would bring in 25,000 gutted pounds of various groupers in a single trip.

But now—a quarter century after the grouper sandwich craze began—this fish has been so dramatically diminished in both size and number that the sandwich is more typically made with imposters masquerading as the goliath of yesteryear. In the fall of 2006, when fisheries officials began DNA testing of seafood sandwiches being offered to Florida's sport fishers and beachcombers, they were astonished to find a dozen other kinds of fish—including farm-raised catfish and tilapia from Panama—being passed off as native grouper. They have determined that at least a tenth of the 12,000,000 pounds of so-called grouper that were being imported into the United States each year was not even remotely related to this family of fish. Their sting operations targeting unscrupulous fish brokers and retailers only underscore the tremendous pressure on the ocean to meet the insatiable desires of fish consumers; these very pressures have brought the goliath and a half-dozen other groupers to the verge of collapse.

Floridian Ken Daniels Jr., whose family owns three fishing boats that have used longlines to catch grouper, has admitted that the writing is on the wall—fishermen will not survive very long if all the groupers become overharvested the way the goliaths were:

> It's not 1989 anymore. It's not 1996 . . . It's 2006, and if I am ever going to get my kids to college then I am going to have to take care

© SeaPics.com

of this resource and work responsibly. Ten years ago it was wide open, kill everything, do whatever you want to do. It's just not like that today.

Today, whether they are ethical fishermen like Daniels or curious naturalists snorkeling around coral reefs and shipwrecks, plenty of people are giving goliath groupers a second look. Ironically, goliaths are curious about humans as well and often come right up to scuba divers, including spear fishermen. Divers have found goliath groupers among the top predators of snappers and amberjack along the Atlantic coast. They range from the Carolinas in the north past the Florida Keys and well into the Caribbean and throughout the Gulf of Mexico. There, in the Gulf, they appear to have been most abundant in shallow waters with rocky bottoms from Pensacola to Key West within a hundred miles out from the shore. However, goliaths may also frequent mangrove habitats, which have been diminished and degraded by a half century of rapid coastal development in Florida.

Oddly, until four decades ago, English-speaking sportsmen and commercial fishermen disdained the goliath grouper, selling its flesh for half the price of that of other groupers. Instead, they concentrated their energies on landing red snapper, the fish that beach-town restaurants preferred during the heyday of that fish. However, Spanish- and French-speaking fishermen in the Caribbean and the Gulf gave the goliath more respect. Most of them were Catholic and wished to offer their neighbors plenty of fish to consume—smoked, dried, or fresh—during Lent. For centuries, Cubans harvested a few tons of goliath grouper each year to smoke on makeshift grills and then preserve for the Lenten season. A map from the 1840s, made with the help of a French-speaking fisherman, includes one place name that referred to this long-standing tradition: Passe aux Grilleurs, where the firm flesh of groupers was grilled and smoked.

Ironically, this Lenten tradition is now just as imperiled as the fish themselves.

The goliath grouper has been recognized as a critically endangered species by the World Conservation Union (IUCN), which reports that its populations declined by at least 80 percent over the first decade of the grouper sandwich craze. That occurred just prior to the U.S. Marine Fisheries Service banning any commercial take in 1990, and several countries in the Caribbean closed their fisheries as well in 1993. Although there has been some recovery, none of the goliaths that have been incidentally landed over the last decade reach even half the size of their massive forebears. Virtually all the modest-sized goliaths landed today have been born since the fisheries were closed in the 1990s, and the species will require another quarter century to reach the ages that once characterized the populations in the Caribbean and the Gulf. Nevertheless, there are plenty of fishermen in Florida who are pressuring officials to let them harvest this grouper once more, arguing that there are already some signs of population recovery.

Among the slowest-growing fish species in the Gulf, the goliath grouper also has one of the lowest reproductive rates of any fish found along the coast of Gumbo Nation. It is not expected to recover to population levels high enough to allow sustainable harvesting for many decades to come.

The following recipe for goliath grouper chowder can be prepared using most other groupers as well; just make sure what you have is truly a grouper!

Further Readings

Nohlgren, Stephen. "Giant Groupers Gobble Angler's Catch." *The St. Petersburg Times*, November 24, 2006.

Nohlgren, Stephen, and Terry Tomaslin. "The Grouper Catch." *The St. Petersburg Times*, August 6, 2006.

GOLIATH GROUPER CHOWDER

1½ pounds legally harvested grouper, deboned
¼ cup Key lime juice
4 slices bacon, chopped
1 medium Bermuda onion, chopped
2 stalks celery, chopped
¼ datil chile pepper, chopped
2 Southern Queen yams, peeled and diced
8 Creole tomatoes, chopped, and their juices
4 cups hot water or fish stock
½ teaspoon salt
½ teaspoon dried thyme leaf
1 bay leaf

Dice the grouper into ½-inch cubes and marinate in lime juice for 1 hour. In a large stew pot placed over medium heat, fry the bacon until light brown. Add the onion, celery, datil pepper, and yams, cooking and stirring until these vegetables are tender. Add the marinated fish and all remaining ingredients. Bring to a boil, and then reduce the heat to low.

Simmer the chowder for 1 hour, stirring occasionally. Season with datil pepper sauce or additional Key lime juice. Serve with hot Seminole pumpkin bread.

Pre–Civil War Peanut

Kept by a family that lived and farmed in Pearl River County, Mississippi, for over a century and a half, the heirloom pre–Civil War peanut produces a medium-sized peanut with a light pinkish skin. It is grown from Tennessee to Texas and down to Washington Parish, Louisiana. Found in Chestnut, Gumbo, and Cornbread Nations, the pre–Civil War peanut matures in 100 to 120 days. It is excellent for eating roasted and for making peanut butter.

Also known as goobers, groundnuts, and pinders, peanuts may have reached North America by 1602, but Columbus had seen them growing in Haiti and Cortés in Mexico well before that date. Never one to be timid about trying to propagate a new plant, Thomas Jefferson was busy planting peanuts by the 1790s. Soon this tropical groundnut became popular in the temperate zones of America, where it was traditionally used to make peanut soups and peanut cream gravies.

And then—exactly a century after Thomas Jefferson's nutty experiments—George Washington Carver brought peanuts into his efforts at Alabama's Tuskegee Institute, as a nitrogen-fixing cover crop to replace the cotton that had been recently devastated by boll weevils. He elaborated hundreds of new uses for the lowly peanut and created dozens of new recipes himself. The following recipe is adapted from one inked by Carver's own pen using peanuts grown in his own peanut patch. Unfortunately, you'll have to look long and hard to find sources for this historic peanut. Only three Seed Savers Exchange members offered them in 2007, and at most two specialty seed catalogs, Horus Botanicals and Seed Dreams, have offered them in recent years.

PEANUT CAKE WITH BLACKSTRAP MOLASSES

1 pint pre–Civil War peanuts, finely ground
1 heaping teaspoon baking soda
4 cups unbleached pastry flour
2 teaspoons freshly ground cinnamon or sassafras bark
½ teaspoon cloves
¼ teaspoon each freshly grated nutmeg and mace
2 cups blackstrap molasses
1 cup turbinado sugar
1 cup sunflower oil
2 cups hot water
1 egg from a free-ranging Dominique hen, beaten
1 tablespoon powdered (confectioners') sugar

Preheat the oven to 350 degrees F. In a glass mixing bowl, combine the peanuts, baking soda, flour, and spices, then add the molasses, sugar, oil, and water. Stir this batter until the flour is fully moistened, then add the egg last. Bake in a shallow 10-inch-diameter pan until golden brown on top, approximately 40 minutes, testing with a toothpick to see if the batter is no longer sticky inside. Pull from the oven and sprinkle the top with powdered sugar just prior to serving hot.

Further Readings

National Council of Negro Women. *The Historical Cookbook of the American Negro*. Boston: Beacon Press, 2000.

Whealy, Kent, and Joanne Thuente. *Garden Seed Inventory*, 6th ed. Decorah, Iowa: Seed Savers Exchange, 2004.

David Cavagnaro

Gulf Coast Native Sheep

The first domesticated sheep to touch ground in Gumbo Nation were likely Churro types, which accompanied Pedro Menéndez de Avilés in 1565 when he founded the mission of Saint Augustine in Florida. But soon Merino-Rambouillet types were imported as well, and from 1800 onward they gradually mixed with the Churros already established in Florida, Georgia, Louisiana, and Texas. Later, British breeds such as Southdown, Hampshire, Cheviot, and Dorset Horn were thrown into the mix, and all of these were interbreeding by the time that Florida was ceded to the United States in 1821. It was from this gene-rich cauldron that Southern sheep farmers brewed up the breed now known as Gulf Coast Native, Louisiana Scrub, Pineywoods Native, or simply Gulf Coast sheep.

The many color and size variants of this landrace all have a few traits in common: small bone structure, early maturity, hardiness in subtropical climes, resistance to bloodworms and stomach worms, and clean faces, legs, and underlines. The lack of wool on their faces, necks, legs, and bellies may be an adaptation to heat and to humidity. The Gulf Coast Native rams sometimes reach 180 pounds at maturity, but the ewes seldom attain weights of 100 pounds or more. Their medium-length fleeces range in color from white to tan to dark brown, and their faces can also vary in hue.

Wherever they have survived for some time in Gumbo Nation, they have become opportunistic foragers on the likes of honeysuckle, kudzu, and other invasive plants. They are renowned for their resistance to gut parasites and their adaptation to hot, wet climates and logged-over scrublands.

Jeannette Beranger; courtesy American Livestock Breeds Conservancy

CREOLE STEW WITH GULF COAST NATIVE LAMB

1 pound Henderson lima beans
2 tablespoons shortening
2 pounds Gulf Coast Native lamb shoulder, cut into 1-inch cubes
3 Louisiana shallots, chopped
2 teaspoons salt
¼ teaspoon freshly ground black pepper
½ teaspoon Tabasco pepper sauce
6 stalks celery, chopped
6 Creole tomatoes, chopped
¼ cup unbleached whole-wheat flour
2 cups water

Sort and clean the lima beans, then place them in a Dutch oven. Cover them with 2 inches of water and soak them overnight. The next morning, drain and rinse them, then set the limas aside. Next, melt the shortening in a skillet and add the cubed lamb meat. Sauté it over medium heat until all the meat is brown. Add the water and lamb to the beans in the Dutch oven, then toss in the minced shallots, salt, pepper, and Tabasco sauce. Bring the ingredients in the Dutch oven to a boil and then immediately reduce the heat to low. Cover the Dutch oven and let its contents simmer for 1 hour.

Next, add the chopped celery and tomatoes. Cook the stew for another half hour or until the lamb is tender. Remove the lamb and the vegetables with a slotted wooden spoon, reserving all the broth in the Dutch oven for making a roux. Set the stewed lamb and beans aside while you are preparing this roux.

Combine the flour with water, then add the mix to the Dutch oven that contains the broth from the lamb and beans. Simmer over medium heat, stirring frequently, until the roux thickens into a rich brown sauce. Return the lamb, beans, and vegetables to the pot and simmer 4 minutes more over low heat. The 3 quarts of Creole stew this recipe makes will be enough to serve 9 people.

Further Readings

Christman, Carolyn J., D. Phillip Sponenberg, and Donald E. Bixby. *A Rare Breeds Album of American Livestock.* Pittsboro, North Carolina: American Livestock Breeds Conservancy, 1997.

Dohner, Janet Vorwald. *The Encyclopedia of Historic and Endangered Livestock and Poultry Breeds.* New Haven, Connecticut: Yale University Press, 2001.

Eakin, Katherine, ed. *The Southern Heritage Beef, Veal and Lamb Cookbook.* Birmingham, Alabama: Oxmoor House, 1984.

Before World War II, this uniquely American breed provided most of the raw wool sent to textile mills in the Gulf South. In Louisiana alone, as many as 300,000 of these native sheep grazed scrublands and pastures prior to the war, and tens of thousands of their kin inhabited the farmlands and forests in the adjacent states.

After the war, economic pressures to industrialize meat production had the same adverse effects on Gulf Coast Native sheep as they did on many other breeds. Not only did the breed itself suffer rapid declines, but the low-input farming regimes that nurtured them also underwent a deep depression. Fortunately, both Florida State University and Louisiana State University established flocks of Gulf Coast Natives in the 1950s and occasionally exchanged rams as means to broaden their gene pools.

However, it was not until 1994 that the Gulf Coast Sheep Breeders Association established a breeders network and a strategy for more broadly promoting this landrace. This new registry incorporated the open flock book or breed registry initiated earlier by the American Livestock Breeds Conservancy. While some observers worry that too many of the best individuals of Gulf Coast Natives are still being crossbred with other breeds, the number of registered individuals continues to grow. Because its registered population has reached as high as 2,000 individuals in some years, the Gulf Coast Native is now considered to be rare rather than critically endangered. In 2006 it was boarded onto the Slow Food Ark of Taste as a prime example of the recently successful efforts in Gumbo Nation to "save it by eating it" through farmer–chef collaborations to develop new market demand for recovering breeds.

The recipe for Creole stew above is adapted from one elaborated by Katherine Eakin and features the lean lamb shoulders of the Gulf Coast Native.

Seminole Pumpkin

There is a story behind the Creek Indian name for the Seminole pumpkin, *chassa-how-itska,* which means "hanging pumpkin," for such a simple description encodes a rich ecological, cultural, and culinary history. The history of this heirloom vegetable can definitively be traced back as far as the Creek, who historically migrated southward from Georgia and Alabama into the Florida Everglades in the early 1700s to the join the Hichiti-speaking Mikasuki (I'laponathi) and the last remaining Calusa near Lake Okeechobee. There, they apparently found a domesticated variety of *Cucurbita moschata* squash that had either been grown in raised fields by the prehistoric Calusa or been traded in during early historic times from Cuba. These three peoples—Creek, Mikasuki, and Calusa—collectively became known as the Seminole, a term derived from the Creek word for "free beings" or "runaways on the loose."

The Seminoles and their predecessors would plant their pumpkin seeds at the base of girdled custard apple trees, so that the vines would climb up the tree trunks and the fruits would hang from the bare limbs. Reducing contact with soggy ground ripe for powdery mildew, this natural trellising technique allowed the pumpkins to escape disease but also to mature almost out of reach of their cultivators. To harvest them, Seminole boys used to shoot at the pumpkins with guns, until they swayed enough to break the vines and fall to the ground. Seminole boys used to say that the ones they couldn't shoot from the trees were "for the coons." The natural trellising was so successful for growing healthy pumpkin patches that Florida Crackers settling around the Everglades also adopted this "native permaculture" method, producing hundreds of Seminole pumpkins per acre. Will Pierce planted a few seeds on Hypoluxo Island in Florida in 1873, and ten years later his Seminole plants were found to be still alive and going strong.

Seminole pumpkins seem to possess qualities that make them superior to most other squashes and pumpkins that gardeners have attempted to grow in Gumbo Nation. They tolerate heat, drought, insects, and powdery mildew in places where other cucurbits

David Cavagnaro

Further Readings

Divina, Fernando, and Marlene Divina. *Foods of the Americas: Native Recipes and Traditions.* Berkeley, California: Ten Speed Press, 2004.

Goldman, Amy. *The Compleat Squash.* New York: Artisan Books, 2004.

Morton, Julia F. "The Sturdy Seminole Pumpkin Provides Much Food with Little Effort." *Proceedings of the Florida State Horticultural Society* 88 (1975): 137–142.

Nabhan, Gary Paul. "Lost Gourds and Spent Soils on the Shores of Lake Okeechobee." In *Enduring Seeds: Native American Agriculture and Wild Plant Conservation*, pp. 125–154. San Francisco: North Point Press, 1989.

West, Patsy. "The Native Way." *The Everglade Magazine*, 1997. Available at www.evergladesnationalpark.nps.gov.

Whealy, Kent, and Joanne Thuente. *Garden Seed Inventory,* 6th ed. Decorah, Iowa: Seed Savers Exchange, 2004.

SEMINOLE PUMPKIN FRITTERS

1 cup pureed flesh from a Seminole pumpkin
3 cups unbleached, all-purpose whole wheat flour
½ teaspoon hazelnut or peanut oil
¼ teaspoon freshly ground cinnamon or sassafras bark
½ teaspoon sea salt or kosher salt
2 ½ teaspoons baking powder
1 teaspoon baking soda
1 cup water
⅓ cup cane sugar, tupelo honey, or blackstrap molasses
1 quart corn or sunflower oil for frying

After cracking open the pumpkin and separating its flesh from seeds and rinds, steam or bake for ½ hour and mash the cooked pulp into a puree. Set aside to cool. Meanwhile, sift into a large bowl the flour, ground cinnamon or sassafras, salt, baking powder, and baking soda. Gradually add the cooled pumpkin puree, along with the water, nut oil, and the sugar, honey, or molasses; mix the ingredients together to form a soft dough. Knead the dough with your hands until it is elastic enough to hold together. Divide the dough into 6 equal parts and then divide them again to obtain 12 lumps. Dust your hands with flour and roll each divided portion into a small ball. Place the 12 balls of dough onto a floured surface, flour your hands, then pat each ball flat until it forms a fritterlike cake ¾ of an inch thick and 3 inches across, pinching the edges into a ruffled pattern.

In a large iron skillet, pour the corn or sunflower oil until it is an inch in depth and then heat it on medium heat until it is hot but not smoking. Lay 1 fritter in the oil, brown it for about 3 minutes on one side and then turn it over with a long-handled fork or a slotted wooden spoon. Brown the other side for about 3 minutes as well, until it puffs up and develops a crisp, golden-brown texture. Using tongs, remove the fritters from the oil, drain, and place on a paper towel. Serve warm, for 6 to 12 people.

wither altogether. Under the unforgiving sun of the subtropics, the silvery hairs on the plant's leaves create an almost shiny reflective surface, repelling many flying insects that would otherwise carry viruses onto the vines. Heirloom squash expert Amy Goldman describes the fast-growing vines as "irrepressible" because she witnessed their survival during bug infestations and windstorms that devastated other pumpkin varieties grown in the same garden.

The Seminole pumpkin is not merely prolific; the fruit of this cucurbit also has distinctive forms, flavors, and textures. Usually pear shaped, it sometimes has a graceful, swanlike neck. It is a sturdy, hard-shelled "winter squash," with a rind so hard that it sometimes takes an axe to chop it open. The tough protective skin varies from a light salmon to a pink-tinged gold, but inside the thick orange-beige flesh is so fine grained that some folks describe it as "powdery." When it is baked, its flavor is so distinctive that it is legendary among Seminoles and Crackers as well. Amy Goldman claims that when a Seminole pumpkin is cut in half and simply baked, the resulting flavor is so phenomenal that it can be regarded as "the treat of a lifetime."

Among the Seminole, this heirloom has typically been reserved for making certain breads and soups that have been part of Creek and Mikasuki cuisine for centuries. Seminole pumpkin bread is much like a fritter or empanada, and it is still featured at tribal ceremonies in Gumbo Nation and at the tribally owned restaurant at the Seminole Casino Brighton, on the edge of the Everglades. Descendants of the Seminole spiritual leader Osceola continue to use the same historic recipe for this bread as they did at the time of Osceola's tragic death in 1837. A version of the bread has also been adopted by other tribes in Gumbo Nation and, more recently, by Anglo and Hispanic immigrants to the region. Unfortunately, some of these newcomers now use the name "Seminole pumpkin bread" for pastries no longer made with the original heirloom variety, which has declined in cultivation as canned pumpkin has become so readily available in grocery stores.

For most of the last five decades, the true Seminole pumpkin has been maintained only by a few Florida old-timers and by a number of squash breeders scattered across the continent. In recent years, its seed has been available through as many as five or as few as one catalog per year, making its long-term availability to the public problematic. The variety is now critically endangered in its historic range within Gumbo Nation, due to the dramatic land- and water-use changes that have devastated the Everglades. The recipe above has been shared at intertribal events in Gumbo Nation for decades and is adapted from one collected by Patsy West, who has served as the historian for the Seminole tribe of Florida. Fernando and Marlene Divina's tips on making good pumpkin fry bread have added extra quality to these fritters.

Pineywoods Cattle

Among the oldest remnant breeds of cattle grazing the grassy face of the North American continent, Pineywoods cattle emerged out of the Criollo herds brought to the New World by the Spanish in the early sixteenth century. Meeting the peculiar parasites and diseases in the heat and humidity of Gumbo Nation, these nimble cattle adapted a set of distinctive traits that have kept them hardy and resistant over the last four and a half centuries. They have thrived where the coastal plains are covered by long-leafed "yellow" pines, with an understory of silkgrass, big bluestem, little bluestem, and carpetgrass offering them excellent forage. They have also adapted to traditional ways of farming and timber utilization in what has become known as the pine barrens of the Deep South, or the Pineywoods. The so-called Cracker cultures of Alabama, Mississippi, and Georgia have a multigenerational legacy of keeping the Pineywoods cattle as a source of meat, hides, draft power, and household dairy products. Were it not for the tenacity of these people to stick with their traditions and remain on the lands that their ancestors had farmed and forested, it is doubtful that even the remnants of Pineywoods cattle would be with us today.

Even in comparison to other descendants of the Spanish Criollo, the Pineywoods are small, lean, and resilient, with cows seldom weighing more than 800 pounds and bulls averaging about 1,000. Pregnant cows drop their calves without any need for human assistance, while their strong maternal behaviors and sharp horns can ward off any predator. There is an angularity to their conformation and a rainbow-like variety to the colors and patterns of their hides. Different strains of Pineywoods kept by different families have altogether distinctive colors and markings. The Carter strain of Mississippi—herded across the Pearl River by a sixteen-year-old named Printer Carter in the 1860s—started off as a ruddy-red herd but now includes several other colors as well. Those of the Holts in Georgia are solid-colored duns and black-sided roans. Those tended by the Conways of Mississippi tend to be red and white, while those of the Griffins are yellow.

Whatever the color of their hides, the Pineywoods have all been selected to be triple-purpose cattle, providing meat, milk, and traction or "draft power." As Mississippi farmer and folk historian Justin Pitt recalls, the oxen of the Pineywoods breed were

> . . . used for logging, pulling cotton and corn wagons during harvest, and for heavy land clearing, while mules generally were used for cultivation. Many are the pictures of ox teams hauling out the massive yellow pines that once covered the Deep South . . . President Jefferson Davis had Pineywoods cattle on his Briarfield Plantation, as is evidenced by a photograph taken by Union troops during the Civil War. There is one cow lying at the end of the front gallery that looks like a twin to one of my cows.

And yet, within a few decades following the Civil War, the Pineywoods breed had already gone into decline, as carpetbaggers from the North took control of more and more lands in Gumbo Nation and introduced "improved" English and European cattle. These cattle either were crossed with Pineywoods or replaced them altogether. Less than a dozen extended families persisted with purebred Pineywoods well into the twentieth century, and each of their herds became a unique strain with a self-contained gene pool.

Despite the efforts of these families, the breed was nearly extirpated from the pine barrens by the last decades of the twentieth century. Again, Justin Pitt offers us the best explanation of just how and why this decline has advanced:

> Our culture has changed tremendously in the last two decades. Virtually no young people are staying on the farm to raise any form of livestock, much less heritage breeds . . . but who will take up the mantle, as it were, when these older [caretakers] are gone? . . . And gone they are. My notes read almost like a casualty list after a battle, as I mark those herds that are gone. The following herds are either gone or are no longer held by the original family: Batson, Holt, Morrow, Ezell, Ladner, Hickman, Bayliss, Conway, and the list grows. The Clark strain is now gone as well—sold over the scales only a year or so before renewed interest would have assured its survival. Other herds [still] face the threat of crossbreeding.

Nevertheless, there are other families, like the descendants of Printer Carter, who have kept their own strain of Pineywoods pure—without any blood coming in from other breeds—since as far back as 1810. They did not always meet with the favor of extension agents, range scientists, and livestock breeders, who were aggressively promoting either the hybridization or the wholesale replacement of the Pineywoods strains with highly bred "improved"

Further Readings

Beranger, J., and D. Phillip Sponenberg. "A Southern Revival: Report on the Mississippi Pineywoods Cattle Workshop." *American Livestock Breeds Conservancy News* 24:1 (2007).

Brown, Julie. *More about Pineywoods Cattle.* Carnesville, Georgia: Pineywoods Cattle Registry and Breeders Association, 2007.

Christman, Carolyn J., D. Phillip Sponenberg, and Donald E. Bixby. *A Rare Breeds Album of American Livestock.* Pittsboro, North Carolina: American Livestock Breeds Conservancy, 1997.

Dohner, Janet Vorwild. *The Encyclopedia of Historic and Endangered Livestock and Poultry Breeds.* New Haven, Connecticut: Yale University Press, 2001.

Eakin, Katherine, ed. *The Southern Heritage Beef, Veal and Lamb Cookbook.* Birmingham, Alabama: Oxmoor House, 1984.

Pitt, Justin. "Is There a Next Generation for Pinewoods Cattle?" *American Livestock Breeds Conservancy News* 22:1 (2006).

Pitt, Justin. "What Good Are They?" *American Livestock Breeds Conservancy News* 22:1 (2006).

Rouse, John E. *The Criollo: Spanish Cattle in the Americas.* Norman: University of Oklahoma Press, 1977.

Sponenberg, D. Phillip. "Pineywoods Developments." *American Livestock Breeds Conservancy News* 23:6 (2006).

Phillip Sponenburg; courtesy American Livestock Breeds

breeds. Some programs explicitly set as their goal the elimination of such a "wild, inefficient" hand-me-down breed from the Southern pine barrens altogether.

By the time the collective numbers of individuals in the herds of various Pineywoods strains had dropped to fewer than 200 breeding animals, a call went out to save this unique heritage breed. Dr. Phillip Sponenberg, an advisor to the American Livestock Breeds Conservancy, made field visits over a fifteen-year period to assess and document family lines of Pineywoods cattle, developing relationships among these relictual herds. Sponenberg convinced the last breeders that their stock was still worth saving, even though many strains had already been lost. Realizing it was time to join forces to save the breed, the Pineywoods Cattle Registry and Breeders Association was formed, and Sponenberg developed a registry system to document the pedigrees of breeding cattle.

A recent breeders' workshop sponsored by the ALBC at Hattiesburg, Mississippi, was attended by more than seventy-five current and potential herd owners. Some old-timers made new commitments to pure breeding, and new allies were recruited. Today,

Pineywoods cattle numbers are at last increasing. Several New Orleans chefs have become smitten with their story, as well as the flavor of this nearly forgotten regional treasure of the table, and are turning to the farmers for advice on cooking the meat. Justin Pitt has offered these comments to the chefs, some of them tongue-in-cheek:

The meat produced by these cattle is excellent and very lean. Because they are so lean they must be cooked in ways that preserve the moisture, such as slow-roasting with ample basting. However, I know that the cook has much to do with the eating experience. No one can surpass Mrs. Matie Lee Bayliss in preparing a roast, and no one can ruin one any better than my sister. I like to tell my sister that her roasts are so dry they have been known to ask for a glass of water before being served!

The following recipe from Alabama is adapted from Katherine Eakin's collection of Southern heritage meat recipes.

CARPETBAG STEAK WITH MAÎTRE D'HÔTEL BUTTER

2 1½-pound Pineywoods strip steaks, cut with pockets
12 ounces shucked Apalachicola oysters
½ teaspoon sea salt
¼ teaspoon freshly cracked peppercorns

For maître'd hôtel butter
Mix together:
½ cup unsalted butter, melted
2 tablespoons lemon juice
2 tablespoons chopped parsley
¼ teaspoon salt
8 drops Tabasco pepper sauce

Slice each of the strip streaks so that it has a "pocket" on one side. Stuff each of the pockets full of half of the oysters, then close the opening of the pockets with toothpicks. Set the steaks on a rack and sprinkle each with salt and pepper. Place the rack on a broiler pan that is set 5 to 6 inches beneath the heating element. Broil the steaks for 8 to 10 minutes on each side. Remove the rack from the oven and place the steaks on a cutting board. Slice them diagonally across the grain, removing the toothpicks as you go. Place the sliced steaks and oysters onto four plates and drizzle the herb butter over them. Serves 4.

MAPLE SYRUP NATION

As E. B. White is said to have quipped, in Vermont a Yankee is "somebody who eats pie for breakfast," but to the rest of us, a Yankee is a New Englander of English descent. In the hills and mountains of the northeastern United States and eastern Canada, an enduring tradition based on small-scale orchard and vegetable crop production, dairy livestock pasturing, and forest product extraction has evolved over centuries. Drawing on Algonquian, English, Québecois, and French Acadian traditions, the inland Yankees and other ethnic enclaves have shaped a distinctive cuisine from cheeses, dry beans, root crops, smoked meats, and maple syrup. Although the regenerative capacity of maple forests is now in question due to climate change and acid rain, maple syrup remains the signature flavor of this region. Nonetheless, as the mixed farm economy declined in the region following World War II, many traditional foods began to be abandoned. Today, more than 180 traditional foods are threatened or endangered in this region by changing land uses and waning cultural practices.

Sugar Maple of the Allegheny Plateau

The maple has always been ranked among the loveliest of trees to see in the autumn—with its yellow-orange and pinkish-red lobed leaves brightening the forest floor—but it is also the sweetest of trees to visit in late winter. Reaching heights of ninety feet and canopy spreads of eighty feet, the sugar maple is one of the ecological and cultural keystones of Maple Syrup Nation. The flow of its sap in late winter has always been a time for collective efforts between and among rural families. From the Algonquian of Ontario and Quebec and the Micmac of New Brunswick through the Iroquois of New York and the Mohegan of Connecticut, the boiled-down syrup and dried sugar made from maples have been used as both food and medicine, while the sugar maple wood has been elaborated into bowls, paddles, ladles, oars, and furniture. The sugar maple has been a constant presence in the lives of the residents of eastern deciduous forests for centuries.

How, then, is it possible that a tree that still grows in six Canadian provinces and thirty-four U.S. states can now be considered to be "at risk"? Can't maple syrup still be found in nearly every grocery store across the entire continent? Is this another case of environmentalists "crying wolf," trying to worry the public about a threat that is little more than a myth at best?

The rapid decline of both sugar maple populations and maple syrup production quantities is no myth, however, especially in the heart of Maple Syrup Nation: the Appalachian plateau of northern Pennsylvania and adjacent New York State. As Pennsylvania forester William E. Sharpe has documented, "The reality is that unprecedented, protracted sugar maple decline and mortality exists on hundreds of thousands of acres of the Allegheny National Forest and other forest lands across the north-central portion of Pennsylvania."

Sharpe is not alone in making such pointed pronouncements. A team of six scientists who evaluated the health of sugar maples in more than forty stands on the Allegheny plateau concluded that "mortality of sugar maple has reached unusually high levels across northern Pennsylvania since the

early to mid-1980s." And the decline in productivity and survival of sugar maples is not restricted to the Allegheny plateau but extends across New York State into New Hampshire and Vermont.

"It appears to be a rather dire situation for the maple industry of [the] Northeast," noted Tim Perkins, director of the Proctor Maple Research Center. "One hundred or two hundred years from now, there may be very few maples here, [leaving] mainly oak, hickory, and pine."

Clearly, something is happening in Maple Syrup Nation, but scientists are only now honing in on the causes of these declines. The changes in forest soil chemistry resulting from acid rain deposition are the major cause of the declines that have been occurring since the 1980s. Drought, overtapping, heavy grazing intensities of livestock and deer, and heavy traffic by farm machinery have aggravated die-offs in certain localities. But recently global warming has also been identified as a contributing factor, for winter temperatures in Maple Syrup Nation have increased by 2.8 degrees since 1971. This is forcing the region's sugar makers to collect the sap from their sugarbushes three to five weeks earlier than the traditional harvest time of a century ago. As a result of trying to cope with the changing seasonality and volume of sap flow from the sugarbushes, Vermont sugar tapper Burr Morse told the *New York Times:*

> The way I feel, we get too much warm. How many winters are we going to go with Decembers turning into short-sleeve weather before the maple trees say, "I don't like it here any more"? We can't rely on tradition [for the timing of sugaring season] like we used to.

Older sugarbushes appear increasingly stressed: They may have dead branches in the upper canopies of the trees and reduced foliage, which now begins to turn color four to six weeks earlier than it did at any time within human memory. Many of the oldest sugar maples are dying at accelerated rates, but new seedlings are not growing up to take their place. In the 1950s U.S. forests like those on the Allegheny plateau produced 80 percent of the world's supply of maple syrup, but now the bulk of production has moved northward, with Canada now providing 75 percent of the world's supply. Although the species of sugar maple (*Acer saccharinum*) is not yet biologically endangered, the syrup-making traditions associated with sugarbushes on the Allegheny plateau are approaching the point of collapse.

The following recipe for maple baked beans is adapted from Dale Carson, a member of the Abenaki Nation, who originally hails from the "Republic of Missisquoi" but now lives around Madison, Connecticut.

Further Readings

Bullock, Pam. "Winter Weather Upsets Rhythms of Maple Sugar." *New York Times,* March 3, 2007.

Carson, Dale. *New Native American Cooking.* New York: Random House, 1996.

Horsley, Stephen B., Robert P. Long, Scott W. Bailey, Richard A. Hallett, and Thomas J. Hall. "Factors Associated with the Decline Disease of Sugar Maple on the Allegheny Plateau." *Canadian Journal of Forestry Research* 30:9 (2000): 1365–1378.

Moerman, Daniel E. *Native American Ethnobotany.* Portland, Oregon: Timber Press, 1998.

Peattie, Donald Culross. *The Natural History of Trees of the Eastern and Central North America.* Boston: Houghton Mifflin, 1991.

Sharpe, William E. "Acid Deposition Explains Sugar Maple Declines in the East." *BioScience* 52:1 (2002): 5.

MAPLE BAKED YELLOW-EYE BEANS

1 pound dried yellow-eye or molasses face beans
1 tablespoon unsalted butter
1 medium Red Wethersfield onion, sliced
1 cup dark amber Grade A (or Grade B) maple syrup
1 teaspoon dried mustard
1 teaspoon powdered ginger
1½ teaspoons sea salt
2 cups water

Preheat oven to 375 degrees F. In a 2-quart pot, begin to boil the yellow-eye beans in as much water as will cover them. When they come to a boil, reduce the heat and let them simmer, uncovered, for 2 hours. Next, drain the beans but reserve 2 cups of their liquid. In a small skillet, melt the butter, then sauté the onion slices in it until they are golden brown and crispy. Transfer the browned onions to a gallon-sized bean pot or large clay baking dish with a cover, then add the reserved liquid, 2 cups water, maple syrup, mustard, ginger, and sea salt. Bring to a boil and pour over the beans until they are just barely covered in the pot. Bake covered in the middle of the oven for 2 hours, uncovering the beans for the final half hour to allow the beans to absorb nearly all the liquids. Let the baked beans stand for 10 minutes after removing from the oven, then ladle them into bowls, to eat alongside pumpkin bread and wild grapes. Serves 8.

Java Chicken

Archaeologists have recently confirmed that chickens arrived in the Americas prior to the voyages of Columbus, perhaps through seafarers traveling to South America from Polynesia or Southeast Asia. It is in Southeast Asia that chickens appear to have first been domesticated from wild jungle fowl much like the ancestors of the Java chicken. But the Java itself had a later arrival in North America, being brought directly from the Indonesian island of Java in the early nineteenth century. Immediately following its introduction into Clambake and Maple Syrup Nations, it became one of the most popular poultry breeds on the continent. However, the changing fads among poultry fanciers and the industrialization of chicken production left the Java in the dust by the onset of World War II, so that this heritage breed has become critically endangered.

Javas are single-combed birds of medium size, with broad backs, deep breasts, and legs that are largely free of feathers. They may have either glossy black or mottled plumage, but their skin and the bottoms of their feet are always a brilliant yellow. Their beaks are typically black, but their shanks come in black, willow, or leaden blue hues, underlain by yellow. Their thighs, like their breasts, are large and meaty, with a subtly gamy flavor when Javas are raised as free-rangers. The roosters weigh as much as nine pounds, while Java hens seldom reach seven pounds in weight.

Jan Strasma; courtesy American Livestock Breeds Conservancy

By the 1840s, this dual-purpose poultry breed had become one of the most common barnyard birds in Maple Syrup Nation, with tens of thousands being raised for market sales each year in New York and New Jersey alone. The famous American politician and orator Daniel Webster entered his Java cocks and hens in the Boston Poultry Show of 1849, further drawing attention to the breed. They spread westward with Manifest Destiny, as far as Missouri by the time of the Civil War. Their heyday in North America continued through the 1880s, when both the Black and the Mottled Javas were accepted into the American Poultry Association's *Standard of Perfection* registry. Within the next two decades,

The Garfield Farm Museum in La Fox, Illinois, which mounted a campaign to conserve and interpret the Java Chicken. Jan Strasma; Garfield Farm Museum

Further Readings

Dohner, Janety Vorwald. *The Encyclopedia of Historic and Endangered Livestock and Poultry Breeds.* New Haven, Connecticut: Yale University Press, 2001.

Edge, John T. *The Southern Belly: The Ultimate Food Lover's Guide to the South.* Chapel Hill, North Carolina: Algonquin Books of Chapel Hill, 2007.

Howard, George E. *Standard Varieties of Chickens.* Washington, D.C.: U.S. Government Printing Office, 1916.

Malmberg, Peter. "Javas: An Ideal Homestead Bird." Accessed July 4, 2007, from www.feathersite.com/Poultry/CGD/Java/JavaHomestead.html.

Platt, June. *June Platt's New England Cook Book.* New York: Atheneum, 1971.

Sokolov, Raymond. *Fading Feast.* New York: Farrar, Strauss & Giroux, 1982.

Wilford, John Noble. "First Chickens in Americas Were Brought from Polynesia." *New York Times/Science,* June 5, 2007. Accessed July 5, 2007, from www.newyorktimes.com.

JAVA CHICKEN BRUNSWICK STEW

2 Java chicken breasts (about 1½ pounds)
4 slices Canadian bacon, chopped
2 tablespoons butter
1 large New York Early yellow-skinned onion, peeled and chopped
4 large Roma paste tomatoes, chopped
¼ teaspoon sea salt
¼ teaspoon freshly ground black pepper
1 bay leaf
½ teaspoon dried basil
1 cup chopped Early Dwarf green okra
2 cups Baxter's sweet corn kernels, shelled and steamed
2 cups Henderson or Fordhook lima beans, precooked
4 medium-sized new Seneca Horn blue potatoes, peeled and sliced
dash of Fish Pepper sauce
2 teaspoons Worcestershire sauce

Wash the chicken breasts, then dry on paper towels and set aside. Spread the bacon out in a large casserole pan, place over medium-low heat, and fry until it begins to brown while still remaining limp. Add the butter to the bacon grease, then add the chopped onion and sauté, stirring with a wooden spoon for 5 minutes or until a caramelized brown. Add the chicken breasts to the pan and cook 3 minutes on each side. Add the chopped tomatoes, seasoning them with salt and pepper, bay leaf, and basil. Cover the casserole pan and simmer on low heat for 40 minutes, occasionally stirring. When the chicken breasts are tender, add the chopped okra, simmering for another 15 minutes. With a slotted spoon, remove the chicken breasts, temporarily setting them aside.

Next, add the shelled sweet corn and lima beans, cooking with the onions, okra, tomotoes, spices, and juices for 15 minutes. Add the potato slices and cook for another 20 minutes. While simmering the stew, turn your attention to the chicken breasts, removing and discarding their skin and bones while keeping the meat as intact as possible. Bury the chicken breasts back into the juices of the stew and, when piping hot, add the Fish Pepper sauce and the Worcestershire sauce. When it reaches a pale amber color, stir into a froth with the wooden spoon one last time and serve in four warmed bowls.

however, the popularity of the Java began to slip as the U.S. Department of Agriculture intensified efforts to introduce additional breeds to the continent and to release their own improved breeds that were better suited to market production of eggs and meat. Few large flocks of Javas could be found anywhere by 1940. With the onset on World War II, the government promoted the "factory farming" of different chicken breeds for meat or for eggs, and the remaining flocks of heritage breeds on the nation's family farms were clearly in decline.

Nevertheless, certain poultry scientists and agricultural historians continued to see the merits of the Java, for its genes were used to develop new varieties such as the Black Jersey Giant, the Barred Plymouth Rock, and the Black Australorp. In the mid-1980s, the staff of the Garfield Farm Museum in La Fox, Illinois, decided that, because Javas had been kept in the Chicago area almost continuously since 1840, the museum should mount a campaign to conserve and interpret them. The staff obtained birds from the last commercial supplier of Black Javas, Dwane Urch of Turnland Poultry. In 1992, after learning that this one commercial hatchery and only five family farmers in all of North America continued to breed Javas, they formalized their conservation project with these breeders. Four distinct strains of Black Javas and two of Mottled Javas were found among these breeders, and blood-testing of their breeding herds confirmed that they were uncontaminated by improved breeds originally derived from the Java. Over the last two decades, efforts to breed more Javas have involved at least fifty farmers, museums, and backyard poultry enthusiasts, so that more than 500 Black Java hens now contribute to the gene pool each year. Nevertheless, some of the Java strains suffer from low fertility, so they remain of critical concern.

The recipe for Brunswick stew above features Java chicken meat. Food historian Ray Sokolov calls Brunswick stew "the most famous dish to emerge from the campfires and cabins of pioneer America" and places its origin in Brunswick County, Virginia, around 1828. That is where Creed Haskins and his cook Jimmy Mathews were said to have first dubbed their traditional hunter's dishes a "Brunswick stew." Others place its origin in a cast-iron cauldron from Brunswick County, Georgia, where the stew is still served as a side with barbecue sandwiches, but its fame has been widespread for more than a century and a half. Although the stew is often made with squirrel or wild fowl rather than domestic chicken, Java chicken is just gamy enough to make a memorable and authentic Brunswick stew.

Cayuga Duck

Perhaps the only domesticated duck of North American origin to gain much currency, this breed has origins that are shrouded in myth and mystery. The story goes that two strange black ducks landed in a pond by a mill, and the miller removed a joint from their wings to prevent their flight and then bred them. The breed spread in Maple Syrup Nation in the 1840s and was further developed by Mr. J. S. Clarke in the county of Cayuga, New York, not far from Cayuga Lake. Its ancestry remains unknown, but the Cayuga first attracted newspaper attention in 1851. It first achieved recognition in the American Poultry Association's *Standard of Perfection* in 1874 but never became very common. That seems odd, for the prevailing temperament of this breed is quiet and calm, so that Cayugas are usually good companions and can be hand-raised by children.

The Cayuga is a big bird with upright posture and glossy greenish-black feathers. Most Cayugas have black feet, legs, and bills as hatchlings, but their bills turn slate-colored and their legs become mottled with orange as they mature. Drakes can achieve weights of eight pounds or more, but female ducks seldom gain more than seven pounds before slaughter. Remarkably hardy, they can endure winter weather in Maple Syrup Nation without much special care. Cayuga meat is of fine flavor, texture, and quality, especially when roasted with their skins on.

For all their merits, Cayugas remain rare. The 2000 American Livestock Breeds Conservancy census of domestic waterfowl in North America found only 1,013 breeding Cayuga. Only seven people reported breeding Cayugas, and just one primary breeding flock with fifty or more breeding birds existed.

The following recipe is adapted from the Lee brothers' fine repertoire of Southern-style preparations.

Further Readings

Chrisman, J., and Robert O. Hawes. *Birds of a Feather: Saving Rare Turkeys from Extinction.* Pittsboro, North Carolina: American Livestock Breeds Conservancy, 1999.

Dohner, Janet Vorwald. *The Encyclopedia of Historic and Endangered Livestock and Poultry Breeds.* New Haven, Connecticut: Yale University Press, 2001.

Lee, Matt, and Ted Lee. *The Lee Bros. Southern Cookbook.* New York: W. W. Norton, 2006.

Photo Courtesy of Living History Farms, Des Moines, IA

ROAST CAYUGA DUCK WITH SCUPPERNONG GRAPE PRESERVES AND HOT PEPPER

This is a cross-cultural recipe, with northern duck and southern grapes!

1 5-pound Cayuga duck
1 tablespoon crushed dried datil chile or Fish Pepper pods
2 tablespoons sea salt
1 teaspoon freshly ground black pepper
⅓ cup Scuppernong grape preserves
1 teaspoon white wine vinegar
1 tablespoon sorghum molasses

Preheat the oven to 275 degrees F. Trim the fat off the duck, rinse it, and dry it inside and out. With a paring knife cut vents into its breasts and legs. In a small wooden bowl, mix the crushed red pepper pods with salt and pepper, and sprinkle this mixture onto the breasts and legs and in the cavity. Next, position the duck breast-side down on a rack in roasting pan and sprinkle more of the spice mixture on top of the duck's side and legs (and reserve some for later). Roast the duck for 1 hour before removing it to roll it over, cutting more vents in the other side to release excess fat. Roast for 1 more hour or until golden on all sides.

Next, remove the duck from the pan and increase the heat in the oven to 375 degrees F. Pour off the fat into a measuring cup and baste the duck breast and legs with the Scuppernong preserves, vinegar, and molasses, which have been mixed together in a bowl. Sprinkle the glazed skin with more of the chile spice seasoning and roast 1 final hour, basting frequently. When the roasted duck is chestnut brown, remove it from the oven, cool, and then serve it after 15 minutes.

Oldmixon Free (Clearstone) Peach

This peach has a flavor described as "rich and luscious." Its look must be just as memorable, for it was described by William Coxe in 1817 as "a beautiful, large flat peach, with a white skin and a red cheek." Large and round, it has sweet, richly flavored freestone flesh marbled with red streaks, pale and subtly blushing. When Slow Food USA recently put it on the Ark of Taste, its judges described the Oldmixon Free as one that "bursts with a vanilla flavor and a hint of sugary mint. The meat is delicate with a tart finish." It is the gem of Maple Syrup Nation.

The English historian Sir John Oldmixon is credited with having introduced the variety to America by planting a pit, or stone, while on a visit in the early 1700s. Today, Sir John must be rolling in his grave, for his generous gift to American fruit connoisseurs is now available from only one nursery on the entire continent, Southmeadow Fruit Gardens in Michigan.

How can it be that such a fine fruit falls into neglect, when so many Americans still love peaches? Perhaps the greater disease resistance, shorter time to fruit production, and greater shippability of modern peach cultivars answer that question, but on the tree or off, these new varieties are hard to tell apart. The Oldmixon, though, remains distinctive, unparalleled, and possibly unsurpassed.

OLDMIXON PEACHES AND CREAM

4 Oldmixon Free peaches, skinned and pitted
½ cup heavy cream
½ teaspoon pure vanilla extract
¼ teaspoon maple syrup

Dice the peaches into half-inch bites and place half of them in each of two bowls. Measure out the cream into a mixing cup, add the vanilla and maple syrup, and pour the mixture over the peaches in the bowls. It cannot get any simpler or better than that!

Further Readings

Barry, Patrick. *The Fruit Garden: A Treatise.* Rochester, New York: Charles Scribner, 1883.

Coxe, William A. *A View of the Cultivated of Fruit Trees and the Management of Orchards and Cider.* Philadelphia: Carey and Son, 1817.

Reproduced from U.P. Hedrick's *The Peaches of New York* (Albany: J.B. Lyon, 1917).

Seneca Hominy Flint Corn

Pearly white kernels form eight rows on the short, lean cobs of this flint corn, called *ha-gó-wa* among the Seneca. These pearls are sometimes mixed with a scattering of red and blue kernels, but the ears are not as variegated as the calico flint and flour corns that were historically grown in what we now call Maple Sugar Nation. Here, by the middle of the fourteenth century, many farmers in the Iroquois Confederacy were intercropping flint corns, beans, and squash together in mounds, referring to them as the *dioheka*, or "three sisters."

This particular heirloom flint corn is the legacy of Nettie Watt, a Seneca elder and gardener on the Allegheny Reservation that once straddled the New York–Pennsylvania border. Mrs. Watt lived on what was known as the Seneca's Cornplanter Grant until it was destroyed by the building of the Kinzua Dam in the 1960s. The Kinzua Reservoir—nicknamed "the Lake of Perfidy"—eventually inundated about 10,000 acres of Seneca farms and woodlands, a third of the reservation's land, forcing the relocation of Watt and hundreds of Seneca by 1964. The broken treaties leading to this tragic event evoked protest songs such as *As Long as the Grass Shall Grow,* popularized by Johnny Cash, and *Now That the Buffalo's Gone,* penned by Buffy Sainte-Marie. Until they were forced to relocate, the Watt family and their Seneca ancestors had grown this flint corn in their homelands for more than 1,000 years. Today, this heirloom maize is kept accessible to Native Americans only by those who received its seed through the Eastern Native Seeds Conservancy before it closed its doors. Because neither nonprofit seed catalog nor tribal nursery keeps it on their lists, it can be considered to be critically endangered.

Seneca Hominy flint is one of perhaps a dozen distinctive northern flint corns surviving in Maple Syrup Nation that trace their ancestry back to maize introductions that made their way into the region around A.D. 1040. Although Seneca Hominy flint may seem superficially similar to other flints and flours persisting among the Iroquois Confederacy members—Tuscacora White flour, Longfellow flint, Mohawk Round Nose, Narragansett White Cap, and Seneca Blue Bear Dance—each of these maize vari-

Courtesy Mark Millard, USDA-ARS, Ames, Iowa

eties has diverged from the others enough to have its own particular climatic adaptations and peculiar culinary uses.

Most of these corns became relatively scarce after World War II, but thanks to the late great Native American activist and historian John Mohawk, there was a revival of interest in them beginning around 1992, some 500 years after the continuous colonization of the Americas. John Mohawk worked with the Pinewood Community Farm to promote several Iroquois corns, including Tuscarora White hominy corn, which received rave reviews at high-profile tastings from New York City to Albuquerque and San Francisco. Mohawk has since passed away, but at about the same time, agricultural scientist Jane Mt. Pleasant—herself of Tuscarora ancestry—had begun to involve Native American students at Cornell University in developing a seed bank as a safety net for such native corn varieties of Maple Syrup Nation. Mt. Pleasant also documented the science behind the three-sisters mound system of intercropping. Despite the passing of Watt and Mohawk, Seneca

Hominy flint corn lives on and will hopefully land in the hands of another generation tenacious enough to nurture it along.

The following recipe has been adapted from one version of "corn not quite ripe soup" recorded by Frederick Wilkerson Waugh in 1913 and another by Iako-Nikohn-Rio, who learned its basics from Mohawk tribal members.

Further Readings

Bilharz, Joy A. *The Allegany Senecas and Kinzua Dam*. Lincoln: University of Nebraska Press, 1998.

Doebley, John F., Major M. Goodman, and Charles W. Stuber. "Exceptional Genetic Divergence of Northern Flint Corn." *American Journal of Botany* 73:1 (1986): 64–69.

Mt. Pleasant, Jane. "The Science behind the Three Sisters Mound System: An Agronomic Assessment of an Indigenous Agricultural System in the Northeast." In Bruce F. Benz, Robert H. Tykot, and John. E. Staller, eds., *Histories of Maize*, pp. 529–537. Burlington, Massachusetts: Academic Press, 2006.

Nabhan, Gary Paul. "35 Who Made a Difference: Jane Mt. Pleasant; Iroquois Tradition Plus Western Science Equals a More Sustainable Future." *The Smithsonian* 36:8 (2005): 45.

Parker, A. C. "Iroquois Uses of Maize and Other Food Plants." In W. N. Fenton, ed., *Parker on the Iroquois*. Syracuse, New York: Syracuse University Press, 1968.

Rio, Iako-Nikohn. "Mohawk Corn Soup." On the website of NativeTech: Indigenous Food and Traditional Recipes. 2005. Accessed August 15, 2007, from www.nativetech.org/recipes.

Waugh, F. H. "Iroquois Foods and Food Preparation." Geological Survey Memoir 86, Anthropological Series Number 12. Ottawa, Ontario: Canada Department of Mines, 1916. (Reprinted in 1991 by Irocrafts, Ltd., Ohsweken, Ontario, Canada.)

SENECA-MOHAWK HULLED HOMINY CORN SOUP

2 cups hulled corn, of Seneca Hominy flint or Tuscarora White flour

2 teaspoons fine dry wood ashes (or hydrated lime)

1½ cups Duane Baptiste potato beans, boiled until tender

½ pound venison backstrap, cut into chunks like stew meat

4 smoked venison sausage, diced

4 large Oxheart carrots

1 Waldoboro Green Neck rutabaga

2 Gilfeather turnips

¼ Early Wakefield cabbage

½ teaspoon sea salt

freshly ground black pepper to taste

Harvest the corn when it is firm but not fully ripe.

To make hominy, boil it with the wood ashes until the hulls are loosened. Rinse the kernels thoroughly in a sieve under cold running water, then boil them for another half hour and rinse them again until the kernel seedcoats are completely free of the hominy grains.

Add the potato beans (and their cooking juices) to the pot and let the corn and beans sit together while you prepare the other ingredients. In a skillet, brown the chopped venison and the sausage, then add them to the pot. Next, dice the carrots, rutabaga, and turnips and chop the cabbage, then add them as well.

Finally, add enough water to cover all the ingredients by an inch, season with salt and pepper, and gently boil until all of the vegetables are tender. Serve in bowls.

Buckeye Chicken

The only American chicken breed known to have been developed entirely by a woman, the Buckeye owes its existence to Mrs. Nettie Metcalf of Warren, Ohio, an expert in genetically selecting poultry for backyard production in the late nineteenth century. Nettie Metcalf first bred several Barred Plymouth Rock hens to a Buff Cochin rooster and then bred these half-Cochin pullets to a Black-Breasted Red Game rooster. The resulting offspring were rather fluffy, with a lustrous sheen to their red plumage, underlain by slate-colored barring. This slate undercolor distinguished Buckeyes from their pea-combed competitor, the Rhode Island Red, which had either a red or a white undercolor beneath its own red plumage.

Metcalf named her unusually crimson birds after her Ohio homeland, the Buckeye State. She selected the Buckeyes to be free-range foragers that could withstand Ohio's cold, wet winters, for such climatic tolerance was hardly found in the poultry of her era.

Courtesy American Livestock Breeds Conservancy

They soon caught on among farmers and backyard poultry fanciers in Maple Syrup Nation.

To this day, Buckeyes retain the stocky shape and assertive behavior of their game fowl ancestors. They have rather stout legs and broad, well-rounded chests, producing substantial thigh and breast meat.

As Craig Russell, past president of the Society for the Preservation of Poultry Antiquities, has observed, "It is a good dual-purpose bird, more than the simple meat bird that Metcalf tried to create. They are big enough to produce generous portions of meat, but are also pretty good layers." When they reach sexual maturity, Buckeye hens lay brown, medium-sized eggs.

By 1896, Metcalf was recognized by the American Poultry Association for producing consistently meaty, red-feathered Buckeyes that seemed destined to compete for popularity against Rhode Island Reds in local, regional, and national poultry shows. But within a few years, it became clear that Rhode Island Reds had somehow cornered the market, and by 1904 Buckeye production began to decline. It is now considered one of the five most endangered American chicken breeds and has been added to the Slow Food Ark of Taste. This recognition has prompted RAFT—led in this case by the American Livestock Breeds Conservancy—to offer a number of workshops and tastings that are helping return this bird to our tables. In 2007 over 1,000 chicks were hatched and distributed to new breeders. The following recipe hearkens back to a 1794 volume of *The Experienced English Housekeeper* and is adapted from Elverson and McLanahan's collection of recipes from early American cooks, *A Cooking Legacy*.

BUCKEYE CHICKEN CURRIED IN SAVORY JELLY

8 medium-sized Buckeye chicken breasts
2 tablespoons onion salt
2 tablespoons curry powder
½ teaspoon salt
2 freshly ground white peppercorns
2 cups strong chicken broth
2 envelopes unflavored gelatin
¼ cup cold water
¼ cup heavy cream
8 strips pimento peppers
4 parsley sprigs

Place the washed Buckeye chicken breasts in a shallow 14-inch baking pan, breast-side down. Sprinkle onto each of the breasts a light coating of onion salt, curry powder, salt, and pepper. Place the covered pan of chicken breasts in the refrigerator overnight to season. Late the next morning, turn the skin side down, pour chicken broth over the breasts until each is half-covered, and place aluminum foil over the pan. Place in a preheated 350-degree F oven and poach until the juices run clear. Remove and cool the chicken breasts, then remove their skins and reserve the broth.

Next, soften the gelatin in a saucepan of cold water, add the hot broth, and stir until all the gelatin is dissolved. Take out ½ cup of broth, and add heavy cream to it in a bowl. Pour the rest of the clear broth into a shallow pan to reserve in the refrigerator. Cool the thickened broth with cream until it almost sets, then place the chicken breasts on a serving platter and glaze with this creamy jelly. Just before serving, cut each breast into half-inch cubes, and decorate them with strips of pimentos and bouquets of parsley. Serve cold with pawpaw or persimmon chutney. Serves 8.

Further Readings

The American Standard of Perfection. Burgettstown, Pennsylvania: American Poultry Association, 2001.

Bender, Marjorie, Robert O. Hawes, and Donald E. Bixby. *Counting Our Chickens: Identifying Breeds in Danger of Extinction.* Pittsboro, North Carolina: American Livestock Breeds Conservancy, 2004.

Dohner, Janet, and Vorwald Dohner. *The Encyclopedia of Historic and Endangered Livestock and Poultry Breeds*. New Haven, Connecticut: Yale University Press, 2001.

Elverson, Virginia T., and Mary Ann McLanahan. *A Cooking Legacy.* New York: Walker and Company, 1975.

Heinrichs, Christine, and Don Schrider. "Enjoy Heritage Chickens." *Mother Earth News*, February–March 2005. Available at www.motherearthnews .com/Livestock-and-Farming/2005-02-01/Enjoy-Heritage-Chickens.aspx.

MOOSE NATION

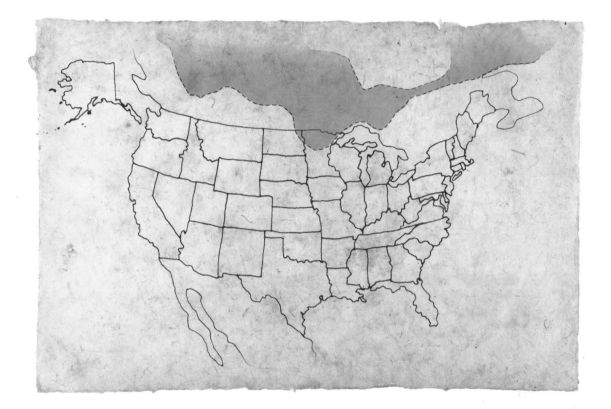

Exemplifying the North Woods of north-central Canada through the Upper Midwest of the United States, Moose Nation hosts the highest percentage of subsistence hunters and fisherfolk of any region in North America. Moose meat may be the mainstay in the larder of hunters and trappers, but many other species of game abound. Some, such as the musk oxen of the Arctic Circle, have suffered severe declines historically. Nevertheless, the long summer days of Moose Nation offer an abundance of wild berries, big game, and oil-rich fish. The extent and health of this region are already being reshaped by the effects of global warming. At least five of its traditional foods are already threatened or endangered, and many more may soon be added to that list.

Moose of Northwestern Minnesota

While they are the largest living member of the deer family, moose are surprisingly timid and quite vulnerable to a variety of stresses, from soaring temperatures to miniscule parasites. With gangly, knock-kneed legs, humped shoulders, homely faces, big ears, and enormous snouts, moose win few beauty prizes. What they lack in prettiness, however, they make up for with stature, weights of up to 1,000 pounds, and laconic character.

The moose of northwestern Minnesota are among the southernmost populations of this species on the continent, and perhaps that's why they are so vulnerable to the consequences of global warming. Already, moose have retreated from Michigan, Wisconsin, Pennsylvania, and New York during recent historic times. Nevertheless, the moose of northwestern Minnesota around Agassiz National Wildlife Refuge still evoke in us that classic recognition of the wonders of the North Woods. Indeed, moose populations extend from Minnesota and Maine all the way northward to Hudson Bay and Alaska's tundra. In the south, they frequent forests, muskegs, and woodland patches on the edges of farmlands. There, the moose of Minnesota are now in trouble, and many wonder whether their awesome character might soon vanish altogether from the North Woods of Minnesota, the southern periphery of Moose Nation.

The term *moose* comes from an Algonquian word meaning "eater of twigs." Many indigenous communities as well as non-Indian trappers have used moose meat as their mainstay. Hundreds of variations on moose meat stew exist, but all are hearty enough to warm a hunter or trapper on a cold winter's night.

In the mid-1980s both hunters and wildlife biologists first noticed that the moose of northwestern Minnesota were suffering from some kind of die-off. There were about 4,000 moose in the state in 1984, but by 1993, only 3,500 were alive. That prompted wildlife researchers to radio-collar 150 moose in 1995, not merely to track their movements and mortality rates but to take necropsies to determine the causes of any further die-offs.

What the wildlife biologists found over the following five years was rather unsettling. More than half of the radio-collared moose died while under study, and at least another eighty-four individuals from the same herds died as well. The immediate causes of death varied, but parasites, diseases, mineral deficiencies, and outright starvation had all taken their toll. Many of the moose succumbed to parasitic infestations of liver flukes and brainworms. The moose that died from an unidentified infectious disease and the parasites were probably susceptible to them because of chronic malnutrition. By 2005, only 250 moose were left in northwestern Minnesota, and many of those also showed signs of mineral deficiencies, illness, and parasites.

Mike Schrage, who has helped census the two largest moose herds in Minnesota for years, suggests

Malene Thyssen; courtesy Wikimedia Commons

Further Readings

Chapman, Joseph A., and George A. Feldhamer. *Wild Mammals of North America.* Baltimore: Johns Hopkins University Press, 1982.

Gunderson, Dan. "The Dying Moose Herd in Northwestern Minnesota." Minnesota Public Radio, February 10, 2005.

Hunter, Alice. *Alice Hunter's North Country Cookbook.* Yellowknife, Northwest Territories, Canada: Northwest Publishers/Outcrop Ltd., 1986.

Murray, Dennis L., Eric W. Cox, Warren B. Ballard, Heather A. Whitlaw, Mark S. Lenarz, Thomas W. Custer, Terri Barnett, and Todd K. Fuller. "Pathogens, Nutritional Deficiency, and Climatic Influences on a Declining Moose Population." *Wildlife Monographs* 166:1 (2006): 1–30.

that the reasons the population in the Northwest has "crashed" are all the indirect effects of global warming. Over the past four decades, the growing season has significantly lengthened, and the peak summer temperatures have dramatically risen throughout the Minnesota range of moose herds. The animals cannot bear the additional heat loads, and so they dissipate much of their energy panting or seeking out water. The die-off is most severe during midsummer's heat surges. And even the moose that survive the heat itself become plagued with parasitic buildups over the following months. Their mortality rates are now twice the continentwide average of all herds across North America.

Although moose are in no way endangered as a species, the populations at the southern limits of their range are blinking out. By the end of the twenty-first century, Minnesota summers are predicted to be six to twelve degrees warmer than they are now. That will mean that moose populations may survive several hundred miles north of the boundary waters in Canada but may vanish altogether from the United States.

The following recipe for stuffed moose heart is adapted from Alice Hunter of the Northwest Territory.

M. Gifford

STUFFED MOOSE HEART

1 moose heart
2 tablespoons lard
1 celery stalk, chopped
1 medium onion, peeled and chopped
½ cup diced Canadian bacon
1½ cups cubed rye bread
¼ cup milk
¼ teaspoon dried sage
¼ teaspoon caraway seeds
¼ teaspoon dill seeds
½ teaspoon sea salt
½ teaspoon coarsely ground black
   peppercorns

Wash the moose heart and pat dry with paper towels. Melt 1 tablespoon of the lard in a skillet and then brown the moose heart on all sides over medium-low heat. Remove the heart from the skillet and set aside. Add the remaining lard to the skillet and then add the chopped celery and onion and the Canadian bacon. Sauté until these ingredients are soft, then add the rye bread cubes to the skillet. Stir with a wooden spoon until the lard and bacon fat have been absorbed into the bread.

At this point, preheat the oven to 325 degrees F. Remove the stuffing from the skillet and place in a glass bowl. Pour the milk over the stuffing, add all the spices, and mix with the wooden spoon. Using your hands, mix the stuffing one last time and then insert it into the moose heart. Place the stuffed heart into a baking dish and bake in the oven for 2 hours. Slice and serve while still warm.

Northern Giant (McFayden) Cabbage

The seeds of giant drumhead cabbages were first brought across the Atlantic in 1541 on the third voyage of French explorer Jacques Cartier, and they have been a staple vegetable for the inhabitants of Moose Nation ever since. By the time Fearing Burr Jr. cataloged the field and garden vegetables of North America in 1863, there were several varieties of drumhead cabbages that were widely available to farmers and gardeners, including the Bergen or Great American Quintal, the Early, the Early Low Dutch, and the Large Late or American, many of which yielded sixty tons of edible mass per acre in cold climates. It appears that the Northern Giant or McFayden emerged from this group of drumheads to become exquisitely adapted to the far north. The alternate name McFayden suggests some Scottish heritage associated with this heirloom cabbage. It has a huge drumhead that is firm and rather solid, thereby resisting most cabbage worms. Its heads are composed of crisp, glossy, greenish-white leaves that are excellent for sauerkraut.

Over most of the last two centuries, the Northern Giant produced the largest cabbage heads in both Canada and Alaska, where up to twenty-one hours of sunshine fuel their growth on the longest summer days. Since 1941, when the first Great Cabbage Contest was held at the Alaska State Fair in the town of Palmer, north of Anchorage, Northern Giants have won awards many times. In 2000, gardener Barb Everingham from Wasilla, Alaska, broke the record for the heaviest cabbage ever grown on North American soil, producing a leaf mass from Northern Giant seed that weighed in at 105.6 pounds *without having yet formed a mature head!* Ms. Everingham may have grown one of the largest leaf vegetables ever produced, and she used her prize winnings to build a cabin in the wilds of Talkeetna, Alaska. Curiously, the seed of Northern Giant heirlooms has become commercially scarce, being offered only by P. P. Seed of Hamburg, New York; otherwise the variety is simply passed from hand to hand by Canadians and Alaskans enamored by its drumheads.

The following traditional recipe for country sauerkraut—adapted for the use of Northern Giant drumheads and heirloom apples—comes to us via Beth Dooley and Lucia Watson's fine book, *Savoring the Seasons of the Northern Heartland.*

The French explorer Jacques Cartier, and the river in eastern Canada that bears his name. Library and Archives Canada (engraving); Josyan Pierson (photo)

COUNTRY SAUERKRAUT WITH NORTHERN GIANT CABBAGE

1 medium White Portugal onion, peeled and sliced
2 tablespoons rendered Canadian bacon fat
1 pound Northern Giant cabbage, fermented into sauerkraut then drained
2 tart Canada Red apples, peeled, cored, and sliced
½ cup apple cider
1 teaspoon caraway seeds
2 tablespoons granulated maple sugar or maple syrup

¼ teaspoon salt
¼ teaspoon freshly ground black pepper

In a large skillet, sauté the onion slices in the bacon fat until they are caramelized and translucently brown. Add the sauerkraut, apple slices, cider, and caraway seeds. Stir to combine them in the skillet. Simmer, uncovered, for 20 minutes, then add the maple sugar (or syrup), salt, and pepper. Serve atop moose or caribou sausage or pork chops or with dumplings.

Further Readings

Burr, Fearing Jr. *The Field and Garden Vegetables of America*. Chillicothe, Illinois: American Botanical Booksellers, 1994. (Originally published in 1863.)

Dooley, Beth, and Lucia Watson. *Savoring the Seasons of the Northern Heartland*. New York: Random House, 1994.

Shackle, Eric. "Can Alaskans Grow a 125-Pound Cabbage?" 2004. Available at www.bdb.co.za/shackle/articles/alaskan_cabbage.htm.

Courtesy Lazy Mountain Bed and Breakfast

Short and Thick Parsnip

Short and Thick is an early-maturing hollow-crowned parsnip that is well adapted to the short growing seasons and shallow soils of Moose Nation. Hollow-crowned parsnips were introduced from Europe to Canada and the United States by 1609, and they became a popular staple among English, Dutch, French, and German colonists attempting to farm in Canada's northern climes. Sweeter and nuttier in texture than their close relatives the carrots, parsnips are said to have a flavor that mingles well with honey and spices; alternatively, they serve well as a side dish to salt cod.

Short and Thick has a stubby but exceedingly tender root that tapers very rapidly in its first six inches belowground. The main root can grow up to three inches in diameter within one hundred days after planting, but it seldom attains lengths of more than eight inches in that time. Its attractive white flesh retains its excellent cooking quality even when pulled from the ground before full maturity, and it can be kept in cold cellars for weeks, if not months. If hard freezes arrive while it is still in the ground, its starches are converted to sugars, and the entire root can be eaten without being peeled. While an old adage claims that "parsnips are poison unless they are first frozen," the truth is that their sweetness and flavor are simply enhanced when they remain underground until after the first snow blankets the garden beds of Moose Nation.

This oddly semisweet parsnip is easy to pull from the ground and can be immediately braised, steamed, or parboiled, then mashed for a variety of uses. Unfortunately, its commercial availability is now extremely limited, with Prairie Garden Seeds in Saskatchewan and Seeds of Diversity in Toronto being among its only regular outlets. Parsnip use has declined in many parts of Canada due to the availability of fresh vegetables that are transported from further south during most winter months.

The following recipe for parsnip chowder is adapted from the 1947 classic *Secrets of New England Cooking,* written by Ella Shannon Bowles and Dorothy S. Towle.

SHORT AND THICK PARSNIP CHOWDER

⅓ cup diced salt pork
4 medium-sized Barletta white onions, sliced
2 cups sliced Short and Thick parsnips, cleaned but not peeled
1 cup cubed Green Mountain potatoes
2 cups boiling water
4 cups hot milk
2 tablespoons canola (rapeseed) oil
salt and pepper to taste
¼ cup rolled cracker crumbs

In a deep skillet, render the fat from the salt pork, then add the onion slices and sauté until they are caramelized and translucently brown. Remove the pork scraps and then pour the remaining grease and onions into a large kettle. Add the sliced parsnips and cubed potatoes, then immerse in 2 cups of boiling water. Cook these root vegetables until they are fork tender. Add the milk, canola oil, and seasonings. Bring the chowder almost to the boiling point, but just before reaching that point, toss in the cracker crumbs and take the kettle off the heat. Ladle the chowder into wooden bowls and serve at once.

Further Readings

Bowles, Ella Shannon, and Dorothy S. Towle. *Secrets of New England Cooking.* Mineola, New York: Dover Publications, 2000.

Smith, Andrew F. *The Oxford Companion to American Food and Drink.* New York: Oxford University Press, 2007.

Whealy, Kent, and Joanne Thuente. *Garden Seed Inventory,* 6th edition. Decorah, Iowa: Seed Savers Exchange, 2004.

PINYON NUT NATION

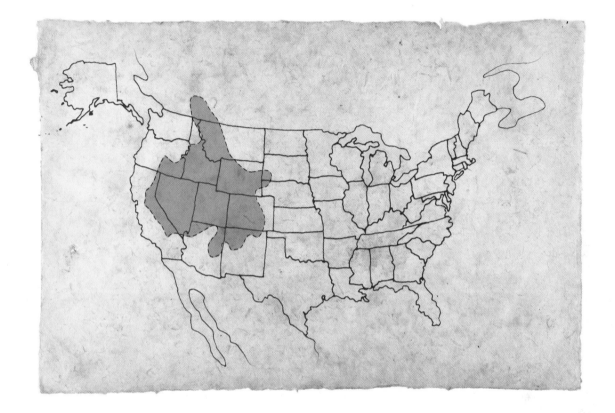

Much of the semiarid Intermountain West lies within Pinyon Nut Nation. From the Front Range of the Rockies to the eastern flanks of the Sierra Nevada, pinyon nuts have been gathered for millennia but are now declining due to the insidious combination of drought, bark beetles, and wildfires. Ranching and sheepherding traditions remain strong in this region, which hosts the annual National Cowboy Poetry Gathering, an event that features Basque and other cowboy cuisines. The region is rich in freshwater fish, many of them endangered, and in berries, bulbs, and grasses. More than fifty-two of its traditional foods are now threatened or endangered.

Nevada Single-Leaf Pinyon Nut

Pinyon nuts were one of the first American tree harvests ever to be described in a European language; the Spanish explorers Alvar Núñez Cabeza de Vaca and Estevan el Moro apparently stumbled upon a traditional gathering ground of pinyon nuts in 1536.

Of the many admirers of Nevada pinyon nuts, naturalist John Muir was the astute observer who has perhaps given us the richest, *loveliest* description of how significant this wild crop was to the Paiutes in the 1870s:

When the crop is ripe, the Indians make ready their long beating-poles; bags, baskets, mats, and sacks are collected; the women . . . assemble at the family huts; the men leave the ranch work; old and young, all are mounted on ponies and start in great glee to the nut-lands, forming curiously picturesque cavalcades; flaming scarfs and calico skirts stream loosely over the knotted ponies; two squaws usually astride of each, with baby midgets bandaged in baskets slung on their backs or balanced on the saddle-bow; while nut-baskets and water jars project from either side, and the long beating-poles make angles in every direction . . . Then the beating begins right merrily, the burrs fly in every direction, rolling down the slopes, lodging here and there against rocks and sage-brushes, cached and gathered by the women and children in fine natural gladness.

Producing a delicious, soft-shelled nut, the Nevada Single-Leaf Pinyon is a tree that most would call a shrub, for it may hardly reach twenty-five feet in

David Cavagnaro

height after 500 years of growth in the Great Basin Desert. The soft, yellow-orange, nearly translucent meat of this pinyon is so costly for the tree to produce under arid conditions that it is produced only once every few years. However, a decade of drought and bark beetle infestation has knocked back nut production even more and has killed millions of trees that formerly dominated the plant cover on the mountain slopes in Nevada, Utah, and eastern California. Even so, whenever the nuts are ripe in pinyon-juniper woodlands, both wildlife and human inhabitants still head for the hills to partake of their delights. As such, the contemporary citizens of Pinyon Nut Nation are honoring a cultural and ecological keystone of the region that has provided food, fuel, and shelter for upwards of 10,000 years.

A Paiute woman winnowing pinyon nuts in the 1950s or '60s. Courtesy University of Nevada

MEXICAN WEDDING COOKIES WITH NEVADA SOFT-SHELLED PINYON NUTS

8 tablespoons (1 stick) unsalted butter, softened
$\frac{1}{3}$ cup powdered (confectioners') sugar, plus extra for coating cookies
1 teaspoon vanilla extract
1 teaspoon grated orange rind
$1\frac{1}{4}$ cups all-purpose flour
$\frac{1}{8}$ teaspoon salt
1 teaspoon anise seeds
$\frac{1}{2}$ teaspoon freshly ground cinnamon
$\frac{1}{2}$ cup Nevada Single-Leaf Pinyon nuts, toasted and ground
48 whole pinyon nuts, shelled

In a medium-sized glass mixing bowl, beat the butter with $\frac{1}{3}$ cup of powdered sugar, the vanilla, and the orange rind until fluffy. Mix in the flour, salt, anise seeds, and cinnamon. Next, fold in the ground pinyon nuts. Refrigerate this dough until it is firm, which typically takes 2 hours or more. Remove the dough and roll it into crescent or round shapes, using about 2 rounded teaspoons of dough for each cookie.

Preheat the oven to 350 degrees F. Place the cookies an inch apart on greased baking sheets and firmly set two whole pinyon nuts atop each cookie. Bake the cookies until they are lightly browned, about 12 to 15 minutes. Roll the warm cookies in powdered sugar and cool on wire racks. Makes 2 dozen cookies for the next family wedding!

Further Readings

Frazier, Penny. "History of American Pine Nuts and the People of the Great Basin." On the Goods from the Woods website, 2004. Available at www.pinenut.com/history.htm.

Lanner, Ronald. *The Pinyon Pine: A Natural and Cultural History.* Reno: University of Nevada Press, 1991.

Compared to other pine nuts from Asia and Europe, the nuts from Nevada are large in size and soft in the shell and have an almost fruity complexity of flavors, which is enhanced by roasting. They are rich in unsaturated, cholesterol-free fats and store extremely well. Nevertheless, imported pine nuts now meet more than 80 percent of consumer demand in the United States. How is it that such a natural culinary treasure—one recently boarded onto Slow Food USA's Ark of Taste—could be underutilized in its own backyard, while there remains a strong demand for nuts of inferior quality?

The answer to this question is complex, but it reminds us that, historically, most any food prized by hunter-gatherers was looked down on by agricultural and urbanized peoples. Although the Shoshone, Paiute, Washoe, and other indigenous communities had detailed knowledge of this resource and celebrated sophisticated "first fruits" ceremonies at harvest time, just as some farmers do for their crops, pinyon nuts were relegated to the status of poor man's food. Since the nineteenth century, more than 1,300,000 acres of pinyon trees have been cleared away from lands in the Great Basin simply to make more grassy pasture for cattle, even though the value of a 75- to 250-pounds-per-acre harvest of pinyon nuts dwarfs the income that could be made by grazing livestock on the same amount of land. In addition, mines scattered across the Great Basin sent out men to cut pinyon trees for fuel wood to fire their smelters. By the end of the twentieth century, less than a tenth of all lands formerly dominated by pinyon pines retained enough cover to sustain any nut harvest.

Nevertheless, the remaining gathering grounds of the Shoshone and other tribes are visited by traditional harvesters to this day. Timing their harvest to optimize the ease of collecting and cracking open the cones, they use long willow poles to knock the opening cones free of the trees, then gather the cones and loose nuts up in wicker baskets to carry to their campfires. There, the cones and nuts are roasted and cracked open on an anvil-like stone. Historically, the nuts were used in soups, stews, and porridges, as well as being traded and bartered to neighboring Anglo and Mexican cultures not so fortunate to have their own prime pinyon habitats.

Just as the demand for an in-country source of pine nuts was increasing—and land managers began to recognize their cultural and culinary value—a drought triggered the infestation of stressed pinyon trees with bark beetles, which can kill a 500-year-old tree in a matter of months. By 2010, it is projected that more than 80 percent of all pinyon trees of various species on the Colorado Plateau will have been killed by bark beetles. This loss has greatly increased the value of the nut harvests in the adjacent region of the Great Basin Desert. Perhaps for the first time in history, Shoshone nut harvesters are receiving close to fair trade value for the nuts they sell to wholesalers. The soft-shelled pine nuts from Nevada are now being marketed for a retail value of $25 per pound. Thanks to grassroots organizers Bonnie Babb and Penny Frazier, upwards of 20,000 pounds of Shoshone-harvested nuts have entered the U.S. marketplace in recent years.

One of the most widely used recipes for these nuts in Pinyon Nut Nation is for the preparation of "Mexican" wedding cookies as described in the recipe on the preceding page.

Cui-ui Sucker

In the midst of the Great Basin Desert, the Northern Paiute of Pyramid Lake, Nevada, have long referred to themselves as the Cui-ui-dakado, "those who feasted on *cui-ui*." Pronouced "kwee-wee," the once-abundant big-mouthed sucker that lives in Pyramid Lake, the Lower Truckee River, and nowhere else has perhaps been a staple of the Paiute diet since they moved to the shores of the lake some 2,000 years ago. Archaeological evidence from a cave on the eastern shore of the lake demonstrates that cui-ui were prehistorically caught, decapitated, skinned, and eaten. Today, both the cui-ui and the Paiute traditions associated with it are considered to be endangered, after a century of water diversions from Pyramid Lake, which was once the second-largest natural lake in the West.

The cui-ui is one of a dozen suckers that inhabit the lakes and streams of Pinyon Nut Nation. It is a slow-growing but long-lived fish, with the same individuals known to remain allegiant to particular habitats in Pyramid Lake for forty years or more. While the females are plump and grayish in cast, the breeding males turn brilliant reds and brassy oranges. They reach up to twenty-seven inches in length and can weigh up to six pounds.

When John Charles Fremont became the first European-American to visit Pyramid Lake in 1844, he giddily described its gorgeous setting:

> It broke upon our eyes like the ocean . . . The waves were curling in the breeze, and their dark-green color showed it to be a deep body of water. It was set like a gem in the mountains, which from our position, seemed to enclose it almost entirely . . . We encamped on the shore, opposite a very remarkable rock in the lake, which had attracted our attention for many miles . . . [for] it rose . . . 600 feet above the water.

There, Fremont met Paiute fishermen who caught the spawning cui-ui along the Lower Truckee River with nets, traps, harpoons, set lines, and weirs woven like baskets. They not only used the cui-ui fresh, dried, and smoked as a staple in their own diet but traded these fish to other tribes in and beyond Pinyon Nut Nation. Consuming the cui-ui along with the inland Lahontan cutthroat trout that also frequented the Truckee, the Paiute had a flavorful and abundant supply of juicy fish flesh that kept them healthy and prosperous. Compared to other indigenous peoples of the Great Basin, Fremont found that the Pyramid Lake Paiute "appeared to live an easy and happy life."

That all changed within the decade after Fremont's visit to the lake, when Forty-Niners attracted by the California Gold Rush began to compete with the Paiute for land, water, and food. Fortunately, the government protected nearly a half million acres surrounding Pyramid Lake and the lower Truckee for the Pyramid Lake Band of Paiutes in 1859, and within two decades they were canning part of their fish harvests for distribution to restaurants and trading posts from San Francisco to Salt Lake City. But as more and more white settlers became neighbors of the Paiute, they built eleven diversion dams along the Truckee, only two with ladders to aid the migratory fish. They also contaminated the river and the lake with wastes from timber mills and pulp mills.

Somehow, the cui-ui survived these insults and

Glenn Clemmer, Nevada Natural Heritage Program

still ran so thick at the mouth of the Truckee at the turn of the twentieth century that their bodies sometimes dammed the river there. But then, in 1902, the Reclamation Act was used to form the Truckee-Carson Irrigation District to grow crops on what local whites referred to as the Newlands Project. By 1905, the Derby Dam built on the Truckee was diverting half of all its flow out of the riverbed into canals that led to white farmers' fields and pastures. These diversions reduced the size of the lake by a quarter, and the water level of the once-deep, azure-colored lake dropped some seventy feet.

At the south end of the lake bed, Pyramid Lake's remaining reserves no longer connected with the Truckee. After Derby Dam was built, the cui-ui and Lahontan cutthroat trout could no longer spawn in most years. The strain of Lahontan cutthroat trout unique to Pyramid Lake eventually died out, while the more adaptable cui-ui learned to spawn on gravel beds above the dam. Despite efforts to recover its populations, its numbers have never again approached the historic abundance known by the nineteenth-century Paiute. The cui-ui is federally listed as as an endangered species, and its once-magnificent commercial fishery has been closed indefinitely. For that reason, we offer no recipe for this imperiled fish.

Further Readings

Fowler, Catherine S. *Tule Technology: Northern Paiute Uses of Marsh Resources in Western Nevada.* Smithsonian Folklife Studies 6. Washington, D.C: Smithsonian Institution Press, 1990.

Fremont, John C. *Report on the Exploring Expedition to the Rocky Mountains in the Year of 1842 and to Oregon and California in the Years of 1843–1844.* Washington, D.C.: Gales and Seaton, 1845.

Sigler, William C., and John S. Sigler. *Fishes of the Great Basin.* Reno: University of Nevada Press, 1987.

Wheeler, S. H. *The Desert Lake: The Story of Nevada's Pyramid Lake.* Caldwell, Idaho: Caxton Printers, 1974.

Wilkinson, Charles F. *Crossing the Next Meridian: Land, Water, and the Future of the West.* Washington, D.C.: Island Press, 1992.

Colorado Pikeminnow

One of the largest "minnows" in the world, this torpedo-shaped fish of Pinyon Nut and Chile Pepper Nations can grow up to six feet in length and weigh in at more than ninety pounds. Known in different eras of American history as the Colorado squawfish or white salmon, it has been recognized not merely for its size and pikelike shape but also for its fine flavor. Each year in May and June, the fish formerly began a migration hundreds of miles long to spawn, just as salmon do, laying their eggs in backwater eddies within the deep canyons of the region. Its current scarcity in the Colorado River gives most visitors to the Grand Canyon no clue of its former ubiquity in rivers, streams, and irrigation ditches. As Robert Rush Miller has noted, the pike minnow:

> . . . was an important food source for the aborigines that lived along the lower Colorado and Gila rivers . . . At one time, this predatory, pike-like fish was common in river channels throughout the Colorado River basin, wherever there was sufficient depth and current. Until about 1911, the species was so abundant in the lower Colorado that individuals got into the irrigation ditches and were pitch-forked out onto the banks by the hundreds to use as fertilizer . . . In the early days, the Indians tied two sticks together, with netting in between, to dip "salmon" out of the river.

This bronze-backed, silver-sided torpedo was indeed an effective predator, for it was known to steal mice, birds, and even rabbits from anglers' baited hooks. It too was preyed on, not only by native cultures but by immigrants as well. Before 1900, it was being caught and shipped to Denver, Salt Lake City, and San Francisco as featured restaurant fare. It was the highlight of Brewster Stanton's 1889 Christmas dinner at Lee's Ferry, Arizona, when he paused from his attempt to identify a railroad route through the Grand Canyon to partake of "Colorado River salmon," among other delights. Spencer Johnson, who grew up at Lee's Ferry in the Grand Canyon between 1921 and 1931, recalls that when he first began fishing, the pikeminnow population had not yet declined to the point where fish could no longer be caught. As a boy, he caught pikeminnows along the Paria River, providing them as an important source of food for

Further Readings

Fradkin, Phillip. *A River No More: Colorado River and West.* Berkeley: University of California Press, 1996.

Miller, Robert Rush. "Man and the Changing Fish Fauna of the American Southwest." *Papers of the Michigan Academy of Sciences, Arts and Letters* 46 (1961): 365–404.

Minckley, W. L. *Fishes of Arizona.* Phoenix: Arizona Game and Fish Department, 1973.

Smith, D. L., and C. G. Crampton. *The Colorado River Survey: Robert B. Stanton and the Denver, Colorado Canyon & Pacific Railroad.* Salt Lake City: Howe Brothers, 1987.

his family. But when the cofferdam was constructed around 1929 at the site of Hoover Dam as a means to harness the Colorado River's energy and water supplies, it brought the migratory runs of pikeminnows to a halt. Then, in the 1960s, pikeminnows were intentionally killed with fish toxins to make room in the rivers for trout.

Some long-lived individuals hung on tenaciously in the reservoirs above their former habitats, however. The last wild river-running Colorado pikeminnow in the lower basin (from the Grand Canyon downstream) was taken at the mouth of Havasu Creek in 1976, some thirteen years after Glen Canyon Dam harnessed the river upstream. The proliferation of dams in the Colorado and Green watersheds has gradually decreased the range of this pikeminnow from two countries, including nine states, to just three states. At the same time, forty nonnative fish have been introduced to these watersheds, driving ten native fish into extinction and further imperiling the four remaining natives, including the pikeminnow. It was federally listed as endangered in 1967 and was one of the first fish given full protection by the Endangered Species Act in 1973. Today, Arizona, Utah, and Colorado all offer it some state-level protection as well.

Although no historic recipe has been found for this species, the following menu for Christmas dinner was included in Brewster Stanton's field notes from his Grand Canyon expedition. It appears that the explorers were not exactly fasting for this holiday.

Glenn Clemmer, Nevada Natural Heritage Program

Colorado pikeminnow caught in the Grand Canyon, 1911. Emery Kolb; used with permission of the Kolb Family; courtesy Northern Arizona University Special Collections

CHRISTMAS MENU, LEE'S FERRY, GRAND CANYON, 1889

Soups
Oxtail, Tomato, Chicken

Fish
Colorado River Salmon

Meats
Roast Turkey, Roast Beef
Ox Heart, Braised Chicken
Game Pie

Vegetables
Mashed Potatoes, Stewed Onions
Tomatoes, Rice
Potato Salad
Wheat, Corn, and Graham Bread
Tea, Coffee, Chocolate Milk

Dessert
Plum Pudding, Hard Sauce
Mince Pie, Apple Pie
Apple and Cherry Sauce
Chocolate Cake
Bents Crackers and Cheese (Utah)
Fruit
Arizona Apples, Peaches, Pears
Raisins and Nuts
Havana Cigars
Turkish Cigarettes

Death Valley Devil's Claw

There are two species of devil's claw that have been cultivated in the United States, and each has its own peculiar history and culinary value. When you first look at their tough, dry pods with curving black horns, they might seem like the most improbable sources of food on the entire North American continent. Their alternative folk name—the unicorn plant—refers to the appearance of their still-green, unopened pods, which have a single curved horn.

The first of the two species is the pinkish-flowered Louisiana unicorn plant, which grows wild in floodplain patches across a wide range of states in the southern United States and northern Mexico. As early as 1805, their immature pods were marketed and pickled as if they were a substitute for okra or cucumbers. Native Americans also parched and then dried their oil-rich seeds as a trail food. However, since the late nineteenth century selections have been made that have higher seed germinability and greater tenderness of flesh. African-, Anglo-, Hispanic-, and Native American gardeners have shared a legacy of exchanging seeds and recipes of the unicorn plant since at least the 1840s.

The second major species of devil's claw was once restricted to Chile Pepper and Pinyon Nut Nations, where Native American basketmakers selected a strain that has white seeds and extremely long claws—fifteen inches in length—useful as coiled basketry splints. The oil-rich seeds of both species have been pried out of the pods and used as a snack for centuries; a distant kin of sesame, their fatty-acid composition compares favorably to that of sunflower and canola seeds. Devil's claw is one of the few plants fully domesticated in North America by indigenous peoples, but since the 1940s, it has been experimentally grown by non-Indians as a potential oilseed crop.

The cultivation of devil's claw, which historically reached up into Shoshone and Northern Paiute territory around the Death Valley region of Nevada and California, is but one more indication of the extensive plant trade routes shared by indigenous peoples in late prehistoric and early historic times. Perhaps basketmakers in Pinyon Nut Nation first received seeds of this crop from related tribes in Chile Pepper Nation, but after that they made the most of it on their own. Today, however, as Tupperware replaces the traditional use of baskets in the region, there are fewer indigenous basketweavers and still fewer who grow their own devil's claw. Nearly all devil's claw seed in trade is from selections derived from Chile Pepper Nation or Bison Nation; it is time to seek out the selections from Pinyon Nut Nation, an area that many historians dismissed as being too difficult for native cropping to occur there. The Paiute and Shoshone proved them wrong.

The following recipe, verbatim, is the oldest known record of unicorn plant or martynia pickles. It was included in Mrs. Abel's 1846 advice to "skilled housewives":

> Martinoes. The salt and water, in which they should be soaked two or three days, must be changed every day or they will become soft. Use allspice, cloves, and cinnamon, and scald the martinoes with the spices in the vinegar. Secure them from air.

Further Readings

Abel, M. *Mrs. Abel's Skilled Housewife's Book, or Complete Guide to Domestic Cookery.* New York: D. Sewell, 1846.

Armstrong, Wayne P. "A Gourmet's Guide to Unicorns." *Desert Magazine* 43 (1980): 36–39. Accessed on May 19, 2007, from http://waynesword.palomar.edu/worthypl.htm.

Bretting, Peter K. "Morphological Differentiation of *Proboscidea parviflora* ssp. *parviflora* under Domestication." American *Journal of Botany* 69 (1981): 1531–1539.

Moerman, Daniel E. *Native American Ethnobotany.* Portland, Oregon: Timber Press, 1998.

Nabhan, Gary Paul, and Amadeo M. Rea. "Plant Domestication and Folk Biological Change: The Upper Piman/Devil's Claw Example." *American Anthropologist* 89 (1987): 57–73.

Nabhan, Gary Paul, Alfred Whiting, Robert Euler, Richard Hevly, and Henry Dobyns. "Devil's Claw Domestication: Evidence from Southwestern Indian Fields." *Journal of Ethnobiology* 1 (1981): 135–164.

Russian ethnobotanist N.I. Vavilov examing a cultivated devil's claw plant, 1931. Homer Schantz; courtesy Center for Sustainable Environments, Northern Arizona University

David Cavagnaro

Paiute (Speckled) Tepary Bean

Few historic records remind us that the native peoples of Pinyon Nut Nation practiced farming for centuries, but the speckled tan, chocolate brown, and burnt orange tepary beans of the Shivwits band of Paiutes are a living testament to this legacy. Although tepary beans were undoubtedly first domesticated somewhere in the dry subtropics of western Mexico, their center of diversity is in Chile Pepper Nation, where over a dozen desert cultures have grown them since prehistoric times.

The Southern Paiute were perhaps the northernmost traditional farmers of teparies, growing them in small fields fed by springs and streams north of the Grand Canyon, where the Colorado Plateau and Great Basin deserts meet. The Southern Paiute of the Shivwits Indian Reservation have been irrigating crops like teparies along the Virgin, Santa Clara, and Muddy rivers for centuries. They probably received their first teparies through trade with the Mohave, who extensively farmed them along the Colorado River not too far south of Las Vegas, Nevada. The Paiutes first inhabited the lands now known as Utah around A.D. 1100.

All tepary beans are among the most drought-, salt-, and heat-tolerant legumes in the world, producing flowers and fruit in searing temperatures that make other beans wither and die. They were typically grown with the floodwaters diverted out of desert washes in the peak heat of the summer and have been known to germinate, set pods, and produce dry seed on the residual soil moisture left by a single drenching rainfall.

Their water-conserving, alkalinity-tolerating, and heat-resisting adaptations to desert conditions are not the only qualities that make tepary beans worth their salt. Their rich, nutty flavor as a bean that is boiled or baked is also distinctive. The dry teparies were also toasted, ground, and rehydrated with a little water to make "instant bean" gruel. Pinyon Nut Nation chefs such as John Sharpe at the Turquoise Room at La Posada in Winslow, Arizona, have found them to be well suited to cassoulets, combining them with wild game meat, sausage, and spices for a deeply satisfying main dish.

In the heyday of dry farming (1890–1920)—just prior to the introduction of gas-driven pumps for groundwater mining—teparies were a staple crop for Native, Hispanic, and Anglo-American farmers alike. Then, as energy- and water-intensive irrigation agriculture allowed other crops to be introduced to Pinyon Nut and Chile Pepper Nations, the hardy tepary was all but forgotten. Tragically, tepary beans nearly fell out of commercial availability throughout the United States in the latter half of the twentieth century. Only one farmer of desert cash crops, the late W. D. Hood of Coolidge, Arizona, maintained a supply of them for sale to trading posts and groceries on Arizona Indian reservations during this era.

After Hood retired, the responsibility of keeping teparies in the marketplace fell on his neighbors, Terry and Ramona Button of the Gila River Community, in central Arizona. Since then, Native Seeds/SEARCH, the San Xavier Co-op, the Maricopa Agricultural Center, and the Tohono O'odham Community Action Farm have taken up the gauntlet of keeping teparies in culinary currency. Brown and white teparies

Further Readings

Bye, Robert A. Jr. "Ethnobotany of the Southern Paiute Indians in the 1870s, with a Note on the Early Ethnobotanical Contributions of Dr. Edward Palmer." In Don D. Fowler, ed., *Great Basin Cultural Ecology: A Symposium.* Desert Research Institute Publications in the Social Sciences 8. Reno: University of Nevada Desert Research Institute, 1972.

Kavena, Juanita Tiger. *Hopi Cookery.* Tucson: University of Arizona Press, 1980.

Nabhan, Gary Paul, and Richard Stephen Felger. "Tepary Beans *(Phaseolus acutifolius* Gray) in Southwestern North America." *Economic Botany* 32:1 (1978.): 2–19.

Rainey, K. M., and P. D. Griffiths. "Identification of Heat Tolerant *Phaseolous acutifolius* Gray Plant Introductions Following Exposure to High Temperatures in a Controlled Environment." *Genetic Resources and Crop Evolution* 52:2 (2005): 117–120.

PARCHED PAIUTE SPECKLED TEPARY BEANS

3 cups dry tepary beans, rinsed
1½ cups water
1 tablespoon "sea" salt from the Grand Canyon
1 tablespoon dried and crushed wild bush-mint or oregano leaves

In a cast-iron pot or Dutch oven, place ½ to 1 inch of clean, fine-grained sand. Heat the sand in the pot until it becomes coffee-brown in color and obviously hot to the touch. Test its readiness for roasting beans by dropping a single tepary onto the sand surface: If it quickly browns, the sand is sufficiently hot to roast the beans. Alternatively, sprinkle a few water droplets onto the sand and wait for them to sizzle.

Next, pour the rinsed tepary beans into the sand and, with a wooden spoon, stir them frequently to keep them from charring. When the beans have browned lightly to a uniform color, pour the sand and the parched beans into a sieve and shake vigorously until all the sand has fallen through the screening. Pour the beans out into a glass bowl. Sprinkle them with a cup of water mixed with sea salt and crushed bushmint or oregano leaves and stir these ingredients together until the beans are coated. Let dry and eat as a snack or grind into a parched bean *pinole* that can serve as a trail food for long-distance runners. The runners can take a pinch of this *pinole* with them and add it to their drinking water while out on the trail.

are now listed on Slow Food USA's Ark of Taste. They have been embraced by James Beard Award–winning chefs in Chile Pepper Nation including Janos Wilder in Tucson, Lois Ellen Frank and Mark Miller in Santa Fe, and Fernando Divina, formerly of Scottsdale.

Of the eighteen tribes in five U.S. states that formerly cultivated teparies, only five—the Tohono

O'odham, Gila River Pima, Hopi, Cocopá, and Yaqui—still regularly grow them today. Of some forty-four local varieties of various shapes, colors, and sizes, roughly five survive in cultivation north of the U.S./Mexico border. Only two seed catalogs have ever made the Paiute tepary bean from Pinyon Nut Nation available to the public, but neither of these has offered it on a regular basis in the last few years. The Paiute speckled tepary bean is clearly endangered, as are most crops that were prehistorically and historically grown by Native Americans in Pinyon Nut Nation.

The recipe at left for parched beans—an ancient means of preparing a traditional trail food among many Native Americans—is adapted from one recorded by Juanita Tiger Kavena, a Creek woman who lived among the Hopi and neighboring tribes of Pinyon Nut Nation for decades.

Courtesy Native Seeds/SEARCH

SALMON NATION

From coastal Alaska southward into northern California, Salmon Nation encompasses all the watersheds whose streams and rivers flow into the North Pacific. The Columbia River, in particular, has served as an effective trade route for foods between the coastal bays and tidelands and the montane headwaters to the east. Since time immemorial, several species of salmon have run the gamut of habitats between these two extremes, but in modern times their migratory pathways have been disrupted by dams and degraded by pollution from pulp mills. Today, nearly ninety-five of Salmon Nation's traditional foods are threatened or endangered. Despite these losses, it remains the richest region on the continent in terms of the numbers of fish, shellfish, berries, mushrooms, wild corms, bulbs, and tubers it supports. Its First Nations cultures include many master fisherfolk and retain many of their ancient food traditions, although some, such as the preparation of fermented ooligan grease, a highly prized trade item, have nearly disappeared.

Snake River Chinook Salmon

Chinook are the largest species of salmon in all of Salmon Nation, and the fall run along the Snake River is perhaps the most endangered of all the remaining populations of this species. Also called kings or tyees, Chinooks commonly weigh in at more than thirty pounds per fish, but a few of over one hundred pounds have been landed. Their large-flaked, oil-rich, pinkish or ivory flesh can be a feast for the palate, but while still alive, their sleek bodies and spotted, lobed fins are feasts for the eye. When the salmon are swimming the ocean, their backs are bluish green and their sides silvery; when running and spawning in freshwater, their body colors chimerically shift from blood red to copper to dull black.

The traditional spawning grounds of fall Chinook are in the stretches of the Snake River below Hells Canyon and in several of the larger tributaries of the Snake as well. Once they've left their birth streams in Salmon Nation for a three-year stint in the North Pacific prior to spawning, they may be spotted anywhere from southeast Alaska to Baja California.

Chinooks have been integral to the tribal traditions in Salmon Nation. Even today, as noted by Jake Jones, tribal fisherman of the Pacific Northwest, "for us, this is everything. It's our food and our money. These fish, this river . . . it's all we have." In prehistoric and early historic times, hundreds of millions of Chinook would run up the Columbia and its tributaries; the Yakima, Umatilla, Nez Perce, and Warm Springs communities would gather along the Hanford Reach near Richland, Washington, to catch them from scaffolds mounted with hoops and nets. But as James Kash Kash—a Umatilla fisherman born in 1863—later explained, his people restrained themselves from catching all the Chinooks accessible to them:

> It was customary for the Indians not to catch the salmon in the tributaries until after they had spawned, for the reason that they knew

Snake River at Hell's Canyon.

Further Readings

Barker, Rocky. "Tribes Cast for Tradition, Catch Controversy." *High Country News*, December 20, 1999. Available at www.hcn.org.

Butler, Virginia L. "Where Have All the Native Fish Gone? The Fate of Fish That Lewis and Clark Encountered on the Lower Columbia River." *Oregon Historical Quarterly* 105:3 (2004): 438–463.

Divina, Fernando, and Marlene Divina. *Foods of the Americas: Native Recipes and Traditions.* Berkeley, California: Ten Speed Press, 2004.

Faris, Tamra. "Snake River Fall Chinook Salmon *(Oncorhynchus tshawytsch)*." Alaska Department of Fish and Game, Division of Wildlife Conservation, 1997. Available at www.wildlife .alaska.gov/index.cfm?adfg=concern.chinook.

Martin, Glen. "A Disappearing Way of Life: Yuroks Fear Klamath River Water Grabs Are Devastating Salmon and Tradition." *San Francisco Chronicle*, September 2, 2003. Available at www.sfgate.com.

Montgomery, David R. *King of Fish: The Thousand-Year Run of Salmon*. Cambridge, Massachusetts: Westview Press, 2003.

TallMountain, Mary. *The Light on the Tent Wall*. Los Angeles: University of California American Indian Studies Center, 1990.

Top: Drying Snake River Chinook on hooks. Both photos Nancy Turner

there would be no salmon in the future if they did not permit the females to lay their eggs to be hatched and available in future years.

Then, in 1867, the first cannery was established in the watershed, and the "mining" of Chinook began. From canning 4,000 cases of salmon the first year, the industry peaked in less than two decades, canning 630,000 cases in 1883. That year, 43,000,000 pounds of Chinook were caught in the Columbia, but from then on landings of Chinook steadily declined. By the 1940s, roughly 70,000 Chinook would gather for the fall run up the Snake. Then, beginning in the 1950s, a series of dams blocked their migration routes and kept most of them from ever reaching their primordial spawning grounds. In 1958, hundreds of thousands of Snake River salmon of all species died when the river dried up completely below the Oxbow Dam at the Hells Canyon stretch of the watershed. In the 1990s, four of the Snake River's historically abundant runs of salmon had to be federally listed, with the fall run of the Chinook declared to be threatened. Tom Wilson, a Yurok fisheries technician, has recently lamented ongoing fish die-offs caused by agricultural diversion of irrigation water from the rivers of Salmon Nation. Seeing one such die-off of 35,000 salmon, he mourned, "It felt like death, not just for the fish, but for the People. The Maker never intended fish to die here. He meant them to go all the way up the river."

Once the number of salmon spawning in a watershed has been dramatically reduced, any sizeable harvest by commercial, recreational, and even subsistence fishermen puts the population at further risk. It is therefore not surprising that introduced diseases and parasites from hatcheries and genetic contamination by escapes from fish farms have also taken their toll. During the last three decades, barely 500 Chinook per year make the fall run up the Snake.

Worse yet, the flesh of some Chinooks now harbors high levels of industrial contaminants.

Native American poet Mary TallMountain has praised the Chinook and lamented their loss in her poem "Ggaal Comes Upriver":

> . . . Strong in the brown river
> She cleaves the miles.
> Her fearless eyes
> Know swoop and nip of gulls,
> Menace of rolling logs,
> Black waiting shapes of Bear.

> With one compulsion
> She will not feed again
> On the ancient pilgrimage
> To the tiny creek of spawning
> Only her genes remember . . .

The following recipe is an adaptation of a Coastal Salish version documented by Marlene and Fernando Divina, who are now at the Tendrils at SageCliffe, a restaurant overlooking the Columbia River; Marlene is of Chippewa, Cree, and Assiniboine ancestry.

POTTED CHINOOK SALMON

⅓ cup ooligan grease or
  unsalted butter
2 tablespoons hazelnut oil
⅔ cup smoked Chinook salmon, flaked
¼ teaspoon sea salt
dash of freshly ground black pepper
4 tablespoons lime juice
2 juniper berries, finely crushed

In a large mortar or *molcajete,* cream the butter or ooligan grease and the hazelnut oil, whipping with a wooden spoon. Next, add the salmon flakes and work with the pestle until the mixture is smooth and creamy. Add the salt, pepper, lime juice, and crushed juniper berries. Mix one last time and place this paste in a decorative bowl to use as a dip or condiment.

Gillette Fig

It seems as though the Salmon Nation's Gillette fig suffers from a lack of charisma. Its reviewers haven't been especially kind. "Fruits pale yellow, small, pulp . . . nearly white, without a lot of character," reads one description, on the website of the California Rare Fruit Growers. "Flavor is fair, but not memorable," writes Ray Givan, on another website dedicated to figs.

The Gillette does have something to offer, though. Also known as the St. John, Croisic, Cordelia, or Pingo de Mel fig, the Gillette fig has sweet, yellow flesh that is decent for fresh eating, canning, or drying. Gillette trees fruit early—in July or August—though only fruits of the first crop, the *brebas,* are useful. It is frost tolerant and is the only known fig with an edible caprifig. That's the developmental stage at which the flesh is usually spoiled by an abundance of fig wasp eggs. (It's biologically a fair trade, as the wasps are figs' primary pollinators.) Finally, the fig boasts a charming little history.

Jim Gilbert, at One Green World plant distributors in Molalla, Oregon, says the Gillette fig can be traced to the early 1900s, when an Oregon man named Bert Amend started a fig nursery. His goal was to find figs that would ripen around his home in Salmon Nation because figs from Southern California hadn't enjoyed a good track record there. He started with one hundred varieties and discovered a few that worked.

The Gillette fig was one, but another—the Marseilles or White Marseilles, which Amend called Lattarulla—took center stage. "You can find really old trees of Lattarulla around, in backyards in Portland neighborhoods," Gilbert says. Figs in general are oblivious to most pest problems, so they're good candidates for organic growing. Both the Gillette fig and the Lattarulla ripen by early fall, which makes them good fits for Oregon's maritime climate.

At one point, Amend maintained a small orchard with the assistance of his son, Ford. But its very success was also its undoing. The pair would pack egg cartons with fresh figs and deliver them to local stores. Then they started making fig jam, and Meier and Frank, a department store, immediately wanted 500 cases of it. The little business was overwhelmed, and that was the end of the fig jam. The fig nursery winked out sometime in the 1930s. Seed Savers Exchange lists the Gillette fig as having one source in 1992 and one in 2000. That single source, Oregon Exotics in Grants Pass, Oregon, may remain the only outlet for the Gillette fig.

Besides the Amend family, Gilbert credits Italian immigrants for bringing some of the fig varieties that are now grown in the Pacific Northwest. Lattarulla's other common name is Italian Honey fig. It's a green-skinned fig with sweet, honey-colored flesh. The ribbed fruit is flattened on the base and juicy. It's great for fresh eating and decent for canning. As such, it's fairly widespread. Both the Gillette and Lattarulla have been superseded by another summer-ripening variety, the Desert King, which is cosmetically more appealing. There's also the matter of the plug. Gillette figs produce a dry little plug at the end where the "eye" is. An attractive feature for pollination by wasps, the plug isn't good for eating, and it's somewhat unsightly.

Further Readings

California Rare Fruit Growers. "Fig," 1996. Available at www.crfg.org/pubs/ff/fig.html.

Givan, Ray. "Ray's Figs," 1997. Available at http://home.planters.net/~thegivans/.

Waters, Alice, Alan Tangren, and Fritz Strieff. *Chez Panisse Fruit.* San Francisco: HarperCollins, 2002.

GILLETTE FIGS POACHED IN ANGELICA

12 sun-dried Gillette figs
2 cups sweet Angelica wine made from Mission grapes (see page 32)
½ cup citrus honey
1 cinnamon stick
4 teaspoons peeled and finely chopped orange zest
¼ cup juice from a Moro blood orange
¼ vanilla bean

Toss the figs into a saucepan, splash with water, and cover with Angelica. Drizzle the honey over them and then add all other ingredients to the saucepan. Simmer over very low heat until the figs inflate and are tender. Remove them from the heat but let them continue to bulge up. When ready to serve, drain away the remaining liquid and the cinnamon stick. Serve them with ice cream, pork, or custard.

Eulachon Smelt

The rivers of Salmon Nation awake from their deep winter slumber with the arrival of the eulachon smelt—the first sign of spring, the first infusion of oceanic flavors after a harsh winter fueled by preserved foods. As legend tells it, this small oily fish saved whole villages on the brink of starvation after long, unforgiving winters. But the eulachon, once central to trade, ceremony, and sustenance for the Northwest coastal tribes, is moving toward extinction and gaining a new name—the ghostfish smelt. Eulachon (or, depending on your geography and dialect, ooligan, candlefish, oolichan, Columbia River smelt, or oilfish), like other smelt, is a long, thin fish, bluish above with a silvery sheen on its sides and belly. The eulachon is most prized for its oily nature. The smelt is so full of oil that, when preserved and dried and then placed upright and lit with a match, it will burn from end to end like a candle.

This particular silvery smelt spends most of its life in the oceans between northern California and the Bering Strait before ascending into rivers, like

Nancy Turner

Ruby Alexander (left—now Ruby Anderson), the eulachon festival Queen, and Lynne Lewis, a member of the festival queen's court, dipping smelt from the Cowlitz River at Kelso, Washington, in 1944. Courtesy Cowlitz County Historical Museum

salmon, to lay thousands of eggs before dying on the gravelly bottoms of small tributary streams.

These fish embark on their annual journey up the ice-cold rivers of the Northwest, from Canada and Alaska to Washington and Oregon. The ooligan smelt travel in huge schools along rivers weaving amid towering mountain ranges cloaked in green. Traditional Native American fishermen take part in this annual journey of birth and death, catching the ooligan smelt with dip nets or long funnel-shaped nets.

The eulachon catch is brought to shore for a centuries-old community event—fermenting and rendering the oil from the prized smelt. Tsimshian, Tlingit, Haida, Nisga'a, and Bella Coola tribes once gathered in oil camps near the river mouths of the Northwest coast each spring. It took anywhere from ten days to three weeks to ripen or ferment the harvested fish in cedar chests or in canoes before extracting the oil. The resulting oil was so highly prized for its flavor and healing qualities that it was traded in ceremonial cedar boxes hundreds of miles inland, forming the great "grease trails" of the Northwest.

Sadly, this tradition is slowly vanishing as the ancient, orally transmitted knowledge of fishing and preparing the ooligan fish fades and the smelt runs dwindle. According to eighty-year-old June Allen, a

Smoked eulachon smelts. Nancy Turner

former reporter from the *Ketchican Daily News* with a keen interest in the ooligan smelt, there are only a handful of Tlingit ooligan fishermen left in Ketchican, Alaska. The same smelt run, on the Unuk River, that "just boiled with ooligan" when Allen watched fisher-

folk fifteen years ago has become so meager that it's been closed to both commercial and subsistence fishing for the past two years.

Tribal elders still love the flavor of the fish, whether it's smoked or cooked in the rendered eulachon oil as in butter. Sometimes the oil is whipped with wild berries. The eulachon is not only tasty but highly nutritious. This smelt provides essential vitamins to the Northwest coast native food web as well as much needed calcium and protein. June Allen enjoys them best "cooked hot and fast fresh from the river."

Lewis and Clark also enjoyed roasted eulachon on their famed journey of discovery. In 1806, Meriwether Lewis wrote of the eulachon, alongside a beautiful sketch of this fish, "They are so fat they require no additional sauce, and I think them superior to any fish I ever taste[d], even more delicate and luscious than the white fish of the lakes which have heretofore formed my standard of excellence among the fishes." The grease itself has a smell like no other; some people describe it as mild ocean breeze, whereas others say it has an overwhelmingly strong, cheesy smell. This variance in flavor and aroma changes with each ooligan run.

OLYMPIA OYSTERS TUCKED INTO EULACHON-OILED PATTIES OF OZETTE POTATOES AND CAMAS

24 Olympia oysters, shucked and washed

2 sage grouse eggs

⅔ cup wild onions or ½ cup roasted Inchelium garlic

2 tablespoons sea salt

2 teaspoons steamed and chopped nettles

2 cups camas root, precooked or pit-roasted and mashed

2 cups cooked and mashed Ozette potatoes

2 tablespoons Indian ricegrass flour (Montina brand)

4 tablespoons eulachon grease (or flaxseed oil)

Preheat oven to 275 degrees F. Slightly brown the oysters in a pan, then remove from the heat. In a bowl, mix the eggs, onions or garlic, salt, and the precooked nettles, camas, and Ozette potatoes; mash and blend them into a batter of even consistency. With ricegrass flour on your hands, shape the batter into patties 4 to 5 inches in diameter and ½ inch thick. Place a browned oyster in the middle of each patty, burying it in the batter until it is fully hidden. Drizzle ooligan grease (or flaxseed oil) in a nonstick skillet, set at low to medium heat, and fry two patties at a time until golden brown, for no more than 6 minutes each. Serves 5.

While historically unpredictable, the eulachon smelt runs have declined precipitously over the past twenty years, with some runs disappearing altogether. Although commercial smelt harvests in the Columbia River watershed historically weighed in between 3,000,000 and 5,000,000 pounds, they dropped to only 234 pounds in 1994, the smallest recorded harvest since 1935. Catches from the remaining runs throughout the Northwest have become highly regulated. According to the Alaska Department of Fish and Game, in 2005 there were fewer than a hundred eulachon fish in Burroughs Bay, located in southeastern Alaska. As of April 2007, ooligan fisheries in southeastern Alaska sustained a second year of closures.

These dramatic declines may be the result of a whole host of problems—bycatch of other fisheries, water pollution, habitat destruction caused by dredging and construction, and a rise in water temperature due to climate change. Yet thus far this smelt has garnered little attention from the conservation community, so little is known about its status. Perhaps with more scientific research, combined with traditional knowledge and a concerted effort to sustain this fish throughout Salmon Nation, there will be plenty of eulachon to harvest and make the absolutely distinctive eulachon grease for years to come.

The recipe on the preceding page highlights eulachon grease as a flavoring for other foods unique to Salmon Nation, while the recipe at right describes the processing of the grease in the traditional manner learned by chef Dolly Watts of the Gitk'san of the Nass River in Canada.

Eulachon festival fish fry in the 1940s or early '50s. The chef is Carlton Moore. Courtesy Cowlitz County Historical Museum

Further Readings

Kuhnlein, Harriet. "Ooligan Grease: A Nutritious Fat Used by Native People of Coastal British Columbia." *Journal of Ethnobiology* 2:2 (1982): 154–161.

Stewart, Hilary. *Indian Fishing: Early Methods on the Northwest Coast.* Seattle: University of Washington Press, 1977.

Watts, Dolly, and Annie Watts. *Where People Feast: An Indigenous People's Cookbook.* Vancouver, British Columbia: Arsenal/Pulp Press, 2007.

GITK'SAN-STYLE EULACHON OIL

To extract eulachon grease, place freshly caught candlefish smelt in a cedar box or canoe placed on a riverbank. The box or canoe should have its bottom lined with cedar boughs. Fill this cedar container with fish, cover it, and leave the fish there to decompose and ferment for 7 to 10 days. Transfer this mixture of oil and flesh to a large cast-iron cooking pot hung over a bed of red-hot coals. Bring the oil, flesh, and juices to a boil and, every few minutes, stir with a large wooden spoon or a metal whisk to release more oil from the flesh. Remove large pieces of fish and scum and then add several cups of ice-cold water to arrest the boiling process. Remove the pot from the heat and add more cold water, and the oil will rise to the surface. Let sit for 2 to 4 hours so that the remaining solids sink as the oil or grease rises. Skim off this oil with ladles, then strain it through a cheesecloth covering a large-mouthed sterilized pitcher or large-mouthed glass jug. Seal the jugs or pitchers and store them in a cool, dry place.

Marshall Strawberry

Once declared the finest eating strawberry in America, the finicky yet flavorful Marshall strawberry has almost vanished from our farms and our palates. According to the venerable American agricultural encyclopedia *The Small Fruits of New York,* the Marshall strawberry was the standard of excellence for the entire northern strawberry industry. With rich, dark red flesh to its very center, the Marshall strawberry is also described as exceedingly handsome, splendidly flavored, aromatic, and juicy—words beyond the reaches of imagination when biting into the strawberries found on most contemporary grocery shelves.

In this era of food homogenization, the unique flavors of our heritage crops are at risk. The remarkable texture and taste of the Marshall strawberry are on the verge of disappearing as its important historical role fades from the history books and our heirloom seed catalogs. A chance seedling, the Marshall strawberry was discovered by Marshall F. Ewell of Massachusetts in 1890 and introduced to the public in 1893. The Marshall took root in Salmon Nation; until the 1960s this strawberry was the backbone of the Northwestern berry industry. The Marshall thrived particularly on the San Juan Islands off the coast of Washington State, becoming the central crop there during the first half of the twentieth century.

In fact, it is on Bainbridge Island that the Marshall strawberry has its greatest champions, in both historical preservation and its current revival. Through the diligence of Jerry Elfendahl, a seventh-generation islander, the Bainbridge Island Historical Society has an incredible collection of writings, photos, and histories of the island and its rich Marshall strawberry industry. Beginning in 1908, Japanese strawberry farmers began to plant hundreds of acres of strawberries on the island; the soil and the weather are perfect for producing delectable berries. Berry production on the island peaked prior to World War II, when 500 fifty-five-gallon barrels were shipped off the island per day. Filipino settlers looked after the farms during the Japanese internment during World War II, and Native Americans from British Columbia would come to work during harvest season. This help, along with the work of the islanders, was essential: At just two weeks, the Marshall season isn't much longer than a blink of an eye.

In the aftermath of World War II, berries were debilitated by crop diseases inadvertently imported from other countries. The delicate Marshall, requiring exacting climatic and soil conditions, proved to be extremely susceptible to these introduced viruses. It was phased out of production in the 1960s, occupying only 4,000 acres of Oregon and Washington's strawberry market.

As we begin the twenty-first century, the essential flavor of strawberries has been all but eliminated in industrial, chemically intensive agricultural systems. Now, even fruit aficionados such as David Karp—the self-styled "fruit detective" who writes for the *New York Times* and *Gourmet* magazine—struggle to find any producers willing to maintain the exquisite Marshall strawberry. But thanks to the Bainbridge Island Historical Society's Marshall Strawberry Project, the Marshall is being revived on the same land that nurtured these plants fifty years ago. A handful of old-timers on the island have continued to grow the Marshall strawberry in their home gardens; from these strawberry plants a small plot was started on the grounds of the historical society to preserve the history of Bainbridge Island and also serve as a fund-raiser for the small museum.

The strawberry plants have proven to be immensely popular, and the revival of this project has moved beyond the grounds of the historical society to support a budding food and farming movement on the island. Carol McCarthy, a volunteer with the historical society, manages the Marshall Strawberry Project, caring for the plants on-site and offering starter plants to schools and community groups. In particular, she has worked closely with the Trust for Working Landscapes and Global Source, local community groups that are revitalizing agriculture on the island and nurturing its connection with education. Participants at Voyager Montessori School, for example, restored a portion of the school's property back to its historical use as a Marshall strawberry farm from plants grown at the historical society. These stewards on Bainbridge Island are bringing this remarkable strawberry out of the history books and back to our tables.

Further Readings

Darrow, George McMillan. *The Strawberry: History, Breeding, and Physiology*. New York: Holt Rinehart and Winston, 1966.

Hedrick, U. P. *The Small Fruits of New York*. Albany, New York: J. B. Lyon Company, 1925.

Makah Ozette Potato

"It tastes the way good earth smells." Gerry Warren has found the perfect description for the flavor of the Makah Ozette potato. It is this distinctive taste, coupled with its unique story rooted in the Salmon Nation, that inspired Gerry and Slow Food Seattle to revive this potato that was so close to extinction.

Salmon Nation is incredibly lush and bountiful, providing an unparalleled wealth of wild foods ranging from roots to fruits; yet terroir enthusiasts find little in the way of cultivated plants in the Northwest that can be considered natives. But when Slow Food Seattle began to look into the food traditions of the Northwest, they found a gem in the backyard gardens of the Makah.

The Makah, who attracted worldwide attention for their recent revival of a whaling hunt, live on the extreme northwestern tip of the continental United States: Neah Bay, Washington. In the fertile soils of the Olympic Peninsula, the Makah have nurtured the Ozette potato for over 200 years. Unlike most potatoes, the Makah Ozette variety came directly from South America to Neah Bay, where Spaniards were attempting to stake out territory along the northern Pacific Coast in the late 1700s. While every other potato variety in the United States has its origin in the Andes, most took a detour through Europe, brought there by early Spanish explorers, before making it to the shores of New England aboard colonists' ships.

The Makah Ozette has remained on the Olympic Peninsula because the Makah cherish its distinctive flavor. In doing so, the Makah have protected a rare example of a truly local potato. This knobby fingerling potato with its rich, creamy texture may be unusual to us, but it is an example of the incredible variety of shapes, colors, and tastes found in South American potatoes. Your average potato from the grocery bin does little to inspire because it is seldom meant to. Instead, the average potato is chosen for its ability

David Cavagnaro

Further Readings

Brown, C. R. "The Potato of the Makah Nation." NSF Potato Genome Project. Accessed on August 7, 2007, at www.potatogenome.org/nsf5/potato_biology/history.php.

Cutter, D. C. Malaspina, and D. Galiano. *Spanish Voyages to the Northwest Coast, 1791 and 1792.* Seattle: University of Washington Press, 1991.

Divina, Fernando, and Marlene Divina. *Foods of the Americas: Native Recipes and Traditions.* Berkeley, California: Ten Speed Press, 2004.

Gill, S. J. *Ethnobotany of the Makah and Ozette People, Olympic Peninsula, Washington (USA).* Pullman: Washington State University Department of Botany, 1983.

to survive the rigors of cross-continental shipping and exhibit the marketable quality of uniformity. But the Makah Ozette potato has a flavor so rich you may resist the temptation to slather it in butter or fry it up in oil. Instead, Gerry Warren cooks the delicious Makah Ozette tubers simply—first steaming them until just tender, then pan-roasting them with a hint of olive oil, salt, and pepper.

This inspiring potato might never have made it to Gerry Warren's table were it not for the curiosity of a scientist, Dr. Chuck Brown, who was keen on the mysterious history of the Ozette. In collaboration with high school and college youth from the Makah Nation, Dr. Brown was able to match science with history to verify that the Makah Ozette came directly from South America. It was also Dr. Brown who introduced Slow Food Seattle and Gerry Warren to the Makah community, to tell them of a new revival

DUNGENESS CRAB HASH WITH MAKAH OZETTE POTATOES

8 Makah Ozette potatoes
zest of 1 lemon
2 tablespoons unsalted butter
2 tablespoons corn oil
1 leek bulb, the white part only, finely chopped
2 tablespoons minced White Portugal onion
2 tablespoons minced Canada Cheese Pimento pepper
12 ounces (1½ cups) Dungeness crab meat
1 tablespoon chopped fresh dill weed
½ teaspoon sea salt
½ teaspoon coarsely ground black peppercorns

Preheat the oven to 400 degrees F and then place the Makah Ozette potatoes on the oven rack and bake them for 30 to 40 minutes, until they are fork tender. Remove them from the oven to cool, then peel and grate them into a bowl. Set aside.

Next, place the lemon zest in a small saucepan, with just enough water to cover. Place over medium-high heat and bring to a boil. Drain and repeat the process twice, then rinse the zest in cold water and pat dry with paper towels. Mince, then set aside.

In a large nonstick skillet, melt the butter over medium heat and add the corn oil and then the grated potatoes, spreading them out evenly and sautéing them for 5 to 7 minutes without mixing or flipping. Spread the leek, onion, and pepper out on top of the grated potatoes and cook for 5 minutes more or until the bottom is golden brown. Spread the crabmeat atop this mix and sprinkle with the minced zest and dill, salt, and pepper. Turn the entire hash cake over with a spatula and cook for 7 more minutes or until the hash cake is evenly heated to a crisp, golden hue. Serve on four plates with poached eggs mounted onto the hash cake slices.

afoot—a Slow Food Presidium project dedicated to the Makah Ozette potato.

To bring the Makah Ozette back from the edge of extinction, the Presidium's objectives are twofold: to create a sustainable supply of the delectable Ozette and to create a market for it. This effort began in 2006, when Slow Food Seattle distributed 500 pounds of Makah Ozette seed potatoes to locals and to a select group of farmers. These farmers have in turn helped supply enthusiastic Seattle-based chefs with this heirloom fingerling steeped in the history of

Salmon Nation. Thanks to this effort, you'll find the Makah Ozette on tables throughout Seattle and at farmers' markets in Seattle's Ballard and University District neighborhoods.

Chef Fernando Divina of the Tendrils at SageCliffe in Quincy, Washington, not only serves the Makah Ozette potato as part of his seasonal menu but grows it in the gardens of the Inn at Cave B, overlooking the Columbia River. In the recipe above the Makah Ozette is featured in an adaptation of Fernando's recipe for Dungeness crab hash.

Orcas Pear

The story goes that a man named Joseph C. Long discovered some young pear seedlings growing next to a farm building in 1966, and he noticed over a couple of years that one of the seedling trees was producing a lot of good-sized, attractive fruit. More importantly, it didn't seem to show any sign of pear scab *(Venturia pyrina),* which is a common fungus disease of pears in the maritime climate of the Pacific Northwest.

In the early 1970s, Long—who was then a septuagenarian—contacted Robert Norton at the Washington State University Research and Extension unit at Mount Vernon. They arranged to grow and evaluate some trees. The pear's parentage remains a mystery, but it's earned a good reputation in the intervening years. It was formally introduced as the Orcas pear in 1986. The Orcas pear is a large, yellow fruit with a carmine blush. It's shaped like a Bartlett pear. The Orcas is juicy, with a buttery texture. It's also versatile; people who grow it say it works well for fresh eating, canning, or drying. The Orcas tree tends to bloom in mid-April and produces every year, though its yield sometimes takes a hit when spring rains curb pollination by bees.

Seed Savers Exchange listed only two sources for this pear in the late 1980s and four in more recent years. One of these is the Cloud Mountain Farm & Nursery in Washington, one county over from Orcas Island. For nursery manager Terry Maczuga, the Orcas is a favorite because it has shown more disease resistance than the Bartlett. He says people who grow it feel as though it's one of the best canning pears there is.

Nick Botner, who maintains an extensive orchard in Yoncalla, Oregon, said the Orcas pear looks like a Bartlett but tastes better. This energetic man grows more than 400 pear varieties, 500 types of grape, and 3,500 varieties of apple on his 125 acres, and "it's getting worse all the time," he says. "I have 500 new varieties in my house ready to graft." He says conservation is part of his motive, but the obsession has its own legs: "It's like collecting stamps, you know, you just keep on collecting them."

Enthusiasts can drive to Botner's farm and pick produce or buy plant trees. Locals visit, as well as travelers from Idaho, Nevada, Utah, and California. He keeps varieties they can't find anywhere else, he points out, which means his operation is helping to conserve rare heirlooms like the Orcas. Once visitors taste and see this variety, then hear Botner's stories, the Orcas is no longer an abstraction, but a unique presence in Salmon Nation.

Joseph Postman, with the USDA Agricultural Research Service's National Clonal Germplasm Repository in Corvallis, Oregon, said he suspects the Orcas pear may be an old European cultivar that happened to thrive in the maritime climate on Orcas Island, but he hasn't made a serious effort to try to match it to the other European pears in the collection. Orcas Island was settled by Europeans in the 1800s, though, and there are many remnant orchards and fruit trees scattered on the island that date back to that period.

This recipe is dramatically revised from a version by Waters, Tangren, and Strieff that relies on Asian pears.

Further Readings

Norton, Robert A., J. King, and G. Moulton. "'Orcas' Pear." *HortScience* 23:6 (1988): 1090.

Norton, Robert A., J. King, and G. Moulton. "'Rescue' Pear." *HortScience* 24:1 (1989): 170.

Postman, J. D. "Pear." In *The Brooks and Olmo Register of Fruit & Nut Varieties*, 3rd ed. Alexandria, Virginia: ASHS Press, 1997.

Washington State University. "About Us; Pear Evaluations," 1999. Available at http://mtvernon.wsu.edu/frt_hort/about_us.htm.

Waters, Alice, Alan Tangren, and Fritz Strieff. *Chez Panisse Fruit.* San Francisco: HarperCollins, 2002.

ORCAS PEAR AND CALIFORNIA BLACK WALNUT SALAD

⅔ pound black walnuts, shelled
3 tablespoons fig vinegar
½ cup Mission olive oil
¼ teaspoon sea salt
black pepper to taste
6 Orcas pears
1 cup watercress
edible flowers for garnish

On a baking sheet, toast the walnuts for 5 minutes in a 350-degree F oven until they are golden. Set them aside to cool and meanwhile make a vinaigrette of the fig vinegar, olive oil, salt, and pepper. Peel the pears, then cut lengthwise, removing the core. Slice the pears, then toss them with the watercress in the vinaigrette. Crumble the toasted walnuts over them and serve with edible flowers edging them on a platter. Serves 10.

Courtesy Mark DuPont, Sandy Bar Ranch & Nursery

Olympia Oyster

The only true oyster native to Salmon Nation, the Olympia, or Oly, nearly died in its beds before a concerted effort was made to restore its habitats and reduce the threats of industrial contamination. Thanks to collaborations undertaken by the Olympia Oyster Restoration Project, which includes seven tribes as well as municipalities, schools, and family-owned businesses, the Oly is on its way to recovery, but it is still on federal lists of species of concern in the United States and Canada and a candidate for listing as threatened in Washington State.

The Olympia is a small but delicious oyster, one whose shell is barely the size of a fifty-cent piece; it takes 250 of its hand-harvested meats to fill up one pint. Nevertheless, its flavor and texture have been enough to attract the attention of the inhabitants of both Salmon Nation and Acorn Nation for thousands of years. Formerly ranging from Southern California through southeastern Alaska, its greatest abundance is and has been around Puget Sound. Since 1878, the Olympia Oyster Company has been managing several hundred acres of marine tidelands edging Totten Inlet on southern Puget Sound, not far from Olympia, Washington. It was the Washington Territorial Legislature that dubbed this already-famous local oyster the Olympia in 1889.

Although its commercial harvesting began around the San Francisco Bay Area during the Gold Rush, one bay after another was overharvested and contaminated, until Puget Sound became the last refuge for the oyster's commercial production. Production declined after the 1920s, when paper pulp mills began to contaminate many of the prime habitats for Olympia oysters within the bays and sounds of the Pacific coast. The impacts of pollution on Olympia oysters were exacerbated by the introduction of the Pacific oyster from Japan in 1903 and its subsequent spread into habitats formerly dominated by the Olympia. From 1927 until 1999, when the Olympia Oyster Restoration Project began, there was a slow decline in the number of both natural oyster beds and diked tidelands where the Olympia cultivated. Fortunately, the project has since released at least 5,000,000 propagated oysters at some eighty

Dr. Kay McGraw with the NOAA Restoration Center monitoring a native Olympia oyster enhancement site with Puget Sound Restoration Fund. Tristan Peter-Contesse

Olympia Oyster Company employees working in company oyster beds located in Totten Inlet, Washington State, circa 1929.

OLYMPIA OYSTER HANGTOWN FRY

9 eggs

16 Olympia oysters, shucked

¼ cup unbleached whole-wheat flour

½ cup bread or cracker crumbs

¼ teaspoon sea salt

⅛ teaspoon freshly ground black pepper

16 strips of bacon

1 teaspoon olive oil or butter

¼ cup whipping cream

1 cup freshly grated Parmesan cheese

In a glass mixing bowl, crack open one egg and beat it. Add the oysters and lightly coat them in the egg batter, then add the flour, bread crumbs, salt, and pepper, breading each oyster with a thick coating. Next, place two large skillets over medium heat and fry the bacon in the first skillet until each strip is almost crisp. Remove the bacon, place on paper towels, and set aside, while draining the grease from the skillet to use again.

In the other skillet, pan-fry all the oysters in olive oil or butter for three minutes, or until they are golden brown, then remove and place them on a paper towel. Again, ready the second skil-let, adding a bit of bacon grease or butter to it. In the glass bowl, mix the eight remaining eggs, the whipping cream, and half of the Parmesan cheese. Heat both skillets, then lay out the strips of bacon in the skillets as if they were railroad tracks, and place the oysters between them. Pour the batter over the bacon and Olympia oysters, and cook as you would any omelets, folding them over and cutting each skillet's Hangtown fry into four sections. Garnish with the rest of the cheese. Serves 8 people, who can enjoy it with sourdough bread and strong coffee or whiskey.

sites around Puget Sound, involving more than one hundred partners in this fieldwork. The White House Conference on Cooperative Conservation in 2006 featured the collaborative efforts of tribes, schools, nonprofits, and state and local agencies to ensure that the Olympia oyster never leaves our tables again.

According to some folk historians, the world-famous multicultural cuisine of the Pacific coast of Salmon Nation began with the preceding page's traditional recipe, which has always featured Olympia oysters in its peculiar breakfast dish. Hangtown fry originated either in the gold fields around Placerville, California—formerly known as Hangtown or Old Dry Diggins—or at a saloon called Parker's Bank Exchange in San Francisco.

Legend has it that a prospector who had just struck it rich came into the saloon and exclaimed, "Gimme your most expensive grub, I'm tired of eatin' beans!" The saloon cook took his three most costly ingredients—Olympia oysters (then brought live in barrels of saltwater from San Francisco Bay), eggs, and bacon—and fixed up the prospector an omelet that continues to be featured at many West Coast restaurants. One of the longest-running Hangtown fry purveyors was the Blue Bell Café, formerly a watering hole for miners on Main Street in Placerville. Even in the nineteenth century, Hangtown fry could fetch as much as six dollars a plate, an astronomical price for those times. It is the official dish of both Placerville and surrounding El Dorado County.

Further Readings

Fisher, M. F. K. *Consider the Oyster*. New York: Duell, Sloan and Pearce, 1941.

Herter, George Leonard, and Bertha E. Herter. *Bull Cook and Authentic Historic Recipes and Practices.* San Francisco: Herter's Inc., 1960.

Noble, Doug. "The Original Hangtown Fry." *Mountain Democrat,* July 31, 2000.

Olympia Oyster Company website. Accessed February 14, 2007, at www.olympiaoyster.com.

Reardon, Joan, and Ruth Ebeling. *Oysters: A Culinary Celebration*. Orleans, Massachusetts: Parnassus Imprints, 1984.

Pacific Herring Roe on Hemlock Boughs and Kelp

Although herring remain relatively common compared to other fish along the coasts of Salmon Nation, the ancient sustainable practice of harvesting herring spawn on hemlock boughs placed in tidal waters is a tradition under considerable threat. Practiced by First Nations peoples scattered along the North Pacific coast from Vancouver Island in southern Canada to Sitka Sound in southeastern Alaska, the herring spawn harvest is a time of great celebration in the early spring. Following the spring equinox—in late March or early April—the hundreds of thousands of herring come into the quiet bays and fjordlike inlets along the rocky coast. They tend to spawn at mean low water associated with a full moon, with most fish arriving between the flood and the ebb tides. The water turns milky with the milt of the males, the eggs or roe of the females, and the scales of both.

For centuries, coastal tribes such as the Tlingit and Haida have used the arrival of golden eagles, harbor seals, sea lions, and glaucous-winged gulls as indicators that the herring are soon to spawn. Today, both native and nonnative harvesters participate in this subsistence harvesting tradition. Selecting secluded

Drying herring roe on k'aaw (giant kelp). Nancy Turner

inlets where others might not notice their handiwork, they have traditionally hidden branches or whole trunks of hemlocks (*haaw* in Tlingit, *k'aáng* in Haida, *siihmu* at Barkley Sound) in the tidal waters, anchoring them down with stones to depths of twenty to thirty feet. Some coastal peoples also submerge Sitka spruce and fir branches, or giant kelp (*daaw* or *k'aaw*) and hair seaweed (*ne* in Tlingit, *Xuya sgyuuga* or "Raven's mustache" in Haida) as other substrates on which to catch the herring roe. The Haida still tell a story about how the Herring People laid their spawn in Raven's mustache, which he threw away so that it became seaweed suitable for collecting herring roe.

As explorers Aurel and Arthur Krause described on their arrival in Sitka Sound in April of 1882,

> At this time the Indians plant hemlock twigs at the low water mark, where they become covered with spawn, after which they are gathered in canoe loads. The spawn is heaped upon the twigs, to which it adheres in grapelike clusters, which are sometimes called "Alaskan grapes."

One smooth-barked, twenty-foot-long hemlock trunk immersed in the tidal waters might capture as much as 1,000 pounds of herring eggs, but smaller trunks and boughs seldom hold more than 300 pounds of roe. The harvesters keep their "sets" of hemlock boughs out in the water for two to three days after the spawning begins, hoping that the roe will completely saturate the surface of the substrate. Then, arriving in canoes, skiffs, roundabouts, or Boston whalers, they carry the boughs full of hundreds of pounds of herring roe back to their villages. There, the roe is immersed briefly in boiling water, then removed, so that it retains its translucent sheen; if overcooked, the roe turns creamy white and rather rubbery. It is then dried, salted, and bundled; frozen for later use; or eaten fresh.

Herring eggs on kelp or hemlock have long been as valuable as ooligan grease (see page 242) and are sometimes bartered to obtain this delicious fermented oil from other tribes. Each substrate

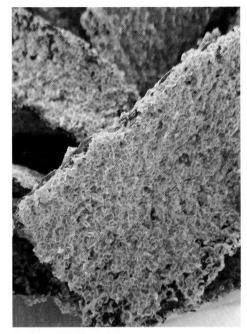

Herring roe on k'aaw. Nancy Turner

(conifers and seaweeds) offers its own flavor to the herring eggs. The roe can be eaten with oil, soy sauce, honey, vinegar, butter, mayonnaise, or spices. Since the late 1980s, however, fewer and fewer Tlingit families invest the considerable time in the harvest within Sitka Sound, and twenty families now bring in the majority of the roe. Some of these remaining families have suffered theft of their boughs and kelp in recent years.

In addition, an untold number of families from the Haida and Nuu-Chah-Nulth nations have tried to maintain this tradition in Canada, but it showed signs of disruption beginning around 1988, when there was a complete cessation of spawning by herring at some of their historically important mating sites on the west coast of Vancouver Island. As the Nuu-Chah-Nulth Tribal Council wrote to Fisheries and Oceans Canada in November 1989: "We are extremely alarmed that there has been virtually no intestinal spawning in Barkley Sound in the past two years. Something is terribly wrong when a fish species that has evolved to spawn intestinally has suddenly abandoned this behavior."

As one wildlife biologist, Thomas Thornton, has suggested, the season of . . . .

Sitka Sound in northeastern Alaska, where herring run. Elaine Bontempi

... the herring spawn is shorter and spottier, and the small subsistence herring roe harvest has been overshadowed by an intense, lucrative, and globalized commercial fishery, which Sitka Tlingits fear is harming the species and the ecosystem. Unlike the Native herring roe harvest, which spares the herring to spawn again, the commercial fishery kills the fish—up to 11,000 tons each year in Sitka—to get the *roe en sac,* as the Japanese markets prefer, paying up to $100 per pound for the final product.

A Tlingit elder, Herman Kitka, warned that the commercial harvest of *roe en sac* to provide Japanese consumers with gift packs of salted *kazunoko* roe is affecting not only his people, but wildlife as well:

Before the herring roe fisheries in Alaska, the fur seals used to come into all the inlets along the Pacific Coast. Today you no longer see any fur seals at all. If we don't control the roe fisheries in Alaska I am afraid even our salmon will also be gone forever. The salmon fingerlings leave the streams in time to move into herring spawning areas to feed on the eyed floating herring. The fish ducks and Dolly Vardens also move in to feed on the small salmon fingerlings. The salmon [is] also part of the fur seals' diet. The fur seals, sea lions, whales and all fish ducks will be gone forever . . . if we don't cut back on the roe fisheries in Alaska.

To date, Alaska's governor has not agreed to curtail the commercial extractive harvest of *roe en sac* to conserve either the sustainable traditions of herring roe on hemlock harvest or the native wildlife of Alaska.

The following recipe is adapted from Tlingit elder and educator Pauline Kokeesh Duncan.

Further Readings

Allen, June. "A Biography of Alaska's Herring: A Little Fish of Huge Importance." *Stories in the News,* Ketchikan, Alaska, March 14, 2004. Available at www.sitnews.net/JuneAllen/Herring/031404_herring.html.

Carlson, Stefanie. *Changes in Roe Herring Markets: A Review of Available Evidence.* Commercial Fisheries Entry Commission Report Number 05-5N. Juneau, Alaska: CFEC, 2005.

Duncan, Pauline. *A Sitka Herring Spawn.* Sitka, Alaska: Children of the Tideland, 1993.

Duncan, Pauline. *Tlingit Recipes of Today and Long Ago, Sitka, Alaska.* Sitka, Alaska: Cookbook Publishers/Paula Duncan, 2003.

Schroeder, Robert F., and Matthew Kookesh. "The Subsistence Harvest of Herring Eggs in Sitka Sound, 1989." Alaska Department of Fish and Game Technical Paper No. 173. Anchorage, Alaska: Alaska Department of Fish and Game, 1990.

Thornton, Thomas F. "Last of the Sealers or Last of the Seals? A Special Report, Fifty Years Later." *Natural History Magazine,* 1999. Reprinted as a "Pick from the Past: June 1955." Available at www.naturalhistorymag.com.

Turner, Nancy J. *Plants of Haida Gwaii.* Winlaw, British Columbia, Canada: Sononis Press, 2004.

TLINGIT HERRING EGG SALAD

2 cups herring egg clusters on hemlock boughs
½ cup fresh shelled green peas
½ cup diced Northern Giant cabbage
½ medium-sized red onion, diced
1 green Quadrato D'Asti Giallo pepper, diced
¼ cup diced kelp or watercress
¼ cup sour cream
2 tablespoons mayonnaise
4 tablespoons apple cider or salmonberry vinegar
1 sprig fresh dill, sliced
1 pinch sea salt

In a colander, rinse the herring eggs and pick the grapelike clusters from the hemlock branches. Place the peas, cabbage, onion, and pepper in a glass bowl. Separately, dice the kelp and the herring roe, blanch for less than 20 seconds in hot water, then remove and drain through a colander. Add the roe, kelp, sour cream, mayonnaise, vinegar, dill, and salt to the diced vegetables in the glass bowl. Mix with a wooden spoon and serve as a main dish or as a side salad to a meal of grilled black cod collars.

White Sturgeon

The largest freshwater fish in North America is also among the most threatened. Once abundant in Salmon Nation from the Aleutian Islands southward to central California, the white sturgeon is a slow-growing fish that ultimately reaches sizes of twenty feet in length over its century-long lifespan. Because of the sturgeon's longevity, its wild populations are also the ones that are slowest to recover from the relentless overfishing that began in the 1880s.

It is easy to see why fishermen immigrating to the Columbia River watershed would have pursued this stately fish, for its firm, fatty flesh was excellent for smoking or grilling, and a single individual might weigh as much as 1,500 pounds. By 1892, the commercial fishery peaked with a 5,000,000-pound harvest of both white and green sturgeon. However, by the turn of the twentieth century—less than two decades after commercial exploitation began—it was clear that any sturgeon population within reach of major fishing villages had already been depleted. Their numbers were further thinned by the construction of dams, which limited sturgeon movement among the rivers, the estuaries, and the ocean. If those insults were not enough, in recent decades toxins such as dioxins, PCBs, and mercury have begun to accumulate in their flesh, so that the consumption of any meat or eggs (caviar) from older individuals or any organ meat from younger ones is no longer recom-mended. Pesticides, paper mill wastes, discarded paints, and raw sewage spewed into rivers are among the sources that contribute these toxins.

Despite these many environmental impacts on sturgeon health and reproduction, both commercial and sport fisheries for the white sturgeon have remained open in Salmon Nation. In some recent years, the commercial catch from legal permits has been valued at more than $10,000,000, and that has encouraged some unscrupulous fishermen to poach sturgeon to sell through the black market.

Although several First Nations communities in Salmon Nation have treaty-guaranteed subsistence rights as well as commercial permits to catch sturgeon, some have voluntarily shortened or suspended their season when numbers are predictably low. When tribal fishermen do pursue sturgeon, some

Anna, a female white Sturgeon that was captured, spawned, and—as shown here—released to support conservation based fish-culture activities on the Nechako River. Courtesy Carrier Sekani Tribal Council

Further Readings

Baldwin, Carole, and Julie H. Mounts, eds. *One Fish, Two Fish, Crawfish, Bluefish: The Smithsonian Sustainable Seafood Cookbook.* Washington, D.C.: Smithsonian Books, 2003.

IUCN Red List of Threatened Species. Assessment of *Acipenser transmontanus* (white sturgeon), 2004 Available at www.iucnredlist.org.

Nabhan, Gary Paul, ed. *Renewing the Food Traditions of Salmon Nation.* Portland, Oregon: RAFT/Ecotrust, 2006.

still use traditional hoop-nets off platforms built along the shore, while others use gillnets, hooks, and setline gear. Both states and tribes have set size limitations on allowable catches, with release required for undersized "shakers" as well as any "oversized" individuals reaching five feet or more in length. Because all egg-bearing females are larger than this latter size, they are excluded from any commercial, sport, or subsistence takings.

If caught amid white sturgeon, the more globally threatened green sturgeon must be released unharmed. Most of the remaining commercial fishing for white sturgeon in Salmon Nation occurs on the Columbia River below Bonneville Dam, although some tribes still fish for it between the Bonneville and McNary dams. In Canada, the entire Fraser River fishery was closed in 1994 after the harvest had dwindled down to a few thousand pounds. There are, however, commercially lucrative efforts to farm white sturgeon in California, where both meat and caviar are being produced.

The following recipe is adapted from a much more elaborate one developed by Chef Bob Hurley, of Hurley's Restaurant and Bar in Yountville, California, featured in *One Fish, Two Fish, Crawfish, Bluefish: The Smithsonian Sustainable Seafood Cookbook.*

PAN-ROASTED FARMED WHITE STURGEON WITH MUSHROOMS

7 tablespoons olive oil
3 cups chopped wild, seasonally fresh mushrooms, including chanterelles, morels, lobsters, and oysters
1 clove Inchelium Red garlic, chopped
2 shallots, chopped
¼ cup Pinot Noir or Madeira wine
½ cup chicken broth
¼ teaspoon sea salt
¼ teaspoon coarsely ground black pepper
4 6-ounce farmed white sturgeon filets

Preheat the oven to 400 degrees F. Drizzle 4 tablespoons of the olive oil into a large oven-proof sauté pan placed over medium heat and then add the chopped mushrooms, garlic, and shallots. Stir them vigorously with a wooden spoon as you sauté them for 4 to 5 minutes. Add the wine, chicken broth, salt, and pepper and then simmer until the liquids are reduced to half their original volume. Pour the contents of the pan out into a bowl and set them aside, keeping them warm, then add the other 3 tablespoons of the olive oil to the pan. Season the sturgeon filets with salt and coarsely ground pepper on both sides, then add them to pan and brown them on both sides. Next, place the pan in the oven and cook the sturgeon 6 more minutes, until the filets are done in the center. Remove the pan from the oven, place a filet on each of four plates, and then ladle the mushrooms, garlic, and shallots in wine and broth over the fish.

A juvenile white sturgeon in a stretcher as part of annual Carrier Sekani Tribal Council sampling activities on the Nechako River to assess the level of juvenile recruitment into the white sturgeon population in the river. The fish are measured, weighed and normally tagged with Passive Integrated Transponder (PIT) and in some instances, radio transmitters. Courtesy Carrier Sekani Tribal Council

WILD RICE NATION

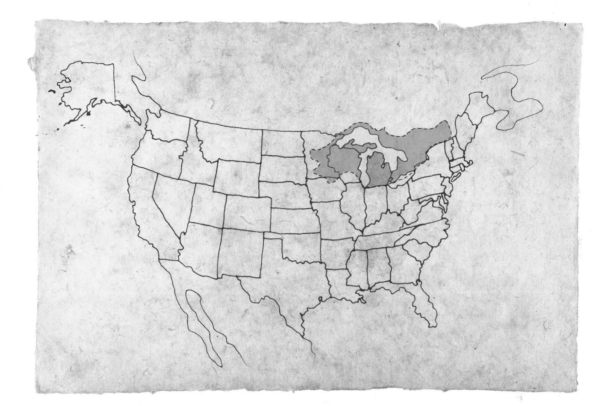

Spanning the watersheds surrounding the Great Lakes in the midwestern United States and southern Canada, Wild Rice Nation has strong extant traditions of ricing, fishing, and hunting. Although farming occurs at many sites within the region, orchard production, wild foraging, and meat procurement are its most distinctive traditions. The rituals associated with wild rice persist among most of the Anishnabe, Chippewa or Ojibwa, Cree, and Menominee peoples of the region, although cheap California-grown rice still economically threatens the economic well-being of authentic ricers. Immigrant cultures, including the French, Scots, English, Germans, Belgians, Norwegians, and Swedes, have also had a profound impact on the region's land use and culinary history. In the seventeenth century, the Métis culture unique to the region evolved among the descendants of marriages between indigenous peoples—woodland Cree, Ojibwa, Saulteaux, and Menominee—and Europeans—French Canadians, Scots, and English. Their foodways have remained relatively stable, although a number of fish stocks have declined due to introduced invasive species. At least 32 traditional foods are now at risk in Wild Rice Nation.

Hand-Harvested Wild Rice (*Manoomin*)

Anishinabe oral tradition has it that the People—now often recognized as the Ojibwa in Canada and Chippewa in the United States—were directed long ago by the Great Spirit to move west from the Atlantic coast, following the melting ice, until they found food growing on the water. They found wild rice, which grows naturally on rivers and lakes in northern Minnesota, Wisconsin, and Michigan. This native grain is celebrated in Anishinabe culture as well as the hybrid cultures of the Métis and others who arrived hundreds of years later. The Anishinabe word for the rice is *manoomin.* The name of a county in northern Minnesota uses an English-language version of the spelling, Manohmen. Wild rice is the official grain of Minnesota.

The plant is so central to the tribal culture and experience that many of today's elders have spent nearly every season of their entire lives harvesting it. Often, they can taste or look at rice grains and tell

Harvesting wild rice in Minnesota. Sarah Alexander/White Earth Land Recovery Project

whether they came from a river or a lake—sometimes even which lake. Rice has been the focus of many celebrations, including the "first-fruits" offerings that traditional cultures set aside to ensure that the spirits will continue gifting this bounty year after year. As John Quaderers of the Lac Court Oreilles band once explained,

> [Our] People come to visit the Bear [Spirit] and bring things for it like a bowl of wild rice or maple sugar or syrup or blue berries . . . If this is done in the evening, the first person coming in the morning could eat the food on the mat [and] talk to the bear.

"It's not just about food," explained Kathy Hoagland, a tribal member who is working to restore the use and awareness of wild rice on Minnesota's White Earth Reservation. "It's about preserving our way of life, our stories."

The Anishinabe people view rice as a gift from the Creator. They know it is a nutritious, important food source for their people. And they worry about it in the face of several daunting threats. For starters, hand-harvested wild rice has fallen out of favor with the younger generations, who are tempted by the ease and convenience of fast food. Consequently, many of the younger people have lost sight of the cultural importance of the rice.

"When I was little," said Earl Hoagland, "you couldn't even pee in the water. You had to go to shore. Now, you even see a lot of beer cans in the lake, people ricing to pay for beer. There's a loss of respect for wild rice."

Besides that, some of the naturally growing rice is downwind from agricultural fields where pesticides are applied. Earl Hoagland said Big Rice Lake, near the White Earth Reservation, used to be full of rice from shore to shore. "Now it's uncommon to see 50 percent of the lake growing rice," he said. He and others suspect that changing weather patterns and even beavers, with populations swollen from a lack of natural predators, are also causing damage.

The biggest fears regarding the wildness of their

rice among the people who value it in its natural form are the potential impacts of technology and bio-technology. Hand-harvesting is difficult. Two people must go out in a canoe. One person uses a pole to arch the rice plants over the boat, and the other uses a second pole to knock the grains into the bottom of the boat—carefully, so as not to damage the plant and the grains that aren't yet ready for harvest. Today, traditionalists still place iron kettles over woodfires to slowly toast the green rice into fire-cured black rice, while some now substitute other mechanized processing techniques. By the late 1960s, agricultural engineers found easier but more environmentally and culturally problematic ways to produce rice in flooded paddies that could be mechanically harvested after the paddies were drained. By 1986, California was outproducing Minnesota two to one, but its product could hardly be called "wild" anymore.

Earl Hoagland says he doesn't like the rise of paddy rice, but he believes that it isn't in itself the worst-possible hit to true wild rice. "When people start to eat paddy rice, then taste the real stuff, they want the real thing," he said.

The worst threat, as far as he and others are concerned, is genetic manipulation. Researchers have long been interested in making certain modifications to wild rice—so all the grains ripen at the same time, for example. But the tribal people are aware that contamination can happen, and they don't want to pollute a food source that is so crucial to their history, culture, and health.

As a way to head off the threat of such contamination, Minnesota state senators Satveer S. Chaudhary and Mary Olson introduced Senate Bill 2301 in the spring of 2007, requiring an environmental impact statement and advance notification about the release of genetically engineered wild rice in the United States, along with other controls.

To those who are most alarmed by such efforts, the idea of genetically modifying wild rice amounts to cultural genocide. That's a radically different view from that of researchers, who see heroism in the idea that they could one day harvest a nutritious food more efficiently. And it's an altogether different viewpoint from that of agricultural entrepreneurs, who see the grain primarily as a cash crop.

Earl and Kathy Hoagland say there are three

Steve Hurst, USDA-NCRS PLANTS Database

in Minnesota and—more recently—Michigan and Wisconsin. University of Minnesota researchers have even begun funding a minicamp, following the fall rice camp that's meant mostly for tribal members, but where nontribal members can also come to experience the harvest for themselves.

Craig Hassel, an associate professor and extension nutritionist at the University of Minnesota, has been working on the scientific front to test wild rice and other native foods for nutritional content, as compared to their mass-produced equivalents. Wild rice is a good source of protein, iron, and manganese and has a low glycemic index, which means it's an especially good choice for people at risk for diabetes. Hassel says the lab diagnostics for native foods can go only so far, however, and that indigenous knowledge is another legitimate way to understand the value of traditional foods.

Earl Hoagland agrees: "There is a spiritual gift that goes along with the rice," he says. "They probably will look and look and probably never find it, unless they learn how to pray."

Further Readings

Hassel, Craig. "Good Nutrition at Harvest Time." *Harvest Newsletter of the Dream of Wild Health Network*, October 2003.

Hauser, Susan Carol. *Wild Rice Cooking*. Guilford, Connecticut: Lyons Press, 2000.

LaDuke, Winona, and Brian Carlson. *Our Manoomin, Our Life*. Ponsford, Minnesota: White Earth Land Recovery Project, 2003.

Miller, Matthew. "Gains in Grain: Better Rice Growth—Through Science." *Lansing State Journal* (Michigan), March 30, 2006.

Nabhan, Gary Paul. "Wild Rice: The Endangered, the Sacred and the Tamed." In *Enduring Seeds: Native American Agriculture and Wild Plant Conservation*, pp. 109–122. Berkeley, California: North Point Press, 1989.

Vennum, Thomas Jr., *Wild Rice and the Ojibway People*. St. Paul: Minnesota Historical Society Press, 1988.

Wente, Scott. "Legislative Proposal Seeks to Protect Native Wild Rice." *Bemidji Pioneer* (Minnesota), March 31, 2006.

realms where work needs to be done to restore respect for traditional, hand-harvested wild rice: the political, the scientific, and the cultural. "We have to deal with all three," Kathy said. "We concentrate on the cultural part." For seven years, the Hoaglands have been hosting annual wild rice camps to teach the tribe's young people about the harvest and its importance in the culture. Mostly, their motive is to reestablish rice as a healthy food source for their people, who are in dietary and spiritual need of it. But the Hoaglands are reaching out, too, by welcoming interest and help from university researchers

WILD RICE WITH TOASTED PECANS AND HICKORY NUTS

⅔ cup pecans
⅔ cup hickory nuts
1 small onion or ramp (wild leek), finely chopped
4 tablespoons butter
4 cups precooked wild rice (*manoomin*)
1 teaspoon sea salt
½ teaspoon dried wild oregano leaves
2 teaspoons minced parsley or watercress

Preheat the oven to 350 degrees F. Spread the pecans and hickory nuts on half of a baking sheet, and on the other half spread the chopped onion or ramp. Place the sheet in the oven and bake for 10 minutes, until the nuts are toasted and the onion or ramp is caramelized. In a skillet, melt the butter and then add the precooked rice, nuts, onions, salt, and oregano. Sauté until warm, then remove from heat, place in a serving bowl, and sprinkle with minced parsley or watercress.

Chantecler Chicken

Bill Beard, of Illinois, almost didn't respond to a query about his late father, Irving Beard, and the latter's long track record of winning poultry contests with Chantecler chickens at the Illinois State Fair. Beard is one of the few remaining people who can speak with some knowledge about the breed in the United States, which is sometimes spelled Chanticler elsewhere. It remains the national poultry breed of Canada but is considered a rare breed of critical status both by Rare Breeds Canada and by the American Livestock Breeds Conservancy.

It turns out the delay in Beard's response was somewhat personal. "All I did was chores," he said. "I was a kid when Dad was doing all this stuff, and he was . . . he wasn't a very good teacher." But Beard remembers quite a bit about his father's chicken-raising hobby—which was actually an obsession for the eccentric man. He remembers that Irving Beard was an accomplished, though self-taught, geneticist and breeder of the chicken, a man who spent whole days sitting on upside-down feed buckets and watch-

Courtesy Cherry Creek Canadians

ing his flock. He kept meticulous notes. Sometime after Bill Beard went off to college, though, his father lost all of the notebooks.

Printed information about the Chantecler is scarce, and that may be one reason it's at risk. The breed was developed at the Abbey of Notre Dame du Lac in Oka, Quebec. Founded in 1881, the abbey is a monastery of the Order of Cistercians of the Strict Observance, with members commonly called Trappists. Though Trappists don't necessarily take vows of silence, they tend to be silent except when necessary for their work or their devotion. Fr. Bruno-Marie's response to an e-mail inquiry was suitably brief. "We have in our archives pictures and books about the Chantecler and Brother Wilfrid who created it," he wrote. "We don't work on it anymore."

According to Hans Schipper of Holland, the full name of the monk who first developed the breed is M. Wilfred Chatelaine, who lived from 1876 to 1963. He wanted to produce a breed with good meat and egg production. In the process, he also bred chickens with modest combs and wattles to suit the colder Canadian climate. The Oka Agricultural Institute in La Trappe, Quebec, first showed them, and in 1921 they were officially recognized as a breed, Schipper reports. Probably as a result of their very low profile, Chantecler chickens have been the subject of extinction rumors in the past. One H. Gordon Green countered such a rumor in a 1988 article about the breed for the *Toronto Star* newspaper. Apparently, an unnamed academic had pronounced dead "the only breed of chicken ever to originate in Canada," Green wrote. "There are at least half dozen chicken fanciers in this province who have them in their henyards right now. The professor could have seen them at the Ormstown Fair last month."

Fanciers say the Chantecler is friendly, quiet, and well mannered. The birds are famous among those who have tasted their high-quality breast and thigh meat. The chicks grow quickly on little food, and the hens can lay as many as 200 eggs a year. They're well adapted to cool climates and make beautiful show birds. Still, efforts to maintain flocks of them have been sporadic. One such attempt was made by a horsemen's group called the Cherry Creek Canadians, out

CRANBERRY-ROASTED CHANTECLER CHICKEN

chicken giblets
1 pound bread, crumbed to use for stuffing
2 cups Searle's or Early Black cranberries, mashed
¼ pound morel mushrooms, chopped
1 pound Damson plums, mashed
1 teaspoon sea salt
½ teaspoon freshly ground black pepper
1 quart water
2 whole Chantecler chickens, plucked and cleaned
2 cups hard apple cider, as a basting liquid

Preheat an oven to 350 degrees F. In a pot, simmer the giblets in salted water for ½ hour, then skim off the fat and save for preparing the stuffing. In a glass mixing bowl, combine the bread crumbs, mashed cranberries, chopped morels, mashed plums, giblets, and seasonings, then add the quart of water and mix thoroughly with your hands. Using a small wooden spoon, stuff the chickens with the dressing and place them on a rack in a large roasting pan. Place remaining dressing in aluminum foil on the side. Roast both the chicken and the dressing for 3 hours, basting every 15 minutes with hard cider and drippings. Let cool for 5 minutes, slice, and serve.

of Kamloops, a city in the southern interior of British Columbia. That group's short-lived breeding experiment provided them with an abiding affection for the birds but not much stock to contribute. Other efforts have yielded similar results, although Glen Drowns at the Sand Hill Preservation Center in Calamus, Iowa still offers Chantecler chicks in the original white and partridge varieties as well as a newer buff version.

Chantecler enthusiasts like the late Irving Beard are a disappearing breed themselves. Beard's family still regrets that he couldn't be bothered with multimillion-dollar offers from the likes of Kentucky Fried Chicken and Ralston-Purina. When Beard finally

Gina Bisco; courtesy American Livestock Breeds Conservancy

closed down his Hickory Hill Hatchery, he distributed his stock to a Leo P. "Huck" Finn, whose poor hearing precluded anything but shouted compliments about the bird, and another man named Tom Pierceall. Tom's wife, Carla, said she remembered receiving a few of Beard's birds, but the couple certainly doesn't raise Chanteclers now. "I think we butchered them," she said. The recipe on the facing page combines the cranberries of the North Country with this rare bird.

Further Readings

American Livestock Breeds Conservancy. "Chantecler Chicken." Available at http://albc-usa.org/cpl/chantecler.html.

Cherry Creek Canadians. "Chantecler Chickens." Available at www.cherrycreekcanadians.ca/chanteclers.htm.

Green, Gordon H. "A Breed Apart." *The Toronto Star* (Ontario), July 16, 1988.

Hunt, David. *Native Indian Wild Game, Fish and Wildfoods Cookbook.* Lancaster, Pennsylvania: Fox Chapel Books, 1992.

Sand Hill Preservation Center. "Chickens: Chantecler." In *Sand Hill Preservation Center Poultry Catalog*, 2006. Available at www.sandhillpreservation.com/catalog/chickens.html.

Schippers, Hans L. "Chantecler," 2000. Available at http://jubileeacres.net/chantecler.html.

American Eels of Lake Ontario and the St. Lawrence River

The eel is, as aficionado Richard Schweid concedes, "one of the most unlikely of fish . . . shaped like a serpent, with a long fin on top running almost the entire length of its body, ending in a semblance of a tail . . . Its slimy, mucous-covered skin is made up of tiny scales . . . so small that ancient rabbis judged it to be without scales and therefore deemed it non-kosher, prohibiting its consumption." And yet the current global market for eels is so voracious that it has already extracted most of the American eels that once reached the Great Lakes, bringing these and other populations to the verge of collapse.

For tens of thousands of years, American eels have slithered and swum a pathway that they now find to be quite perilous; it runs from the emptiest, least-known depths of the Atlantic to the inland lakes and streams of North America. Their migration cycle is the exact opposite of that of salmon, which spawn and hatch in streams, then migrate out to sea for most of their lives. Even today, after hatching in the warmth of the Sargasso Sea not far from the Bermuda Triangle, eels gradually make their way up the St. Lawrence River to mature in streams and marshes surrounding Lake Ontario; those that are among the lucky few later return to their birthing grounds in the Sargasso to spawn and die. This, the only species of freshwater eels in the Western Hemisphere, has recently suffered innumerable insults throughout much of its natural range. It is now nearly absent from its former haunts in Lake Ontario, where historically it was the lake's most abundant fish. What has been an unbroken chain of migrations over many millennia is now close to being broken by hydropower plants, dams, habitat loss, pollution, and overfishing. That rupture could possibly terminate a relationship between eels and humans that has endured thousands of years.

Fisherfolk from the First Nations have sought, caught, and consumed American eels from the waters of Wild Rice, Clambake, and Crabcake Nations since the last Ice Age. A prehistoric fish weir, found at the mouth of Alder Lake near Newport, Maine, attests to the antiquity of eel harvests in Clambake Nation. The sharpened wood stakes driven into the

This engraving, published in 1588, illustrates the fishing techniques of Native Americans, including a fish weir.

streambed range in age from 1,700 to 5,800 years old, making it the oldest known fish weir in North America. Archaeologists have little doubt that it was used to slow female American eels for capture during their fall migration out of Alder Creek, into the Sebasticook, then to the Kennebec River and ultimately to the Atlantic Ocean. It was in a place such as this that Tisquantum, a Pawtuxent fisherman, patiently trained the Pilgrims from the *Mayflower* how to spear American eels.

Further Readings

Atlantic States Marine Fisheries Commission. "Interstate Fishery Management Plan for American Eel *(Anguilla rostrata)." Fishery Management Report No. 36, 2000.*

Busch, W. D. N., S. J. Lary, C. M. Castilione, and R. P. MacDonald. "Distribution and Availability of Atlantic Coast Freshwater Habitat for American Eel *(Anguilla rostrata)." U.S. Fish and Wildlife Service Administrative Report 98-2.* Amherst, New York: 1998.

Dohne, Douglas. "Are We Seeing the End of the American Eel?" *Patriot-News* (Harrisburg, Pennsylvania), October 24, 2004.

Eckstorm, Fanny H. *Indian Place Names of the Penobscot River and Maine Coast.* Orono: University of Maine Press, 1938.

Fondation Culinaire. *L'Art Culinaire au Pays des Bleus et de la Ouananiche.* Quebec City, Canada: Fondation Culinaire, 1967.

"The Quebec Declaration of Concern: Worldwide Decline of Eels Necessitates Immediate Action." Declaration issued at the 2003 International Eel Symposium, held in conjunction with the 2003 American Fisheries Society Annual Meeting. Quebec City, Canada: August 14, 2003.

Schwabe, Calvin W. *Unmentionable Cuisine.* Charlottesville: University Press of Virginia, 1979.

Schweid, Richard. *Consider the Eel: A Natural and Gastronomic History.* Chapel Hill: University of North Carolina Press, 2002.

ANGUILLE AU VIN BLANC OU CIDRE DE GLACE (EELS IN WHITE WINE OR CIDER)

1½ to 2 pounds eel meat, cleaned
1 to 2 cups white wine or *cidre de glace*
12 large Romaine lettuce or watercress leaves
¼ cup small green peas, freshly harvested and shelled
1 tablespoon chopped sage leaves
1 tablespoon chopped spearmint leaves
1 bay leaf
3½ ounces butter
1½ tablespoons unbleached whole-wheat flour

To clean an eel:

Stun the eel by whacking its head against a hard rock or wood block. Loop a string around its head and tie it to a beam to suspend its body in the air. Cut an incision just below the string and peel back the skin from that level downward, grabbing hold of it with needle-nose pliers and pulling the skin inside out in one piece. Gut the eel through a cut in its belly and then bring it down off the beam and chop off the head.

To prepare the eel:

Cut the eel meat into inch-long segments and place them in a casserole dish or deep frying pan, covering them with either white wine or apple ice wine. Cook the meat for 15 minutes, then transfer it with the remaining wine and meat juices to a heavy cast-iron cooking pot. Put the romaine lettuce leaves or watercress, shredded into strips, on top of the eel meat. Add the peas, sage, mint, bay leaf, and butter and simmer gently for 15 minutes more. Remove some of the cooking liquid, let cool for 2 minutes, then whisk in the flour to form a roux. Add the roux to the pot and stir it into the rest of the juices, covering each piece of eel meat. Simmer 5 minutes more, until the sauce has thickened, then serve.

Since the eighteenth century, female eels have been traditionally harvested at a similar spot in the Sebasticook drainage—named "Eel Weir Rips." On still another stream in Maine—the Kenduskeag, a tributary of the Penobscot River that enters the tidal waters at Bangor—the historic Penobscot eel harvest was frequent enough for them to name it "Place Where Eels Are Speared." After being speared or caught by hand at a weir, the eels were smoked on alder wood to be preserved as a storable trail food. They were, of course, highly prized as "human fuel" because their caloric value is six times that of any other freshwater fish. Though somewhat bony, the flesh of the American eel tastes like that of waterfowl or poultry; when smoked, its oiliness retains a rich complex of flavors and fragrances. Because the flesh of the eel offers one-fifth more protein than a T-bone steak (with only one-fourth the fat), it is the ideal winter ration.

Of course, Canadians and Americans were not the only people on Earth who savored the eel. Because a plate of young "grass" eels might run as much as fifty dollars in Asian and European seafood restaurants, they have been aggressively harvested along the Atlantic seaboard for export from Canada and the United States since 1960. Until 2004, between 850 and 3,500 metric tons of eels were annually harvested from U.S. waters, and between 500 and 1,200 metric tons were harvested from Canadian waters, with over half of that coming from Lake Ontario and the Upper St. Lawrence River.

If such harvests were the only pressures on American eels, many populations would still have plummeted, but dams, locks, and hydro-turbines wreaked further havoc on their numbers. By 2001, eel populations in both countries had suffered such dramatic declines that the fisheries in Lake Ontario and the Upper St. Lawrence were closed down. Most notably, the number of juvenile eels migrating into Lake Ontario fell from close to a million in the early 1980s to fewer than 10,000 in 1993 and finally to levels approaching zero in 2001. Over the same period, significant drops in eel harvests occurred in New York, Virginia, New Brunswick, and Prince Edward Island. This prompted eel biologists from eighteen countries meeting in Canada in 2003 to unanimously endorse "The Quebec Declaration of Concern: Worldwide Decline of Eels Necessitates Immediate Action." This declaration noted:

> The steep decline in populations of eels endangers the future of these legendary fish. With less than 1 percent of major juvenile resources remaining, precautionary efforts must be taken immediately to sustain these stocks. In recent decades, juvenile abundance has declined dramatically; by 99 percent for the European eel . . . by 80 percent for the Japanese eel . . . [while] recruitment of American eel to Lake Ontario—near the species' northern limit—has virtually ceased.

Although decades passed with virtually no fisheries management of the American eel relative to the conservation efforts that targeted other fish, there are signs that this situation may be changing. Recently, the St. Regis Mohawk tribe initiated a collaboration with the U.S. Geological Survey's Tunison Biological Laboratory in Cortland, New York, to identify means of recovering the American eel populations in their home waters of Lake Ontario and the St. Lawrence. They are not merely ascertaining the causes of the recent depopulation but are considering means of reversing it. By 2005, commercial aquaculture projects had begun in Maryland, New Jersey, and Pennsylvania, marketing farm-raised American eels to gourmets around the world for handsome prices. And yet, as food historian Calvin Schwabe has lamented, "probably most present-day Americans under 30 have never seen an eel except in an aquarium somewhere . . . For animals that are such delicious eating and are prized in so many cuisines . . . it is remarkable how little demand now exists in America for eel meat."

Schwabe then offers some twenty-nine recipes for this "most unlikely of fish," and his notes on preparing eel are integrated into the recipe on the preceding page. The core of the recipe is attributed to an old French-Canadian fisherman and included in the 1967 edition of *L'Art culinaire au pays des Bleuts et de la Ouananiche,* but it can be prepared with either white wine or a Canadian apple-based ice wine, *cidre de glace.*

EPILOGUE

Gone but Not Forgotten: The Continentwide Extinction of the Passenger Pigeon

There are some traditional foods of North America that have become endangered and extinct on a continentwide basis, reminding us that our consumption patterns can either deplete diversity on a grand scale or help save it. The passenger pigeon is an especially poignant example, for the bird was not at all rare even a half century before its widespread demise. As has been the case for many other species, the vicious synergies of overharvesting and habitat fragmentation combined to wipe this species out of its habitats and off our grandparents' plates. At the same time, however, we have seen how sportsmen and resource managers have learned from that tragic lesson, allowing the return of wild turkeys, bobwhite quail, prairie chickens, and many ducks to their former ranges. Nevertheless, Canadians, Americans, and Mexicans must be reminded that we continue to see widespread declines in other species once thought to be beyond anyone's capacity to deplete them, from cod to sturgeon to ramps to ginseng. We offer this profile of passenger pigeons as a historic food animal to remind us that some animals and plants may never return to our plates and that we should not rush to consume those that are in recovery until it is absolutely sure that they can withstand any harvesting pressure.

Once the most numerous bird in North America, if not on the entire planet, the passenger pigeon reminds us that a species once so common—numbering 4,000,000,000 or more in the nineteenth century—can be completely lost; Martha, the last survivor, died in 1914. Unfortunately, rare species of limited range are not the only ones that can be driven to extinction by gluttony, greed, and habitat loss. From the Atlantic seaboard to the Front Range of the Rockies, flocks once contained so many individual pigeons that hunters believed they could not make a dent in them. How

could humankind have any impact at all on a game bird so abundant that a single flock might be a mile wide and 300 miles long?

The passenger pigeon was a pretty bird, larger and more gaily colored than a mourning dove. Its head and rump were both a slate blue, but its breast was a deep wine red. Its eyes were scarlet. As is usually the case, the males were a bit showier than the females, boasting more brilliantly illuminated feathers.

Yet individuals did not much stand out as distinctive unless they were dead in the hand. Passenger pigeons were exceedingly social, with hundreds nesting in a single tree and millions in a single forest. Flocks comprising billions of individuals would migrate south in the fall to winter in Gumbo Nation, Cuba, or even Mexico. Their stopovers during migration were often named in honor of their seasonal presence: Mimico ("place of the passenger pigeons") in Ontario; Pigeon Lakes in Minnesota and Wisconsin; White Pigeon, Michigan; Pigeon Roost, Indiana; Pigeon Forge, Tennessee; and Crockford Pigeon Mountain in Georgia.

Being so numerous that they were commonly considered "countless," passenger pigeons were also easy to kill by the clumsiest of hunters. Their ultimate extinction was due to a convergence of many causes, but their numbers were thinned primarily by those who sought to sell pigeon flesh on a massive commercial scale. By the early 1800s, as cities grew to the point that their residents no longer farmed, foraged, or hunted for themselves, a breed of market hunters developed. They killed, plucked, salted, and shipped pigeons by the boxcar load into Baltimore, Philadelphia, Boston, and New York, where a single pigeon sold for a penny in 1805. Rich folks offered pigeon to their slaves and servants as the cheapest meat they could buy for them. By 1878, a single market hunter was shipping 3,000,000 pigeons a year to New York for sale.

As early as the 1850s, there were already signs that these birds were declining. They were losing food, roosts, and refuges as the oak and beech forests were leveled to make room for new farms. When the pigeons left the forest remnants to feed on grain planted in the newly plowed fields, farmers took to shooting as many as they could. A rather slow decline in pigeon numbers occurred between 1800 and 1870, but then the rate of loss accelerated. Between 1870 and 1890, the passenger pigeon decline could only be called catastrophic, for several states and provinces were left without a single bird. They became absent from Wild Rice Nation along the shores of the Great Lakes in the 1890s. By 1900, they were also gone from most of Maple Syrup Nation, Bison Nation, Clambake Nation, Crabcake Nation, Cornbread Nation, and Gumbo Nation. Hunters in the United States, Canada, and Mexico were stunned. By September 1, 1914, when Martha died alone in captivity in a cage at the Cincinnati Zoo, Americans stood in disbelief. As early as 1909, organizations began to offer rewards for a living specimen taken from the wild, but those prizes were never claimed. The last unconfirmed reports of small flocks in the wild came in around 1930, largely from the backwaters of Louisiana and Arkansas. And yet no more birds appeared in the hand, on the table, or over the grill.

The following recipe is taken verbatim from M. H. Mitchell's book, *The Passenger Pigeon in Ontario:*

Passenger Pigeon Pot Pie
To make a pot pie of them, line the bake-kettle with a good pie crust; lay out your birds, with a little butter on the breast of each, and a little pepper

shaken over them, and pour in a tea cupful of water—do not fill your pan too full; lay in the crust, about half an inch thick, cover your lid with hot embers and put a few below. Keep your bake-kettle turned carefully, adding more hot coals to the top, till the crust is cooked. This makes a very savoury dish for a family.

Further Readings

Eckert, Allan W. *The Silent Sky: The Incredible Extinction of the Passenger Pigeon*. Lincoln, Nebraska: One Universe Books, 1965.

Mitchell, M. H. "The Passenger Pigeon of Ontario." Contribution No. 7 of the Royal Museum of Zoology. Toronto, Ontario, Canada: University of Toronto Press, 1935.

Passenger Pigeon Society website, www.passengerpigeon.org.

Schorger, A. W. *The Passenger Pigeon: Its Natural History and Extinction.* Madison: University of Wisconsin Press, 1955.

APPENDIX 1
RAFT List of Foods at Risk in North America

The following list inventories more than 1,080 heirloom seed, fruit, and nut varieties; heritage breeds; and populations, subspecies, and species of fish, game, and wild foods known from North America as of November 2007. Periodic updates of this list will appear on websites of Slow Food and other organizations, including one that lists the states and provinces within which these foods occur. The food-nation designations refer to each ecological and agricultural region by a totemic or iconic keystone species and should not be confused with sovereign nations of indigenous peoples residing on this continent, many of whom have "farmer's rights" to some of these varieties that we honor. The rarity values for each listing are interpreted as follows: **T,** or **threatened,** means that it is regularly available in four to eight known local farmers' markets, community fairs, seed catalogs, nurseries, hatcheries, or wild natural populations; **E,** or **endangered,** means it is available through only one to three of these outlets; and **X,** or **functionally extinct,** indicates that it is no longer recorded in any current catalogs, fairs, or markets that bring it to the table, although it still may exist in government repositories or private collections of individual citizens or tribes. Those marked with asterisks are boarded on the Ark of Taste. We welcome your input in correcting or amplifying this list; please contact the editor, Gary Nabhan, for making changes in distributions or status.

Food Group	Specific or Generic Type	Variety, Breed, or Wild Population	Rarity	Food Nation
BERRIES				
	Blackberry	Cape Cod	E	Clambake
	Blackberry	Eclipse	E	Chestnut
	Blackberry	Hane's	E	Wild Rice
	Blackberry	Kellogg's	E	Cornbread
	Blackberry	Marshland	E	Clambake
	Blackberry	Morgantown	E	Chestnut
	Blackberry	Northwestern	E	Salmon
	Blackberry	Olympic	T	Salmon
	Blackberry	Posey County	T	Wild Rice
	Blackberry	Toland County	E	Clambake
	Blackberry	Trailing	E	Salmon
	Blueberry	Brunswick Lowbush	E	Clambake
	Blueberry	Gulfcoast Highbush	E	Crabcake, Gumbo
	Blueberry	Rubel Highbush	T	Clambake
	Blueberry	Upright Maine	E	Maple Syrup
	Cranberry	Berry Berry	E	Clambake
	Cranberry	McFarlin	E	Wild Rice
	Currant	Buffalo	E	Salmon
	Currant	Red	E	Maple Syrup
	Dewberry	Kansas City	E	Bison
	Dewberry	Pineland	E	Chestnut
	Dewberry	Pocono Plateau	E	Chestnut
	Dewberry	Rhode Island	E	Clambake
	Grape	Agawam	E	Maple Syrup
	Grape	Alicante Bouschet	E	Acorn
	Grape	Barry	E	Clambake
	Grape	Bell	E	Chestnut
	Grape	Berckmans	E	Salmon
	Grape	Brilliant	T	Salmon
	Grape	*Bronx Seedless	E	Acorn, Maple Syrup
	Grape	Campbell's Early	T	Salmon
	Grape	Canandaigua	E	Maple Syrup
	Grape	*Charbono	E	Acorn
	Grape	Concord, California	E	Acorn, Salmon
	Grape	*Cynthiana/Norton	E	Cornbread
	Grape	Delaware	T	Maple Syrup, Clambake
	Grape	Dutchess	E	Maple Syrup
	Grape	Goff	E	Maple Syrup
	Grape	Hopi	E	Chile Pepper
	Grape	Kishwaukee	E	Wild Rice
	Grape	Liberty	E	Gumbo
	Grape	Magoon Muscadine	E	Cornbread
	Grape	Mission	E	Acorn
	Grape	Muscat of Alexandria	T	Acorn, Salmon
	Grape	*Napa Gamay/Valdaguie	E	Acorn
	Grape	Red Malaga	T	Chile Pepper
	Grape	Suelter	E	Wild Rice
	Grape	Tokay Seedless	E	Acorn
	Hawthorn	Mission	T	Chile Pepper
	Hawthorn	Succulent	E	Wild Rice, Maple Syrup
	Hawthorn	T.O. Warren's Opaca	E	Gumbo
	Hawthorn	Western Mayhaw	E	Gumbo
	Huckleberry	Bear Lake	E	Pinyon Nut
	Huckleberry	Jenny Lake	E	Bison, Pinyon Nut
	Huckleberry	Low Growing Mountain	E	Salmon
	Passionfruit	White Maypop Passionfruit	E	Crabcake
	Pawpaw	Zimmerman	E	Maple Syrup, Clambake
	Raspberry	Boulder	E	Pinyon Nut
	Raspberry	Honey Queen	E	Bison
	Serviceberry	Nantucket	E	Clambake
	Strawberry	*Daybreak	E	Gumbo
	Strawberry	*Headliner	E	Gumbo
	Strawberry	*Klondike	E	Gumbo
	Strawberry	Marshall	E	Salmon
	Strawberry	Seaside (Chilean) Coastal Populations	X, E, T	Salmon
	Strawberry	*Tangi	E	Gumbo
	Strawberry	Tennessee Beauty	T	Crabcake, Chestnut
FISH AND SHELLFISH				
	Abalone	Black	E	Acorn
	Abalone	Flat	T	Salmon
	Abalone	Pinto	E	Salmon, Acorn
	Abalone	*Red	T	Acorn
	Abalone	White	E	Acorn
	Bass	Giant Sea	E	Acorn
	Chub	Bonytail	E	Pinyon Nut
	Chub	Humpback	E	Pinyon Nut
	Chub	Owens Valley Tui	E	Pinyon Nut
	Chub	Virgin River	E	Pinyon Nut
	Clam	*Geoduck	T	Salmon
	Clam	Horse, Gaper, or Great Washington	T	Salmon
	Clam	Quahog	T	Clambake
	Clam	Tomales Bay	T	Acorn
	Cod	Atlantic	E	Maple Syrup
	Cod	Cow	T	Salmon, Acorn
	Cod	Cusk	T	Clambake
	Cod	Pacific Black	T	Acorn, Salmon
	Conch	Queen (Atlantic)	E	Gumbo
	Crab	Blue Crab of Chesapeake Bay	E	Crabcake
	Croaker	Striped	T	Clambake
	Eel	American Eels of Lake Ontario and the St. Lawrence River	E	Wild Rice
	Flounder	Atlantic Yellowtail	T	Clambake, Crabcake
	Flounder	Summer (Fluke)	T	Clambake, Crabcake
	Flounder	Winter	E	Clambake, Crabcake
	Grouper	Goliath	T	Chestnut
	Grouper	Gulf/Cabrilla	T	Chile Pepper
	Grouper	Nassau	T	Crabcake
	Grouper	Spotted Cabrilla	E	Chile Pepper
	Grouper	Spotted Junefish/Mero Guasa	E	Chile Pepper
	Grouper	Warsaw	T	Crabcake, Gumbo
	Grunion	California	T	Acorn
	Haddock	Atlantic	T	Clambake
	Hake	Pacific	T	Salmon
	Halibut	Atlantic	T	Clambake, Crabcake
	Herring Roe	Pacific Herring Roe on Western Hemlock Boughs and Kelp	E	Salmon
	Lamprey	Pacific or Trident	E	Salmon
	Lingcod	Lingcod	T	Salmon, Acorn
	Monkfish	Atlantic	T	Crabcake, Clambake
	Oyster	*Delaware Bay	T	Clambake
	Oyster	Galveston Bay	T	Gumbo
	Oyster	*Olympia	T	Salmon
	Pikeminnow	Colorado River	T	Pinyon Nut
	Redfish	Redfish/Red Drum	T	Gumbo, Crabcake
	Rockfish	Boccacio	T	Salmon
	Rockfish	China	T	Salmon
	Rockfish	Pacific	E	Acorn
	Salmon	*Columbia River Chinook	T	Salmon
	Salmon	Columbia River Chum	T	Salmon
	Salmon	Gulf of Maine Atlantic	E	Clambake
	Salmon	Lower Columbia River Coho	T	Salmon

Food Group	Specific or Generic Type	Variety, Breed, or Wild Population	Rarity	Food Nation
	Salmon	Northern California Coho	E	Acorn, Salmon
	Salmon	Olympia Peninsula Chum	T	Salmon
	Salmon	Ozette Lake Sockeye	E	Salmon
	Salmon	Pink, Southern	X	Salmon
	Salmon	*Puget Sound Chinook	T	Salmon
	Salmon	*Russian River Chinook	T	Salmon
	Salmon	*Sacramento River Chinook	E	Acorn
	Salmon	Sacramento River Chum	X	Salmon
	Salmon	*Snake River Chinook, Fall Run	T, E	Salmon
	Salmon	Snake River Sockeye	T	Salmon
	Salmon	Southern Oregon Coho	T	Salmon
	Scallops	Peconic Bay	E	Clambake
	Scallops	Penobscot Bay	T	Clambake
	Scallops	Saco Bay	T	Clambake
	Sea Trout	Gulf Corvina	T	Chile Pepper
	Sea Trout	Totoaba	E	Chile Pepper
	Shad	Alabama	T	Gumbo
	Shad	Hickory	E	Clambake
	Shrimp	Ohio/Mississippi River	T	Gumbo, Cornbread
	Smelt	Delta	T	Acorn
	Smelt	Eulachon, Ooligan	T	Salmon
	Smelt	Rainbow	T	Clambake
	Snapper	Red	T	Gumbo
	Steelhead	Columbia River	T	Salmon
	Steelhead	Northern Oregon/Washington	T	Salmon
	Steelhead	Puget Sound	T	Salmon
	Steelhead	Sacramento-san Joaquin	T	Acorn
	Steelhead	Snake River	T	Salmon
	Steelhead	Southern California	E	Acorn
	Steelhead	Southern Oregon	T	Salmon
	Steelhead	Upper Columbia	T	Salmon
	Sturgeon	Alabama	E	Gumbo
	Sturgeon	Green	E	Salmon
	Sturgeon	Gulf	T	Gumbo
	Sturgeon	Pallid	E	Bison, Cornbread, Gumbo
	Sturgeon	Shortnose	E	Clambake, Crabcake
	Sturgeon	White	E	Salmon
	Sucker	Cui-ui	T	Pinyon Nut
	Sucker	Razorback	E	Pinyon Nut
	Trout	Apache	T	Chile Pepper
	Trout	Bull	E	Salmon, Pinyon Nut
	Trout	Coastal Cutthroat	E, T	Salmon
	Trout	Gila	T	Chile Pepper
	Trout	Greenback Cutthroat	E	Pinyon Nut
	Trout	Lahontan Green Cutthroat	E	Pinyon Nut
	Trout	Little Kern Golden	T	Pinyon Nut
	Trout	Paiute Cutthroat	T	Pinyon Nut
FRUIT TREES				
	Apples	*American Beauty	E	Clambake
	Apples	*American Golden Russett/Bullock	T	Maple Syrup
	Apples	*American Pippin	T	Maple Syrup
	Apples	Amy	E	Crabcake
	Apples	August Sweet	E	Cornbread
	Apples	Aunt Rachael	E	Crabcake
	Apples	Bailey Sweet	E	Maple Syrup
	Apples	Baker Sweet	E	Cornbread
	Apples	Baldwin	E	Maple Syrup
	Apples	Belmont	E	Cornbread
	Apples	*Bethel	T	Maple Syrup
	Apples	Bevan's Favorite	E	Maple Syrup
	Apples	*Black Ben Davis	E	broad range

Food Group	Specific or Generic Type	Variety, Breed, or Wild Population	Rarity	Food Nation
	Apples	Black Oxford	E	Maple Syrup
	Apples	Bottle Greening	T	Maple Syrup
	Apples	Brushy Mountain Limbertwig	E	Chestnut
	Apples	*Buckinham Buff/Cherokee Buff	T	Chestnut
	Apples	Campfield	E	Maple Syrup
	Apples	Carter's Blue	E	Crabcake
	Apples	Cauley	E	Gumbo
	Apples	Champlain	E	Maple Syrup
	Apples	Chandler	E	Maple Syrup
	Apples	Charette/The Donut	E	Maple Syrup
	Apples	Chimney	E	Maple Syrup, Crabcake
	Apples	*Coles Quince	E	Maple Syrup
	Apples	Crow Egg	E	Chestnut
	Apples	*Davey	E	Maple Syrup
	Apples	Doctor	E	Maple Syrup
	Apples	*Fall Harvey	E	Clambake
	Apples	*Fall Wine	E	Bison
	Apples	*Gano	T	Chestnut
	Apples	*Garden Royal	T	Clambake
	Apples	*Gilpin	E	Chestnut
	Apples	*Gloria Mundi/Ox	T	Maple Syrup
	Apples	*Graniwinkle	E	Clambake
	Apples	*Gravenstein (Sonoma)	E	Acorn
	Apples	Hackworth	E	Gumbo
	Apples	Hammond's	E	Chestnut
	Apples	*Harrison	E	Maple Syrup
	Apples	*Hawkeye/Red Delicious Old Line	T	Bison
	Apples	*Henry Clay	T	Chestnut
	Apples	Hewes Virginia Crab	E	Chestnut, Crabcake
	Apples	*Hightop Sweet	T	Cornbread
	Apples	*Honey Cider	E	Chestnut
	Apples	*Horse	T	Chestnut, Crabcake
	Apples	Hunt Russett	E	Clambake, Maple Syrup
	Apples	*Huntsman	E	Cornbread
	Apples	*Hyslop (Hyssop) Crab	E	Maple Syrup
	Apples	*Ingram	E	Cornbread
	Apples	*Johns (Original York)	E	Chestnut
	Apples	*Kinnard's Choice	E	Chestnut
	Apples	*Late Strwberry	E	Maple Syrup
	Apples	*Limbertwig	T	Chestnut
	Apples	*Lowry	E	Chestnut
	Apples	*Lyman's Large Summer	T	Wild Rice
	Apples	*Magnum Bonum	E	Chestnut
	Apples	Manzanitas Mexicanas	E	Pinyon Nut, Chile Pepper
	Apples	Mattamuskeet	T	Chestnut
	Apples	*McAffee	E	Chestnut
	Apples	*McLellan	T	Clambake
	Apples	*Melon	E	Maple Syrup
	Apples	*Milam	E	Chestnut
	Apples	*Missouri Pippin	E	Cornbread
	Apples	Mrs. Bryan	E	Chestnut, Crabcake
	Apples	*Newtown Spitzenburg	T	Maple Syrup
	Apples	Nickajack	E	Chestnut
	Apples	*Nova	T	Acorn
	Apples	*Novascotia Gravenstein	E	Clambake
	Apples	*Ohop Nonpareil	E	Cornbread
	Apples	Okabena	T	Bison
	Apples	Oliver	T	Cornbread
	Apples	Orenco	T	Salmon
	Apples	*Ortley/Greasy Pippin	E	Maple Syrup
	Apples	Park's Pippin	E	Chestnut

Food Group	Specific or Generic Type	Variety, Breed, or Wild Population	Rarity	Food Nation
	Apples	*Pearmain, Cannon	T	Chestnut
	Apples	*Pearmain, Summer	E	Maple Syrup
	Apples	*Peck's Pleasant	T	Maple Syrup, Clambake
	Apples	*Pilot	T	Chestnut
	Apples	*Porter/Yellow Summer Pearmain	E	Clambake
	Apples	*Primate	E	Maple Syrup
	Apples	*Rainbow	E	Chestnut, Crabcake
	Apples	*Rambo (Winter)	E	Maple Syrup
	Apples	Senator	E	Cornbread
	Apples	*Shiawasee Beauty	E	Wild Rice
	Apples	*Shockley	E	Chestnut
	Apples	*Smith's Cider	E	Maple Syrup
	Apples	Somerset of Maine	E	Clambake, Maple Syrup
	Apples	Spokane Beauty	T	Salmon
	Apples	*Starkey	T	Maple Syrup
	Apples	*Stayman	E	Chestnut, Crabcake
	Apples	*Stone	E	Maple Syrup
	Apples	*Summer Banana	T	Chestnut, Crabcake
	Apples	*Summer Sweet/Sidney	E	Maple Syrup
	Apples	*Sutton's Beauty	T	Cornbread
	Apples	*Sweet Winesap	E	Maple Syrup
	Apples	Tanyard Seedling	E	Chestnut
	Apples	Terry Winter	E	Chestnut
	Apples	*Turley Winesap	E	Cornbread
	Apples	*Vine	E	Chestnut
	Apples	*Virginia Crab	E	Chestnut
	Apples	*Virginia Greening	E	Chestnut, Crabcake
	Apples	*Virginia Winesap	E	Chestnut
	Apples	Walker's Pippin	E	Chestnut, Crabcake
	Apples	Wallace Sweet	E	Chestnut, Crabcake
	Apples	*Western Beauty	T	Maple Syrup
	Apples	*Winter Sweet Paradise	T	Chestnut
	Apples	*Winthrop Greening	E	Maple Syrup
	Apples	Wismer's Dessert	E	Wild Rice
	Apricot	Hopi Seedling	E	Chile Pepper
	Apricot	Wenatchee Moorpark	T	Salmon
	Avocado	Mexicola	E	Acorn
	Avocado	*Wilson Popenoe	E	Gumbo
	Banana	Texas Star	E	Gumbo
	Cherry, Sour	Belle of Santa Fe Black Oxheart	X	Chile Pepper
	Cherry, Sour	Evans	E	Bison
	Cherry, Sour	Mesabi	E	Wild Rice
	Cherry, Sweet	Black Republican	E	Salmon
	Cherry, Sweet	Governor Wood	T	Wild Rice
	Cherry, Sweet	Kansas Sweet/Hansen	E	Bison
	Cherry, Sweet	Yellow Spanish	E	Clambake, Maple Syrup
	Citrus	Arizona White Grapefruit	T	Chile Pepper
	Citrus	Atwood Navel Orange	E	Acorn
	Citrus	Campbell Valencia Orange	E	Acorn
	Citrus	Duncan Grapefruit	E	Gumbo
	Citrus	Hamlin Orange	E	Gumbo
	Citrus	Key Lime, West Indies Lime	T	Gumbo
	Citrus	Marsh Seedless Grapefruit	T	Gumbo
	Citrus	*Meyer Lemon	T	Acorn
	Citrus	Newhall Navel Orange	E	Acorn
	Citrus	Olinda Valencia Orange	E	Acorn
	Citrus	*Ojai Pixie Tangerine	T	Acorn
	Citrus	Ponderosa Lemon	E	Gumbo
	Citrus	Redblush Grapefruit	E	Chile Pepper
	Citrus	Thornless Key Lime, Mexican Line	T	Chile Pepper
	Citrus	Washington Navel Orange, Parent/ Old Linr	E	Acorn, Chile Pepper
	Date	Black Mission/Franciscan	E	Chile Pepper
	Date	Black Sphinx	E	Chile Pepper
	Fig	Chicago Black	E	Wild Rice
	Fig	Gillette	E	Salmon
	Fig	Hardy Chicago	E	Wild Rice
	Fig	Long Island	E	Clambake, Crabcake
	Fig	New York City	E	Clambake
	Fig	Panache/Striped Tiger	T	Pinyon Nut
	Jujube	Abbeville	E	Gumbo
	Jujube	Admiral Wilkes	E	Crabcake
	Jujube	*Edhegard	E	Chestnut
	Jujube	Fitzgerald	E	Gumbo
	Jujube	Redlands No. 4	E	Acorn
	Jujube	Sherwood	T	Gumbo
	Jujube	Shui Men	T	Cornbread
	Jujube	Texas Tart	T	Chile Pepper
	Olive	*Mission	E	Acorn
	Pawpaw	Mango	E	Chestnut
	Pawpaw	Sue	E	Cornbread
	Pawpaw	Sweet Alice	T	Cornbread
	Pawpaw	Zimmerman	E	Maple Syrup
	Peach	Amsden	E	Wild Rice
	Peach	Charlotte	E	Salmon
	Peach	*Crawford, Baby	E	Acorn
	Peach	Crawford, Early	T	Clambake
	Peach	Crawford, Late	E	Clambake
	Peach	George IV	E	Clambake
	Peach	Hopi White	E	Chile Pepper
	Peach	*Indian Blood Free	E	Cornbread
	Peach	Iron Mountain	E	Maple Syrup
	Peach	Lola Queen	X	Bison
	Peach	Louisiana Pecher	X	Gumbo
	Peach	Louisiana White	X	Gumbo
	Peach	Muir	E	Acorn
	Peach	Navajo Clingstone	X	Chile Pepper
	Peach	Oldmixon Clearstone	E	Wild Rice
	Peach	*Oldmixon Free	E	Wild Rice
	Peach	Rochester	E	Maple Syrup
	Peach	*Silver Logan	E	Acorn
	Peach	Slappy	E	Maple Syrup
	Peach	Slaybaugh Special	E	Maple Syrup
	Peach	Strawberry Free	E	Acorn
	Peach	Stump-the-world	E	Clambake
	Pear	*Beirschmitt	E	Bison
	Pear	*Bloodgood	E	Clambake
	Pear	*B. S. Fox	E	Acorn
	Pear	*Buffum	E	Clambake
	Pear	Burford	E	Chestnut
	Pear	*Clapp's Favorite Red	T	Clambake
	Pear	*Colonel Wilder	E	Acorn, Salmon
	Pear	*Columbia	E	Clambake
	Pear	*Dana Hovey	E	Clambake
	Pear	*Dearborn	E	Clambake
	Pear	*Dorset	E	Clambake
	Pear	El Dorado	E	Salmon
	Pear	*Frederick Clapp	E	Clambake
	Pear	Golden Boy	E	Gumbo
	Pear	*Howell	E	Bison
	Pear	*Idaho	E	Pinyon Nut

Food Group	Specific or Generic Type	Variety, Breed, or Wild Population	Rarity	Food Nation
	Pear	*June Sugar	E	Chestnut
	Pear	*Lawrence	E	Clambake
	Pear	*Lawson	E	Maple Syrup
	Pear	*Lincoln	E	Cornbread
	Pear	*Lucy Duke	E	Crabcake
	Pear	*Orcas	E	Salmon
	Pear	*Rescue	T	Salmon
	Pear	*Sheldon	E	Maple Syrup
	Pear	*Sudduth	E	Cornbread
	Pear	*Tyson	E	Maple Syrup
	Pear	*Vermont Beauty	E	Maple Syrup
	Pear	*Wilder Early	E	Maple Syrup
	Pear	*Winter Bartlett	T	Salmon
	Pear	Worden Seckel	E	Maple Syrup
	Persimmon	Craggs	E	Cornbread
	Persimmon	Delight	E	Cornbread
	Persimmon	Early Golden	E	Cornbread
	Persimmon	Evelyn	E	Maple Syrup
	Persimmon	Killen	E	Clambake, Crabcake
	Persimmon	Miles	E	Cornbread
	Persimmon	Missouri	E	Cornbread
	Persimmon	Pipher	E	Cornbread
	Persimmon	Tatum	E	Cornbread
	Persimmon	Texas Black	E	Bison
	Persimmon	Wabash	E	Cornbread
	Persimmon	Yates/Jewel	T	Cornbread
	Plum	*American/Klamath	E	Acorn
	Plum	Bird or Oso	T	Salmon
	Plum	Burbank	T	Acorn
	Plum	Chickasaw, Miner	T	Cornbread
	Plum	*Elephant Heart	E	Acorn
	Plum	Flatwoods	E	Crabcake, Gumbo
	Plum	Grave's Beach	E	Clambake
	Plum	*Inca	T	Acorn
	Plum	Jefferson	E	Wild Rice
	Plum	Jesse (Champion)	E	Salmon
	Plum	Kelsey	E	Acorn
	Plum	*Laroda	E	Acorn
	Plum	*Mariposa	T	Acorn
	Plum	Ogeechee	E	Cornbread
	Plum	*Padre	T	Acorn
	Plum	Potawatomi	T	Pinyon Nut
	Plum	Santa Rosa	T	Acorn
	Plum	Shiro	E	Acorn
	Plum	South Dakota	E	Bison
	Pomegranate	North Carolina Seedling	E	Chestnut, Gumbo
	Pomegranate	Papago/sonoran White	T	Chile Pepper
	Pomegranate	Plantation Sweet	T	Chestnut
	Quince	*Meech's Prolific	E	Clambake
	Quince	Sonoran	T	Chile Pepper
GRAINS				
	Amaranth	New Mexico Hispanic Alegria	T	Chile Pepper, Pinyon Nut
	Amaranth	Pueblo Red Dye	E	Chile Pepper, Pinyon Nut
	Barley	Faust	T	Bison
	Corn	Acoma Blue Flour	E	Chile Pepper
	Corn	Acoma Pop	X	Chile Pepper
	Corn	Alabama Coschatta Flint	E	Cornbread
	Corn	Apache Red Flour	T	Chile Pepper
	Corn	Arkansas Red and White Dent	E	Cornbread
	Corn	Assiniboine Flour	E	Bison
	Corn	Baby Rice Pop	E	Wild Rice
	Corn	Bear Island Chippewa Dent	E	Wild Rice
	Corn	Bearpaw Pop	E	Maple Syrup
	Corn	Beasley's Red Dent	E	Cornbread
	Corn	Big Mountain (Dine) Blue Flour	E	Chile Pepper
	Corn	Black Mennonite Pop	E	Maple Syrup
	Corn	Boone County White Dent	T	Wild Rice
	Corn	Carolina Gourdseed Dent	E	Chestnut
	Corn	*Chapalote Flint/Pop	E	Chile Pepper
	Corn	Cherokee Blue And White Dent	E	Chestnut
	Corn	Cherokee White Eagle Dent	E	Chestnut
	Corn	Cherokee White Flour	E	Chestnut
	Corn	Cherokee Long Ear/Pop	E	Bison
	Corn	Cheyenne Agency Striped Flint	E	Bison
	Corn	Chickasaw Dent	X	Bison
	Corn	Cochiti Blue Flour	T	Chile Pepper
	Corn	Cochiti Pueblo Pop	E	Chile Pepper
	Corn	Cocopah Multicolored Sweet	E	Chile Pepper
	Corn	Colorado Blue Flour	E	Pinyon Nut
	Corn	Concho White Flour	E	Chile Pepper
	Corn	Crosby's Early	X	Maple Syrup
	Corn	Delaware Blue Flint	X	Clambake
	Corn	Delaware Lenni Lenape	E	Clambake
	Corn	Delaware White Flour	E	Clambake
	Corn	Duncan Dent	E	Chile Pepper
	Corn	Early Cory	X	Maple Syrup
	Corn	Early Dean Sweet	X	Maple Syrup
	Corn	Early Vermont	X	Maple Syrup
	Corn	Early White Cory	X	Maple Syrup
	Corn	Encinal Blue Flour	E	Chile Pepper
	Corn	Ernest Strubbe's Dents	E	Wild Rice
	Corn	Escondida Blue Flout	E	Chile Pepper
	Corn	Fort Kent Gold Flint	E	Maple Syrup
	Corn	First of All	X	Maple Syrup
	Corn	Ganondaga Flint	E	Maple Syrup
	Corn	Garland Flint	X	Maple Syrup
	Corn	Gaspé Flint	E	Maple Syrup
	Corn	Ha-go-wa (Seneca Flint)	E	Maple Syrup
	Corn	Hasting's Prolific	X	Gumbo
	Corn	Hickory King Yellow	E	Chestnut
	Corn	Hooker's Sweet Indian	T	Salmon
	Corn	Hopi Greasy Hair	E	Chile Pepper
	Corn	Hopi Orange-red Flour/Flint	E	Chile Pepper
	Corn	Hopi Pink Flour	E	Chile Pepper
	Corn	Hopi Red Flour	E	Chile Pepper
	Corn	Hopi Sweet	T	Chile Pepper
	Corn	Hopi White Flour	E	Chile Pepper
	Corn	Hopi Yellow Flour	E	Chile Pepper
	Corn	Howling Mob Sweet	E	Wild Rice
	Corn	Iroquois Calico Flour	E	Maple Syrup
	Corn	Iroquois White Giant Flour	E	Maple Syrup
	Corn	Isleta Blue Flour	E	Chile Pepper
	Corn	Isleta White Flour	E	Chile Pepper
	Corn	Jemez Blue Flour	E	Chile Pepper
	Corn	Jemez White Flour	E	Chile Pepper
	Corn	Jicarilla Apache Concho White Flint	E	Chile Pepper
	Corn	John Haulk Yellow Dent	E	Chestnut
	Corn	King of Early	X	Maple Syrup
	Corn	King Philip Improved Flint	E	Clambake
	Corn	Kokoma, Hopi Purpleback	E	Chile Pepper

Food Group	Specific or Generic Type	Variety, Breed, or Wild Population	Rarity	Food Nation
	Corn	Lady Finger Rainbow Pop	E	Cornbread
	Corn	Lancaster Surecrop	E	Maple Syrup
	Corn	Longfellow Flint	T	Maple Syrup
	Corn	Luther Hill Sweet	T	Chestnut, Maple Syrup
	Corn	Mandan Black Flint	E	Bison
	Corn	Mandan Bride Flour	T	Bison
	Corn	Mandan Clay Red Flint	E	Bison
	Corn	Mandan Red Flour	E	Bison
	Corn	Mesquakie Dent	E	Wild Rice
	Corn	Mexican June "Chico"	E	Chile Pepper
	Corn	Mojave Flour	E	Chile Pepper
	Corn	Mohawk Round Nose Flour	E	Maple Syrup
	Corn	Mohawk White Hominy	E	Maple Syrup
	Corn	Morgan's Mill	X	Maple Syrup
	Corn	Nambe White Flint	E	Chile Pepper
	Corn	Narragansett White Cap Flint	E	Clambake
	Corn	Navajo (Dine) Blue Flour	T	Pinyon Nut, Chile Pepper
	Corn	Navajo (Dine) Gold Flour	E	Pinyon Nut, Chile Pepper
	Corn	Navajo (Dine) Robin's Egg Flour	E	Pinyon Nut, Chile Pepper
	Corn	Navajo (Dine) White Flour	E	Pinyon Nut, Chile Pepper
	Corn	Nothstine Yellow Dent	E	Wild Rice
	Corn	Ohio Blue Claredge	E	Wild Rice
	Corn	Ohio Calico Dent	E	Cornbread
	Corn	Osage Brown Flour	E	Bison
	Corn	Osage Red Flint	T	Bison
	Corn	Pawnee Flour	X	Bison
	Corn	Pennsylvania Dutch Butter	E	Maple Syrup
	Corn	Pima White Flint	E	Chile Pepper
	Corn	Ponca Blue Flour	X	Bison
	Corn	Posole Dry	E	Chile Pepper
	Corn	Puhwem White	E	Bison
	Corn	Quapaw	E	Bison, Cornbread
	Corn	Reventador	T	Chile Pepper
	Corn	Rio Lucio Concho Flour	E	Pinyon Nut, Chile Pepper
	Corn	*Roy's Calais Flint	E	Maple Syrup
	Corn	San Felipe Pueblo Blue	E	Pinyon Nut, Chile Pepper
	Corn	San Felipe Pueblo White	E	Pinyon Nut, Chile Pepper
	Corn	Santo Domingo Blue	E	Chile Pepper
	Corn	Santo Domingo White	E	Chile Pepper
	Corn	Sehsapsing (Delaware Blue)	T	Maple Syrup
	Corn	Seneca Blue Bear Dance	E	Maple Syrup
	Corn	Seneca Hominy	T	Maple Syrup
	Corn	Shaker's Early	X	Maple Syrup
	Corn	Silver King	E	Cornbread, Wild Rice
	Corn	Six Nations	E	Maple Syrup
	Corn	Stowell's Evergreen	T	Maple Syrup
	Corn	Tait's Norfolk Market Dent	X	Crabcake
	Corn	Tait's White Dent	E	Chestnut
	Corn	Taos Blue Flour/Flint	E	Chile Pepper
	Corn	Tennessee Red Cob Dent	E	Chestnut, Cornbread
	Corn	Texas Shoepeg Sweet	T	Chile Pepper
	Corn	Tohono O'odham 60-day Corn (Papago 60-day)	E	Chile Pepper
	Corn	Tohono O'odham June	T	Chile Pepper
	Corn	Tom Thumb Yellow Pop	T	Maple Syrup
	Corn	Tonawanda Calico Flint	X	Maple Syrup
	Corn	*Tuscarora White Hominy	E	Maple Syrup
	Corn	Vadito Blue, Concho, White	E	Pinyon Nut
	Corn	Vermont Yellow Flint	X	Maple Syrup
	Corn	Virginia Gourdseed Dent	E	Chestnut
	Corn	White Rice Pop	E	Crabcake
	Corn	Wisconsin Black Pop	E	Wild Rice
	Grains, Wild	Chia, Golden Chia	X	Chile Pepper
	Grains, Wild	Hand-harvested Wild Rice (*Manoomin*)	E	Wild Rice
	Grains, Wild	Little Barley	X	Chile Pepper
	Grains, Wild	Maygrass	X	Cornbread
	Grains, Wild	Palmers Saltgrass	T	Chile Pepper
	Grains, Wild	*Texas Wild Rice	T	Bison
	Grains, Wild	Wild Rice (Naturally Grown)	T	Wild Rice
	Huazontle (Goosefoot)	Huazontle (Goosefoot)	X	Chile Pepper
	Sonoran Panicgrass	Saugui	T	Chile Pepper
	Sorghum	Apache Red Sugarcane	E	Chile Pepper
	Sorghum	Gila River Hegari	T	Chile Pepper
	Sorghum	Honey Drip	E	Gumbo, Cornbread
	Sorghum	John Coffer/Dale Strain	E	Maple Syrup
	Sorghum	Mennonite Red	E	Cornbread
	Sorghum	Orange Top	E	Gumbo
	Sorghum	Salts Red	E	Cornbread
	Sorghum	San Felipe Pueblo Black Seeded	E	Chile Pepper
	Sorghum	Santa Fe/Santo Domingo Red-seeded	E	Chile Pepper
	Sorghum	Texas Black Amber Molasses	T	Chile Pepper
	Sorghum	Texas Long Sweet	E	Gumbo
	Sorghum	White Mountain Apache Red Seeded	E	Pinyon Nut, Chile Pepper
	Wheat	Early Baart Spring White	E	Chile Pepper
	Wheat	Huron Spring Bread	E	Bison, Wild Rice
	Wheat	Pacific Bluestem No. 47 Hard White Spring	E	Acorn, Salmon
	Wheat	Pima Club	X	Chile Pepper
	Wheat	Red Bobs Hard Red Spring	E	Bison
	Wheat	Red Fife Hard Red Spring	T	Bison
	Wheat	Turkey Red	E	Bison
	Wheat	White Sonora Bread	E	Chile Pepper
LIVESTOCK				
	Cattle	*Canadienne	E	Maple Syrup
	Cattle	*Corriente	T	Chile Pepper
	Cattle	*Florida Cracker	E	Gumbo
	Cattle	*Milking Devon	E	Clambake, Maple Syrup
	Cattle	*Pineywoods	E	Gumbo
	Cattle	*Randall Lineback	E	Clambake, Maple Syrup
	Cattle	Texas Longhorn	T	Bison
	Cattle	White Park	E	Bison
	Goats	San Clemente	E	Acorn
	Goats	*Spanish	T	Bison
	Goats	Tennesee Fainting	T	Bison, Cornbread
	Pigs	Choctaw	E	Bison
	Pigs	Guinea	E	Gumbo
	Pigs	Hereford	T	broad range
	Pigs	*Mulefoot	E	Cornbread, Bison
	Pigs	*Ossabaw Island	E	Crabcake
	Pigs	*Red Wattle	E	Gumbo
	Rabbit	*Silver Fox	E	Cornbread
	Sheep	California Variegated	E	Salmon
	Sheep	Gulf Coast	E	Gumbo
	Sheep	Hog Island	E	Crabcake

Food Group	Specific or Generic Type	Variety, Breed, or Wild Population	Rarity	Food Nation
	Sheep	*Navajo-Churro	T	Pinyon Nut, Chile Pepper
	Sheep	Newfoundland	T	Clambake
	Sheep	Santa Cruz	E	Acorn
	Sheep	St. Croix	T	Gumbo, Salmon
	Sheep	*Tunis	T	Crabcake
NUTS				
	Acorn	Emory (Acorn)/Bellota	E	Chile Pepper
	Acorn	Engelmann's (Acorn)	E	Acorn
	Almond	Dry Farmed	T	Acorn
	Almond	Texas Mission/Prolific	T	Chile Pepper
	Butternut	American Butternut	E	Maple Syrup
	Chestnut	*American	X, E	Chestnut, Maple Syrup
	Hickory	Burlington Hecan	E	Cornbread
	Hickory	*Fayette Shellbark	E	Maple Syrup
	Hickory	*Fox Shagbark	X	Maple Syrup
	Hickory	*Grainger Shagbark	E	Cornbread
	Hickory	*Weschcke Shagbark	E	Bison
	Hickory	*Wilcox Shagbark	E	Cornbread
	Pecan	Centennial	E	Gumbo
	Pecan	Greenriver	T	Cornbread
	Pecan	Texas Wild	E	Bison
	Pecan	Wilcox	T	Cornbread
	Pine Nut	*Nevada Soft-shell Pinyon	T	Pinyon Nut
	Walnut	(Northern) California Black Walnut, Hinds or Claro Walnut	T	Acorn
	Walnut	Spurgeon Special	E	Salmon
POULTRY				
	Chickens	*Buckeye	E	Cornbread
	Chickens	*Chantecler	E	Maple Syrup
	Chickens	Cubalaya	T	Gumbo
	Chickens	*Delaware	E	Crabcake
	Chickens	*Dominique/Dominicker	T	Clambake, Crabcake
	Chickens	Holland	E	Clambake
	Chickens	Java	E	Maple Syrup, Wild Rice
	Chickens	*Jersey Giant	T	Maple Syrup
	Chickens	*New Hampshire	T	Clambake
	Chickens	*Plymouth Rock, Nonindustrial	E	broad range
	Chickens	*Rhode Island Red	E	Clambake
	Chickens	Rhode Island White	T	Clambake
	Chickens	*Wyandotte	T	Maple Syrup
	Ducks	Cayuga	T	Maple Syrup, Crabcake
	Geese	*American Buff	E	broad range
	Geese	*Cotton Patch	E	Gumbo
	Geese	*Pilgrim	T	Bison
	Turkeys	*American (Standard) Bronze	T	Maple Syrup
	Turkeys	*American Buff	E	broad range
	Turkeys	Beltsville Small White	E	Crabcake, Wild Rice
	Turkeys	*Bourbon Red	T	Cornbread
	Turkeys	*Jersey Buff	E	Maple Syrup
	Turkeys	*Narragansett	T	Clambake
	Turkeys	Royal Palm	T	Gumbo
SUCCULENTS				
	Agave	Hohokam/Murphey's Mescal	E	Chile Pepper
	Agave	Page Springs	E	Chile Pepper
	Agave	Sacred Mountain	E	Chile Pepper
	Cactus	Fort Marcy Cholla	E	Pinyon Nut, Chile Pepper
VEGETABLES				
	Bean	Algonquian Red Speckled	E	Clambake, Maple Syrup
	Bean	Aztec Dwarf White Runner	T	Chile Pepper
	Bean	Barnes Mountain Cornfield	E	Chestnut
	Bean	Bearpaw Runner	E	Maple Syrup
	Bean	Bertie Best Greasy	E	Chestnut
	Bean	Big Frosty	E	Gumbo
	Bean	Big John	E	Chestnut
	Bean	Blackcoat Runner	X	Maple Syrup
	Bean	Black Pinto	E	Chile Pepper
	Bean	Bumblebee	E	Maple Syrup
	Bean	Caguama, Tewa Turtle	X	Chile Pepper
	Bean	Champion of England Pea	E	Maple Syrup
	Bean	Charles Murphey's Shell	E	Maple Syrup
	Bean	Cherokee Cornfield	T	Chestnut
	Bean	Cherokee Greasy	E	Chestnut
	Bean	Chester	E	Clambake, Maple Syrup
	Bean	Chickashaw Dry Bush	E	Cornbread
	Bean	*Cocopah Brown Tepary	E	Chile Pepper
	Bean	*Cocopah White Tepary	E	Chile Pepper
	Bean	Dan O'rourke Pea	T	Maple Syrup
	Bean	Del Norte	E	Chile Pepper
	Bean	Deserento Potato	E	Maple Syrup
	Bean	Doyce Chambers Greasy Cutshort	E	Chestnut
	Bean	Duane Baptiste's Potato	E	Maple Syrup
	Bean	Edwards Cornfield	E	Chestnut
	Bean	Fisher	E	Maple Syrup
	Bean	Flagg	E	Maple Syrup
	Bean	*Four Corners Gold	T	Chile Pepper
	Bean	Four Corners Runner	E	Chile Pepper
	Bean	Golden Heirloom	E	Maple Syrup
	Bean	Grady Bailly Greasy	E	Chestnut
	Bean	*Hopi Beige Lima	T	Chile Pepper
	Bean	Hopi Black Dye	E	Chile Pepper
	Bean	Hopi Black Tepary	X	Chile Pepper
	Bean	*Hopi Gray Lima	T	Chile Pepper
	Bean	*Hopi Red Lima	T	Chile Pepper
	Bean	Hopi White Tepary	E	Chile Pepper
	Bean	Hopi Yellow	T	Chile Pepper
	Bean	*Hopi Yellow Lima	E	Chile Pepper
	Bean	Ice	E	Maple Syrup
	Bean	Immigrant	E	Salmon
	Bean	Iroquois Brown	E	Maple Syrup
	Bean	Iroquois Cranberry	E	Maple Syrup
	Bean	Jack Kelly Butter	E	Chestnut
	Bean	Kahnawake Pole	T	Maple Syrup
	Bean	Kearnerly Yellow Eye	T	Clambake
	Bean	Kilham Goose	E	Salmon
	Bean	King of Early	E	Maple Syrup
	Bean	Lazy Housewife	E	Maple Syrup
	Bean	Leather Britches	T	Maple Syrup
	Bean	Lenape Cutshort/Indian Hannah	E	Clambake
	Bean	Lucas Navy	E	Salmon
	Bean	Maine Yellow Eye	T	Clambake, Maple Syrup
	Bean	Marafax	E	Clambake
	Bean	Margaret Best Greasy	E	Chestnut
	Bean	Mary Moore Greasy	E	Chestnut
	Bean	Mayfare Pea	T	Maple Syrup
	Bean	*Mayflower	E	Clambake, Maple Syrup
	Bean	Maygog Early Pea	X	Maple Syrup
	Bean	Mcleans Little Pea	E	Maple Syrup
	Bean	Mostellers Wild Goose	T	Maple Syrup, Chestnut
	Bean	Mull Kidney	E	Maple Syrup
	Bean	Nez Perce	E	Salmon

Food Group	Specific or Generic Type	Variety, Breed, or Wild Population	Rarity	Food Nation
	Bean	Nickell Half-runner	E	Chestnut
	Bean	Northeaster Pole	X	Clambake
	Bean	Old Champion Pea	X	Maple Syrup
	Bean	Onondaga Kidney	T	Maple Syrup
	Bean	O'odham Brown Tepary	E	Chile Pepper
	Bean	Ora's Speckled Pole	E	Chestnut
	Bean	Oregon Giant	E	Salmon
	Bean	Oxford Yellow Eye	E	Maple Syrup
	Bean	Paint	E	Salmon
	Bean	Painted Lady Runner	E	Maple Syrup
	Bean	*Paiute Mixed Tepary	E	Pinyon Nut
	Bean	*Paite Yellow Tepary	E	Pinyon Nut
	Bean	*Pima Beige Tepary	E	Chile Pepper
	Bean	*Pima Lima	X	Chile Pepper
	Bean	Pinacate Black Tepary	E	Chile Pepper
	Bean	Pink Tip Greasy	E	Chestnut
	Bean	Redkloud Red Kidney	E	Maple Syrup
	Bean	Robe Mountain Cornfield	E	Chestnut
	Bean	San Felipe Pueblo White Tepary	E	Chile Pepper
	Bean	Scott's Choice Dry Bush	T	Maple Syrup
	Bean	Seay Cutshort	E	Chestnut
	Bean	Seneca Pinto	E	Maple Syrup
	Bean	Six Nations	T	Maple Syrup
	Bean	Steuben Yellow Eye	E	Clambake, Maple Syrup
	Bean	Striped Hull Greasy Cutshort	E	Chestnut
	Bean	Sulfur	X	Maple Syrup
	Bean	Summer Succotash	E	Maple Syrup
	Bean	Tennessee Cornfield Pole	E	Cornbread, Chestnut
	Bean	Thomas Laxton Pea	X	Maple Syrup
	Bean	Thousand-to-one	T	Maple Syrup
	Bean	Tobacco Worm	E	Chestnut
	Bean	Tohono O'odham Pink	E	Chile Pepper
	Bean	*Tohono O'odham Red-brown Tepary	E	Chile Pepper
	Bean	Tohono O'odham Yellow	T	Chile Pepper
	Bean	*Tohono O'odham White Tepary	E	Chile Pepper
	Bean	Tonawanda Seneca Dry Bush	E	Maple Syrup
	Bean	*True Red Cranberry Bush	E	Maple Syrup
	Bean	Turkey Craw Cvornfield	T	Chestnut
	Bean	Vermont Cranberry	E	Maple Syrup
	Bean	Whatcom Half Runner Lima	E	Salmon
	Bean	Winter Succotash	E	Maple Syrup
	Bean	Yoeme (Yaqui) Beige-brown Tepary	E	Chile Pepper
	Beet	*Early Blood Turnip	T	Crabcake
	Beet	Flat Egyptian	X	Maple Syrup
	Beet	Lane's Imperial Sugar	X	Maple Syrup
	Beet	Long Blood Red	X	Maple Syrup
	Beet	Mennonite Red	T	Maple Syrup
	Cabbage	Danish Ballhead Shortstem	E	Maple Syrup
	Cabbage	Jersey Wakefield Pewt	E	Clambake
	Cabbage	Marblehead Mammoth	X	Clambake, Maple Syrup
	Cabbage	Northern Giant	E	Moose, Salmon
	Cabbage	Red Dutch	T	Clambake
	Cabbage	Stone Mason	X	Maple Syrup
	Cabbage	Winningstadt	T	Clambake, Maple Syrup
	Carrot	Danvers	T	Clambake, Maple Syrup
	Carrot	Early Chantenay	E	Clambake, Maple Syrup
	Carrot	Early Scarlet Horn	E	Clambake, Maple Syrup
	Carrot	Robertson's Scarlet Keeper	T	Maple Syrup
	Carrot	St. Valery	T	Maple Syrup
	Celery & Celeriac	Golden Yellow	T	Cornbread
	Celery & Celeriac	Red Stalk	T	broad range
	Celery & Celeriac	Tall Golden Self-blanching	E	Wild Rice
	Celery & Celeriac	Tehama Sunrise	E	Acorn
	Chayote / Vegetable Pear	Louisiana Mirliton	E	Gumbo
	Chicory	Magdeburg (Louisiana) Coffee	T	Gumbo
	Collards	Carolina	X	Chestnut
	Collards	Florida	X	Gumbo
	Collards	Georgia Blue Stem	E	Gumbo
	Collards	Georgia Green	E	Gumbo
	Collards	Georgia Long Standing	X	Gumbo
	Cowpeas/ Crowders/ Black-eyes	Blue Goose (Gray) Crowder	E	Gumbo
	Cowpeas / Crowders / Black-eyes	Brown Crowder	E	Gumbo
	Cowpeas / Crowders / Black-eyes	Calico Crowder	E	Gumbo
	Cowpeas / Crowders / Black-eyes	Clay Cow	E	Gumbo
	Cowpeas / Crowders / Black-eyes	Clay Field Pea	E	Gumbo
	Cowpeas / Crowders / Black-eyes	Kreutzer	E	Chestnut
	Cowpeas / Crowders / Black-eyes	Mississippi Brown Crowder	T	Gumbo
	Cowpeas / Crowders / Black-eyes	*Mississippi Silver Hull	T	Chestnut
	Cowpeas / Crowders / Black-eyes	Ozark Razorback	E	Cornbread
	Cowpeas / Crowders / Black-eyes	Pigott Family Heirloom	T	Gumbo
	Cowpeas / Crowders / Black-eyes	*Pink Eye Purple Hull	E	Gumbo
	Cowpeas / Crowders / Black-eyes	Rice	T	Cornbread
	Cowpeas / Crowders / Black-eyes	*Rouge Et Noir	E	Gumbo
	Cowpeas / Crowders / Black-eyes	*Running Conch	E	Gumbo
	Cowpeas / Crowders / Black-eyes	Suzanne Cream	T	Gumbo
	Cowpeas / Crowders / Black-eyes	Tohono O'odham (Papago)	T	Chile Pepper

Food Group	Specific or Generic Type	Variety, Breed, or Wild Population	Rarity	Food Nation
Cowpeas / Crowders / Black-eyes		*Washday	T	Chestnut
Cowpeas / Crowders / Black-eyes		Whippoorwill	T	Gumbo
Cowpeas / Crowders / Black-eyes		Zipper Cream	T	Chestnut
	Cucumbers	Boothby's Blonde	T	Maple Syrup
	Cucumbers	Early Cluster Pickling, Russian	T	Maple Syrup
	Cucumbers	True Lemon	T	Maple Syrup
	Devil's Claw	Death Valley White Seeded	E	Pinyon Nut
	Eggplant	Old White Egg	T	Clambake
	Fava	Haba Del Norte	E	Chile Pepper
	Garbanzo	Garbanzo Del Norte	T	Chile Pepper
	Garlic	German Extra Hardy	T	Pinyon Nut
	Garlic	New Mexican Red	T	Pinyon Nut
	Ground Cherry/ Tomatillo	*Aunt Hattie's	T	Bison
	Ground Cherry/ Tomatillo	*New Mexico Native	T	Chile Pepper
	Jack Bean	Jackbean, Chickasaw Lima	X	Bison, Chile Pepper
	Jerusalem Artichoke	Beaveny Valley Purple	E	Maple Syrup
	Jerusalem Artichoke	Clearwater	X	Clambake
	Jerusalem Artichoke	Dave's Shrine (Wolcottian Red)	T	Clambake
	Jerusalem Artichoke	Jack's Copperclad	E	Chestnut
	Jerusalem Artichoke	Maine Giant	T	Maple Syrup
	Jerusalem Artichoke	Stampede	T	Maple Syrup
	Kale	Walking Stick	T	Acorn
	Lentil	O'odham (Papago)	E	Chile Pepper
	Lettuce	*Amish Deer Tongue	T	broad range
	Lettuce	Boston Market	T	Clambake
	Lettuce	*Grandma Admire's	T	broad range
	Lettuce	Limestone Bibb	T	Cornbread
	Lettuce	Speckled Hansen	T	Cornbread
	Lettuce	Spotted Aleppo	T	Clambake
	Melon	Amish Musk	E	Wild Rice
	Melon	Anne Arundel Musk	T	Crabcake
	Melon	Bidwell Casaba	E	Acorn
	Melon	Cassaba	E	Chile Pepper
	Melon	Chimayo	E	Pinyon Nut, Chile Pepper
	Melon	Citron (Green Citron)	T	broad range
	Melon	Crane	E	Acorn
	Melon	Early Christiana	T	Clambake
	Melon	Eden's Gem (Rocky Ford)	E	Pinyon Nut
	Melon	Emerald Gem	T	Pinyon Nut
	Melon	Fordhook Gem	T	Maple Syrup
	Melon	Green Nutmeg	T	Pinyon Nut
	Melon	Hopi Casaba	E	Pinyon Nut, Chile Pepper
	Melon	Jenny Lind	T	broad range
	Melon	*Montreal Nutmeg	E	Maple Syrup
	Melon	New Mexico	T	Chile Pepper
	Melon	Old Time Tennessee	T	Cornbread
	Melon	O'odham Ke:li Ba:so (Old Lady's Knees)	E	Chile Pepper
	Melon	Oregon Delicious	E	Salmon
	Melon	Santo Domingo Casaba	E	Chile Pepper
	Melon	Santo Domingo Native	E	Chile Pepper
	Melon	Schoon's Hardshell	T	broad range
	Melon	Snake in the Shed	T	Chile Pepper
	Melon	Sungold Casaba	T	Maple Syrup
	Melon	Winter Valencia & Maltz	T	Chestnut
	Mustard	Louisiana Green Velvet	T	Gumbo
	Mustard	Southern Giant Curled	T	Cornbread
	Okra	Alice Elliot	E	Cornbread
	Okra	Benoist Blunt	T	Gumbo
	Okra	Choppee	T	Chestnut
	Okra	Louisiana Red	T	Gumbo
	Okra	Star of David	T	Cornbread
	Onion	Egyptian Walking/Tree	T	broad range
	Onion	*I'itoi's Shallot/Papago Onion	T	Chile Pepper
	Onion	Louisiana Shallot	T	Gumbo
	Onion	McCullar's White Topset	T	Cornbread
	Onion	Red Wethersfield	T	broad range
	Onion	Walla Walla Sweet	T	Salmon
	Onion	Yellow Globe Danvers	T	Maple Syrup
	Parsnip	Guinea	X	Maple Syrup
	Parsnip	Short and Thick	E	Moose
	Pea	Alveron de Temporal	E	Pinyon Nut
	Pea	Caribou	E	Maple Syrup
	Pea	New Mexico Field	T	Chile Pepper
	Pea	O'odham Green	T	Chile Pepper
	Pea	*Prussian Blue	T	Crabcake
	Pea	Risser Sickle	E	Maple Syrup
	Pea	Salt River Pima Tan	E	Chile Pepper
	Pea	Tall Arrow	E	Clambake
	Peanut	Black Pindor	T	Chestnut
	Peanut	Pre–Civil War	E	Gumbo
	Pepper	Alcalde	E	Chile Pepper
	Pepper	*Bull Nose Bell	E	Chestnut
	Pepper	*Chiltepin	T	Chile Pepper
	Pepper	*Chimayo/Native New Mexican	T	Chile Pepper
	Pepper	Cochiti	T	Chile Pepper
	Pepper	*Cochiti Pueblo	T	Chile Pepper
	Pepper	*Datil	E	Gumbo
	Pepper	Dr. Greenleaf's Tabasco	E	Gumbo
	Pepper	*El Guique/casados	E	Chile Pepper
	Pepper	Escondida	T	Chile Pepper
	Pepper	*Fish	T	Crabcake
	Pepper	Isleta	T	Chile Pepper
	Pepper	Jarales	E	Chile Pepper
	Pepper	Louisiana Arledge Hot	T	Gumbo
	Pepper	McMahon's Texas Bird Pepper	E	Chile Pepper
	Pepper	Patagonia	E	Chile Pepper
	Pepper	Pico De Pajaro	E	Chile Pepper
	Pepper	Rooster Spur	T	Gumbo
	Pepper	San Felipe	T	Chile Pepper
	Pepper	San Juan	T	Chile Pepper
	Pepper	Santo Domingo	T	Chile Pepper
	Pepper	Short Yellow Tabasco	E	Gumbo
	Pepper	Tabasco	T	Gumbo
	Pepper	Tennesee Spice	E	Cornbread
	Pepper	Tennessee Teardrop	E	Cornbread
	Pepper	Velarde	T	Chile Pepper
	Pepper	Waver's Mennonite Stuffing Sweet	E	Maple Syrup
	Pepper	Wenk's Yellow Hot	T	Chile Pepper
	Pepper	Zia	T	Chile Pepper
	Potato	Abenaki	E	Maple Syrup, Clambake
	Potato	Beauty of Hebron	E	Maple Syrup
	Potato	Early Goodrich	X	Maple Syrup

Food Group	Specific or Generic Type	Variety, Breed, or Wild Population	Rarity	Food Nation
	Potato	Early Ohio	E	Cornbread
	Potato	Early Rose	T	broad range
	Potato	Garnet Chile	T	broad range
	Potato	*Green Mountain	T	Maple Syrup
	Potato	Haida	E	Salmon
	Potato	Harrison	X	Maple Syrup
	Potato	Irish Cobbler	X	Clambake
	Potato	Katahdin	T	Maple Syrup
	Potato	Long John (Long Red)	T	Bison
	Potato	*Makah Ozette	T	Salmon
	Potato	Newfoundland Blue	X	Clambake
	Potato	Newfoundland Jumbo	X	Clambake
	Potato	New Queen	X	Maple Syrup
	Potato	Peach Blow	T	Clambake
	Potato	Pride of Multnomah	X	Salmon
	Potato	Purple Cow Horn	E	Clambake
	Potato	Seneca Horn	E	Maple Syrup
	Potato	Snowflake	T	Maple Syrup
	Potato	Tlingit (Marks)	E	Salmon
	Potato	To-le-ak	E	Salmon
	Potato	Yampa (Gairdner's Yampah)	T	Chestnut
	Radish	Black Spanish Winter	E	Maple Syrup
	Radish	Rand (Black Spanish) Long	T	Maple Syrup
	Rutabaga/Turnip	Canadian Gem	E	Maple Syrup
	Rutabaga/Turnip	*Gilfeather	T	Clambake, Maple Syrup
	Rutabaga/Turnip	Old Jake's	E	Clambake
	Rutabaga/Turnip	Waldoboro Greenneck	E	Maple Syrup
	Salsify	Pennsylvania Dutch (Hawwerwurzel)	E	Maple Syrup
	Squash/Pumpkin	Acoma Pumpkin	E	Chile Pepper
	Squash/Pumpkin	*Amish Pie	E	Maple Syrup
	Squash/Pumpkin	Apache Giant Cushaw	X	Pinyon Nut, Chile Pepper
	Squash/Pumpkin	Arikara Ebony Acer	T	Bison
	Squash/Pumpkin	Arikara Long	E	Bison
	Squash/Pumpkin	Bakery's	E	Maple Syrup
	Squash/Pumpkin	Big Cheese	E	Chile Pepper
	Squash/Pumpkin	*Boston Marrow	E	Clambake, Maple Syrup
	Squash/Pumpkin	Canada Crookneck	T	Maple Syrup
	Squash/Pumpkin	*Choctaw Sweet Potato	E	Gumbo, Cornbread
	Squash/Pumpkin	Cochiti Pueblo Cushaw	E	Chile Pepper
	Squash/Pumpkin	Connecticut Sweet Pie	E	Clambake
	Squash/Pumpkin	Cow Pumpkin	T	Cornbread
	Squash/Pumpkin	Creole Butternut	E	Gumbo
	Squash/Pumpkin	Cuaresma Cushaw	T	Chile Pepper
	Squash/Pumpkin	Cutchogue Cheese	E	Maple Syrup
	Squash/Pumpkin	Essex Turban Long Pie	X	Maple Syrup
	Squash/Pumpkin	Georgia Roaster	E	Gumbo
	Squash/Pumpkin	Gila Cushaw	E	Chile Pepper
	Squash/Pumpkin	Green Delicious	E	Maple Syrup
	Squash/Pumpkin	Hidatsa Hubbard	E	Bison
	Squash/Pumpkin	Hopi Orange	E	Chile Pepper
	Squash/Pumpkin	Hopi Pale Gray	E	Chile Pepper
	Squash/Pumpkin	Hopi Pumpkin	E	Chile Pepper
	Squash/Pumpkin	Hopi Vatnga Cushaw	E	Chile Pepper
	Squash/Pumpkin	Hopi White	E	Chile Pepper
	Squash/Pumpkin	Indian Oblong Long Pie	E	Maple Syrup
	Squash/Pumpkin	Jap	E	Wild Rice
	Squash/Pumpkin	Kentucky Field Cheese	E	Cornbread
	Squash/Pumpkin	King of Mammoth (Mammoth)	T	Cornbread
	Squash/Pumpkin	Lakota	E	Bison
	Squash/Pumpkin	Landreth Cheese	E	Clambake, Crabcake
	Squash/Pumpkin	Long Island Milk Cheese Pumpkin	E	Clambake
	Squash/Pumpkin	Lower Salmon River	E	Salmon
	Squash/Pumpkin	Mandan	E	Bison
	Squash/Pumpkin	Marblehead Mammoth	E	Clambake, Maple Syrup
	Squash/Pumpkin	Minnie's Apache Blue Hubbard	E	Chile Pepper
	Squash/Pumpkin	Mormon Blue-green Hubbard	E	Pinyon Nut
	Squash/Pumpkin	Nanticoke Indian Turban	E	Crabcake, Clambake
	Squash/Pumpkin	Navajo Blue Hubbard	E	Pinyon Nut
	Squash/Pumpkin	Navajo Cushaw	E	Pinyon Nut
	Squash/Pumpkin	North Georgia Candy Roaster	T	Chestnut
	Squash/Pumpkin	Okeechobee Gourd	E	Gumbo
	Squash/Pumpkin	Old-fashioned Tennessee Vining	E	Cornbread
	Squash/Pumpkin	Paydon Heirloom Acorn	E	Gumbo, Cornbread
	Squash/Pumpkin	Penasco Cheese	E	Chile Pepper
	Squash/Pumpkin	Penobscott	X	Clambake, Maple Syrup
	Squash/Pumpkin	*Pike's Peak/Sibley	T	Bison
	Squash/Pumpkin	Red Warren Turban	E	Clambake
	Squash/Pumpkin	San Juan Pueblo Cushaw	E	Pinyon Nut, Chile Pepper
	Squash/Pumpkin	Santo Domingo Pueblo Cushaw	E	Chile Pepper
	Squash/Pumpkin	Seminole	E	Gumbo
	Squash/Pumpkin	Sibley Pike's Peak	E	Maple Syrup, Bison
	Squash/Pumpkin	Taos Hubbard	E	Pinyon Nut
	Squash/Pumpkin	*Tennessee Sweet Potato Cushaw	E	Gumbo
	Squash/Pumpkin	Texas Indian	E	Chile Pepper
	Squash/Pumpkin	Thelma Sander's Sweet Potato	E	Cornbread
	Squash/Pumpkin	Umatilla/Yakima Marblehead	E	Salmon
	Squash/Pumpkin	Warner Turban	E	Maple Syrup
	Squash/Pumpkin	White Pumpkin	E	Chestnut
	Squash/Pumpkin	Winter Luxury Pie	E	broad range
	Squash/Pumpkin	Wisconsin Cheese	X	Wild Rice
	Squash/Pumpkin	Wood's Early Prolific	T	Crabcake
	Squash/Pumpkin	Yellow Mandan	T	Bison

Food Group	Specific or Generic Type	Variety, Breed, or Wild Population	Rarity	Food Nation
	Squash/Pumpkin	Zapallo Plomo	E	Chile Pepper
	Sunflower	Arikara	T	Bison
	Sunflower	Hidatsa No. 1	E	Bison
	Sunflower	Puebloan (Hopi) Dye	X	Chile Pepper
	Sunflower	Seneca	E	Maple Syrup
	Sunflower	Sumpweed	E	Cornbread
	Sweet Potato	Hayman White	E	Crabcake
	Sweet Potato	Nansemond	T	Chestnut
	Sweet Potato	Old Kentucky White	X	Cornbread
	Sweet Potato	Purple (Pumpkin) Wam	X	Cornbread
	Sweet Potato	Red Wine Velvet	X	Cornbread
	Sweet Potato	Southern Delight	E	Gumbo
	Sweet Potato	Southern Queen Yam/White Triumph	T	Gumbo, Cornbread
	Sweet Potato	Spanish White	E	Wild Rice
	Tomato	Acme	X	Maple Syrup
	Tomato	Amish Paste	T	Maple Syrup
	Tomato	Beaut	E	Maple Syrup
	Tomato	Berkshire Polish	T	Maple Syrup
	Tomato	Brandywine Pink	T	Cornbread
	Tomato	Cheerio	E	Maple Syrup
	Tomato	Cherokee Purple	E	Cornbread
	Tomato	Conqueror	X	Maple Syrup
	Tomato	Far North Sea	X	Maple Syrup
	Tomato	John Allen Yellow German	E	Cornbread
	Tomato	Mankin Plum	T	Clambake
	Tomato	Margaret Best Yellow	E	Chestnut
	Tomato	*Mortgage Lifter	T	Broad Range
	Tomato	*Orange Oxheart	T	Chestnut, Maple Syrup
	Tomato	Persimmon	T	Chestnut, Clambake
	Tomato	Power's Heirloom	T	Chestnut
	Tomato	Prescott	E	Chile Pepper
	Tomato	Red Peach	E	Maple Syrup
	Tomato	Tiffen Mennonite	T	Maple Syrup
	Tomato	Trophy	X	Maple Syrup
	Watermelon	Georgia Rattlesnake (Garrison)	T	Chestnut
	Watermelon	*Hopi Yellow-meated	T	Chile Pepper
	Watermelon	*Moon and Stars	T	Cornbread
	Watermelon	Mountain Sweet Yellow	T	Clambake
	Watermelon	Nancy	T	Cornbread
	Watermelon	Pueblo Red-meated Winter	T	Chile Pepper
	Watermelon	Tohono O'odham Yellow	E	Chile Pepper
	Watermelon	Tom Watson	T	Moose
WILD FOODS				
	Assorted Wild Roots	Jepson's Onion	E	Acorn
	Assorted Wild Roots	Munz's Onion	E	Acorn
	Assorted Wild Roots	Passey's Onion	E	Acorn
	Assorted Wild Roots	Pink Fawn Lily	T	Salmon
	Assorted Wild Roots	Prairie Potato (Indian Turnip)	E	Bison
	Assorted Wild Roots	Sandfood	T	Chile Pepper
	Assorted Wild Roots	Yampa (Gairdner's Yampah)	T	Salmon
	Other Wild Foods	Beach Plum	E	Clambake
	Other Wild Foods	Butternut	T	Maple Syrup
	Other Wild Foods	*Chiltepin	T	Chile Pepper
	Other Wild Foods	*Emory Oak Acorn/Bellota	T	Chile Pepper
	Other Wild Foods	Fox Grape	E	Maple Syrup
	Other Wild Foods	Lady's Thumb	E	Maple Syrup
	Other Wild Foods	Nevada Soft-shelled Pinyon	T	Pinyon Nut
	Other Wild Foods	Sassafras Leaves for Handmade Gumbo Filé	T	Gumbo
	Other Wild Foods	Scrub Plum	E	Gumbo
WILD GAME				
	Birds	Atwater's Geater Prairie Chicken	E	Bison
	Birds	Masked Bobwhite Quail	E	Chile Pepper
	Birds	Passenger Pigeon	X	broad range
	Birds	Steller's Eider	E	Moose
	Mammals	Carolina Northern Flying Squirrel	E	Chestnut
	Mammals	Cascade Moose	T	Salmon
	Mammals	Columbia White-tailed Deer	E	Salmon
	Mammals	Grizzly Bear	T	broad range
	Mammals	Key Deer	E	Gumbo
	Mammals	Louisiana Black Bear	T	Gumbo
	Mammals	Musk-ox	E	Moose
	Mammals	Northwestern Minnesota Moose	E	Moose, Wild Rice
	Mammals	Peninsular Bighorn Sheep	E	broad range
	Mammals	Plains Bison, Free-ranging	T	Bison
	Mammals	Roosevelt Elk	T	Salmon
	Mammals	Sierra Nevada Bighorn Sheep	E	Acorn
	Mammals	Sonoran Pronghorn	E	Chile Pepper
	Mammals	Steller's Sea Lion	E	Salmon
	Mammals	Virginia Northern Flying Squirrel	E	Chestnut
	Mammals	Wood Bison	T	Salmon
	Mammals	Woodland Caribou	T	Salmon
	Reptiles	American Alligator	E	Gumbo
	Reptiles	American Crocodile	E	Crabcake, Gumbo
	Reptiles	Desert Tortoise	T	Pinyon Nut, Chile Pepper
	Reptiles	Green Sea Turtle	E/T	Acorn, Gumbo
	Reptiles	Hawksbill Sea Turtle	E	Gumbo
	Reptiles	Kemp's Ridley Sea Turtle	E	Crabcake, Clambake, Gumbo
	Reptiles	Leatherback Sea Turtle	E	Acorn, Chile Pepper
	Reptiles	Loggerhead Sea Turtle	T	Gumbo
	Reptiles	New Mexico Ridge-nosed Rattlesnake	E	Chile Pepper
	Reptiles	Olive Ridley Sea Turtle	T	Acorn

APPENDIX 2
RAFT Toolkit for Community-Based Conservation and Evaluation of Traditional Foods

As one of the food experts or enthusiasts in your community, you inspire those around you to celebrate, partake, and protect traditionally used plants and animals in our food system. Whether you make a living as a fisher hooking Chinook salmon along Washington's Snake River, as a home cook boiling up a pot of hoppin' John for your family every New Year's Day, or as a passionate eater of sustainably harvested ramps, the choices you make influence the success of RAFT.

Take a few moments to consider how to apply what you've learned in this book and how to bring that knowledge to your table. This toolkit is your guide. You've read the manifesto. You've looked up the stories that relate to you and your community. You know that many of America's favorite flavors are endangered and that their loss has biological, economic, environmental, and cultural effects. Now it's time to put it in practice.

RAFT's progress depends on the community of eaters we create together. What can you do specifically to enhance and promote activities that will save America's agricultural and wild food biodiversity?

In broad strokes, our conservation work involves production, creation, and consumption, defined as follows:

- **Production** means cultivating land, lakes, or seas to yield food. Whether you make a living as a farmer, rancher, butcher, or fisher, you know about the soil, the air, the water, and how to provide the best product from your environment.

- **Creation** is about the artistry of releasing the unique flavors, textures, and fragrances of food. Who are the creators? We all are. From the celebrity chef and the artisanal cheesemaker to you and me cooking in our own kitchens, we have the knowledge, motivation, and skill to create delicious meals.
- **Consumption.** Must we spell this out? Sourdough toast topped with maypop passionfruit jelly. Bowlfuls of broken crab and Choppee okra stew. Mexican wedding cookies sprinkled with pine nuts—your hand in the cookie jar! Eater-based conservation is RAFT's centerpiece. Our most enduring food memories motivate us to demand the presence of certain fresh produce, cured meats, and dried ingredients in grocery stores and in restaurants. Our demand, in turn, fuels supply. Said simply, when you eat that cookie, you've completed a cycle that helps ensure an economic return for a producer's work. "Eat it to save it!"

So where do you go from here? Start by questioning your meals. Say you've just had a spoonful of hoppin' John. Will it really bring you good luck? Who said it brought good luck in the first place and why? And what kind of peas are these? Black-eyed? Crowder? Cow? Clay? How much does the inclusion of particular heirloom peas make a difference to its taste?

By asking such simple questions, we can shape our future consumer choices. Below is a list of questions that we hope you will use to understand the particular foods unique to your region and the food traditions unique to your community. These questions give us a starting place from which we move into action in our roles as producers, creators, and consumers.

- What flavors, fragrances, and textures are part of your community? How long have they been there? Who developed them in place or brought them there?
- What taste sensations do you want to ensure future generations have a chance to experience?

- Are there others like you who are taking an active role in maintaining cultural and culinary traditions that surround these foods?
- How can you and your community further safeguard these foods?

Production!

Today, Americans rely on fewer crop and livestock species and varieties than ever before. Fewer than thirty plants provide 90 percent of the world's nutrition. Over the last century, thousands of apple varieties have gone extinct in American orchards. In our roles as producers, breeders, and processors, we must find ways to safeguard agricultural biodiversity so that we can fully *enjoy* the food we produce.

General Tips

- Support (and learn about) the regeneration of agricultural biodiversity by joining the American Livestock Breeds Conservancy, Native Seeds/SEARCH, and the Seed Savers Exchange.
- Become a seed saver or fruit explorer and organize seasonal events for local exchange of varieties adapted to your homeland.
- Nominate one of your endangered foods to the Slow Food Ark of Taste (see page 288).
- Purchase and pasture livestock or poultry breeds from independent hatcheries or registered breed associations.
- Organize a field trip with friends to seek out some of these rare foods on the back roads of your county.
- Create a market for the food you grow by making sure it's prepared deliciously. Partner with a Chefs Collaborative member near you (www.chefs collaborative.org).
- Start a Slow Food Presidium, an endangered food recovery project.
- Write about endangered foods in the *Edible* magazine or associated website that features foods of your locality.

Producers

- Identify your product specifically by variety or breed—for example, not "plums" but "Elephant Heart plums"; not "chicken" but "Buckeye chicken."
- Raise your animals following good husbandry and (when possible) grass-fed practices to ensure high meat quality and consistency.
- Promote regional heirloom seeds and heritage breeds at farmers' markets, county fairs, and food festivals by providing information and samples.
- Choose to work with crops, livestock, and poultry that are adapted to your climate and to a sustainable production system.
- Shape your production system to use local knowledge and resources, reflecting or honoring local cultures.
- Identify how your product was raised—"Natural," "Organic," "Pastured," "Humanely"—and any appropriate "green" certifications.

Breeders

- Select animals of high quality and genetic purity that meet the historic standards for the breed.
- Mentor new breeders who have just become involved with the breed.
- Make sure that some of your good breeding stock is passed on to others or put into bull, ram, or rooster exchanges, to perpetuate the breed and secure a healthy gene pool into the future.

Processors

- Develop a clear understanding of the cultural, historical, or culinary significance of the breeds or fruits you take in.
- Discuss and work with producers to improve preshipping, shipping, and handling methods that can optimize the end-product results and minimize losses in product quality and value.
- Showcase the unique culinary qualities of endangered breeds or fruits by featuring them in value-added products.
- Avoid foods still too endangered to be stressed by premature demand in the marketplace.

Creation!

This is where you take the raw products derived from the art of production and bring them to the table. What does it mean for cooks to participate in agricultural conservation?

- Join (or offer to cook for) local food organizations in your community that focus on endangered foods.
- Identify and support other stakeholders in your community who are working in sustainable agriculture.
- Create a working group or "fresh food network" with these stakeholders to identify who is growing or producing endangered foods to create a purchasing relationship with them.
- Tell the colorful stories of these foods on menus and websites, to customers, and to your friends and neighbors.
- Train your serving staff to tell stories about the menu, from the farm to the table.
- Try out new recipes in your kitchen and introduce these foods to your guests.
- Hold dinners at your restaurant and in your home focusing on the recovery of endangered foods.
- Agree to conduct cooking demonstrations at farms or farmers' markets featuring endangered foods.
- When working with purveyors, ask them to add endangered foods to their lists.
- Pressure purveyors not to carry GMO foods that may contaminate those of nearby producers.
- Engage purveyors in conversations about how to prepare unfamiliar foods.
- Create an endangered foods "Ark of Taste" meal (see page 290).
- Join the Chefs Collaborative.

Consumption!

This is the pleasure page—we all love to eat. Now that we've taken action to secure the supply of endangered fruits, vegetables, fish, and meats, it's time to buy these foods, use recipes that showcase them, and feast on them. If the market is the primary engine for recovering these foods, how can our purchasing and dining choices positively impact the marketplace?

- Think of yourself as a "coproducer"—what you buy and eat directly affects what farmers grow.
- Request specific varieties of fruits, vegetables, and meats from your grocers, your market farmers, and your waitstaff at restaurants.
- Taste new flavors and develop an ability to describe them vividly.
- Make mealtimes the centerpieces of your day.
- Add your favorite local food to the Slow Food Ark of Taste.
- Organize a tasting, not just of wine (which we love) but of beans, chickens, and other Ark of Taste foods.
- Ask local farmers to grow Ark of Taste fruits and vegetables (and be willing to provide seeds if necessary).
- Ask your grocers or CSAs to showcase these varieties.
- Create an endangered foods meal to evaluate which should be "rafted" to the Ark of Taste.

How to Nominate a Food to the Slow Food Ark of Taste

The Ark of Taste aims to rediscover, catalog, describe, and publicize forgotten flavors. It is a metaphorical refuge or sanctuary for excellent gastronomic products that are threatened by industrial standardization, hygiene laws, the regulations of large-scale distribution, and environmental damage. Dozens of countries already maintain a national Ark of Taste listing online. What distinguishes this list from the RAFT list of endangered foods is that foods on the Ark of Taste are filtered for outstanding flavor characteristics and (sustainable) commercial potential. Some RAFT listed foods may still be too endangered to promote in the marketplace, or lack such flavor.

Add to the U.S. list by nominating particular traditional food varieties (not their recipes or preparations) of your region. Once they are on the Ark of Taste, chefs, retail grocers, educators, food producers, and consumers can begin to restore and celebrate these as precious elements of our biocultural and culinary diversity. Nominations for Ark products can be made online at www.slowfoodusa.org.

Ark products range from Navajo-Churro sheep and the Harrison cider apple to geoduck shellfish. All are formerly endangered products that have gained real economic viability and commercial potential.

Criteria:
- Products must be of outstanding quality in terms of taste. "Taste quality" is defined in the context of local traditions and uses.
- Products must be linked to the memory and identity of a community and reflect the terroir of that region.
- Products must be linked environmentally, socioeconomically, and historically to a specific area.
- Products must be produced in limited quantities, by farms or by small-scale processing companies.
- Products must be threatened with either real or potential extinction.

Categories:
- Beverages
- Cereals
- Cheeses
- Fish
- Fruits and Berries
- Game
- Livestock
- Meat Products
- Nuts
- Poultry

- Pulses (beans)
- Shellfish
- Syrups
- Vegetables, Greens, and Herbs
- Vinegars

Ark nomination format:

1. Name the food (supply scientific *and* common names when appropriate).
2. Briefly describe the food.
3. List the food's producers—farmers, harvesters, artisans. Provide name and contact information for each.
4. Describe in a few sentences why you think this food should be on the U.S. Ark of Taste. Include information including taste quality, sustainable production, level of endangerment/underappreciation, and cultural significance
5. If photos or illustrations are available, please submit and include the photographer's name. Please note whether Slow Food has permission to reproduce the image.
6. Include a bibliography.
7. Include the nominator's name and contact information.

How to Create an Endangered Foods "Ark of Taste" Feast

Many fruits, vegetables, and meats initially fall into disuse because they're not economically viable to produce. Although the foods may still be produced on a small scale, their flavors, fragrances, and textures slip into obscurity. For example, the deluge in groceries of thin-skinned, softly sweet, and watery seedless Red Globe grapes means that a generation of Americans has not had the pleasure to experience the deep, chewy, jellylike consistency of a Concord or a Scuppernong grape . . . to say nothing of missing the opportunity to taunt younger brothers and sisters with classic tales of grape vines growing in your tummy if you swallow a seed!

What can we do about such dilemmas? Reintroduce a regional flavor to your friends, your customers, and your neighbors. Host an Ark of Taste dinner or a RAFT American

Heritage picnic! Because some of the ingredients are obscure, these dinners may take a bit more effort than others, so we'd like to share some lessons we've learned after years of throwing dinner parties and community picnics in Great American landscapes:

- Review the Ark and RAFT listings on Slow Food USA's website (www.slow foodusa.org). Read the descriptions of the foods and think about their region and season.
- Creating this event can require extra effort in planning. If you can't locate items you'd like fresh, you may find and store them in another form, as frozen puree, smoked filet, or a chutney.
- Ask local farmers to grow Ark and RAFT fruits and vegetables and poultry producers to grow heritage breeds.
- Time your event according to seasonality to maximize available fresh Ark and RAFT produce.
- Using endangered livestock breeds in particular requires special consideration and can take more than two years of planning. Help to sustain an endangered breed and educate a local producer by asking him or her to raise animals that you provide for your Ark dinner. Refer to the ALBC website (www.albc-usa.org).
- Some hand-processed foods, like filé powder, have very limited production. Find out when they're harvested and order the amount you need before supplies run too low.
- Focus on the historically acclaimed foods of your region. Foods within three hours' reach of your home will be more easily located and especially meaningful to your participants.
- Staples are easy to ship. If the Ark list for your region is thin, use nonlocal fresh foodstuffs only to supplement your local fresh ingredients and nonperishable Ark foods from outside as the basis for the meal.
- Keep the price of the event reasonable to encourage people of all ages and classes to come and taste the food.

- Informal locations such as picnic grounds, botanical gardens, parks, halls-for-hire, or granges work well for Ark and RAFT events, with decoration and table service by attendees and the meal served family-style.
- Cooking together builds community. Plan your menus to delegate kitchen responsibilities across the range of talents your volunteers have to offer. Simple recipes help event participants imagine using Ark foods in their own kitchens.
- Weave wonderful tales around the menu. People are very inspired by the stories of these foods and the efforts needed to produce them. Highlight local heroes. Consider featuring their photos on "table talkers" or explanatory cards for buffets or tables.
- Purchase a bit of surplus and have a table of Ark products for sale. This makes it easy for attendees to try them on their own.
- Have evaluation cards handy to get feedback on the newly encountered tastes and textures from participants.

Tasting Principles
by Poppy Tooker, Chair, U.S. Ark of Taste

- Humans detect five basic tastes: salt, sour, sweet, bitter, and the newly labeled umami ("savory," which is the taste of certain amino acids, such as glutamate, aspartate, and related compounds).
- Our sensitivity to all tastes is distributed across the whole tongue and other regions of the mouth where there are also taste buds (such as the epiglottis and soft palate and laryngeal), but some areas are more specific in response to certain tastes than others.
- The flavors of sour and bitter are detected on the rear two-thirds of the tongue (and sour is also tasted as acid). Salt is detected on the front edges of the tongue, and the tip of our tongue detects sweetness.
- If soy sauce, which is composed mostly of MSG, is present in prepared foods it tricks the taster, as its presence allows less of a particular flavor to be present to taste it.

- Taste is mostly scent. Our sense of smell is responsible for about 80 percent of what we taste. What we often call "taste" is in fact flavor, which is a combination of taste, smell, texture (tongue sensation), and other physical characteristics such as temperature.
- The most thorough tasting methods combine mouth flavor with scent transmitted between your mouth and nose through the back of your palate.

Ark of Taste Criteria

Use all your senses to evaluate the food for the following qualities:

- Appearance
- Aroma
- Texture/Mouth-Feel
- Flavor
- Aftertaste
- Overall impression

ACKNOWLEDGMENTS

Renewing America's Food Traditions, as a project, received early moral and financial support from Martin Teitel of the Cedar Tree Foundation, Amy Goldman of the Lillian Goldman Charitable Trust, Mary Ann Mott of the C.S. Fund, and Agnese Haury.

We dedicated this book to them, and to the Daniel Smith family.

The RAFT team grows as it goes and is made up of many remarkable and knowledgeable individuals. We are especially grateful for the support and enthusiasm of the executive directors of the following nonprofits involved in the maiden voyages of RAFT: Erika Lesser and Patrick Martins of Slow Food USA; Jennifer Hall and Melissa Kogut of the Chefs Collaborative; Kevin Dahl and Bryn Jones of Native Seeds/SEARCH; Melissa Nelson of the Cultural Conservancy; Kent Whealy of the Seed Savers Exchange; Chuck Bassett of the American Livestock Breeds Conservancy; and Laura Huenneke and Gary Deason of Northern Arizona University's Center for Sustainable Environments.

The organization's board members, leaders, or staff who contributed in particular to this book include Deborah Madison, Amy Goldman, Peter Hoffman, Alice Waters, Poppy Tooker, Phillip Sponenberg, Gerry Warren, David Buchanan, Kurt Friese, Matt Jones, Robin Schempp, Leigh Belanger, Neil Hamilton, Don Shrider, Jeannette Beranger, Marjorie Bender, Tami Lax, Jennifer Trotter, Amy Blankstein, Will Engelhardt, Gina Fiorillo-Brady, Barbara Bowman, Jeanette Sherman, Heather Farley, Patty West, Kanin Routson, Steve Buckley, Suzanne Nelson, Diane Whealy, Steph Hughes, Aaron Whealy, and Matt Barthel.

Beyond our organizations, we are particularly grateful for the information exchanges and collaborations with Alex Sando, Amy Trubek, Anthony Boutard, Ashley Rood, Barry Infuso, Ben Watson, Bill Kazoukis, Brett Bakker, Brett Ramey, Cecily Upton, Coll Thrush, Craig Hassel, Dan Bussey, David Buchanan, David Cavagnaro, Debra Sohm-Lawson, Don Bixby, Don Davis, Doug Elliot, Drew Conroy, Elen Eckert Ogden, Elizabeth Kennedy, Elizabeth Woody, Enrique Salmon, Eric Jones, Estevan Arrellano, Fernando Divina, Fred Schneider, Gay Chanler, Gerry Warren, Ginger Nickerson, Glenn Drowns, Jennifer Bloeser, Jennifer Hall, Jessica Harris, Jesus Garcia, Joe McGarry,

Joel Glanzberg, John Elder, John Grahame, John T. Edge, Jon Mortimer, Justin Pitts, Kanin Routson, Kelly Kindscher, Kit Anderson, Kristen Gremellion, Laura Baldez, Larry Stevens, Leigh Belanger, Les Hook, Linda Murray Berzok, Lois Ellen Frank, Lolis Eric Elie, Lora Lea Misterly, Loretta Oden, Lucia Watson, Nancy Turner, Neil Lash, Nicola Wagenberg, Nova Kim, Pamela Hamilton, Patty West, Paul Atkinson, Peter de Garmo, Phil Klasky, Phillip Ackerman-Leist, Randi Seidner, Richard Felger, Richard Nelson, Rick Brusca, Robert Rhoades, Russell Libby, Sandra Oliver, Shawn Kelley, Sinclair Phillip, Suzanne Nelson, Tim Crews, Tom Burford, Tony Forsman, Virginia Nazarea, Wendy Hodgson, Wendy Hodgson, William Dunmire, and Winona LaDuke. Deja Walker assisted with the proofs.

Finally, we are blessed by the extraordinary talents, values, and care given to this manuscript by the Chelsea Green staff, including Ben Watson, Shay Totten, Emily Foote, and Margo Baldwin, and their great designer at Sterling Hill Productions, Peter Holm.

INDEX

Photographs are indicated by italic page numbers. The complete RAFT list of foods at risk in North America appears in Appendix 1, pages 271–281.

the politics and practice of sustainable living

CHELSEA GREEN PUBLISHING

Chelsea Green Publishing sees books as tools for effecting cultural change and seeks to empower citizens to participate in reclaiming our global commons and become its impassioned stewards. If you enjoyed *Renewing America's Food Traditions*, please consider these other great books related to agriculture, food, and the politics of food.

The War on Bugs
WILL ALLEN
ISBN: 978-1-933392-46-2
$35 (PB)

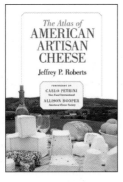

*The Atlas of American
Artisan Cheese*
JEFFREY P. ROBERTS
ISBN: 978-1-933392-34-9
$35 (PB)

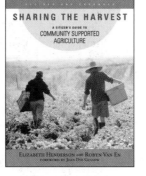

Sharing the Harvest
ELIZABETH HENDERSON
WITH ROBYN VAN EN
ISBN: 978-1-933392-10-3
$35 (PB)

Full Moon Feast
JESSICA PRENTICE
ISBN: 978-1-933392-00-4
$25 (PB)

*The Revolution Will
Not Be Microwaved*
SANDOR ELLIX KATZ
ISBN: 978-1-933392-11-0
$20 (PB)

*The Slow Food Guide
to New York City*
PATRICK MARTINS
& BEN WATSON
ISBN: 978-1-931498-27-2
$20 (PB)

*The Slow Food Guide
to Chicago*
KELLY GIBSON &
PORTIA BELLOC LOWNDES
WITH SLOW FOOD CHICAGO
ISBN: 978-1-931498-61-6
$20 (PB)

*The Slow Food Guide
to San Francisco*
SYLVAN BRACKETT, WENDY
DOWNING, & SUE MOORE
WITH SLOW FOOD
SAN FRANCISCO
ISBN: 978-1-931498-75-3
$20 (PB)

the politics and practice of sustainable living

For more information
or to request a catalog,
visit **www.chelseagreen.com**
or call toll-free **(800) 639-4099**.